Readings in White-Collar Crime

Readings in White-Collar Crime

David Shichor
California State University, San Bernardino
Larry Gaines
California State University, San Bernardino
Richard Ball
The Pennsylvania State University, Fayette

Long Grove, Illinois

For information about this book, contact:
Waveland Press, Inc.
4180 IL Route 83, Suite 101
Long Grove, IL 60047-9580
(847) 634-0081
info@waveland.com
www.waveland.com

10-digit ISBN 1-57766-191-5
13-digit ISBN 978-1-57766-191-7

Printed in the United States of America

10 9 8 7 6 5 4

Contents

◂ Preface ▸

White-collar crime is a nebulous form of crime because it remains in the shadows. It is ever present, but unlike street crimes, there is seldom a clear violator or victim. In many cases the perpetrators of white-collar crimes are faceless corporations, and their crimes are rationalized as necessary. It is likely that all of us have been victimized as a result of white-collar crime. In the vast majority of cases, citizens do not realize that they are being victimized. Their victimization is subtle. It may be in the form of price fixing, the marketing of inferior or dangerous products or services, hidden fees, the manipulation of stocks or bonds, or polluting or destroying the environment. In some cases, victimization becomes fairly obvious, such as the savings and loan debacle in the 1980s that cost taxpayers hundreds of billions of dollars.

There is substantial disagreement among academics as to white-collar crime's definition, and the average citizen has little understanding of it. Perhaps this is the result of laws not keeping pace with business practices, technology, and acts that are sometimes associated with white-collar crime. Whereas the behaviors that are considered street crimes are generally "black and white," white-collar crime is grayer. In other words, people and businesses often commit acts that are morally or ethically wrong, but they *may be* legally permissible. In other cases, governmental regulations, rather than criminal laws are violated. People often confuse ethics and the law. They believe that if it is not right, then it is illegal. However, this is not the case. The law has many cracks, and there are always ways for the unethical to dupe, scam, cheat, or fleece other citizens, businesses, corporations, and even government. White-collar crime, however, must involve a violation of law.

The idea of white-collar crime surfaced in Edwin H. Southerland's address to the American Sociological Society in 1939. For Southerland, white-collar crime was committed by those in the upper, "white-collar" class of respectable businesspeople and professionals. The crimes to which Southerland referred were those that occurred as a result of the "conduct of business." In this regard, white-collar crime was seen as violations of laws that were meant to regulate business. To a great extent, white-collar crime is a violation of trust. Most cases of white-collar crime include some "slight of hand" or activity whereby the victim does not receive that which is expected.

It should be noted that white-collar crime is associated with other forms of criminality—specifically, organized crime and political corruption—and quite frequently a fine and sometimes blurry line separates them. Historically, organized crime concentrated on crimes and activities associated with vice: drugs, gambling, prostitution, alcohol, and tobacco. As organized crime acquired larger amounts of wealth, it had the leverage and the muscle to move into other criminal venues. In many cases, organized crime criminals moved into white-collar crime. With their newfound wealth, they were able to use many of the tactics that had developed in the white-collar crime arena.

In terms of political crime, in many cases there is a direct or indirect relationship between politicians and white-collar crime. Businesses lobby legislative bodies for favorable legislation that allows them to maximize profits or to reduce or thwart government regulation. When corporations are able to influence laws and regulations, they are able reduce the possibility of criminality. Ethics and moral concerns are not at issue here, only the legality of actions. In some cases, white-collar criminals have bribed or performed other favors for politicians in return for favorable legislation. When white-collar criminals are able to control a legislative agenda, they are able to remain legitimate and above the law. Congress, state legislatures, and local legislative bodies often pass such special interest legislation.

The study of white-collar crime is extremely important. For the past several decades, the American people have been fixated on drugs and street crime. Little consideration has been given to white-collar crime. Indeed, most Americans do not recognize that it exists. This lack of recognition and attention contributes to white-collar crime's ability to flourish. Specifically, there is little motivation to pass laws and develop enforcement initiatives. If people recognized that white-collar crime is more costly and possibly results in more harm than drug or street crime, we might develop more effective responses in dealing with it. The bottom line is, white-collar crime continues to cost American citizens far more than other forms of crime.

This collection provides an overview of the white-collar crime problem. We first attempt to define it and differentiate it from other forms of crime. Next, we provide examples or cases of white-collar crime. Our purpose is to communicate that white-collar crime is pervasive, and it touches all facets of life. Finally, we address how the criminal justice system handles white-collar crimes and criminals. Although we have made strides in the law enforcement arena, much more needs to be done. Many of the laws we now have are inadequate, and there are continued pressures to reduce the ability of regulatory agencies to police white-collar crime. We hope this book helps to pull white-collar crime out of the shadows, give it form, and provide a better understanding of it. If this occurs, we may develop a will to enact more effective countermeasures to deal with this nebulous form of crime in the future.

◂ PART I ▸

Defining White-Collar Crime

Public and professional interest in the subject of white-collar crime usually is not as intense as the concern with so-called "street crimes." When the topic of crime is raised, people commonly think of murder, robbery, rape and other offenses that involve actual violence or the threat of violence. Even in the case of property offenses that are considered street crimes, such as burglary, larceny, and motor vehicle theft, the potential for personal confrontation and violence is linked with the images of the crime. The visibility of street crimes, amplified by the media, reinforces the perception that those are the "real crimes" while "white-collar" offenses are more remote and less visible.

Despite these perceptions, during the last quarter of the twentieth century more people became aware of the impact of the various offenses that usually come under the umbrella of white-collar crime. The public was alerted to major financial scandals such as the savings and loan debacle, insider trading in the securities markets, and large-scale investment frauds. Consumers became aware of fraudulent practices against them, telemarketing scams, false billings and a host of other violations. Also, major political corruption cases such as Watergate, ABSCAM, Koreagate, and dubious political fundraising schemes highlighted the omnipresence of "white-collar crime."

Edwin Sutherland, arguably the most known and probably the most widely cited criminologist, very likely could not foresee the controversy that he created with the introduction of the concept of "white-collar crime." In his presidential address to the American Sociological Association in 1939 he suggested including the study of criminal activity in areas, mainly economic in nature, that were rarely studied before. Sutherland was likely influenced by the notion of "the criminaloid" devised by E. A. Ross (1907). Friedrichs (1996: 2) described the criminaloid as a "businessman who committed exploitative (if not necessarily illegal) acts of an uninhibited desire to maximize profit, all while hiding behind a façade of respectability and piety." In his famous address Sutherland coined the term "white-collar crime" and approached it as a separate category of criminal behavior (Sutherland, 1940). His well-known and often cited definition of white-collar crime as: "a crime committed by a person of respectability and high social status in the course of his occupation" opened the door for the study of crimes and criminal behavior that were neglected before. However, this definition has raised a host of questions and initiated many debates concerning the proper use of the term "white-collar crime"—about the theoretical perimeters of it and the practical applicability of this concept.

One of the major problems making the study of white-collar crime difficult is that it is not a legal term. Unlike traditional crimes, there is no legal category of "white-collar crime." Even in the case of legally defined offenses that are usually circumscribed in details in the law, there are often questions whether a certain act does or does not fit into the category covered by a particular statue. In the case of white-collar crimes, this problem is grossly magnified. Another controversial issue concerning Sutherland's definition hovers around the term "respectability." How would a person's respectability be determined? Even the concept of "high social status" is not universally agreed upon.

As a result of these complications, Sutherland's definition of white-collar crime came under criticism by several scholars. For example, Edelhertz (1970) claimed that the definition should not focus only on offenses related to occupational activities and should not be limited only to people of high social status. He suggested white-collar crime should be viewed as "an illegal act or a series of illegal acts committed by nonphysical means and by concealment and guile to obtain money or property to avoid the payment or loss of money or property or to obtain business or personal advantage" (3). Coleman (1998) noted that under this definition every property offense committed through deception could be considered white-collar crime.

Earlier Coleman (1985: 5) proposed a definition of white-collar crime as "a violation of the law committed by a person or a group of persons in the course of an otherwise respected and legitimate occupation or financial activity." This definition covers financial violations such as tax evasion in addition to offenses incidental to everyday occupational activity (the term 'respected' remained vague). Some critics pointed out that both Coleman's and Sutherland's definitions did not include crimes committed by corporations because of its focus only on individual offenders.

Marshall Clinard and Richard Quinney (1973) suggested a new approach to white-collar crime. They introduced the distinction between "corporate" and "occupational" crimes based on the distinction between the principal beneficiaries of the criminal act. In other words, if an individual representing a corporation and/or acting on its behalf commits an offense, that would be considered corporate crime. On the other hand, if an individual violates the law for his/her own benefit in the course of an occupational activity, that would be considered occupational crime. Schrager and Short (1977) refined these concepts by making distinctions between "organizational" and "individualistic" white-collar crime. Robin (1974: 262) referred to "occupational crime" as an offense that included "all violations that occur during the course of occupational activity and are related to employment." In a similar vein Green (1997: 15) suggested "occupational crime is any act punishable by law that is committed through opportunity created in the course of an occupation that is legal." The acceptance of this broad definition departs to a large degree from the initial intent of Sutherland who tried to expose the criminal activities of people in the higher echelons of society.

David Simon's formulation of the concept of "elite deviance" (1999) might be seen as a radical attempt to return to some of the original ideas of white-collar crime. Simon uses this concept to refer to acts committed by upper-class individuals for personal economic or political gains. These acts may be in violation of the law, or they might be considered deviant by generally accepted moral standards. Because of their power and influence, individuals committing such acts often can conceal their harmful behavior with little risk of being punished. Simon's approach focuses mainly on the identity of the individual and only to a lesser degree on the nature of the act.

Susan Shapiro (1990), in contrast, suggests that in the definition of white-collar crime the main focus should be on the nature of the criminal act and not on the perpetrator. She claims that "white-collar criminals violate norms of trust, enabling them to rob without violence and burgle without trespass." (Shapiro, 1990: 346). This author takes issue with the widely held contention that white-collar criminals are handled differently than other offenders because of their higher social standing. According to her definition, white-collar crime is a nonviolent act that involves the violation of trust.

While the "violation of trust" as a basic characteristic of white-collar offenses is widely accepted, there are many who would challenge the blanket assertion of their nonviolent nature. Several scholars point to the actual and potential violent outcomes of some of these crimes, such as the well-known Pinto case, illegal toxic waste dumping, and violation of occupational and safety laws (Cullen, Maakestad and Cavender, 1987; Frank, 1993; Mokhiber; 1988).

In a unique approach Gottfriedson and Hirschi (1990) claim that white-collar crime is not a separate category of criminal acts and should not be distinguished from other crimes. According to them the same explanation, basically the lack of self-control, is as relevant for white-collar crime as for any other offenses and can be studied through a "general theory of crime." This position was challenged by many criminologists who pointed out that the "general theory of crime" does not deal with corporations and their criminal acts; it does not explain why most white-collar offenders are not involved in "conventional offenses"; and it does not account for why they commit only certain types of offenses. In a recent article, Geis (2000: 44) criticizes the self-control approach to white-collar crime. He observes that: "To say that an absence of self-control prods the decisions of top-level business officers who violate the law is to trivialize the roots of their actions."

Recently, a combined effort by the participants of the Academic White-Collar Crime Workshop (convened by the National White-Collar Crime Center) suggested the following definition of white-collar crime; it is a synthesis of several other definitions. White-collar crime constitutes

> planned illegal or unethical acts of deception, committed by an individual or organization, usually during the course of legitimate occupational activity by persons of high or respectable social status, for personal or organizational gain that violates public trust. (Hemelkamp, Ball, and Townsend, 1996, p. III)

This brief review of the various definitions of "white-collar crime" illustrates the problematic and controversial nature of this concept. In the first part of this collection, we present several articles that either directly or indirectly address definitional issues of this theoretical construct.

The first article in this section is by Gilbert Geis, a leading scholar of white-collar crime. The title of the article "White-collar crime: What is it?" reflects the confusion surrounding this concept and the problems of definition facing researchers and practitioners dealing with this area more than half a century after the term was coined. The author reviews some of the less known writings of Sutherland and several definitional attempts by other scholars.

These attempts were aimed at clarifying the conceptual quagmire created by Sutherland's original definition. Geis deals with definitions based on the business-related characteristics of white-collar crime, its similarities to the characteristics of organized crime, and with studies that focus on offenses of organizations as a domain of white-collar crime. The author also explores the earlier mentioned "general theory of crime" forwarded by Gottfredson and Hirschi and Shapiro's conceptualization of white-collar crime as "violation of trust." At the end of his overview Geis arrives at the conclusion that Sutherland's original focus on the abuse of power by persons in high positions having the opportunity for such abuse may be the most relevant definition for the study of white-collar crime.

The next selection in this part is written by two scholars with financial and legal backgrounds rather than social science backgrounds. Maria S. Boss and Barbara Crutchfield George analyze the origins of laws defining white-collar crime, the differences between the treatment of corporate versus individual misconduct, legal and judicial measures designed to deter business misconduct, and nontraditional approaches to control white-collar crime. The authors acknowledge that the concept of white-collar crime is marked by changes in definition and the concept is elusive because its origin is in a nonlegal environment. Following their analysis, one might conclude that the most fruitful way to define what is and what is not white-collar crime is through legislation and legal practice.

Elizabeth Moore and Michael Mills focus on the victims of white-collar crimes. While there is an increasing professional interest in crime victims in general, there are relatively few theoretical and empirical studies that deal with white-collar crime victimization (see, Shichor 1998). Moore and Mills pinpoint the sharp contrast between policies aimed at curbing street crime and white-collar crime and the differential treatment of the victims of these crimes by the criminal justice system. The stark contrast between a harsh response to street criminals and our limp response to white-collar criminals violates our sense of equity. This article provides insight into definitional issues through the study of the victims of white-collar crime.

In the last article in this segment Gary Potter and Larry Gaines point to the convergence of organized and white-collar crime. They remind us that white-collar crime is a complex concept that includes the crime itself, the social context in which it occurs, and the attributes of the offenders. The authors claim that "white-collar crime" is a social construct and similar to other such constructs such as "street crime," "organized crime," or "juvenile delinquency," that have to do more with the unique conditions under which the offense occurs than with specified criminal acts. Thus, according to the authors "white-collar crime" is principally a heuristic devise guiding the study of criminal activity by certain actors in certain social situations. Potter and Gaines in this article try to provide an understanding of the nature of the concept of "white-collar crime" and its usefulness in the study of criminology.

◂ References ▸

Clinard, M. B. and R. Quinney (1973). *Criminal behavior systems: A typology* (2nd ed.). New York: Holt, Reinhart & Winston.

Coleman, J. S. (1985). Toward an integrated theory of white-collar crime. *American Journal of Sociology*, 94, 406–439.

Coleman, J. S. (1998). *The criminal elite* (4th ed.). New York: St. Martin's Press.

Cullen, F. T., Maakstad, W. J., and Cavender, G. (1987). *Corporate crime under attack: The Ford Pinto case and beyond.* Cincinnati, OH: Anderson.

Edelhertz, H. (1970). *The nature, impact and prosecution of white-collar crime.* Washington, D.C.: National Institute for Law Enforcement and Criminal Justice.

Frank, N. (1993). Maiming and killing: Occupational health crimes. *Annals*, 525, 107–118.

Friedrichs, D. O. (1996). *Trusted criminals.* Belmont, CA: Wadsworth.

Geis, G. (2000). On the absence of self-control as the basis for a general theory of crime: A critique. *Theoretical Criminology*, 4 (1), 35–53.

Gottfredson, M. R. and Hirschi, T. (1990). *A General Theory of Crime.* Stanford, CA: Stanford University Press.

Green, G. S. (1997). *Occupational Crime* (2nd ed.). Chicago: Nelson-Hall.

Hamelkamp, J., Ball, R. and Townsend, K. (Eds.). (1996). Definitional dilemma: Can and should there be a universal definition of white collar crime? *Proceedings of the Academic Workshop.* Morgantown, WV: National White Collar Crime Center Training and Research Institute.

Mokhiber, R. (1988). *Corporate crime and violence—big business power and the abuse of public trust.* San Francisco, CA: Sierra Club.

Moore, M. H. (1980). Notes toward a strategy to deal with white-collar crime. In H. Edelhertz and C. Rogovin (Eds.), *A national strategy to deal with white-collar crime.* Lexington, MA: D. C. Heath.

Robin, G. D. (1974, July). White-collar crime and employee theft. *Crime and Delinquency*, 251–262.

Ross, E. A. (1907). *Sin and society: An analysis of latter day iniquity.* New York: Harper & Row.

Schrager, L. S. and Short, J. F. Jr. (1977). Toward a sociology of organizational crime. *Social Problems*, 25, 407–419.

Shapiro, S. P. (1990). Collaring the crime, not the criminal: Reconsidering the concept of white-collar crime. *American Sociological Review*, 55, 346–365.

Shichor, D. (1998). Victimology and the victims of white-collar crime. In H. D. Schwind, E. Kube and H. H. Kuhne (Eds.), *Criminology on the threshold of the 21st century: Essays in honor of Hans Joachim Schneider* (pp. 331–351). Berlin: Walter de Gruyter.

Simon, D. (1999). *Elite deviance* (6th ed.). Boston, MA: Allyn and Bacon.

Sutherland, E. H. (1940). White-collar criminality. *American Sociological Review*, 5, 1–12.

1

White-Collar Crime
What Is It?

Gilbert Geis

Few, if any, legal or criminological terms are surrounded by as much dispute as white-collar crime. Sociologists, who dominate the field of academic criminology, are wont to insist that by "white-collar crime" they mean to pinpoint a coterie of offenses committed by persons of reasonably high standing in the course of their business, professional, or political work. Especially clear illustrations would be an antitrust conspiracy among vice presidents of several major corporations, the acceptance of a bribe by a member of the national cabinet, and Medicare fraud by a surgeon.

Persons with criminal law or regulatory law backgrounds, for their part, are likely to point out that no such designation as "white-collar crime" is to be found in the statute books and that the kinds of criminal offenses that sometimes are embraced within the term—such as insider trading, embezzlement, and a large variety of frauds—are committed by persons who might be located anywhere on a status hierarchy. While antitrust conspiracies are not likely to be carried out by lower-echelon employees (though they could in theory involve executives' secretaries), bribery transactions often

Reprinted with permission from *Current Issues in Criminal Justice*, 3(1): 9–24.

include lower-level go-betweens, and fraud against medical insurance programs is perpetrated by pharmacy employees and ambulance drivers as well as medical doctors. Why, it is asked, should a distinction be drawn between persons who have committed the same type of offense merely because they hold different occupational positions? This is but one of the disputes about definition that both plague and invigorate research and writing on white-collar crime.

Cynics are apt to view jousting about the definition of white-collar crime the same way they regard disputes about the definition of pornography: We all can recognize it when we see it, so why bother overmuch with attempting to pinpoint precise parameters? Those rejecting this viewpoint maintain that it is vital to establish an exact meaning for a term so that everyone employing it is talking about the same thing, and so that scientific investigations can build one upon the other rather than going off in various directions because of incompatible definitions of their subject matter.

On the debit side in this long-standing debate is the fact that a great deal of energy and ingenuity has been dedicated to defending one or another of the supposed characteristics of the term "white-collar crime" that could have been employed to increase our understanding of the behaviors involved and to determine more satisfactory methods for dealing with them. The credit side lists improved insight and understanding that result when good minds ask hard questions regarding precisely what is meant by words and terms that appear to be employed imprecisely. In the remainder of this chapter, I want to indicate the course of the intellectual fray regarding the definition of white-collar crime, so that readers might be better able to decide for themselves what resolution satisfies them.

Sutherland and His Early Disciples

The term "white-collar crime" was introduced to the academic world by Edwin H. Sutherland in 1939 during his presidential address to the American Sociological Society in Philadelphia. Fifty-six years old at the time, Sutherland was at the peak of a distinguished career marked primarily by his authorship of a sophisticated textbook, *Criminology*, that had first been published in 1924. Though he had lapsed from the orthodox religious faith of his father, a Baptist minister and college president, Sutherland had intensely strong moral convictions about commercial, political, and professional wrongdoing. He also had been deeply influenced by the populist ideas that permeated the Nebraska of his youth (Cherney, 1981), ideas that depicted corrupt business practices as undermining the well-being of the hard-working, God-fearing frontier people among whom Sutherland had been brought up.[1]

In Sutherland's presidential address, he insisted that he had undertaken his work on "crime in the upper, white-collar class, which is composed of respectable, or at least respected, business and professional men" only "for the purpose of developing the theories of criminal behavior, not for the purpose of muckraking or of reforming anything except criminology" (Sutherland, 1940, p. 1). This patently disingenuous disclaimer was primarily a bow to the ethos of sociology at the time, an ethos that insisted on a "value-free" and "neutral" research stance. A proper definition of his subject matter did not occupy Sutherland's attention in this paper; rather, he used anecdotal stories of rapacious acts by America's notorious "robber barons" and their successors to flay then-popular explanations of criminal activity such as poverty, low intelligence, and offender psychopathy.

Ten years later, in *White Collar Crime,* Sutherland (1949) fleshed out his presidential address, but did little to pin down with any more precision the definition of his subject matter. That he buried part of his definition in a footnote attests to his indifference to the matter. In the text, Sutherland declared that a white-collar crime "may be defined approximately as a crime committed by a person of respectability and high social status in the course of his occupation" (p. 9). He then added that the definition consequently "excludes many crimes of the upper class, such as most of their cases of murder, adultery, and intoxication, since these are not customarily a part of their occupational procedures" (p. 9). The footnoted observation added that "'white collar' is used here to refer principally to business managers and executives, in the sense that it was used by a president of General Motors who wrote *An Autobiography of a White Collar Worker*" (p. 9). However, within two pages of this pronouncement Sutherland illustrated white-collar crime with examples of thefts by employees in chain stores and overcharges by garage mechanics and watch repairers. It may have been a dearth of material at his disposal that led Sutherland to use these illustrations; more likely, it was the inconstancy of his definitional focus. Sutherland believed that all crime could be understood by a single interpretative scheme—his theory of differential association—and therefore, this being so, he saw no compelling reason to distinguish sharply between various forms of illegal activity.

Besides the ill-considered use of fudge words such as "approximately" and "principally" in his definition, Sutherland further muddied the semantic waters by planting here and there other equally amorphous clues to what he might have had in mind. The year before he published *White Collar Crime*, in a speech at DePauw University in Indiana, Sutherland had said:

> I have used the term white-collar criminal to refer to a person in the upper socioeconomic class who violates the laws designed to regulate his occupation. The term white-collar is used in the sense in which it was used by President Sloan of General Motors, who wrote a book titled *The Autobiography of a White Collar Worker*. The term is used more generally to refer to the wage-earning class which wears good clothes at work, such as clerks in stores. (Sutherland, 1956, p. 79)

The fact that Sutherland, usually a meticulous scholar in such matters, wrongly cites the Sloan book (it was *Adventures of a White Collar Man*) (Sloan and Sparkes, 1941) and that Sloan's book offers no further definitional enlightenment adds to the confusion. A strict constructionist might argue that the fact that Sutherland abandoned the final sentence in the foregoing quotation about the wage-earning class and its dress when he incorporated this material into his monograph the following year indicates that he had second thoughts, and that he intended to confine his focus to upper-class offenders.

The most straightforward definition that Sutherland offered has rarely been noted. It appeared in the *Encyclopedia of Criminology* (1949, p. 511) almost co-terminously with the publication of *White Collar Crime*. Here, Sutherland wrote that "the white collar criminal is defined as a person with high socioeconomic status who violates the laws designed to regulate his occupational activities." Such laws, Sutherland added, can be found in the penal code but also included federal and state trade regulations, as well as special war regulations and laws regarding advertising, patents, trademarks, and copyrights. Thereafter, he observed:

> The white collar criminal should be differentiated, on the one hand, from the person of lower socio-economic status who violates the regular penal code or the special trade regulations which apply to him; and, on the other hand, from the person of high socio-economic status who violates the regular penal code in ways not connected with his occupation. (p. 511)

It has to be an uncertain exegetic exercise to comb these different proclamations in order to try to state what was "truly" meant as the definition of the phenomenon Sutherland had so effectively called to academic and public attention. Certainly, the definitions are uncrystallized and, at times, contradictory. For me, though, what stands out is a sense that Sutherland was most concerned with the illegal abuse of power by upper-echelon businessmen in the service of their corporations, by high-ranking politicians against their codes of conduct and their constituencies, and by professional persons against the government and against their clients and patients.

Particularly significant, I find, is Sutherland's specific exclusion in the last of the definitions quoted of a person from the lower socioeconomic class who violates "special trade regulations which apply to him." It must be granted, however, that this phrase too has its ambiguities. Did Sutherland mean to include lower socioeconomic-class persons who violated regulations that applied *both* to them and to those above them in the power structure—such as the printer's devil and the corporate president who trade on insider information? Was it the law or the status of the perpetrator—or both linked together—that concerned him? It is said that Sutherland once was asked by Edwin Lemert, a noted criminologist, whether he meant by white-collar crime a type of crime committed by a special class of people, and he replied that "he was not sure" (Sparks, 1979, p. 17). Given its progenitor's alleged uncertainty, it is not surprising that those who try to perform as glossarists on the Sutherland definitional text often are befuddled. Besides, it should be stressed that Sutherland's definition, whatever its essence, has no necessary standing if more useful conceptualizations of the subject matter emerge.

In Sutherland's Wake

The focus of this chapter will almost exclusively be on definitional issues raised in the United States, primarily because most writers outside America have rather sanguinely ignored the question of the "proper" parameters for white-collar crime. In part, this is probably because it typically requires a large corps of communicants for some to devote their time to matters that have no immediate utilitarian result. Also, criminology outside the United States has only recently emerged as a social science enterprise distinctive from law and medical faculties, and the concept of white-collar crime is a characteristically social science formulation.

The term "white-collar crime" itself has been widely incorporated into popular and scholarly language throughout the world, though the designation "economic crime" tends to be preferred in socialist countries and is also widely used elsewhere. The United Nations, for its part, has adopted the phrase "abuse of power" for those behaviors that correspond to white-collar crimes. In addition, other designations, such as "upperworld crime," "crimes by the powerful," "crime in the suites," and "organizational crime" have their devotees.

Sutherland's position on white-collar crime elicited some early stinging but off-target critiques from two sociologists (Tappan, 1947; Caldwell, 1958), both of whom also held law degrees. Rather than focusing on Sutherland's definitional imprecision, both castigated him for what they saw as his anti-business bias and his use of a conceptual brush to tar persons who had not been convicted by a criminal court. Sutherland got much the better of this debate by arguing that it was what the person actually had done in terms of the mandate of the criminal law, not how the criminal justice system responded to what they had done, that was essential to whether they should be regarded as criminal offenders (Sutherland, 1945, pp. 132–139).

The pioneering empirical studies that followed in the wake of Sutherland's enunciation of a new area of inquiry did little to clarify the definitional uncertainty. Marshall Clinard (1952), studying black-market offenses during the Second World War, devoted his attention to the issue of whether what he had investigated truly was a crime rather than whether it might mesh with the ingredients necessary to characterize the behaviors as white-collar crime. Clinard also argued that the personalities of the perpetrators—such as egocentricity, emotional insecurity, and feelings of personal inadequacy—were at least as significant as Sutherland's differential association theory in accounting for the black-market violations.

Donald Cressey's (1953) interviews with embezzlers in federal prisons led him to question whether these offenders met the criteria for categorization as white-collar offenders, since they typically cheated their employers, and "[w]hile, with a few exceptions, the persons interviewed were in no sense poverty stricken, neither can they be considered as persons of high social status in the sense that Sutherland uses the phrase."[2]

As had Clinard, Frank Hartung (1950), in the third early major study of white-collar crime, addressed almost all of his definitional remarks to the debate over whether what the violators of the wartime regulations in the meat industry had done could be considered criminal (he believed, with solid evidence, that it could), and not whether, if so, the perpetrators were white-collar criminals. What particularly marked Hartung's contribution, however, was the feisty response it drew from a preeminent sociologist, Ernest Burgess (1950). Burgess insisted that persons violating regulatory laws, such as black marketers, could not be regarded as criminals because they did not so view themselves and were not so viewed by the public. Besides, Burgess maintained, this would mean that half the country's population, given the widespread disregard of rationing during the war, were criminals, a conclusion he apparently found intellectually intolerable. Hartung tried to assuage

Burgess, a power in the discipline, but had understandable difficulty with the idea that a person is not a criminal unless that person thinks of himself or herself as a criminal.

Summarizing these early days of white-collar crime scholarship, Donald Newman (1958) maintained that the chief criterion for a crime to be white-collar is that it occurs as a part of or as a deviation from the violator's occupational role. "Technically," Newman insisted, "this is more crucial than the type of law violated or the relative prestige of the violator, although these factors have necessarily come to be major issues in the white-collar crime controversy" (p. 737). This had happened, he argued, because most of the laws involved were not part of the traditional criminal codes, and because most of the violators were a cut above the ordinary criminal in social standing. Yet, in the same article, Newman notes that "[w]hether he likes it or not, the criminologist finds himself involved in an analysis of prestige, power, and differential privilege when he studies upperworld crime" (p. 746). Writing slightly later, Richard Quinney (1964) maintained that the concept of white-collar crime lacked conceptual clarity, and thought that it ought to embrace the derelictions of persons in all kinds of occupations. This, however, created another dilemma for Quinney—the question of what constitutes an occupational act. Is the filing of a tax return part of a retired person's occupation?[3] Is a welfare recipient who cheats the social services engaged in a white-collar crime because being on the dole is an occupational pursuit? Quinney, thus, added some more riddles, but, like those who had written before him, he was unable to put forward a definitional manifesto that could elicit widespread agreement.

◂ The Middle Years ▸

After the first burst of creative research on white-collar crime, the subject was virtually abandoned by scholars in the United States during the 1960s. Undoubtedly, this was in large part because of the reluctance to tackle iconoclastic ventures with the threat of McCarthyism hanging over the country (Schrenker, 1986). Ultimately, the surge for power by blacks, the challenge to the Vietnam conflict, Watergate, and similar events served to refocus attention on abuses of power. At the same time, as the study of crime in countries other than America moved away from being solely an enterprise conducted by black-letter lawyers and medical doctors, scholars throughout the world began to turn their attention to white-collar crime.[4]

On the definitional front, there was, first, an ineffectual and probably ill-conceived attempt in 1962 by the present author to restrict the term "white-collar crime" to the realm of corporate violations (Geis, 1962). Then, in 1970, Herbert Edelhertz, at the time the chief of the fraud section of the federal Department of Justice, offered a definition that drew exclusively upon legal understanding and, as he indicated, one that differed "markedly" from that advanced by Sutherland, which Edelhertz believed was "far too restrictive." "White collar crime is democratic," Edelhertz asserted, and "can be committed by a bank teller or the head of his institution" (pp. 3–4). Edelhertz proposed that a useful definition of white-collar crime would be "an illegal act or series of illegal acts committed by nonphysical means and by concealment or guile, to obtain money or property, to avoid the payment or loss of money or property, or to obtain business or personal advantage" (p. 3). He set out four subdivisions to embrace diverse forms of white-collar crime: (1) crimes by persons operating on an individual, ad hoc basis, for personal gain in a nonbusiness context; (2) crimes in the course of their occupations by those operating inside businesses, government, or other establishments, or in a professional capacity, in violation of their duty of loyalty and fidelity to employer or client; (3) crimes incidental to and in furtherance of business operations, but not the central purpose of such business operations; and (4) white-collar crime as a business, or as the central activity of the business. The last, Edelhertz indicated, referred to confidence games as forms of crime (pp. 19–20).

Criticism of the Edelhertz position predictably came from sociologists who regretted his slighting of the idea of abuse of power as the key aspect of white-collar offenses and his expansive extension of the term to such a variegated range of behaviors. They were puzzled by the excision of violence from the realm of white-collar crime, noting that crimes such as unnecessary surgical operations, the manufacture of unsafe automobiles, and the failure to label poisonous substances at the workplace could be regarded as white-collar crimes with a strong component of violence. Miriam Saxon (1980), for instance, in challenging Edelhertz's viewpoint, noted that the MER/29 case involved a pharmaceutical corporation that knowingly sold an anti-cholesterol drug that subjected at least five thousand persons to such serious side effects as cataracts and hair loss. Later, the American Bar Association would adopt the term "economic offense" for behaviors within the white-collar crime realm set forth by Edelhertz, and would modify the term "nonviolent" with the footnoted observation that this referred to "the means by which the crime is committed" even though "the harm to society can frequently be described as violent" (p. 5).

In 1973, Clinard and Quinney (p. 188) put forward what has become a widely accepted distinction in scholarship on white-collar crime, that between (1) occupational criminal behavior and (2) corporate criminal behavior. The former is meant to include persons at all levels of the social structure and was defined as the "violation of the criminal law in the course of activity of a legitimate occupation." The category included offenses of employees against their employers. Corporate crime for its part was to consist of offenses committed by corporate officials for their corporation and the offenses of the corporation itself[5] (p. 189).

Seven years later—in 1980—Albert Reiss and Albert Biderman, two particularly sophisticated scholars, suggested the following definition of white-collar crime in a monograph that sought, with a singular lack of success, to establish some basis for counting in a systematic manner the number of such offenses committed annually:

> White-collar violations are those violations of law to which penalties are attached that involve the use of a violator's position of significant power, influence, or trust in the legitimate economic or political institutional order for the purpose of illegal gain, or to commit an illegal act for personal or organizational gain. (p. 4)

What is notable about this stab at achieving definitional order is the return to what I see as Sutherland's clarion point, that the offense involve "the use of a violator's position of significant power, influence, or trust."

Another contribution of note was that by Richard Sparks (1979), who preferred to abandon the law as the essential ingredient of a white-collar offense and, instead, to incorporate both deviancy and illegality within its purview. By white-collar crime (or, as he preferred, "crime as business"), Sparks wrote that he meant acts possessing "all or most of the following features":

1. They are carried out primarily for economic gain, and involve some form of commerce, industry, or trade.
2. They necessarily involve some form of organization, in the sense of more or less formal relationships between the parties involved in committing the criminal acts. This organization is either based on, or adapted to, the commission of crimes.
3. They necessarily involve either the use or the misuse, or both, of legitimate forms and techniques of business, trade, or industry. What distinguishes such things as price-fixing conspiracies, invoice faking, and bankruptcy fraud from robbery, burglary, and shoplifting is that the former do, but the latter typically do not, involve methods and techniques that are also used for legitimate business purposes. (p. 172)

Perhaps the most interesting aspect of Sparks's definitional venture is his linkage of what has been called "organized crime" with white-collar crime. Dwight Smith (1981), in particular, has long insisted, though for the most part he has remained a lone voice, that conceptually there is little to distinguish the two forms of lawbreaking.

◂ Current Controversies ▸

Sentencing Studies

Science, both the social and natural varieties, progresses by testing ideas empirically, preferably by experimental means that utilize control or comparison groups. Some ideas—that there is resurrection after life, for instance—remain impervious to scientific scrutiny; others can be tested with greater or lesser difficulty. The field of white-collar crime, for its part, is notably resistant to experimental work. In some measure, this is because the standing of the perpetrators protects them from the kinds of manipulations that constitute so large a portion of experimental research.

A number of Sutherland's ideas concerning possible judicial favoritism towards white-collar offenders, however, have been converted into testable propositions in ways that have had an important impact on the manner in which white-collar crime is defined. In these instances, the nature of the available information dictated the definition employed.

One of the major studies, by John Hagan, Ilene Nagel, and Celesta Albonetti (1980), used college education and income as proxies for white-collar status in its review of the sentences handed out in ten American federal courts. The roster of white-collar offenses was initially derived intuitively from all acts in the statute books that plausibly might fit the category. Then it was refined by asking U.S. attorneys for their views. Ultimately, thirty-one offenses came to be regarded as white-collar offenses. The list included such arguable acts as failure to file a tax return, embezzlement or theft by bank employees, mail fraud swindles, and fraudulent acceptance of veterans' benefit payments. The research then was directed toward determining whether offenders convicted of committing such acts got tougher sentences than persons who had committed non-white-collar offenses—it was found that they did. In the other major sentencing study, Stanton Wheeler, David Weisburd, and Nancy Bode (1982) employed eight broad categories of federal offenses for their representation of white-collar crime: securities fraud, antitrust violations, bribery, tax offenses, bank embezzlement, postal and wire fraud, false claims and statements, and credit- and lending-institution fraud. They directed their inquiry toward discovering whether persons with higher social status were sentenced more leniently for such offenses than those with lower social status—it was found that they were not.[6]

The conclusions of the Wheeler study have been disputed on the ground, among others, that they fail to take into account the considerable screening that takes places in regard to white-collar offenses prior to the point where the remaining perpetrators go to court to plead or to be tried and, if found guilty, to be sentenced.[7] Perhaps a more basic issue is whether or not either team of researchers truly was studying persons who might reasonably be regarded as white-collar criminals. Kathleen Daly (1989), reanalyzing the data used in the Wheeler et al. investigation to determine the fate of women who committed white-collar crimes, came to the paradoxical conclusion that it was "occupational marginality" that best explained such offenses; virtually all of the bank embezzlers in her sample, for instance, were clerical workers, and as many as a third of the women in some offense categories were unemployed. For the men, Wheeler and his colleagues had reported that among the credit-fraud, false-claim, and mail-fraud offenders, fewer than half were steadily employed and a quarter were unemployed at the time of their offenses (Wheeler et al., 1988). At the end of her study, Daly, in an aside almost plaintive in nature, mused, "The women's socioeconomic profile, coupled with the nature of their crimes, makes one wonder if 'white-collar' aptly describes them or their illegalities."[8]

Responding in part to the criticism that he had corrupted the essential nature of white-collar crime in his sentencing study (Geis, 1984, p. 146), Hagan, in collaboration with Patricia Parker (1985), later refocused his attention on securities violations during a seventeen-year period in the province of Ontario in Canada. He now employed as the determinant of white-collar power what he called "relational indicators," such as ownership and authority, which located individuals in class positions directly relevant to the perpetration of their offenses. Hagan and Parker also looked at regulatory enforcement under the Securities Act, arguing that the majority of the offenses in which they were interested never came before the criminal courts. This research overturned the earlier counterintuitive conclusion that white-collar offenders are treated more leniently; instead, it was found that employers often escaped both criminal-court appearance and regulatory punishment for Securities Act violations and that managers bore the heaviest burden of the sanctioning process. Regarding the importance of their different definitional focus, Hagan and Parker noted: "Empirical results of our work suggest that the substitution of class for status measures [for example, education and income] is crucial."

Organizational Foci

Parallel to the contretemps regarding the definitional boundaries of white-collar crime elicited by the sentencing studies, there has been an increasing focus on offenses by organizations as part of the territory of white-collar crime. Sutherland himself had devoted a major portion of his monograph to a compilation of the official records of wrongdoing by the seventy largest American corporations (and, as a result, had labeled most of them "criminal recidivists"), and Clinard and Quinney had established corporate crime as a separable unit of white-collar crime analysis.

Chief among the proponents of an organizational focus are M. David Ermann and Richard Lundman (1978) who note in their definitional framework that, among other things, to be considered deviant an organizational act must be contrary to norms maintained outside the organization and must have support from the dominant administrative coalition of the organization. Laura Schrager and James F. Short, Jr., (1977) define organizational crime in the following manner:

> The illegal acts of omission or commission of an individual or a group of individuals in a formal organization in accordance with the operative goals of the organization, which have a serious physical or economic impact on employees, consumers, or the general public. (p. 408)

The inclusion of a measure of the consequence of the offense ("a serious . . . impact") as an aspect of its definition seems puzzling, since various forms of illegal economic activity, such as some kinds of antitrust activity (for example, pooling resources by different companies to finance research on serious diseases), are at best arguably detrimental to economic health and vitality, but have been outlawed as a consequence of the force of a particular marketplace philosophy (Kadish, 1963).

Attention to organizational activity in white-collar crime studies has drawn heavy criticism from Donald R. Cressey (1989), who argued that the idea that corporations commit crimes is merely a legal fiction. Cressey maintained that "so-called organizational crime (another name for corporate crime) is committed by corporation executives, not by organizations." Cressey's position, for its part, has been criticized by John Braithwaite and Brent Fisse (1990). They argued that "sound scientific theories can be based on a foundation of corporate action," and noted that "[b]ecause the makeup of a corporation is different from that of a human being, it can do things that are not humanly possible, such as growing from infant to adult in a year, securing immortality." The essence of Braithwaite and Fisse's position appears in the following paragraph:

> The notion that individuals are real, observable, flesh and blood, while corporations are legal fictions, is false. Plainly, many features of corporations are observable (their assets, factories, decision-making procedures), while many features of individuals are not (e.g., personality, intention, unconscious minds).[9] (p. 19)

Finally, Braithwaite and Fisse insist that "[t]he products of organizations are more than the sum of the products of individual actions" (p. 22). Albert K. Cohen (1990) recently has supported the Braithwaite and Fisse viewpoint, and offered some guidelines to white-collar crime students for a better understanding of the "organization as an actor."

General Theory and Abuse of Trust

Two major forays into the definitional realm regarding white-collar crime have emerged in the past few years. Both offer strong arguments for the idiosyncratic stances they adopt. Whether either will have more than a passing influence on the manner in which white-collar crime comes to be viewed seems uncertain.

Travis Hirschi and Michael Gottfredson (1987) maintain that white-collar crime is nothing more than another form of lawbreaking—like rape, vandalism, and simple assault—and readily can be incorporated into an explanatory framework that accounts for the causes of all criminal behavior. For them, there is no relevant distinction that would necessitate white-collar crime being regarded as a special category of offense. They argue that focusing on the class position of the offender precludes all theories except those based on psychological differences between lawbreakers as an explanation for what they have done. Hirschi and Gottfredson maintain that persons studying juvenile delinquency have found no utility in examining as separate entities vandalism, arson, rape, or burglary, and that, therefore, "there is little reason to think that the idea of specialization in white-collar offenses will bear fruit."[10] They also argue, apropos white-collar crime, that crimes have in common features that make those engaging in any one of them extremely likely to engage in others as well, a proposition that could be upheld in regard to white-collar offenders only if the category of behavior is defined extremely broadly, as it is by these authors. Critics of Hirschi and Gottfredson maintain that the pursuit of a single explanation that will permit understanding of all forms of criminal activity is a chimera, doomed to eternal failure.

The second call to reconceptualize white-collar crime—or, as she terms it, to "liberate" the term—is that offered by Susan Shapiro (1990), who insists that white-collar crime ought to refer specifically and only to the violation of trust by which persons are enabled "to rob without violence and burgle without trespass" (p. 346). Such persons manipulate norms of disclosure, disinterestedness, and role competence. Their behaviors involve lying, misrepresentation, stealing, misappropriation, self-dealing, corruption, and role conflict. As a whimsical example of misrepresentation, Shapiro tells the story of "Zoogate"—that the zoo in Houston advertised live cobras but actually displayed rubber replicas, since live cobras could not live under the lights in the area where they would have to be kept. Prosecution of crimes involving abuse of trust is handicapped, Shapiro points out, because of the ambiguity that renders victims unwitting and therefore unable to assist in prosecution, and the fact that the suspects tend to have custody of the crucial evidence against them. Shapiro grants that the Sutherland definitional heritage is not readily cast aside, because the concept of white-collar crime is "polemically powerful" and "palpably self-evident" (p. 357). She also grants that her redesign of the concept has its own problems—for instance, that it excludes antitrust crimes as well as corporate violence that grows out of deliberate decisions or negligence. Nonetheless, Shapiro concludes with a resounding indictment of the consequences of the usual way of looking at white-collar crime, which is said to have

> created an imprisoning framework for contemporary scholarship, impoverishing theory, distorting empirical inquiry, oversimplifying policy analysis, inflaming our muckraking instincts, and obscuring fascinating questions about the relationships between social organization and crime. (p. 362)

◂ CONCLUSION ▸

I proposed at the outset of the chapter to set forth a sample of the major contributions directed toward providing a satisfactory definition of white-collar crime so that readers might be helped to adjudicate the debate for themselves. Most certainly, I have intruded into the presentation of viewpoints a relatively strong indication of my personal preferences. In this final section, I want to formalize how I see some of the issues that have been considered in this chapter.

In writing for newspapers, reporters often strive to tie their stories into a more significant or at least more recognizable overarching framework. This search for a "news peg" has its analog in scientific work: all of us generally attend more readily to things that relate to matters about which we already are concerned rather than to unfamiliar issues. The extensive and excellent work of Wheeler and his colleagues at Yale University was funded by the

U.S. Department of Justice as a response to concern with what was known as "white-collar crime." Therefore, it was incumbent upon the grant recipients to place their research under that heading and, when they gained access to federal court data, to insist that such data represented white-collar crime rather than to regard them as a collection of information about certain kinds of offenses against federal law.

Similarly, Shapiro's contribution most basically asks that a new line of inquiry, that focuses on abuse of trust, be pursued in scholarly work. There is no compelling reason that this call-to-arms be allied to the abandonment of traditional research on white-collar crime. Her blueprint may produce worthwhile scholarly and policy products. Shapiro's argument against the traditional study of white-collar crime, however, seems gratuitous, since it is not—and probably cannot be—accompanied by a demonstration of the truth of the assertion that intellectual, political, or social life would be better served by attending to abuses of trust rather than abuses of power.

My personal belief is that, whatever the loss incurred by the mounting of wayward inquiries, the preferred situation is that which encourages research and policy people to pursue those kinds of inquiries that strike them as offering the greatest personal, professional, and public reward. That position, of course, so stated, has elements both of the platitudinous and the pious, but I know of no other way to convey it. In regard to white-collar crime, I remain persuaded that Sutherland, however errantly, focused on a matter of singular practical and intellectual importance—the abuse of power by persons who are situated in high places where they are provided with the opportunity for such abuse. To my mind, the excellent study by Hagan and Parker of the punishment of securities fraud in Canada illustrates how adherence to the Sutherland tradition can produce valuable findings. In my more ardent, youthful days I predicted that unless the term "white-collar crime" was accorded a tighter definition it would remain "so broad and indefinite as to fall into inevitable desuetude" (Geis, 1962, p. 171). Instead, as this chapter indicates, in my more ancient state, almost thirty years down the line, the concept remains vital and compelling. I find myself today in agreement with John Braithwaite's (1985, p. 19) suggestion that "[p]robably the most sensible way to proceed . . . is to stick with Sutherland's definition." This, he points out, at least excludes welfare cheats and credit-card frauds from the territory. Thereafter, Braithwaite would "partition the domain into major types of white collar crime" in order to generate sound theory (p. 3). If his were a legislative motion, and I a member, I would second it. Then, during debate, I would be certain to read into the record Robert Nisbet's (1965) advice:

> Beyond a certain point, it is but a waste of time to seek tidy semantic justifications for concepts used by creative minds. The important and all-too-neglected task in philosophy and social theory is that of observing the ways in which abstract concepts are converted by their creators into methodologies and perspectives which provide new illumination of the world. (P. 39)

◂ Notes ▸

1 For biographical details regarding Sutherland, see Gilbert Geis and Colin Goff, "Introduction," in Edwin H. Sutherland, *White Collar Crime: The Uncut Version* (New Haven: Yale University Press, 1983), *ix–xxxiii.*

2 Daniel Bell similarly excludes embezzlers from the white-collar territory because of their middle-class status: "Crime as an American Way of Life," in *The End of Ideology* (New York: Free Press, 1960), 382.

3 It has been argued that tax evasion ought to be regarded as a white-collar crime, and that all persons, regardless of their social positions, who evade taxes ought to be studied together. Robert Mason and Lyle D. Calvin, "A Study of Admitted Income Tax Evasion," *Law and Society Review*, 13 (1978), 73–89.

4 A brief sample of non-American writings includes Lin Dong-Mao, *The Study of Economic Crime* (Taipei: Central Police College, 1984); Andrew Hopkins, *Crime, Law and Business: The Sociological Aspects of Australian Monopoly Law* (Canberra, Australia: Australian Institute of Criminology, 1978); Georges Kellens, *Banqueroute et Banqueroutiers* (Brussels: Dessart et Mardaga, 1974); Michael Levi, *The Phantom Capitalists: The Organisation and Control of Long-Firm Fraud* (London: Heinemann, 1981). The most comprehensive white-collar crime bibliography has been produced in Germany: Hildegard Liebl and Karlhans Liebl, *Internationale Bibliographie zur Wirtshcaftskriminalitat* (Pfaffenweiler, Germany: Centaurus-Verlagsgesellschaft, 1985).

5 The two American textbooks on white-collar crime employ slight variants of the Clinard and Quinney position. James S. Coleman defines white-collar crime as a "violation of the law committed by a person or group of persons in the course of their otherwise respected and legitimate occupation or financial activity" (*The Criminal Elite,* 2d ed., New York: St. Martin's Press, 1989, 5). Gary S. Green entitled his text *Organizational Crime* (Chicago: Nelson Hall, 1990), and defined its subject as (1) acts punishable by law; and (2) those committed through opportunity created by an occupational role that is legal (p. 13).

6 A replication of the study using different courts has reached somewhat different conclusions: Michael Benson and Esteban Walker, "Sentencing the White-Collar Offender," *American Sociological Review,* 53 (1988), 294–302.

7 For a defense of the sample, see Stanton Wheeler and Mitchell Rothman, "The Organization as Weapon in White-Collar Crime," *Michigan Law Review,* 80 (1982), 1403–1426.

8 Another writer has more aptly described such offenders as "frayed-collar criminals." Jane Roberts Chapman, *Economic Realities and the Female Offender* (Lexington, MA: Lexington Books, 1980), 68.

9 See also John Braithwaite and Brent Fisse, "Varieties of Responsibility and Organizational Crime," Law & Policy, 7 (1985), 315–343.

[10] A critique is found in Darrell Steffensmeier, "On the Causes of 'White-Collar' Crime," *Criminology*, 27 (1989), 345–358.

◂ REFERENCES ▸

Bell, D. (1960). Crime as an American way of life. In *The end of ideology*. New York: Free Press.

Benson, M. L., and Walker, E. (1988). Sentencing the white-collar offender. *American Sociological Review*, 53, 294–302.

Braithwaite, J. (1985). White collar crime. In R. H. Turner and J. F. Short, eds. *Annual review of sociology*, 1–25. Vol. 11. Palo Alto, CA: Annual Reviews.

Braithwaite, J., and Fisse, B. (1985). Varieties of responsibility and organizational crime. *Law & Policy*, 7, 315–343.

Braithwaite, J., and Fisse, B. (1990). On the plausibility of corporate crime theory. In W. S. Laufer and F. Adler, eds. *Advances in criminological theory*, Vol. 2, 15–38. New Brunswick, NJ: Transaction Books.

Burgess, E. W., (1950). Comment, and concluding comment. *American Journal of Sociology*, 56, 32–34.

Caldwell, R. G. (1958). A re-examination of the concept of white-collar crime. *Federal Probation*, 22, 30–36.

Chapman, J. R. (1980). *Economic realities and the female offender*. Lexington, MA: Lexington Books.

Cherney, R. W. (1981). *Populism, progressivism and the transformation of Nebraska politics, 1885–1915*. Lincoln: University of Nebraska Press.

Clinard, M. B. (1952). *The black market: A study of white collar crime*. New York: Rinehart.

Clinard, M. B., and Quinney, R. (1973). *Criminal behavior systems: A typology* (2d ed.). New York: Holt, Rinehart and Winston.

Cohen, A. K. (1990). Criminal actors: Natural persons and collectivities. In School of Justice Studies, Arizona State University, ed. *New direction in the study of justice, law, and social control*, 101–125. New York: Plenum.

Coleman, J. W. (1989). *The criminal elite: The sociology of white collar crime* (2d ed.). New York: St. Martin's Press.

Cressey, D. R. (1953). *Other people's money: A study in the social psychology of embezzlement*. Glencoe, IL: Free Press.

———. (1989). The poverty of theory in corporate crime research. In W. S. Laufer and E. Adler, eds. *Advances in criminological theory*, Vol. 1, 31–56. New Brunswick, NJ: Transaction Books.

Daly, K. (1989). Gender and varieties of white-collar crime. *Criminology*, 27,769–793.

Edelhertz, H. (1970). *The nature, impact and prosecution of white-collar crime*. Washington, DC: Law Enforcement Assistance Administration, U.S. Department of Justice.

Ermann, M. D., and Lundman, R. J. (1978). Deviant acts by complex organizations: Deviance and social control at the organizational level of analysis. *The Sociological Quarterly*, 19, 56–67.

Geis, G. (1962). Toward a delineation of white-collar offenses. *Sociological Inquiry*, 32, 160–171.

———. (1984). White-collar and corporate crime. In R. E Meier, ed. *Major forms of crime*, 137–166. Beverly Hills: Sage.

Green, G. S. (1990). *Organizational crime.* Chicago: Nelson Hall.

Hagan, J., Nagel-Bernstein, I. H., and Albonetti, C. (1980). The differential sentencing of white-collar offenders in ten federal district courts. *American Sociological Review,* 45, 802–820.

Hagan, J., and Parker, P. (1985). White-collar crime and punishment: The class structure and legal sanctioning of securities violations. *American Sociological Review,* 50, 302–316.

Hartung, F. E. (1950). White-collar offenses in the wholesale meat industry in Detroit. *American Journal of Sociology,* 56, 25–44.

Hirschi, T., and Gottfredson, M. (1987). Causes of white-collar crime. *Criminology,* 25, 957.

Hopkins, A. (1978). *Crime, law and business: The sociological aspects of Australian monopoly law.* Canberra, Australia: Australian Institute of Criminology.

Kadish, S. H. (1963). Some observations on the use of criminal sanctions in enforcing economic regulations. *University of Chicago Law Review,* 30, 423–449.

Kellens, G. (1974). *Banqueroute et banqueroutiers.* Brussels: Dessart et Mardaga.

Levi, M. (1981). *The phantom capitalists: The organisation and control of long-firm fraud.* London: Heinemann.

Liebl, H., and Liebl, K. (1985). *Internationale bibliographie zur wirtschaftskriminalitat.* Pfaffenweiler, Germany: Centaurus-Verlagsgesellschaft.

Lin, Dong-Mao (1984). *The study of economic crime.* Taipei: Central Police College.

Mason, R., and Calvin, L. D. (1978). A study of admitted income tax evasion. *Law and Society Review,* 13, 73–89.

Newman, D. J. (1958). White-collar crime: An overview and analysis. *Law and Contemporary Problems,* 23, 737.

Nisbet, R. A. (1965). *Makers of modern social science: Emile Durkheim.* Englewood Cliffs, NJ: Prentice Hall.

Pepinsky, H. E. (1976). *Crime and conflict: A study of law and society.* New York: Academic Press.

Quinney, R. (1964). The study of white collar crime: Toward a reorientation in theory and research. *Journal of Criminology, Criminal Law, and Police Science,* 55, 208–214.

Reiss, A. J., Jr., and Biderman, A. D. (1980). *Data sources on white-collar lawbreaking.* Washington, DC: Government Printing Office.

Rheingold, P. D. (1968). The MER/29 story: An instance of successful mass disaster litigation. *California Law Review,* 56, 116–148.

Saxon, M. S. (1980). *White collar crime: The problem and the federal response.* Washington, DC: Congressional Research Service, Library of Congress.

Schrager, L. S., and Short, J. F. Jr. (1977). Toward a sociology of organizational crime. *Social Problems,* 25, 407–419.

Schrenker, E. W. (1986). *No ivory tower: McCarthyism and the universities.* New York: Oxford University Press.

Shapiro, S. P. (1985). The road not taken: The elusive path to criminal prosecution for white-collar offenders. *Law and Society Review,* 19, 179–217.

———. (1990). Collaring the crime, not the criminal: Liberating the concept of white-collar crime. *American Sociological Review,* 55, 346.

Sloan, A. P., Jr., and Sparkes, B. (1941). *Adventures of a white collar man.* New York: Doubleday Doran.

Smith, D. C., Jr. (1981). White-collar crime, organized crime, and the business establishment: Resolving a crisis in criminological theory. In P. Wickman and T. Dailey, eds. *White-collar and economic crime: Multidisciplinary and cross-national perspectives,* 23–38. Lexington, MA: Lexington Books.

Sparks, R. F. (1979). "Crime as business" and the female offender. In F. Adler and R. J. Simon, eds. *The criminology of deviant women,* 171–179. Boston: Houghton Mifflin Company.

Steffensmeier, D. (1989). On the causes of "white-collar" crime. *Criminology,* 27, 345–358.

Sutherland, E. H. (1940). White collar criminality. *American Sociological Review,* 5, 1–12.

———. (1945). Is "white collar crime" crime? *American Sociological Review,* 10, 132–139.

———. (1949). The white collar criminal. In V. C. Branham and S. B. Kutash, *Encyclopedia of Criminology,* 511–515. New York: Philosophical Library.

———. (1949). *White collar crime.* New York: Dryden Press.

———. (1956). Crime of corporations. In A. K. Cohen, A. Lindesmith, and K. Schuessler, eds. *The Sutherland Papers,* 78–96. Bloomington: Indiana University Press.

———. (1983). *White collar crime: The uncut version.* New Haven: Yale University Press.

Tappan, P. W. (1947). Who is the criminal? *American Sociological Review,* 12, 96–102.

Wheeler, S., and Rothman, M. (1982). The organization as weapon in white-collar crime. *Michigan Law Review,* 80, 1403–1426.

Wheeler, S., Weisburd, D., and Bode, N. (1982). Sentencing the white-collar offender: Rhetoric and reality. *American Sociological Review,* 47, 641–659.

Wheeler, S., Weisburd, D., Waring, E., and Bode, N. (1988). White collar crimes and criminals. *American Criminal Law Review,* 25, 346.

‹ 2 ›

Challenging Conventional Views of White-Collar Crime

Maria S. Boss
Barbara Crutchfield George

An early perception of "criminal" activity saw it as directing violence and harm to a perceived victim. Business misconduct, however, involved "victimless crimes," and so the same perception did not seem accurate.[1] The first categorization of business misconduct as the commission of a "crime" occurred when the term "white-collar crime" was used by sociologist Edwin H. Sutherland in his 1939 presidential address to the American Sociological Society.[2] His definition of white-collar crime was one "committed by a person of respectability and high social status in the course of his occupation."[3] In his work Sutherland focused almost exclusively on business crimes, particularly on violations of federal economic regulations.[4] He is regarded as one of the founders of American criminology, and one of his most important contributions was to bring the privileged crimes of business and government into a field

Reprinted with permission from *Criminal Law Bulletin*, 28(1): 32–58.

that traditionally focused on the crimes of the poor and disenfranchised.[5] His goal was to liberate traditional criminology from the "cognitive misbehavior" reflected in what he perceived to be the false correlation between poverty and crime.[6]

Although there was apparent acceptance of this expansion of criminality to business activity, prosecutors were unwilling to use the criminal justice system against business defendants. Instead, early attempts to control white-collar crime were mainly handled through the civil system with the imposition of treble damages, such as those imposed in anti-trust violations, and other kinds of damage awards. Later the concept of business crime was broadened and new terminology was introduced. For example, "elite deviance" has been used to refer to representative forms of wrongdoing "by wealthy and powerful individuals and organizations."[7]

The evolution of the concept of white-collar crime has been marked by changes in definition. To some the term still denotes crimes committed by individuals of high status. To others, it refers to illegal actions by organizations or by persons in certain occupations. Some observers concentrate on the nature of the offense, others on its consequences. There are, however, certain actions that virtually anyone would regard as white-collar crime: securities violations, anti-trust violations, bribery, embezzlement, mail and wire fraud, tax fraud, false claims and statements, and credit fraud.[8]

During the last two decades, as white-collar crimes became more prevalent and schemes more sophisticated, legislators and the courts have responded by increasing penalties. Conduct formerly considered merely "sharp business practices" or "sleazy" behavior, which, at most, would have been the basis for a civil suit for damages, became grounds for criminal prosecution and the imposition of increasingly harsh penalties. Prosecutors have been provided with forfeiture penalties, megafines, and prison sentences in their deterrence arsenal. However, it may be pointless to attempt to graft activity encompassed within the definition of "white-collar crime" onto traditional concepts of crime and punishment. It must be recognized that the term "white-collar crime" is flawed and that the wrongdoers within this category cannot be deterred through the application of traditional penalties alone. As a result, those governing the criminal justice system must refocus their attitudes toward business misconduct.

The criminal justice system has failed to separate the common-law precepts that govern "white-collar crime" from those applicable to traditional crime. The rules applicable to common-law concepts of crime may not apply when a corporate entity engages in misconduct. For example, the presence of mens rea is irrelevant when an artificial (as opposed to a natural) person is involved.

There are a number of factors explaining why the traditional criminal justice system fails in its attempts to deter white-collar offenses. The strong natural law component of traditional criminal law makes it very clear that such crimes as murder or robbery should not be committed, but many business crimes lack this intuitive illegitimacy.[9] Traditionally, a criminal act constitutes behavior that society defines as an intolerable threat to the social order. It is less clear that such business crimes as anti-trust violations or illegal insider trading activities present such a threat.[10] One of the underlying reasons for societal disinterest in pursuing corporate crime may be the misplaced "respect" evoked when one "beats the system" or "finds a loophole."[11] Legislators must free themselves from traditional criminal law analysis and place primary emphasis on the utilization of new approaches to solving this problem by rewarding ethical behavior of employees within the business environment and by penalizing employer inaction when an employer knows or should have known that its employees have been engaging in illegal conduct.[12]

Sources of Laws Defining White-Collar Crime

Although white-collar crime manifests itself in diverse ways, there is an underlying commonality in its origins in that its sources can ultimately be found in legislation and judicial interpretation. Many of the laws governing white-collar crime result from a societal desire to legislate ethical business practices; thus legislation usually reflects the mainstream viewpoint of how business "should" be conducted.

Historically, the laws defining white-collar crimes have diverse origins, but all of them can ultimately be traced to the conflicts and dislocations resulting from the growth of industrial capitalism.[13] Anti-trust legislation was a response to the economic pressure put on small farmers and business people by the growth of giant corporations.[14] Consumer protection laws can be seen as substitutes for the informal controls that regulated commerce in small-town America.[15] The effort to maintain and improve democratic institutions in the face of the growing centralization of economic power resulted in legislation regulating political campaigns.[16] Recognition of the dangerous side effects of industrial technology led to worker and environmental protection legislation.[17] The inability of the Federal Savings and Loan Insurance Corporation to cover the enormous losses generated by the savings and loan crisis created the impetus for passage by Congress of the Financial Institutions Reform, Recovery and Enforcement Act of 1989 (FIRREA).[18]

Such conflicts and dislocations, however, have not automatically generated new legislation.[19] Rather, it has been the conflict between organized interest groups that results in legislative change.[20] Thus, most white-collar crime legislation has resulted from the struggle between popular mass movements (with occasional support from some segments of the upper class) and established business interests.[21] The antimonopoly, consumer, and environmental movements all fit a similar pattern.[22] In all three situations the reformers at first faced a unified front of business opposition that frustrated their efforts. When they were able to take advantage of factors such as well-publicized disasters and scandals, widespread popular support, and effective organization and leadership, they were able to win passage of new legislation.[23] However, even when such reform legislation was passed, opponents still exerted great influence in shaping its final form.[24]

Not all rules governing business misconduct are found in legislative enactments resulting from public pressure. Widespread public pressure for enactment of legislation was not required in prohibiting such activities as embezzlement and industrial espionage.[25] These prohibitions were initiated by business interests[26] in a pattern that has been referred to as "reform from the top." When business interests sought recourse through the courts, an extensive body of case law developed, resulting in reforms through judicial interpretations rather than through passage of new statutory law.[27]

Motivation for White-Collar Crime

Peter Drucker, a well known academic, has stated that ". . . executive life not only breeds a parochialism of the imagination comparable to the 'military mind,' but places a considerable premium on it."[28] The corporate environment has been blamed for discouraging initiative and placing a premium on conformity.[29] Such conformity, however, can lead to a willingness on the part of the corporate employee to break the law on behalf of the company.

The change in traditional attitudes of corporations and their employees has had an effect on the extent of white-collar crime. This attitude change is possibly the result of a mainstream acceptance of social materialism. It is now more important to make money than to enjoy one's occupation and contribute to an organization. Without the element of loyalty, employees are less likely to feel a moral restraint on conduct such as divulging trade secrets to a competitor. Ambition, in many cases, has caused the traditional notions of loyalty to one's company to be cast aside. Employees no longer expect to spend an entire career at one firm. This expectation has been replaced with the goal of moving up the corporate ladder, usually accomplished by multiple job moves. Corporations, in turn, have been subjected to threats of takeovers with all the ensuing insecurity and turmoil of the merger upon the employees. Large corporate entities, lacking the safeguard of direct accountability to their owners, present a great temptation for the managers to utilize corporate wealth and power for their own personal gain. The profit-driven 1980s, and an atmosphere of merger mania, only served to increase the temptation for white-collar workers to engage in misconduct. The resulting instability took an ethical toll, providing fertile ground for criminal wrongdoing.

Deregulation has been blamed for the increase in white-collar crime. Ralph Nader asserted, "In 1980, Ronald Reagan promised to get government off the backs of business: few voters suspected that less regulation would mean more corporate crime."[30] Adam Smith believed that restraints on the free market created the climate for business crime, and he relied on pure economic self-interest to keep business men and women honest. However, commerce is no longer dominated by the small entities that were the foundation of Adam Smith's theories. With the advent of giant corporate structures, a deregulated climate results in the relaxation of consumer-protection standards and the temptation for various kinds of white-collar fraud.

Organizations have commonly failed to emphasize the importance of ethics through the adoption of standards and guidelines for employee conduct. In the last decade the trend within the business community has been toward replacing ethical values with personal greed. For public relations purposes and other reasons, many corporations have adopted codes of ethics, but such rules are sometimes not observed. Public confidence in business and political leaders remains low. Many serious questions regarding the role of ethical standards and modern American capitalism are being raised. The ethical standards of American business appear to have plummeted, and business indeed is operating at a lower level of personal and corporate ethics.[31] It has been argued that one reason the law fails to compel ethical conduct in business is that frequently the penalties for violating laws regulating business are weak deterrents.[32] In the last decade, however, law enforcers have taken steps to increase penalties in an attempt to remedy this alleged defect in the system.

Difficulty of detection serves as a temptation. Perpetrators of organizational crime know that their actions are often hard to detect. Top management is able to hide behind layers of middle management, and ultimately the corporation itself.[33] Corporations often prevent detection by refusing to prosecute criminals because they are fearful of exposing loose internal corporate controls, at best an embarrassment and at worst the basis of a shareholder derivative suit or a governmental prosecution.[34]

Some other motivating causes for commission of white-collar crime include: (1) potential for illegal profits; (2) inadequate enforcement of laws regulating business; and (3) complexity of laws regulating business conduct.[35] An example of the latter is the failure of Congress to pass legislation defining prohibited insider trading.

Corporate Misconduct Versus Individual Misconduct

One of the main problems encountered in coping with white-collar crime is the issue of how to deal with corporate criminal liability as opposed to individual misconduct. Although common law recognized the corporation as a legal "person," the question of imposition of criminal liability upon the corporate "person" is still being resolved.[36] Recognition of criminal liability for corporate entities has been slow in coming. Early English common law did not hold corporations liable for criminal actions. It was believed that only natural persons, not artificial persons, could have the capacity to form the intent necessary to commit a wrongful act or could be subject to imprisonment. However, as corporations grew in influence and power, there was increased pressure for courts to hold them criminally liable.[37] In addition, emerging tort concepts of vicarious liability made it easier for courts to accept the concept that corporations as a separate entity could be held liable for the acts of their agents.[38] Initially prosecution only involved violations of regulatory statutes where there was no question of a mens rea component to the crime.[39] When corporations actually became defined as "persons," the courts finally had a basis for finding a corporation guilty of a crime with a mens rea component.[40] Corporate criminal liability was broadened when courts began to accept the concept of imputing the wrongful intent of the corporate agent to the corporation as a whole.[41]

Probably the most famous case in recent history that wrestles with the issues of corporate criminal and civil responsibility is that involving the defective design of the gas tank in the Ford Pinto. Although there was a verdict against Ford in the civil litigation in the case,[42] the criminal charges for reckless homicide against Ford were dismissed. This dismissal was extremely significant because it represents the judicial rejection of the concept that a corporation can be criminally prosecuted for injuries or death resulting from defective products.

One of the most difficult issues the courts had to address in deciding issues of corporate liability, including criminal liability, was whether the employee had to be a high-level employee in order to impose liability or whether liability could be imputed as the result of the acts of a lower-level employee with no policy-making authority.[43] The courts appear to have little problem in using agency principles to impute the criminal act of any employee to the corporation as long as the act was within the scope of employment. Another difficult issue is the question of whether fines and social stigma are effective in deterring corporations from committing future crimes.[44] Burdensome fines may not be the answer, because they could affect the financial position of the company negatively, thus harming employees and shareholders who are innocent parties. Social stigma may have a deterrent effect, especially if the company is concerned about its public image.[45]

The Federal Sentencing Reform Act, addressing penalties for individuals, became effective in 1984 (and was later amended in 1990).[46] However, the passage of a corresponding act for corporate defendants has been slower. It can be concluded that one of the hidden causes for this delay is that it is conceptually difficult for courts and legislators to assign traditional criminal sentencing and punishment to corporate defendants.

In 1990 the U.S. Sentencing Commission began work to establish guidelines for mandatory penalties for criminal corporations, a policy that U.S. Attorney General Thornburgh initially sought as part of his longstanding battle against "crime in the suites."[47] The Commission proposed tough new guidelines for corporate criminal sentencing that would have resulted in sentences of millions of dollars for companies found guilty of certain crimes such as consumer fraud and government contract procurement fraud.[48] Such guidelines were believed to be necessary, because judges currently have wide discretion in punishing corporate defendants, but typically do not impose fines of more than $1 million dollars.[49] However, the work of the Commission was delayed, because of criticism of extensive turnovers and vacancies on the Commission, the lack of data supporting organizational sentencing guidelines, and a general reluctance to accept the guidelines on the part of business, a reluctance shared by the Justice Department.

Current Legislative and Judicial Responses

Because the parameters of white-collar crime are so difficult to establish, evaluating the effectiveness of the existing legislative and judicial responses is a formidable task. As white-collar crimes became more prevalent and more sophisticated, law enforcers were faced first with problems of apprehension and prosecution, but after that, inevitably, questions of deterrence arose. Emphasis was placed on increasing the penalties. Thus, legislators have concentrated their efforts on the retributive aspects of punishment as the necessary consequence of committing a moral wrong. Even before the savings and loan crisis, it was estimated that white-collar criminals were costing the American public between $40 billion and $200 billion a year;[50] in response legislatures and the judicial system began increasing the cost of committing a crime.

There has been some concern that increasing the penalties on the wrongdoer has not been as effective a deterrent measure as originally had been expected. Some legislators admitted during the hearings on the Insider Trading Securities Fraud and Enforcement Act that although the purpose of the law was to "enhance deterrence against insider trading, and where that deterrence fails, to augment the current methods of detection and punishment of this behavior," nevertheless, "[d]espite stiffer penalties enacted by Congress in 1984, the last few years have seen a dramatic increase in insider trading cases, including cases against some of the most prominent officials in Wall Street investment banking firms."[51]

A review of some of the prevailing legislative and judicial responses shows that overwhelmingly the criminal justice system favors the use of conventional retribution for illegal activity without regard to the unique sociological aspects of business misconduct as compared with traditional criminal activity involving violence to person and property.

Significant Legislative Responses

Crime Control Act of 1990. A very recent statute addressing white-collar crime is the Crime Control Act of 1990,[52] which was passed by the 101st Congress in late October, 1990.[53] Two parts of the legislation expand the tools available to federal banking regulators to combat fraud and other criminal activities in the banking and savings and loan industries: the Comprehensive Thrift and Bank Fraud Prosecution and Taxpayer Recovery Act of 1990 and the Financial Institutions Anti-Fraud Enforcement Act of 1990 (together, the "Act").[54] The Act includes some very harsh penalties designed to combat perceived and real fraudulent and criminal activities.[55] There has been criticism, however, that the severity of some of the provisions of the Act may deter financial institutions from being able to attract qualified and competent management.[56] It is interesting to note that this same criticism was effectively made in the wake of the *Smith v. Van Gorkom*[57] decision by the Delaware Supreme Court in 1985; that decision substantially undermined the protection afforded to corporate officers and directors by the business judgment rule, and was used to justify new state legislation limiting officers' and directors' liability for negligence.

The Act contains several significant provisions: (1) private citizens are granted the right to file "declarations" alleging banking law violations with the Attorney General of the United States with rewards for resulting criminal convictions from $5,000 to $100,000;[58] (2) private counsel may be engaged by the Attorney General to bring suit on behalf of the United States on a contingency fee basis;[59] (3) the "Financial Crime Kingpin Statute" imposes fines of $10,000,000 for individuals and $20,000,000 for organizations and for persons whose illegal financial crimes exceed $5,000,000 over a twenty-four-month period, as well as making violators subject to imprisonment for a term of ten years to life.[60]

Mail and Wire Fraud Statutes. These federal statutory laws[61] make it illegal to use the mail or any interstate electronic communications network to perpetrate a fraudulent scheme.

Prosecutors are able to invoke them in any case in which there is criminal activity that entails even peripheral use of the postal system or telephonic communication. Both statutes were employed where a *Wall Street Journal* reporter engaged in a conspiracy to inform a number of people about the content of articles in advance of being published.[63] The statutes have also been used to prosecute such activities as fraudulent practices in commodities trading.[63] In the commodities fraud case the specific act of the defendants in trading ahead did not fall under any existing criminal statutory prohibition,[64] but the defendants had used the telephone and mails extensively in schemes that the court deemed fraudulent. Consequently, the defendants were found guilty under the mail and wire fraud statutes.

"Racketeering" Crimes. The Racketeering Influence and Corrupt Organizations Act (RICO)[65] was passed in 1970 for the purpose of prosecuting organized crime but Congress used such general statutory language that the statute has been used to prosecute a wide spectrum of white-collar crimes far beyond the original target group. Indeed the statute has undergone an interesting evolution during the more than twenty years it has been in effect. During the first decade of its existence it was relatively little used. In the early 1980s practitioners began to see the possibilities of benefits from using RICO, helped in part by the expansive interpretation given by the United States Supreme Court in *Sedima, S.P.L.R. v. Imrex.*[66] Recently there have been challenges to the constitutionality of the statute from a wide range of respected

jurists.[67] There is a very recent federal appeals decision that shows the court's reluctance to expand the use of racketeering laws against white-collar crime.[68] In an action against six officials of Princeton/Newport and one Drexel Burnham Lambert Group trader, the government for the first time criminally prosecuted securities firm officials under RICO.[69] The U.S. Court of Appeals for the Second Circuit set aside the tax convictions that made up the bulk of the case, because it found that the defendants had not received a fair trial.[70] The court held that because the RICO convictions were largely based on the tax counts, the racketeering convictions must also be set aside. Although the appellate court remanded the tax and RICO charges to the district court, it suggested that the government should reconsider whether racketeering charges should again be brought and indicated that RICO may be inappropriate for tax cases.[71]

In essence, RICO prohibits the use of an "enterprise" in "a pattern of racketeering" activity.[72] To constitute a "pattern of racketeering" there must be evidence of two acts within ten years.[73] There is a laundry list of federal and state crimes that constitute "racketeering," including such predicate acts as murder, kidnapping, robbery, arson, extortion, obstruction of justice, mail and wire fraud, securities fraud, and (the recently added) financial institutions fraud. The U.S. Supreme Court held in the *Sedima* case[74] (involving civil charges) that prior convictions for the two alleged acts of "racketeering" were not necessary, that ". . . 'racketeering activity' consists of no more and no less than the commision of a predicate act . . ."[75] and that "[t]here is no room in the statutory language for an additional, amorphous 'racketeering injury' requirement."[76] Also the court clearly stated that the application of RICO was not restricted to use against mobsters and organized criminals but could be brought against legitimate enterprises.[77] Just as with the law governing mail and wire fraud, the courts have a wide leeway in applying RICO to the business sector.

RICO is a powerful force against business, because it includes a long list of predicate acts, covering many varieties of white-collar crime, that can be used as a basis for the allegation of a "pattern of racketeering activity" where the white-collar defendant has committed two or more of such predicate acts within a ten-year period. Like the mail and wire fraud statutes, "racketeering" under RICO can be added as another basis for liability along with other traditional crimes alleged by prosecutors. Section 1963 of RICO includes criminal penalties of up to twenty years imprisonment for each racketeering count, up to $25,000 fine for each racketeering count, and forfeiture of any interest the defendant has acquired in violation of the Act.

Forfeiture has come to the forefront in business crimes. It was established in *Russello v. United States*[78] that forfeiture of "any interest," as required by RICO, but not defined, would include all assets, profits, and proceeds from the illegal activity. Because of the fear that the defendant will no longer be in possession of the assets at the end of the trial, prosecutors usually ask for a pretrial freezing of the assets. Questions have been raised about the constitutionality of forfeiture, but the courts have not yet held that it involves a violation of due process.[79]

The comments of a consultant to a state legislative committee considering a forfeiture statute reflects why forfeiture may be necessary as a deterrent: "One reason that this legislature is turning to asset forfeiture in cases white-collar crime is that existing penalties aren't sufficient to discourage the offense. A $10,000 fine isn't anything to some of these people."[80]

Insider Trading Laws. Disgorgement and the imposition of a fine of up to $10,000 were the punishments traditionally used against inside traders. Congress decided to increase the penalties in an attempt to prevent the illegal activity and in 1984 passed the Insider Trading Sanctions Act (ITSA).[81] After the U.S. Supreme Court decisions in the 1980 case of *United States v. Chiarella*[82] and the 1983 case of *United States v. Dirks,*[83] in which the primary issue was a determination of who would be considered an "insider" for the purpose of the application of the insider trading sanctions, Congress set about the task of developing a definition and increasing the penalties. Congress never reached any agreement about a definition, but in recognition of the increased activity in the insider trading area, both the civil and criminal sanctions were increased. The enactment of ITSA reflected the intent of Congress to expand the range of tools available in combating insider trading. In addition to increasing the civil sanctions (by allowing treble damages rather than simple disgorgement), it increased the maximum fine for a criminal violation from $10,000 to $100,000.

While the U.S. Supreme Court decision was pending in the *Wall Street Journal* case, *United States v. Carpenter,*[84] in which the justices were again faced with the issue of who could be considered to be within the scope of prohibitions of the insider trading law, Congress once more tackled the problem of a definition of insider trading. It considered a bill that recommended the passage of the Insider Trading Proscriptions Act in which the emphasis was on defining the conduct that would be considered insider trading and defining who would be within the purview of the Act. Ultimately Congress did not pass the proposed Insider Trading Proscriptions Act; instead the final legislation was the Insider-Trading and Securities Fraud Enforcement Act of 1988.[85]

Like the Crime Control Act of 1990, the Insider Trading and Securities Fraud Enforcement Act includes a bounty provision, i.e., a reward to those who provide information that leads to convictions for insider trading violations. The act expanded the criminal penalties: the maximum imprisonment was increased from five to ten years, the criminal fine for individuals from $100,000 to $1 million, and the maximum fine for corporate business entities from $500,000 to $2.5 million.[86]

The Financial Institutions Reform, Recovery and Enforcement Act of 1989. Prior to the passage of FIRREA, the maximum penalty for violating some of the main criminal statutes relating to financial institutions was a fine of $5000 and/or imprisonment of up to five years. FIRREA increased the penalties dramatically, with Congress obviously believing that such penalties would have a deterrent effect. The maximum fine was increased two hundred times to $1 million and the maximum sentence for imprisonment was raised to twenty years.[87] Thus, white-collar criminals will assume a substantial risk when engaging in the conduct of bank bribery,[88] misapplication and embezzlement relating to banks and savings and loans,[89] placing a false statement in the books of a bank or savings and loan by an insider,[90] making a false statement to the Federal Deposit Insurance Corporation to induce it to enter into certain transactions,[91] making a false statement to a federally insured institution to obtain credit,[92] mail fraud affecting a federally insured financial institution,[93] wire fraud affecting a federally insured financial institution,[94] and financial institution fraud.[95] It should be noted that financial institution fraud was also made a predicate offense under the definition of "racketeering activities" of the RICO statute,[96] thus invoking the forfeiture provisions of RICO.

The Foreign Corrupt Practices Act. One of the primary statutes governing bribery is the Foreign Corrupt Practices Act (FCPA).[97] Its anti-bribery provisions make it unlawful for any company reporting to the Securities and Exchange Commission (SEC) or domestic concerns to offer, give, or authorize a payment or gift to a foreign official, political party, or its candidates for the purpose of influencing any act or decision in order to obtain or retain business.[98]

International payoffs in the form of bribes, kickbacks, gifts, and political contributions were discovered during the Watergate era. The Watergate Special Prosecutor required President Nixon's campaign officials to release the list of corporate donors in 1973. Enormous sums of both domestic and foreign contributions had been made under the most suspicious circumstances. Nearly 400 American companies had paid approximately $300 million to foreign officials for business favors over a five-year period. Lockheed Aircraft Corporation, for example, had paid $22 million to foreign politicians to ensure that it would receive aircraft contracts. In the same period, Gulf Oil Corporation had secretly paid $4 million to foreign politicians to protect its oil interests. In many cases, the bribery had been facilitated and concealed by falsification of corporate records.

It became glaringly obvious that there was no U.S. law against bribing an official in a foreign country (although it was prohibited within the territorial boundaries of the United States). The congressional response was the passage of the FCPA, which criminalized bribery of foreign officials and required a reasonable internal accounting control system and record keeping. Under a 1988 amendment[99] the FCPA changed the language that imposed criminal liability for "knowing or having reason to know" in order to impose criminal liability only in those cases where a person acted "knowingly." It also increased the corporation fine to $2 million and the individual fine to $100,000 along with the possibility of imprisonment of not more than five years against an officer, director, or stockholder acting on behalf of a corporation. The anti-bribery statute enhanced the authority of the SEC as its enforcement is an added responsibility of the Commission.

The Comprehensive Control Act (Federal Sentencing Guidelines). Congress successfully passed a statute in 1984, later amended in 1990,[100] setting forth sentencing guidelines for persons found guilty of committing a federal crime. It was felt that those contemplating the commission of a crime might be deterred from such conduct if they were aware of a definite mandatory sentence that would be imposed. The U.S. Sentencing Commission, an independent agency in the judicial branch created by Congress in 1984, was delegated the task of developing sentencing policies and practices "that will assure the ends of justice by promulgating detailed guidelines prescribing the appropriate sentences for offenders convicted of federal crimes."[101] Appropriate sentences for each class of convicted persons are set forth, and judges are allowed to depart from the guidelines if a particular case presents "atypical" features.

Significant Judicial Responses

There have been a number of high profile cases in the area of white-collar crime in recent years due to the widespread media attention to the prosecution of inside traders and to the related subject of the abuses of junk bond financing.

Drexel Burnham Lambert Group. Drexel Burnham Lambert Group had been in business for 152 years. It had built its empire into 5,300 employees and $3.6 billion in assets. It had in its employ the "junk bond king," Michael Milken, and it shaped the economic history of this country for almost a decade as it financed hostile takeovers with junk bonds. Dennis Levine, a Drexel investment banker, initiated the downfall of the company by implicating the arbitrager, Ivan Boesky, in massive insider trading schemes. Boesky, in turn, implicated Drexel and Michael Milken. The company's fatal error was its involvement in fraudulent stock practices that included allegations that it forced companies into unwanted takeovers and that Milken gave inside information to a network of traders to manipulate the stocks of target companies.[102] Prosecutors threatened to bring racketeering charges against Drexel Burnham that would have allowed the government to use the RICO freeze on $2 billion of the firm's capital.[103] With the knowledge of the tactics used by the government against Princeton/ Newport and its collapse a few months before, in December 1988, Drexel Burnham capitulated and pleaded guilty to six felonies and settled for $650 million. Legal expenses were also incurred in the amount of approximately $100 million. Drexel Burnham also agreed to fire Milken, to close his Beverly Hills office, to pay him no further compensation,[104] and to forbid any of its employees or clients from ever speaking with Milken.[105]

The saga ended on February 13, 1990, when Drexel Burnham Lambert Group filed a Chapter 11 petition in bankruptcy. There has been criticism of the government's handling of the fraudulent securities practices and accusations against the government for using RICO as a bludgeon to force the firm into pleading guilty to lesser counts, causing Drexel to go into an inexorable slide. During this decline it lost its good reputation and was subjected to severe penalties without a chance to clear its name in court.[106] Perhaps Drexel was forced to settle because the pretrial freezing of assets provided for by RICO meant that the firm might go out of business even before a trial could be held.[107] One report, sympathetic with Drexel Burnham, accused the Justice Department of approving "the RICOing of Drexel even though this gave the prosecutor a rubber hose to beat Drexel into submission."[108] The combination of the rising default rate, a slowing economy, and a new federal law requiring savings and loan institutions to dispose of their junk bonds made bankruptcy inevitable.

Michael Milken. Michael Milken joined Drexel in 1970 at a salary of $25,000; by 1978 he had made his name in junk bonds and had become the company's main profit producer. While Milken was head of Drexel's junk bond department, his compensation increased from $45.7 million in 1983 to more than $550 million in 1987 and his total earnings have been estimated at $1.1 billion.[109]

On March 29, 1989 a ninety-eight-count indictment was entered against Milken for insider trading, illegal stock parking, market manipulation, and a variety of other securities offenses. The indictment included charges arising from (1) insider trading and parking violations involving Ivan Boesky; (2) transactions with Princeton/Newport Partners in which Milken helped the limited partnership carry out tax fraud through sham securities trades and Drexel used the limited partnership to illegally manipulate the price of C.O.M.B. Co. securities; and (3) insider trading in the securities of Lorimar Inc. and Viacom.

With the use of RICO the government forced Mr. Milken to face the possibility of $1.85 billion in forfeitures.[110] The financier's lawyers argued that the acts of which he was accused would have earned at most $20 million for him and $140,000 for his brother. The charges against him were pending for three years, but in April 1990 Mr. Milken pleaded guilty to six of ninety-eight counts of securities violations and agreed to pay a record $200 million in criminal fines and penalties and to place $400 million into a fund to compensate investors hurt by his crimes.[111]

In November 1990, a district court judge sentenced him to ten years in prison for six felony counts.[112] Judge Kimba M. Wood modified this sentence by substituting three years imprisonment and seven years probation.

Beyond Penalties: Additional Solutions

Because of the unique nature of white-collar crime, Congress should change its focus to deterrence instead of the prevailing approach of imposing harsh punishment on acts of misconduct. There must be legislation that places the responsibility for *preventing* the misconduct on the directors, officers, or anyone else in a position to take direct and immediate action within the business enterprise. This was done to some extent in the FCPA, a highly unpopular piece of legislation among businesspeople because of its alleged anti-competitive effect on U.S. companies operating abroad. This concern overshadowed all other aspects of the legislation; as a result, it was never directly evaluated for its long-range effectiveness as a tool in the criminal justice system. The authors recommend a reconsideration of the FCPA approach in the area of white-collar crime, imposing legal duties of accountability on business managers and establishing control systems to deter criminal conduct. The authors also recommend consideration of a statutory compliance system imposed on employers to encourage whistleblowing, which is a step further than the reward and protection system now existing in the Insider Trading Sanctions Act and FIRREA.

Legal Duties of Accountability

Ordinarily, criminal penalties are not imposed for simple nonfeasance or neglect of duty; even in the civil law area courts have been reluctant to impose liability for errors in judgment made by officers and directors.[113] One instance in which Congress showed a willingness to impose a responsibility on corporate management was in the FCPA as it was originally passed in 1977.[114] Although it was later amended, the anti-bribery section of the FCPA initially prescribed criminal liability for "knowing or having reason to know" that all or a portion of a payment would be passed on to a foreign official. Clearly the "having reason to know" standard emphasizes the fact that corporate management has a duty to scrutinize the activities of its agents carefully.[115] Such responsibility has the effect of forcing corporate officers and directors to monitor closely the activities of the corporation's agents in order to avoid personal liability, particularly since Congress took the unusual step of precluding corporations from indemnifying employees for violations of the act.

The "having reason to know" provision was roundly criticized by the business community, which argued that it was too great a burden to be responsible for the activities of subordinates. The anti-indemnification provision was also directly contrary to long-standing legal tradition that employees are entitled to indemnification for liability incurred within the scope of employment. Congress finally capitulated to pressure for changes in the FCPA in 1988 and deleted the "reason to know" standard, leaving corporate management with liability only in instances in which it intentionally disregards notice that illegal payments are being made.[116]

The deleted language holds management to a much higher standard of awareness of the conduct in which corporate agents are engaging. Fear of assessment of criminal liability, based on situations in which company officials "have reason to know" that a crime is being committed, will force officers and directors to investigate any suspicious activities within the organization. This imposition of high level accountability is necessary to prevent crime. Perhaps legislation that imposed personal liability upon corporate directors and officers for "knowing or having reason to know" of fraudulent activities would have prevented some of the savings and loan executives from engaging in misconduct themselves and given the directors more of an incentive to actively carry out the role of watchdogs within their organizations.

The Insider Trading and Securities Fraud Enforcement Act of 1988 includes provisions that place responsibility (and ultimately the liability) upon "the controlling person"[117] to take appropriate action if the person knows or recklessly disregards indications that a controlled person is engaging in illegal conduct.[118] The duty is incumbent upon the controlling person, where there are indications of misconduct, to prevent the act before it occurs. Congress intended, through the broadening of controlling person civil penalty liability, to increase the economic incentives for such persons to vigorously supervise their employees.[119] Effective supervision by securities firms of their employees and agents is a foundation of the federal regulatory scheme of investor protection.[120] This level of supervisory accountability should be applied widely across the wide spectrum of corporate business.

Control Systems to Deter Criminal Conduct

The authors advocate, as a model, the internal accounting controls section of the FCPA. The act creates a statutory affirmative duty for corporations, under the jurisdiction of the SEC, to create and maintain financial records. It requires that the directors of a corporation insure the integrity of the internal accounting system to prevent fraud from occurring. Reasonable detail is required, because detailed records insure accurate records and this, in turn, makes the audit process more reliable. Congress used this method to insure that the issuer's records reflected transactions in conformity with accepted methods of recording economic events, thus effectively preventing off-the-books slush funds and secret payment of bribes. The overall effect of this kind of early deterrence is to reduce situations in which business misconduct is likely to occur.

Work Environment

If whistleblowers are protected within the organization and are rewarded for their conduct (i.e., encouraged by the employer), a white-collar worker contemplating a crime will be less likely to commit the crime for fear of disclosure by fellow workers.[121] It is in the employer's best interest to protect whistleblowers, thereby exerting positive control over the workplace. This concept is articulated in the Consumer Product Safety Act,[122] which is structured to provide "front-end protection" *before* injury has occurred rather than providing remedies *after* the injury has occurred as is the case under traditional theories of product liability. Similarly, the whistleblowing legislation the authors propose would provide "front-end" deterrence rather than focusing on punishment after the crime is committed.

The current law directly applicable to the reward incentive for whistleblowing, the Federal False Claims Act of 1986,[123] is a type of "qui tam"[124] legislation. A recent "qui tam" lawsuit involved Northrop Corporation and raised interesting issues involving disclosure by an employee of some variety of white-collar crime by the employer. The Northrop Corporation agreed to pay almost $9 million to settle a civil suit brought in 1987 by two former employees under provisions of the Federal False Claims Act in which the employees alleged that the company falsified tests on the air-launched cruise missile.[125] Under the law, the whistleblowers will share 15 percent to 25 percent of that amount, as determined by the court.[126] The company also was indicted on test-falsification charges, and its Precision Products Division has been suspended from doing business with the government since July 1989.[127] In addition, the company agreed to pay the two employees $750,000 to settle additional claims involving allegations of harassment and wrongful termination.[128] Such a settlement is an example of the application of the public policy exception to at-will employment. Under this exception employees allege that their discharge violates some aspect of public policy and, therefore, the employer is not free to discharge them. Under traditional notions of at-will employment, employers are free to discharge employees for any reason, even if the employer's motivation is improper, i.e., to punish a whistleblowing employee. The public policy exception to the right to discharge is the one most likely to be recognized by courts, and whistleblowing is the most common situation involving issues of public policy.

Another whistleblowing case involving violation of state law was recently decided in Los Angeles Superior Court.[129] Punitive damages of $270,000 were assessed against the employer where a woman alleged she was fired for pointing out racially discriminatory practices by her employer. She was also awarded $239,000 in compensatory damages. The jury found that the employer violated the state's Unruh Civil Rights Act by adopting and ratifying its employees' discriminatory conduct by failing to investigate the purported racist remarks and by firing the woman.[130]

◂ Conclusion ▸

Passage of legislation[131] may augment existing statutory protections and rewards that require employers or "controlling persons" to implement procedural safeguards for whistleblowing employees in order to encourage whistleblowing to government agencies. Procedural safeguards should include hotlines guaranteeing anonymity, reward incentives, and publicizing procedures. Only the existence of a committed and efficient compliance agency will insure consistent availability and provide employees with the security of knowing that there cannot be any retaliation. The governmental agency created to enforce whistleblowing statutes would be analogous to the Equal Employment Opportunity Commission's enforcement of Title VII of the Civil Rights Act of 1964 to effectuate equal employment opportunity. Although there may be legitimate concerns about the creation of yet another government agency, the savings generated to both public and private employers should more than offset the agency's costs.

Studies have indicated that employees are more likely to be whistleblowers when they perceive their organizations to be relatively responsive to allegations of wrongdoing.[132] Therefore, it is important that a statutory duty be imposed upon employers to put in place a system that clearly indicates to employees that they are fully protected if they blow the whistle. Such a system should not be feared by employers because of the overall benefits to be gained through revelation by whistleblowing of activities detrimental to the employer's interest.

It can be seen that the concept of white-collar crime is elusive in many respects, as its definition has its origin in a nonlegal environment. Although both legislatures and courts have sought to deal with the problem, these efforts have often fallen far short (if their aims, as white-collar crime continues to increase in its scope and financial consequences. Legislators should consider taking corporate crime completely out of the current context of common-law practices and should focus their efforts on creating laws specific to white-collar crime that utilize nontraditional penalties and standards imposing accountability and "front-end" compliance requirements. These laws must be clear and specific, allowing the multitude of varied business owners, managers and consumers to understand their application, meaning, and importance.

◂ NOTES ▸

1 The traditional crimes attributable to business people included such acts of malfeasance as anti-trust violations. kickbacks, embezzlement, and larceny. During the last two decades, however, these activities were expanded to include more sophisticated "victimless" crimes.

2 Coleman, *The Criminal Elite* 2 (1989).

3 *Id.*

4 *Id.*

5 Coleman, note 2 *supra*, at 2.

6 Shapiro, "Collaring the Crime, Not the Criminal: Reconsidering the Concept of White-Collar Crime," 55 Am. Sociological Rev. 346 (1990).

7 D. Simon, D. Eitzen, *Elite Deviance* at xiv (1990).

8 Wheeler, Weisburd, Waring, Bode. "White Collar Crimes and Criminals," 25 *Am. Crim. L. Rev.* 331 (1998).

9 E. Conry, *The Legal Environment of Business* 38 (1990).

10 *Id.*

11 One only has to think of the admiration given to one who has avoided paying income tax after finding a particularly recondite loophole.

12 E.g., the 1988 Insider Trading and Securities Fraud Enforcement Act imposes civil penalties on violating persons and persons "controlling" those violators and has provided for broker-dealer and investment advisor employee supervision. It should be noted, however, that recent amendments to the Foreign Corrupt Practices Act removed the language that made the employers liable if they "should have known"; now they are penalized only if they have actual knowledge.

13 Coleman note 2 *supra*, at 244.

14 *Id.*

15 *Id.*

16 *Id.*

17 *Id.*

18 Pub. L. No. 101–73, 103 Stat. 183 (1989) (codified in scattered sections of 12 and 15 U.S.C.).

19 Coleman, note 2 *supra*, at 244.

20 *Id.*

21 *Id.*

22 *Id.*

23 *Id.*

24 *Id.*

25 *Id.*

26 *Id.* at 244–245.

27 *Id.* at 245.

28 P. Drucker, *The Concept of the Corporation* (1972), cited by P. Fiorelli, "White-Collar Crime, Fundamental Causes and Possible Solutions" at 168 in *Readings in Business Law and the Legal Environment of Business*, Whitman, Ed. (1990).

29 *Id.* at 170.

30 Bennett, "The Future of White-Collar Crime." *Nat'l L. J.*, Mar. 23, 1987, at 15, col. 1.

31 In Japan it is common to see executives resign over a simple accusation of wrongdoing. The social implications of dishonor in that country dictate the ethical responsibilities of business in many cases.

32 Conry, note 9 *supra*.

33 See *Grimshaw v. Ford Motor Co.*, 119 Cal. App. 3d 757 (1981).

34 P. Fiorelli, "White-Collar Crime, Fundamental Causes and Possible Solutions," *Readings in Business Law and the Legal Environment of Business*, Whitman, Ed. (1990).

35 Conry, note 9 *supra*.

36 Foerschler, "Corporate Criminal Intent: Toward a Better Understanding of Corporate Misconduct," *L. A. Daily J. Report*, May 31, 1991 at 43.

37 Spiro, *The Legal Environment of Business* 393 (1989).

38 *Id.*

39 *Id.*

40 *Id.*

41 *Id.*

42 See *Grimshaw v. Ford Motor Co.*, 119 Cal. App. 3d 757 (1981), in which punitive damages were assessed against the corporation because management was aware that the fuel tank and rear structure of the Pinto would expose consumers to serious injury or death in a low-speed collision, but nevertheless (after doing a cost-benefit analysis balancing human lives against corporate profits) chose to place the car in the market.

43 Spiro, note 37 *supra.*
44 *Id.*
45 *Id.*
46 Pub. L. No. 98–473 § 212(a)(2), 98 Stat. 1987 (codified as amended by Pub. L. No. 101–647 § 1602, 104 Stat. 4843 at 119 U.S.C. § 3552). Also see P. Fiorelli, note 34 *supra.*
47 Anderson, "White-Collar Sanctions (Business Brouhaha)," 76 *ABA J.* 15 (July 1990).
48 Barrett and Harlan, "Tough New Guidelines Proposed For Corporate Criminal Sentencing," *Wall St. J.*, at B8, Oct. 29, 1990.
49 *Id.*
50 Bennett, note 30 *supra.*
51 H. R. Rep. No. 910 to Accompany H. R. 513, 100th Cong. 2d Sess. 11.
52 Pub. L. No. 101–647, 104 Stat. 4789 (codified in scattered sections of 11, 12, 18, and 28 U.S. C.).
53 Olson, "1990 Legal Developments Relevant For Commercial Banks And Their Holding Companies," published by the Business Law Section of the State Bar of California.
54 *Id.*
55 *Id.*
56 *Id.*
57 488 A.2d 858 (Del. 1985).
58 Olson, note 53 *supra*, at 4.
59 *Id.*
60 *Id.*
61 18 U.S.C. §§ 1341 and 1343.
62 *United States v. Winans*, 612 F. Supp. 827 (S.D.N.Y.).
63 *United States v. Dial*, 757 F.2d 163 (7th Cir. 1985).
64 The court stated in the *Dial* case that "It is true that the Board of Trade has no express rule against trading ahead of a customer . . . and that there is no other specific prohibition (relevant to this case) of insider trading on commodity futures exchanges. . . . But it is apparent that such a practice, when done without disclosure to the customer, is both contrary to a broker's fiduciary obligations and harmful to commodities futures trading. . . ." *Id.* at 168.
65 18 U.S.C. §§ 1961–1968 (1982).
66 473 U.S. 479 (1985).
67 Continuing Education of the Bar, *Civil Actions Under RICO and the California Business and Professions Code*, Presented in Los Angeles, California on March 2, 1991.
68 *United States v. Regan*, 937 F.2d 823 (2d Cir. 1991). See also Lambert & Charlier, "RICO Convictions Scrapped in Fraud Case," *Wall St. J.*, July 1, 1991, at B2, col. 3.
69 *United States v. Regan*, 726 F. Supp. 447 (S.D.N.Y. 1989), *aff'd in part and vacated in part.*
70 *United States v. Regan*, note 68 *supra*, at 827.
71 *Id.*
72 18 U.S.C. § 1961.
73 *Id.* at § 5.
74 Sedima, *S.P.L.R. v. Imrex*, note 66 *supra.*
75 *Id.* at 495.
76 *Id.*

77 *Id.* at 499.
78 464 U.S. 16 (1983).
79 Shaw, "Fifth Amendment Failures and RICO Forfeitures," 28/2 *Am. Bus. L.J.* 169 (1990).
80 Inman, "Commit a Crime, Lose Your Ox (Or, Perhaps, Some Other Asset)," *L.A. Times*, Aug. 19, 1990, at D2, col. 1, quoting from Steve Suchil, consultant to the California Assembly Finance and Insurance Committee.
81 Pub. L. No. 98–376, 98 Stat. 1264 (1984) (codified as amended at 15 U.S.C. §§ 78c, 78t–1, 78u, 78u–1, 78o, 78ff, and 78kk).
82 445 U.S. 222 (1980).
83 459 U.S. 1013 (1983).
84 484 U.S. 19 (1987).
85 Pub. L. No. 100–704 (1988) (codified as amended at 15 U.S.C. §§ 78c, 78t–1, 78u, 78u–1, 78o, 78ff, and 78kk.)
86 Referred to in the Act as "non-natural persons."
87 FIRREA § 961, 103 Stat. at 215 (codified at 12 U.S.C. § 215).
88 18 U.S. C. § 215 (1990).
89 *Id.* at §§ 656, 657.
90 *Id.* at §§ 1005, 1006.
91 *Id.* at § 1007.
92 *Id.* at § 1014.
93 *Id.* at § 1343.
94 *Id.* at § 1344.
95 12 U.S.C. § 1847(a) (1989) for bank holding companies and 12 U.S.C. § 1467(a)(1) (1989) for savings and loan holding companies.
96 FIRREA § 968(1) (codified at 12 U.S.C. § 1961 (1)).
97 15 U.S.C. §§ 78m, 781, 78n, 78o, 78dd–1, 78dd–2, and 78ff (1979).
98 15 U. S. C. § 78dd–1(a) (1988).
99 Pub. L. No. 100–418 §§ 50001 et seq., 102 Stat. 1415 (1988) (codified as amended at 15 U.S.C. §§ 78m, 78dd–1, 78dd–2, and 78ff).
100 Pub. L. No. 98–473 § 212(a)(2), 98 Stat. 1987 (codified as amended by Pub. L. No. 101–647 § 1602,104 Stat. 4843 at 119 U.S.C. § 3552).
101 *U.S. Federal Sentencing Guidelines Manual*, West Publishing Company (1989).
102 Greenwald "Predator's Fall," *Time*, Feb. 26, 1990, at 16.
103 *SEC v. Drexel Burnham Lambert Inc.*, 88 Civ. 6209 (1988–1989 Transfer Binder) Fed. Sec. L. Rep. (CCH) ¶ 93,999, consent decree entered (1989 Transfer Binder) Fed. Sec. L. Rep. (CCH) ¶ 94,474.
104 Milken's attorneys claim that this agreement between Drexel and the government deprived their client of $200 million in earned compensation in violation of due process and constituted an unconstitutional taking of property. See "Plea Bargain, RICO-style," *Nat'l L.J.*, Apr. 10, 1989, at 13.
105 "Drexel: Prosecution and Fall," *Wall St. J.*, Feb. 15, 1990, at A14, col. 1.
106 Paltrow, "All Eyes Are on Michael Milken after Drexel's Bankruptcy," *L.A. Times*, Feb. 17, 1990, at D1, col. 2.
107 Paltrow, "Will Wall St.'s New Cop Keep Heat on Fraud?" *L.A. Times*, Jan. 7, 1990, at 1, col. 5.
108 Note 105 *supra.*
109 "Baby, You're a Rich Man Still," *Time*, May 14, 1990, at 72.
110 Sontag, "Princeton/Newport Case: RICO Stretched Too Far?" Nov. 20, 1989, at 3, col. 2.
111 "Judge Asks Lawyers to Total Fraud Losses in Milken Case," *L.A. Times* (Orange County Edition), Nov. 29, 1990 at D9. In January 1991, in a suit

filed in federal district court in Manhattan, the Federal Deposit Insurance Corp. accused Michael Milken and other defendants "of a scheme of coercion, extortion and bribery" in the junk bond market, and sought damages of six billion dollars. Lambert and Stevens, "FDIC Suit Accuses Milken, Others of Duping S&Ls; Seeks $6 Billion," *Wall St. J.*, Jan. 21, 1991, at B2, col. 3–4.

112 "Hard Time: White Collar Offenders in Toils of Law Finds Little Mercy, Gets Sentenced to Tough Prison," *Wall St. J.*, Dec. 18, 1990, at A6.

113 Under the doctrine of the business judgment rule, courts did not get involved in second-guessing good-faith business decisions made by corporate management. Although this doctrine was considerably undermined by the 1985 Delaware Supreme Court decision of *Smith v. Van Gorkom*, 488 A.2d 858, the protection was later provided pursuant to state legislation limiting officer and director liability.

114 15 U.S.C. §§ 78m, 781, 78n, 78o, 78dd–1, 78dd–2, and 78ff (1979).

115 George, "The U.S. Foreign Corrupt Practices Act: The Price Business Is Paying for the Unilateral Criminalization of Bribery," 4 *Int'l J. of Mgmt.* 393 (1987).

116 Pub. L. No. 100–418 §§ 50001 *et seq.*, 102 Stat. 1415 (1988) (codified as amended at 15 U.S.C. §§ 78m, 78dd–1, 78dd–2, and 78ff).

117 As set forth in H. R. Rep. No. 910 to Accompany H. R. 513, 100th Cong. 2d Sess. 17, a "controlling person" may include not only employers, but any person with power to influence or control the direction or the management, policies, or activities of another person. The Committee expects the Commission and courts to continue to interpret the term "controlling person" on a case-by-case basis according to the factual circumstances.

118 H. R. Rep. No. 910 to Accompany H.R. 513, 100th Cong. 2d Sess. 18.

119 *Id.* at 17.

120 *Id.*

121 The emphasis of existing law is to protect the whistleblowers after the information has been given. The approach being recommended is to place the responsibility on employers to encourage the act of whistleblowing.

122 15 U.S.C. §§ 2051 *et seq.* (1972 & Supp. 1990).

123 18 U.S.C. §§ 1001, 1005 (1982).

124 Allows lawsuits brought by private individuals against government contractors in which the person bringing the action shares in any monetary award to the United States. Waldman, "Time to Blow the Whistle?" *Nat'l L.J.*, Mar. 25, 1991, at 13.

125 Wartzman, "Northrop Agrees to Pay About $9 Million to Settle Suit by Two Whistle Blowers," *Wall St. J.*, June 24, 1991, at A4, col. 2–3.

126 *Id.*

127 *Id.*

128 *Id.*

129 Smith, "Woman Fired for Reporting Racial Bias Wins $509,000," *L.A. Daily J.*, July 2, 1991, at 2, col. 3.

130 *Id.* at col. 4.

131 A suggested title for the legislation is the Conscientious Employee Reporting Act.

132 Miceli & Near, "Individual and Situational Correlates of Whistle-blowing." 41 *Personnel Psychology* 267–282 (1988).

‹ 3 ›

The Neglected Victims and Unexamined Costs of White-Collar Crime

Elizabeth Moore
Michael Mills

For decades the victims of crime were all but ignored by researchers, criminal justice professionals, and policymakers. Recent years have seen a dramatic reversal of this situation. As public officials and a victims' movement focused unprecedented attention on the financial loss, physical injuries, and suffering caused by street crimes, victim-rights legislation and assistance programs were developed across the nation. Although this victims' movement has spawned significant policy reforms, white-collar crime victims have been ignored and what was true 15 years ago remains true today: "The subject of victims of [white-collar] crime has scarcely been addressed [by investigators and policymakers]" (Vaughan and Carlo 1976, p. 154). This article begins with brief comments on the problems of crime victims, the development of programs for victims, and the nature of these programs. We then

Reprinted from *Crime & Delinquency*, 36(3): 408–418.

discuss the costs of white-collar crime to victims and some reasons why the victims' movement has ignored them. We conclude with a call for more research and policy attention to the costs of white-collar crime.

Victims' Problems, Progress, and Programs

Research has documented the disruptive and sometimes devastating effects of street crime on its victims. Victims often report psychological and somatic problems triggered by their victimization, including stress, diminished self-esteem, and helplessness. Many alternate between intense anger and increased feelings of vulnerability and fear (Burt and Katz 1985; Fischer 1984; Janoff-Bulman 1985; Leyman 1985; Maguire 1980; Wortman 1983). These reactions can be trivial or devastating, transitory or enduring.

The problems faced by crime victims do not end once their plight becomes known to authorities. Victims who come to criminal justice officials expecting protection and remedy often find something very different:

> They discover . . . that they [are] treated as appendages of a system appallingly out of balance. They learn that somewhere along the way the system has lost track of the simple truth that it is supposed to be fair and to protect those who obey the law while punishing those who break it. Somewhere along the way, the system began to serve lawyers and judges and defendants, treating the victim with institutionalized disinterest. (President's Task Force on Victims of Crime 1982, p. vi)

The past 15 years have seen increasing official attention to the problems faced by victims. The first action came in the form of 1964 federal legislation establishing guidelines for victim compensation programs. The following year, California created the first state program (U.S. Department of Justice 1988a). By 1974 the Law Enforcement Assistance Administration was contributing $50 million to eight victim/witness assistance programs.

Ronald Reagan's victory in the 1980 presidential election boosted the visibility and political strength of the victims' movement. In 1980 he appointed a Victims of Crime Task Force to investigate the problems of crime victims and to recommend new policies. The task force report led to passage of the Victim and Witness Protection Act of 1982. This Act protects and assists victims and witnesses of federal crimes by (a) making it a felony to threaten or intimidate a victim or witness, (b) providing for inclusion of a victim impact statement in presentence reports, (c) furnishing explicit authority for Federal trial courts to order offenders to make restitution to victims, and (d) requiring judges to state on the record the reasons for not ordering restitution (Finn n.d.). Also in 1982, California voters amended the state constitution to incorporate a victim's bill of rights. In the next 5 years, 28 states followed California's lead and enacted similar bills of rights (Viano 1987, pp. 440–441).

The Victims of Crime Act of 1984 (VOCA) authorized the U.S. Attorney General to make grants to states to establish programs for victim compensation and assistance. By 1987, 38 states had done so (U. S. Department of Justice 1988b; Finn n.d.). These programs offer monetary compensation and other assistance; for example, counseling for victims of crime who suffer physical injury, emotional injury, or lost wages (U. S. Code 1983–1985, p. 1102).

VOCA also established a Crime Victims Fund that is replenished through revenues collected from criminal fines, penalty assessments, and sales of property seized from convicted federal defendants. The principal crimes for which victims are compensated by state programs are assault, homicide, "other," sexual offenses, and child sexual abuse. In 1987, $55 million was paid to victims of assaults and other violent crimes, $6.1 million was paid to families of homicide victims, and $5 million was paid to victims of sexual offenses. The average compensation award was $1,864 (U.S. Department of Justice 1988a, p. i). The 1984 VOCA also made available grants to states for programs to assist victims of designated crimes, including sexual assault, spouse abuse, and child abuse.

Victims of White-Collar Crime

Whereas street crimes disproportionately victimize the poor and marginal, white-collar crime is more democratic in its impact. It harms not only well-heeled financial speculators but couples and individual citizens with few if any assets beyond a modest savings account. We know little or nothing about its impacts on victims. The type of victimization surveys that have enhanced our knowledge of street crime victimization do not lend themselves easily to studies of white-collar crime, and the National Crime Survey (NCS) does not collect data on incidents of white-collar or corporate victimization. These and other aspects of the problem of white-collar crime present obstacles to research that are absent or attenuated where street crimes are concerned. As a result, what was true a decade ago remains true today: "Little systematic attention has been paid to the white-collar crime victim" (Duncan and Caplan 1980; National Institute 1977; Walsh and Schram 1980).

Although statistical data are scarce, many excellent case studies of corporate and white-collar crime document the sufferings of their victims (collections include Douglas and Johnson 1977; Ermann and Lundman 1987; Heilbroner 1972; Hills 1987; Hochstedler 1984; Johnson and Douglas 1978). Much of what we have learned about the costs and victim impacts of white-collar crime come from these very important investigations.

Neglect of white-collar crime victims seems particularly unfortunate in light of its enormous physical, economic, and social toll. No one disputes that it "produce[s] far more destruction and cost than conventional crime" (Elias 1986, p. 115). Victims of some white-collar crime suffer death; others sustain serious injuries, or exposure to unsafe working conditions that cause long-term, progressively debilitating illness; and financial losses may leave still others with a lowered standard of living. Oftentimes the victims include those now "past their prime working years, with perhaps very small savings to piece out the submarginal existence afforded by social security payments. Such victims have just about worked out their life schemes to avoid becoming public charges in their old age" (Edelhertz 1970, p. 10). Aside from its emotional impact, loss of modest savings or retirement funds virtually impoverishes victims such as these. They may be forced to make do with less frequent medical checkups, to forego elective surgery, to eat out less often or to purchase less, and less nutritious, food. The *primary* costs of white-collar crimes appear in the physical, psychological, and monetary suffering of its victims.

Like victims of street crimes, there is reason to believe that white-collar crime victims who seek redress by notifying public officials of their apparent victimization receive less than a satisfactory response (Geis 1975; McGuire and Edelhertz 1980). It may be necessary for them to negotiate a maze of agencies and institutions, most of uncertain jurisdiction and commitment. Often the process produces little beyond frustration and, eventually, angry resignation. Vaughan and Carlo (1975) discovered that a group of citizens victimized by an appliance repairman, hardly the most serious of white-collar offenders, "repeatedly expressed their indignation at being cheated and their frustration at being unable to get satisfaction from the offender, or from anyplace else" (p. 158). A study of fraud in California that victimized many elderly citizens pointed to the "callous indifference that the system demonstrates toward those whom it is particularly charged with assisting" (Geis 1976, p. 14):

> Many [victims] . . . feel their needs have extremely low priority and that, at best, they are tolerated and then often with ill humor. Their role, they say, seems much like that of the expectant father in the hospital at delivery time: necessary for

> things to have gotten underway in the past but at the moment rather superfluous and mildly bothersome. . . . the offender, at least, is regarded by criminal justice functionaries as a doer, an antagonist, someone to be wary of . . . The victim, on the other hand, is part of the background scenery. (Geis 1976, p. 15)

Interviews with a sample of 42 individuals who filed complaints with the consumer fraud bureau of the Illinois Attorney General's office revealed that "dissatisfaction with and even hostility toward the Bureau were widespread." The Bureau was seen as "too slow, unaggressive, biased, disorganized, and 'bureaucratic'" (Steele 1975, p. 1179). In short, "just as the criminal justice system has been termed a 'nonsystem,' the approach taken by the criminal justice system to white collar-crime containment might be considered a 'nonapproach'" (Edelhertz and Rogovin 1980, p. 78). The fact that white-collar crime victims have been ignored by the justice system is only the latest example of this.

◂ UNDESERVING VICTIMS ▸

Like the post-1975 wave of criminal sentencing reform that swept over the nation, the victims' movement drew support from diverse sources. By focusing attention on women as targets of violence, the womens' movement promoted a new definition of their plight as victims. Angered by liberal U.S. Supreme Court decisions expanding the rights of the accused, politically conservative citizens and public officials seized the opportunity to redress this perceived imbalance by promoting *victims'* rights. This was not extended to victims of white-collar crime.

For conservative politicians, the victims' rights movement offered an opportunity to do something positive about crime, thereby undercutting criticisms that their crime control policies amount to nothing more than repression. By establishing restitution and compensation programs, conservatives could show they were willing to fund programs that would benefit women and minorities, groups typically not part of the conservative constituency. These political gains could be achieved at limited political cost and the only group not benefiting from expanded victim rights was street criminals.

The politics of government programs may explain the failure of the victim rights legislation to take explicit account of white-collar crime victims. Compensation and restitution programs for victims of street crime seem a natural extension of the traditional government responsibility to preserve public order. Innocent victims of street crime deserve to be compensated, if only because the state has failed in its responsibility to protect them. Street criminals, however, typically are poor and have few prospects of ever being able to repay their victims. Hence it follows that the state should help make good victims' losses.

This reasoning is harder to apply in the case of white-collar crime. Whereas its victims may or may not be poor, the offenders may, but need not, be part of the wealthy and powerful business establishment. In this situation, the argument that the state owes it to victims to defray the costs of victimization is not persuasive. If the offenders are not poor, why not have them pay for the costs of victimization? Why not set up programs requiring that perpetrators of consumer fraud, bank scams, securities fraud, and other such crimes automatically pay restitution to their victims? But at this point, we confront certain political and economic realities.

New programs facilitating victims' ability to recover from corporate white-collar offenses would necessarily impose costs on the business community. Attempts to legislate such programs will encounter resistance. The business community will point to the existing network of laws, regulations, and agencies and argue that mechanisms for redressing the wrongs suffered by white-collar crime victims are already in place; no new ones are needed. Given the antiregulation, probusiness sentiments increasingly evidenced by public officials, these arguments likely would be well received by many state and federal legislators. Ironically, the conservative political philosophy underpinning the original victims' rights movement may be responsible in part for its continued failure to address white-collar crime victimization.

Other reasons for continued neglect are rooted in prevailing notions about white-collar crime and its victims. Walsh and Schram (1980) suggested that white-collar crime, like the crime of rape, raises "double standard issues." Both crimes are characterized by widespread ambivalence toward the proscribed conduct, victim involvement, and victims' claims for redress. As a result, many white-collar victims do not "arouse the general sympathy reserved for those who have suffered harm, loss, or injury. Instead, these victims often are viewed with a mixture of skepticism, suspicion, and disbelief" and they are seen as "unworthy of society's protection" (pp. 46–47). Little wonder that simply reporting white-collar crime and seeing one's complaint through to resolution can be both exhausting and disillusioning.

Beyond the Primary Costs of Crime

Although the primary costs of white-collar crime are obvious, its *secondary* costs may be equally harmful. Sutherland (1949) noted, some 40 years ago, that white-collar crime is harmful to the social fabric in ways uniquely its own. Because most white-collar offenses violate trust, they breed distrust, lower social morale, and "attack the fundamental principles of the American institutions" (p. 13). These secondary costs

> are far more significant than mere dollar losses—no matter how great—because they go to the very heart of the issue of integrity of our society and to that confidence in our private and public institutions that is essential to their usefulness and effectiveness in serving the public. (Edelhertz 1980, p. 124)

Three areas of potentially significant secondary impact have been identified: (a) diminished faith in a free economy and in business leaders, (b) loss of confidence in political institutions, processes, and leaders, and (c) erosion of public morality.

Many have expressed fears about the potential impact of white-collar crime on our nation's economic life. They reason that restraint of trade, for example,

> tends to undermine the principles of free enterprise that the antitrust laws are intended to protect. [Thus,] the damage from the price-fixing conspiracy in the electrical equipment industry was not limited to the direct extra costs imposed. As Judge T. Cullen Ganey declared in sentencing a defendant: "This is a shocking indictment of a vast section of our economy, for what is really at stake here is the survival of the kind of economy under which this country has grown great, the free enterprise system." (President's Commission 1967, p. 48)

American citizens must have faith and confidence that corporate and business leaders are motivated by an ethic of responsible concern for others and for the common good. To the extent citizens believe otherwise, believe that business decisions are motivated by greed and selfishness, they may withhold financial support and economic investment.

Another secondary cost is the effect of white-collar crime on faith in and support for political institutions, public officials, and governmental processes. Citizens, for the most part, expect public officials to be honest themselves and also to deal unflinchingly with those who employ deceit and exploitation to prey on the public. In a word,

> [citizens] want to see evidence that the criminal-justice system will treat deception and abuses of institutional position as harshly as stealth and physical attack and that it is willing to punish privileged and powerful offenders as well as those who are relatively powerless. (Moore 1980, p. 44)

This is true especially in the U.S., whose economy is based largely on trust in the honesty and legitimacy of agencies that regulate financial markets and activities. The Internal Revenue Service, for example, depends greatly on voluntary, honest compliance by American citizens. The viability of banks and thrifts greatly depends on citizens' confidence in regulatory officials and agencies. Whenever citizens see corrupt public officials and other white-collar offenders violate the law with impunity they inevitably must question official integrity and commitment to fairness. In many ways, the greatest harm to the victims of white-collar crime may be this loss of faith in the very possibility of fair, impartial government. Surely this problem is exacerbated and cynicism intensified when victims' efforts to enlist the aid of political officials in the pursuit of simple justice lead only to frustration. The result may be increased citizen apathy and feelings of *delegitimation.* In one of the few empirical investigations of this hypothesized relationship, Peters and Welch (1980) found that charges of corruption apparently had little effect on net voter turnout and election outcomes in five Congressional elections from 1968 to 1978. They suggested, however, that individual-level studies would be more appropriate for examining whether official corruption or other forms of white-collar crime cause delegitimation.

The state's failure to mete out swift and appropriately severe punishment to white-collar criminals may erode not only victims' confidence in and support for American political and social institutions but also their commitment to and willingness to play by "the rules." Thus, the final secondary impact of white-collar crime is its potentially deleterious effect on public morality. As the President's Commission on Law Enforcement and Administration put it:

> It is reasonable to assume that prestigious companies that flout the law set an example for other businesses and influence individuals, particularly young people, to commit other kinds of crime on the grounds that everyone is taking what he can get. If businessmen who are respected as leaders of the community can do such things as break the antitrust laws or rent dilapidated houses to the poor at high rents, it is hard to convince the young that they should be honest. (1967, p. 48)

In other words, by violating citizens' sense of equity, lenient treatment of white-collar criminals may provide them with easy rationalizations for personal misconduct. This reaction may be understandable particularly among poor and minority citizens who see the stark contrast between our harsh response to street criminals and our limp response to white-collar criminals. Moore (1980) suggests that, "given the intensity of our attack on street crime, there seems to be a *special* obligation to prosecute respectable people who use their position and reputation to steal through deception and exploitation" (p. 30).

White-Collar Crime Victims and Public Policy

Many times, official response to white-collar crime includes agencies that play little or no part in responding to street crimes. For example, use of bankruptcy proceedings to distribute any remaining defendants' assets is a common occurrence in white-collar crime cases (Kusic 1989). We do not know if the complex of agencies, personnel, and legal processes set in motion by white-collar crimes present obstacles and problems for victims that are different from those experienced by street crime victims. Currently, victim assistance programs in the U.S. work almost exclusively with *individual* victims of interpersonal criminal violence and street property crimes. Because these street crimes usually harm individuals and their immediate social networks, this is a reasonable policy response. By contrast, some white-collar crimes victimize thousands of individuals.

This important difference between street crime and white-collar crime victimization constrains investigation, prosecution, and settlement of the latter. There is reason to believe that it constrains intelligent and reasoned responses to victims as well (Edelhertz; and Rogovin 1980). Nonetheless, the absence of systematic data on these matters means that we do not know if existing procedures and programs could be modified or new ones developed to provide assistance to white-collar crime victims.

It does seem clear that lack of concern for white-collar crime victims is not cost free. As a former federal prosecutor suggests, the "inadequate concern to provide remedies for the victims of white-collar crime" undermines efforts to control it (Edelhertz 1980, p. 123).

References

Burt, Martha R. and Bonnie L. Katz. 1985. "Rape, Robbery, and Burglary: Responses to Actual and Feared Victimization, with Special Focus on Women and the Elderly." *Victimology* 10:325–358.

Douglas, Jack D. and John M. Johnson, eds. 1977. *Official Deviance.* Philadelphia: J. B. Lippincott.

Duncan, J. T. Skip and Marc Caplan. 1980. *White-Collar Crime: A Selected Bibliography.* Washington, DC: U.S. Department of Justice, National Institute of Justice.

Edelhertz, Herbert. 1970. *The Nature, Impact and Prosecution of* White-Collar *Crime.* Washington, DC: U.S. Department of Justice, National Institute of Law Enforcement and Criminal Justice.

_____. 1980. "Appendix B: White-Collar Crime." Pp. 119–31 in *A National Strategy for Containing White-Collar Crime*, edited by H. Edelhertz and C. Rogovin. Lexington, MA: D. C. Heath.

Edelhertz, Herbert and Charles Rogovin, eds. 1980. *A National Strategy for Containing White-Collar Crime.* Lexington, MA: D. C. Heath.

Elias, Robert. 1986. *The Politics of Victimization.* New York: Oxford University Press.

Ermann, M. David and Richard J. Lundman, eds. 1987. *Corporate and Governmental Deviance* 3rd. ed. New York: Oxford University Press.

Finn, Peter. n.d. *Victims.* Washington, DC: U.S. Department of Justice, Bureau of Justice Statistics.

Fischer, Constance T. 1984. "A Phenomenological Study of Being Criminally Victimized: Contributions and Constraints of Qualitative Research." *Journal of Social Issues* 40:161–178.

Geis, Gilbert 1975. "Victimization Patterns in White-collar Crime." Pp. 89–105 in *Victimology: A New Focus. Exploiters and Exploited.* Vol. 5, edited by I. Drapkin and E. Viano. Lexington, MA: D. C. Heath.

_____. 1976. "Defrauding the Elderly." Pp. 7–19 in *Crime and the Elderly*, edited by J. Goldsmith and S. Goldsmith. Lexington, MA: D. C. Heath.

Heilbroner, Robert L., ed. 1972. *In the Name of Profit.* New York: Warner.

Hills, Stuart L., ed. 1987. *Corporate Violence.* Totowa, NJ: Rowman & Littlefield.

Hochstedler, Ellen, ed. 1984. *Corporations as Criminals.* Beverly Hills, CA: Sage.

Janoff-Bulman, Ronnie. 1985. "Criminal vs. Non-criminal Victimization: Victims' Reactions." *Victimology* 10:498–511.

Johnson, John M. and Jack D. Douglas, eds. 1978. *Crime at the Top.* Philadelphia: J. B. Lippincott.

Kusic, Jane Y. 1989. *White Collar Crime 101 Prevention Handbook.* Vienna, VA: White Collar Crime 101.

Leymann, Heinz. 1985. "Somatic and Psychological Symptoms after the Experience of Life Threatening Events: A Profile Analysis." *Victimology* 10:512–538.

Maguire, Mike. 1980. "The Impact of Burglary upon Victims." *British Journal of Criminology* 20:261–275.

McGuire, Mary and Herbert Edelhertz. 1980. "Consumer Abuse of Older Americans: Victimization and Remedial Action in Two Metropolitan Areas." Pp. 266–292 in *White-Collar Crime: Theory and Research*, edited by G. Geis and E. Stotland. Beverly Hills, CA: Sage.

Moore, Mark H. 1980. "Notes toward a National Strategy to Deal with White-Collar Crime." Pp. 21–53 in *A National Strategy for Containing White-Collar Crime*, edited by H. Edelhertz and C. Rogovin. Lexington, MA: D. C. Heath.

National Institute of Law Enforcement and Criminal Justice. 1977. *White Collar Crime: A Selected Bibliography.* Washington, DC: U.S. Department of Justice.

Peters, John G. and Susan Welch. 1980. "The Effects of Charges of Corruption on Voting Behavior in Congressional Elections." *American Political Science Review* 74:697–708.

President's Commission on Law Enforcement and Administration of Justice. 1967. *The Challenge of Crime in a Free Society.* Washington, DC: U. S. Government Printing Office.

President's Task Force on Victims of Crime. 1982. *Final Report.* Washington, DC: U.S. Government Printing Office.

Steele, Eric H. 1975. "Fraud, Dispute, and the Consumer: Responding to Consumer Complaints." *University of Pennsylvania Law Review* 123:1107–1186.

Sutherland, Edwin H. 1949. *White Collar Crime.* New York: Holt, Rinehart & Winston.

United States Code. 1983–1985. *Containing the General and Permanent Laws of the United States, Enacted During the 98th Congress* Vol. 3, Title 28–Title 42. Washington, DC: U.S. Government Printing Office.

U.S. Department of Justice. 1988a. *Report to Congress.* Washington, DC: Office for Victims of Crime.

______. 1988b. *Report to the Nation on Crime and Justice.* 2nd ed. Washington, DC: Bureau of Justice Statistics.

Vaughan, Diane and Giovanna Carlo. 1975. "The Appliance Repairman: A Study of Victim Responsiveness and Fraud." *Journal of Research in Crime and Delinquency* 12:153–161.

______. 1976. "Victims of Fraud: Victim-Responsiveness, Incidence, and Reporting." Pp. 79–95 in *Victims, Criminals and Society,* edited by E. Viano. Leiden, Netherlands: A. W. Sijthoff.

Viano, Emilio. 1987. "Victim's Rights and the Constitution: Reflections on a Bicentennial." *Crime and Delinquency* 33:438–451.

Walsh, Marilyn E. and Donna D. Schram. 1980. "The Victim of White-Collar Crime: Accuser or Accused?" Pp. 32–51 in *White-Collar Crime: Theory and Research,* edited by G. Geis and E. Stotland. Beverly Hills, CA: Sage.

Wortman, Camille B. 1983. "Coping with Victimization: Conclusions and Implications for Future Research." *Journal of Social Issues* 39:195–221.

‹ 4 ›

Underworlds and Upperworlds

The Convergence of Organized and White-Collar Crime

Gary Potter
Larry Gaines

"White-collar crime" is not a precise, sociologically or legally defined category of criminal offenses. Rather, it is a social construct used to delineate a set of characteristics which identify the crime itself, the social context of the crime, and the attributes of the criminal actors. Much like similar social constructs, such as "street crime," "organized crime," "juvenile crime," and "political crime," the concept of white-collar crime has more to do with the unique conditions under which criminality occurs than with a specified criminal act. For example, fraud and theft may be white-collar crimes, or may be analyzed under constructs emphasizing "property crime," "street crime," or "organized crime," depending on the social and occupational positions of the offenders involved, the degree of legitimacy that can be ascribed to offenders and/or their respective organizations, the centrality of criminal acts to the offenders' livelihood, and the self-perception of the offender. So,

Reprinted from the Proceedings on Defining White Collar Crime, National White Collar Crime Center, Morgantown, WV.

white-collar crime is less a precise definitional classification of offenses or offenders and more a heuristic device guiding the study or analysis of crimes by certain actors in certain social settings. The key issue becomes one not of definitional precision but of explanatory power, and this issue may be tested only in comparison with other heuristic devices.

"Organized crime" as a similar social construct seems an especially propitious device against which to assess the utility of the white-collar crime construct. There are similarities between the two concepts. Both involve some level of organization; both accentuate issues of self-perception, legitimacy, and the centrality of the criminal act. Both are evolving concepts benefiting from extensive scholarly study that has modified their original forms. The question to be asked, however, is whether our increased understanding of these phenomena has led to a diminution of their utility as separate and unique social constructs placing crime in context.

The Characteristics of White-Collar Crime

The most important characteristic ascribed to "white-collar crime" as a social construct is the idea of social status or social class position of the criminal actor. Sutherland referred to "white-collar crime" as crime "committed by a person of respectability and high social status in the course of his occupation" (Sutherland, 1940). Ever since Sutherland's classic statement first defined the concept, the white-collar crime literature has ascribed great importance to the concept of social class position as both a definitional device and an explanatory device in articulating the components of the criminal act itself. It is suggested that this social class position differentiates the fraud, theft, perjury, bribery, etc., of the organizational and occupational actor from similar acts by the "dangerous classes."

> In the purest "white-collar" crimes, white-collar social class position is used (1) to diffuse criminal intent into ordinary occupational routines so that it escapes unambiguous expression in any discrete behavior; (2) to accomplish the crime without incidents of effect that furnish presumptive evidence of its occurrence before the criminal has been identified; and (3) to cover up culpable knowledge of participants through concerted action that allows each to claim ignorance. (Katz, 1979: 435)

Social class position defines not only the criminal actor but the very ability to commit the crime in question in the social context within which that crime occurs.

When Edwin Sutherland first introduced white-collar crime as a social construct, he placed great emphasis on the offender's occupational and role social class position. But Sutherland also recognized the ambiguity of the construct when compared with similar heuristic devices. For example, Sutherland found several similarities between "white-collar criminals" and professional thieves, another group he studied in depth. Sutherland found that both classes of criminals exhibited a "persistence of behaviors" over time and a propensity for widespread recidivism. Sutherland asserted that both white-collar crime and professional theft are ubiquitous in society and seriously underestimated by officially produced data. In both cases offenders who are caught and prosecuted do not lose social status among their day-to-day and intimate associates. Both professional theft and white-collar crime are deliberate acts involving some degree of organization and criminal intent. Sutherland made distinctions between the two categories of crime: self-conception and public perception. Thieves were thieves and proud of it. The public viewed a professional thief as a criminal. In contrast, white-collar criminals did not view themselves as criminal actors. Rather, they were caught up in the competitive rhythm of the business world or in personal problems that caused them to commit aberrant indiscretions, or they were people victimized by unfair and ambiguous laws and regulations. Similarly, the public viewed white-collar criminals primarily as legitimate actors who strayed or made mistakes (Pontell, Rosoff and Goode, 1990: 290). While Sutherland did not explicitly make such a comparison between white-collar and organized criminals, it is clear that many of the same similarities and dissimilarities could be identified. While status, position, public and self-perception, and occupational context are all vital to understanding white-collar crime as well as to understanding organized crime and professional theft, it would be misleading to assert that such characteristics can be identified with precision. Rather, all forms of crime occur on a continuum of legitimacy, status, public and self-perception, and embeddedness in occupational routines (Smith, 1980).

Modifying White-Collar Crime as a Social Construct

In the years since Sutherland's classic statement prescribing the parameters of white-collar crime as a social construct, scholarly investigations have in some cases added modifications to those parameters, in other cases expanded those parameters, and in some cases introduced new components to the construct. This scholarly work, along with a recognition that all the constituent variables making up this social construct occur on a continuum, leads us to the consideration of several important concepts embedded in the white-collar crime construct. Among the most important of these modifications are the concepts of (1) the organizational dimensions of deviance, (2) front activities, (3) inauthenticity, and (4) criminal corporations.

The Organizational Dimensions of Deviance

Because white-collar crime invariably occurs within some kind of organizational context, even a rudimentary one, the importance of organizations to the social context of the criminal act must be considered. Organizations, both formal and informal, offer various settings and opportunities for deviance that differ appreciably from the settings and opportunities available to individuals. So, members of the organization, particularly new recruits, must be socialized to accept the justifications for behavior that are contrary to norms outside the confines of the organization. Because the deviance is organizational rather than individual, the behavior must be supported by others in the organization. Others must engage in similar behavior or must tolerate it. Organizational deviance must be supported by the dominant administration of the organization (Ermann and Lundman, 1978: 7–8).

Organizational deviance may develop in two ways: (1) it may develop when the organization adopts goals, either formally or informally, that deviate from societal norms, and (2) it may develop when deviant means are adopted as ways to attain otherwise legitimate organizational goals.

These dynamics may be seen most clearly in Clinard and Yeager's articulation of the forces that create an impetus toward corporate criminality (Clinard and Yeager, 1980). The corporation may place more emphasis on profits than on ethics. There may be a strong desire for organizational expansion, security or the maintenance of a successful operation, coupled with a fear of failure and high levels of group loyalty. There may be strong organizational pressure for high levels of performance by members. Finally, some market structures are inherently criminogenic. Although Clinard and Yeager were writing about corporations, there is little in their discussion that would preclude the application of the same principles to organized crime groups. Similarly, while Ermann and Lundman were addressing the organizational dynamics of legitimate organizations, very little difference is discernible when looking at organizations falling on the other end of the spectrum of legitimacy.

Front Activities

Modern organizations are characterized by centralization of authority; the creation of specialized vocabularies producing an organizational ideology that "sanitizes" misconduct, allows for the denial of responsibility and victimization, and condemns the condemners; and a routinization and fragmentation of tasks through specialization. All of these characteristics facilitate the use of front activities by corporations and formal organizations. Front activities hide organizational deviance behind ideology or a public posture. They facilitate management by manipulation. Austin Turk has articulated these front activities in looking at governmental intelligence agencies (Turk, 1981). Turk argues that intelligence agencies lie as a "routine activity," regulated only by political expediency. Similar front activities can be identified in the business world. For example, businesses and corporations provide only specific information requested by regulators, even though other information at their disposal would more fully inform the truth. Corporations and businesses destroy or lose potentially embarrassing or incriminating information prior to any request to produce the information. Corporations fragment information so that documents turned over to regulators are incomplete, out of sequence, and difficult to recreate in context. Finally, corporations and businesses routinely portray deviance occurring with the organization as the work of a deviant or overzealous individual, not as the result of organizational norms (Bernstein, 1976). So, deceit is routinized in formal organizations of all types, intelligence agencies, corporations, small businesses, and organized crime syndicates.

Inauthenticity

Inauthenticity is the organizational practice of maintaining an overt positive appearance in the face of a problem or a revelation of wrongdoing (Seeman, 1966: 67–73; Baxter, 1982; Etzioni, 1968, 1969). An oil company may run ads emphasizing its commitment to the environment after an oil spill at sea. A pharmaceutical manufacturer may focus on its research to cure an incurable illness after having been caught falsifying test results or withholding data from the FDA. A chemical company may stress its people-oriented management style after having been found responsible for a toxic dump site. In fact, Presthus has noted that one type of social character is particularly successful in making it to the top of organizations: an individual with a superficial sense of warmth and charm, who views things in black and white. This type of individual finds it easy to make decisions and is able to categorize and dehumanize individuals (Presthus, 1978)—in other words, an individual adept at the implementation of the strategies of inauthenticity.

Criminal Corporations

Some organizations have no need for the niceties of fronting activities or inauthenticity; they are simply criminal from the start. Scholarly investigations by Block and Bernard (1988) and Levi (1981) have added the concept of criminal corporations to the parameters of white-collar crime as a social construct. Criminal corporations are organizations that are either created, run, or assumed as means of committing crime.

The waste-oil business has produced a classic example of such a criminal corporation. Block and Bernard's case study (1988) details the operations of four waste-oil refineries owned by an entrepreneur named Russell Mahler. Mahler managed the refineries for almost three decades, successfully capturing over 5 percent of the U.S. market for re-refined lubricants. In the 1970s, however, Congress passed the Resource Conservation and Recovery Act that established minimum standards for the disposal of hazardous waste. The new regulations dramatically increased the cost of waste disposal and made the re-refining of waste oil into lubricants very expensive, thereby threatening the economic health of the entire waste-oil business. The net effect of these increased costs was to create:

> economic pressure to dispose of toxic wastes by cheap but illegal means. Waste-oil dealers already had facilities for the storage and disposal of waste products and could illegally sell a mixture of toxic waste as fuel with minimal chances of being caught. Thus, a new illegal means for making money was presented to waste-oil dealers at the same time that their traditional, legal means for making money suddenly disappeared. (Block and Bernard, 1988: 116–117)

Michael Levi's (1984) work centers on what he calls long-firm fraud. Long-firm fraud results from a corporation using its good credit to obtain supplies or resources from legitimate suppliers and then reselling those goods or resources at a profit without paying the suppliers. Levi classifies long-firm fraud in two ways. The first is preplanned long-firm fraud, in which the corporation is set up with the express intention of committing fraud against suppliers. The second, slippery-slope long-firm fraud, is a situation in which a heretofore legitimate corporation turns to fraud primarily as a result of market demands.

Long-firm fraudsters have two main goals. The first is to obtain the goods in question on credit. The second is to efficiently dispose of those same goods as a profit before their suppliers take action against them. Achieving these goals is considerably easier for the slippery-slope fraudster because he or she already has established suppliers and established lines of credit with those suppliers. In addition, the slippery-slope fraudster has well-established outlets through which to sell his or her goods. In preplanned long-firm fraud, these relationships must be established as the corporation itself is created. Lines of credit from suppliers are attained by creating phony references from nonexistent businesses that give the appearance of having actively engaged in commerce with the criminal corporation. Levi found that preplanned long-firm fraud involved a high level of organization and coordination with criminal actors already in the field. The criminal corporation, for example, usually seeks out a number of professional "organizers," "bent bank managers," "shady businesspersons" and "big-time criminals" in order to facilitate its phony credit paper trail and in order to obtain startup capital. Once this assistance has been obtained the participants simply:

> purchase an existing perfectly respectable firm or limited company, preferably on credit terms, and then, usually without informing suppliers of the change in ownership, obtain extensive credit on the basis of the former owner's reputation before finally absconding with the proceeds. (Levi, 1984: 8)

Levi's description of long-firm fraud in the corporate world bears startling resemblances to organized crime's bankruptcy scams. Usually organized criminals will purchase an already existing corporation paying only part of its value in cash. The rest of the sale price is set to be paid in installments. The organized criminals then order from the company's usual suppliers goods that are quickly sold off at a profit. Other company assets may be disposed of as well and the cash from the sale of goods and assets is transferred to a second corporation also controlled by the organized crime syndicate.

The concepts of inauthenticity, front activities, and criminal corporations significantly alter the classic description of white-collar crime. What was originally conceived of as crime by individuals of high status committed in the course of their occupations or professions now takes on the added dimension of criminal intent. Long-firm fraud, ignoring toxic waste disposal regulations, withholding and resequencing information, and creating a corporate front all are acts requiring deliberation and intent. When organizational deviance is planned, premeditated, and designed for criminal purpose, the organization becomes a criminal organization and the lines of demarcation between white-collar and organized crime become extremely difficult to discern. But the imprecision of these demarcations is made even clearer when we look at the criminal law itself, particularly the RICO Act.

The RICO Act of 1970

Of the all the statutes that have impacted organized crime (i.e., the Hobbs Act, conspiracy laws, the Mann Act) none has had a greater impact than the RICO (Racketeer Influenced and Corrupt Organizations) Act. RICO imposes draconian penalties on any organization involved in a pattern of criminal acts (defined as two or more crimes in a ten-year period). Interestingly, while RICO has been used successfully against dozens of organized crime groups, it has also been successfully invoked against corporations like Shearson/American Express, Lloyd's of London, E. F. Hutton and General Motors (Mokhiber, 1985: 23). In these cases and many others the criminal acts of respectable people and organizations have looked very much like the machinations of organized crime syndicates (Pontell and Calavita, 1993).

In this regard, a case study by Peter Reuter (1987) may be instructive. Reuter studied garbage collection in the New York City area. Reuter found that private garbage collectors are members of a garbage cartel that allocates territories in New York City to each cartel member. As a result, garbage haulers do not have to compete against each other and therefore can charge higher prices than the market would ordinarily dictate. The very substantial profits realized from this arrangement are divided among members, with a small percentage set aside to retain the services of local organized crime groups who in return facilitate the business and discourage competition from outside the cartel (Reuter, 1987). This arrangement is a classic organized crime enterprise and would be easily recognized as such by most observers. However, it is difficult to understand how it differs from the same arrangement maintained by the U.S. oil industry, an arrangement also resulting in high prices and excessive profits (Blair, 1976; Coleman, 1989: 22–30).

The New York City garbage collection business is not the only example of organized crime following the lead of corporate entities (or is it the other way around?). As in the example of Russell Mahler's waste-oil business, companies that haul toxic wastes have engaged in wanton violation of environmental laws, often dumping their poisons in city sewers, on the side of a road, in a stream or lake, or in abandoned strip mines. These haulers have also found that alliances with organized crime syndicates facilitate the business of business (Block and Scarpitti, 1985).

In the meat-packing business, companies controlled by organized crime have been known to use rotting or diseased meat to make ground beef, hot dogs, and sausages (Kwitny, 1979: 1–46). Once again, it is often difficult to discern the mob from the corporate managers. Take the case of Hormel, one of the largest meat processors in the world. Hormel bribed inspectors from the Department of Agriculture to ignore persistent violations in their production and packaging of meat (McCaghy, 1976: 216). In fact, in addition to producing unsafe food products for original consumption, the company recycled spoiled meat and sent it back to the market:

> When the original customers returned the meat to Hormel, they used the following terms to describe it: "moldy liverloaf, sour party hams, leaking bologna, discolored bacon, off-condition hams, and slick and slimy spareribs." Hormel renewed these products with cosmetic measures (reconditioning, trimming, and washing). Spareribs returned for sliminess, discoloration, and stickiness were rejuvenated through curing and smoking, renamed Windsor Loins and sold in ghetto stores for more than fresh pork chops. (Wellford, 1972: 69)

Similarly, the Beech-Nut Nutrition Corporation mislabeled its baby food, claiming that a substance which was primarily colored sugar water was apple juice for babies. The company entered guilty pleas to 215 criminal counts charging that it had intentionally defrauded and misled the public (Eitzen and Zinn, 1992). Despite all of this, law enforcement officials rarely if ever speak of the Hormel criminal syndicate or the Beech-Nut Baby Crime Family.

Corporate Collaboration with Organized Crime

Despite the careful distinctions attempted in the criminological literature to differentiate white-collar and organized crime, the fact is that it has been common throughout U.S. history for a series of exchanges between the under- and upperworlds to develop into long-term corrupt relationships. In the private business sector, respected institutions such as Shearson/American Express, Merrill Lynch, the Miami National Bank, Citibank, and others have eagerly participated in illicit ventures with organized crime syndicates (Lernoux, 1984; Moldea, 1986; President's Commission on Organized Crime, 1984: 31–42). For example, in the infamous "Pizza Connection" case in which Southeast Asian heroin was distributed through a series of pizza parlors located in the United States, tens of millions of dollars were laundered through New York City banks and then transferred by those banks to secret accounts in Switzerland, the Bahamas, and other countries. In addition to using banks to launder money, the "Pizza Connection" heroin traffickers also used the brokerage firm of Merrill, Lynch, Pierce, Fenner, and Smith, depositing $5 million (all in $5, $10, and $20 bills) over a six-week period. In addition to accepting these highly dubious deposits, Merrill Lynch provided extraordinary security to the couriers carrying the heroin money. At the same time, couriers from the "Pizza Connection" were laundering $13.5 million through accounts at another brokerage house, E. F. Hutton, which also provided private security services for the couriers.

The affinity of major brokerage houses for heroin money is not new; it has long historical precedents. For example, in the 1930s and even into the 1940s, illegal gambling syndicates were among the largest customers of the fledgling AT&T corporation and played a key role in insuring its subsequent survival and financial health (King, 1975: 40). In another case, in the 1960s both Pan American Airways and Hughes Tool corporations entered into partnerships with organized crime syndicates in gambling casino ventures both in Las Vegas and the Caribbean (Reid, 1969: 138–139). During the 1940s, Detroit automobile manufacturers used organized crime syndicates in an effort to suppress organizing drives by the United Auto Workers. At Ford Motor Company an organized crime syndicate was given a monopoly over the haulaway business in return for taking over the newly established autoworkers union. Even after the AFL successfully organized the industry, Ford still hired organized crime figures to act as strike breakers (Pearce, 1976: 140). Contrary to the official portrait of organized crime, under- and upperworld criminals form close, symbiotic bonds. Business is not the pawn of organized crime; it is, in fact, an integral part.

The organization and coordination of crime is very much like the structure of legitimate business. Finance, investment, capitalization, and credit all matter just as much for organized crime as for McDonalds. In both cases, "bankers" have a great deal of say in the structure of the enterprise. Money enters the banking system from a great variety of sources, usually in used bills, the profits of gambling, vice, narcotics, burglary. In the system, they can be laundered through Las Vegas, Miami, Mexico, Liechtenstein, Switzerland, the Caribbean, and other places. They can be invested and give the businessperson a level of return on profit impossible without the connection to organized crime.

After almost a century, organized crime enterprises have thoroughly penetrated legitimate businesses. The scale of the multinational money-moving conglomerate is suggested by two things: the vast profits of gambling must go somewhere, and the tiny proportion of drug operations that actually come to light involve a substantial capital investment. Cressey gives a good account of such "money movers." The money mover must hide illegally obtained cash and put it to work. "Importing, real estate, trust funds, books, stock and bonds, are his typical undertaking" (1968: 234). Of course, money movers come in various shapes and sizes. Some are glorified loan sharks. Others are men of wealth and international prestige; it is this latter category we describe here. It would be virtually impossible to try to catalogue all of the cases of corrupt relationships between business and organized crime in U.S. history. In fact, it would be impossible to outline all such relationships even in a single city. We will content ourselves with a discussion of two important illustrations of alliances between white-collar and organized criminals: (1) an historical view of Meyer Lansky's attempts to integrate organized crime and corporate America, and (2) the role of organized crime in the savings and loan scandals of the 1980s.

◂ THE WORLDS OF MEYER LANSKY ▸

The remarkable career of Meyer Lansky has been frequently retold, most comprehensively by Hank Messick (1973). A brief synopsis is useful here. Lansky was born in Grodno, Russia, as Maier Suchowljansky in 1902 and migrated with his family to New York in 1911. By 1918 he had formed acquaintanceships with Bugsy Siegel and Lucky Luciano. Prohibition gave him his greatest opportunity, and the "Bugs and Meyer" gang gained prominence as a bootleggers' mercenary force. By the late 1920s, with Lepke Buchalter and Luciano, he pieced together the outlines of a bootlegging syndicate that would be the dominant influence in organized crime for the next three decades. After Prohibition, he and Siegel cast their eyes further afield—to the West, the Sunbelt, the Caribbean. In Miami, Lansky initiated the "Gold Coast" with its hotels and casinos; in Cuba he created Batista's leisure empire; in Nevada and California, Siegel used syndicate money to create a network of enterprises. Siegel was shot and killed in 1947, probably because of a dispute over cost overruns on the Flamingo hotel and casino, but Las Vegas lived on to flourish and prosper. Lansky's business enterprises were now sufficiently far flung to withstand any one setback like that which would be dealt him by Fidel Castro's revolution. When Havana fell, he turned back to Las Vegas and opened new enterprises in Haiti, the Bahamas, and even in London.

Attempting to describe Lansky's activities is an almost impossible task; some authors credit him with virtually every financial scam since 1925. So with this caveat, we can begin to describe Lansky's activities on behalf of organized crime. First, let's take a look at the cast of characters which so frequently are participants in Lansky-inspired activities.

Lansky associates can broadly be divided into two categories: (1) the old-time veterans of the gangs of the 1920s and 1930s; and (2) newer associates, usually relatively clean lawyers and businesspeople. Lansky appears to have preserved his friendships and business partnerships over many decades. For example, after the hit on Bugsy Siegel, control of his Flamingo Hotel passed to three old Lansky cronies: Moe Sedway from the Lower East Side of New York, Morris Rosen, and "Gus" Greenbaum from Phoenix (Fried, 1980: 253–254). Some other examples of these long-standing relationships are instructive:

1. The Minneapolis mob headed by Isadore Blumenfeld ("Kidd Cann") in the 1920s provided Lansky with some of his most durable business partners. Blumenfeld's brother "Yiddy Bloom" held substantial investments in Miami area real estate and controlled a large portion of the New York gambling market. Probably his best known financial coup was the early 1970s stock fraud surrounding the artificial boosting of Magic Marker shares. Bloom was joined in this by his son Jerold and some fifteen fellow conspirators (Pennsylvania Crime Commission, 1980: 195–198).
2. Also from the Blumenfeld Mob was John Pullman, long used by Lansky in his banking ventures for organized crime. Pullman had lived in Canada and Switzerland and was an expert in the use of numbered accounts and dummy corporations. He was the head of the "Bank of World Commerce" in Nassau (Bahamas) in the 1960s, a highly effective "laundry" for Mob money (Pennsylvania Crime Commission, 1980: 198; Fried, 1980: 276–277).
3. "Dandy" Phil Kastel was part of the 1930s move to the Sunbelt from the New York mobs. In New Orleans, Kastel bridged the years from the early bootlegging and gambling syndicates to Carlos Marcello, and through it all, he was never far from Lansky's interests (Messick, 1969: 105, 205, 247).
4. "Doc" Stacher (born 1902), emerged from New Jersey organized crime to become a leader in organized crime's western empire (Fried, 1980: 281–282; Cook and Carmichael: 62).
5. Sydney Korshak (born 1907) was patronized early in his career by the Capone mob. He enjoyed a very successful career representing labor unions and directed the flow of Teamster money into the Nevada casinos. Korshak apparently accumulated enormous wealth from legitimate sources as well (Fried, 1980: 285–286).
6. Harry Teitelbaum was a prominent figure in the New York gangs of the 1920s, who was also associated with the "Bugs and Meyer" and "L and G" (Lepke Buchalter and Gurrah Sha-

piro's labor racketeering gang) gangs. By the 1950s, Teitelbaum was associated with Philadelphia syndicate boss Nig Rosen in a massive Lansky-inspired heroin trafficking operation (Fried, 1980; Cook and Carmichael).

7. Sam Cohen was a Los Angeles bookmaker who was closely associated with the Flamingo Hotel in Las Vegas in the 1960s and was accused with Lansky of operating a major skim operation at the Fremont and Riviera casinos. With his sons Alan and Joel, he was involved in some interesting deals in both Florida and the Pocono Mountains of Pennsylvania. These real estate deals were conducted in association with Alvin Malnik, Lansky's attorney and supposed "heir." Sam Cohen fits the pattern of continuity from the Prohibition gangs to the financial world of the 1970s and 1980s. He moved from New York to Florida in the 1920s and joined the exodus to Nevada in the 1950s (Messick, 1969: 326–331, 363; Mollenhoff, 1973: 186).
8. Benjamin Siegelbaum was a financial manipulator very close to Lansky, who was involved in a Swiss money-laundering operation in the 1960s called the Exchange Bank of Geneva. Siegelbaum had been a partner of Nig Rosen, John Pullman, Yiddy Bloom, and others in his career.
9. Morris Lansburgh was a Lansky associate who was extremely powerful in Miami, where he controlled substantial hotel interests in Miami Beach. He was alleged to have been a partner with Lansky and Sam Cohen in the Flamingo skim (Mollenhoff, 1973: 186).

Other prominent figures in the Lansky orbit were newer and more respectable figures. For example: Delbert Coleman came to prominence in the late 1960s in the "Parvin-Dohrman" affair. In 1968 Coleman was associated with Korshak in an attempt to purchase the Parvin-Dohrman casinos in Las Vegas—and to artificially float that company's stock shares. Coleman and Korshak were also involved in Bernie Cornfeld's Investor's Overseas Services (IOS) scam (Fried, 1980: 282–286; Raw et al.: 229; Demaris, 1981: 247). Alvin Malnik (born 1932) was picked by some observers of organized crime to be Lansky's probable successor. He first came to prominence in the early 1960s with the attempt to establish a gambling resort at Paradise Island in the Bahamas. He had already established himself in the banking and real estate businesses in Miami but soon become Lansky's public "front man." The Paradise Island venture led to the establishment of Resorts International, the entertainment and gambling conglomerate which was the subject of intense law enforcement scrutiny for years as charges of control by Meyer Lansky surfaced (Mahan, 1980).

In the early 1970s, Malnik was also involved with Sam Cohen's sons in land deals in Florida and the Poconos. Their companies—COMAL and "Cove Associates"—dealt with Caesar's World and the Teamsters Pension Fund (Fried, 1980: 282–286; Pennsylvania Crime Commission, 1980: 252–254). Finally, Allen R. Glick (born 1942) of Pittsburgh attracted a great deal of attention when his firm Argent (A. R Glick Enterprises) seemingly came from nowhere to secure a vast Teamsters loan (about $146 million). This enabled him to take over the Stardust casino in Las Vegas and much of the plundered Parvin-Dohrman company. In 1979 he was implicated in a skimming operation, which led to his being forced to sell out for a comfortable profit (Fried, 1980: 284–285; Demaris, 1981: 318, 320, 365–366, 391, 445, 525–526). The operations in which these and other organized crime money-men were involved recycled the profits of organized crime and in turn generated immense new profits—which were, however, almost wholly clean.

Las Vegas

"Bugs and Meyer" pioneered Las Vegas on behalf of east coast organized crime interests, investing money from New York, New Jersey, Philadelphia, Cleveland, and other areas. The first great hotel in Las Vegas was Siegel's Flamingo (1946). After his murder, the hotel passed to three old Lansky cronies: Sedway, Rosen and Greenbaum. Gus Greenbaum would later manage the Riviera, but he fell out with his Chicago based employers. He and his wife were murdered in 1958. Thereafter, new casinos appeared in swift succession:

- The Thunderbird (1948) was fronted by Clifford Jones, a former Lieutenant-Governor of Nevada, but was really a Lansky operation.
- The Desert Inn (1950) was run by the Cleveland Four (Mo Dalitz, Louis Rothkopf, Sam Tucker, and Morris Kleinman), who had dominated bootlegging and illegal casino gambling in the Midwest and Kentucky.
- The Sands (1952) was owned by an awesome list of organized crime backers including Lansky, Joe Adonis, Frank Costello, Doc Stacher, Ed Levinson, Kid Cann, and Frank Sinatra.
- The Sahara (1952) was backed by Chicago, Cleveland, and New York "money men."
- The Riviera was backed by the Chicago mob.
- The Dunes was opened by representatives of Raymond Patriarca of Rhode Island.
- The Stardust (1958) was a Dalitz operation, as was the Sundance.
- The Tropicana (1957) was backed by Kastel and Costello.

- The Palace was opened by Patriarca, Chicago mob investors, Lansky, and Teamster Union money. Teamster money also flowed into Caesar's Palace, the Landmark, the Dunes, and the Fremont (Hammer, 1975: 224–225).

By the late 1950s, the casinos were doing an admirable job of making old-time gangsters quite respectable—particularly in the case of the old Cleveland Four. For instance, Cleveland Four veteran Lou Rothkopf's nephew Bernie was a legitimate businessman, director of the MGM Grand Hotel (Demaris, 1981: 56–59). Moreover, the casinos provided wonderful opportunities for "skimming" to defraud the IRS. In a major scandal at the Flamingo in the 1960s, Lansky was indicted along with partners Morris Lansburgh and Sam Cohen. Estimated "skimmed" profits amounted to several million dollars a year. By the 1970s, Nick Civella and the Kansas City mob apparently controlled the Tropicana and the Dunes, in the latter case through Jimmy Hoffa's attorney Morris Shenker. At the Aladdin, Delbert Coleman and Ed Torres, both Teamster Union operatives, were believed to be representing someone who wished to remain hidden.

The ownership of a Las Vegas casino is often frighteningly complex. However, we might recount the history of one casino in order to give some idea of the sort of problems involved. In the mid-1950s, the Parvin-Dohrman company bought the Flamingo. In the 1960s, it bought the Fremont and sold the Flamingo to a consortium headed by Morris Lansburgh, with Lansky receiving a finder's fee. The Parvin-Dohrman empire then expanded to include the Aladdin, and also the Stardust, purchased from Moe Dalitz. In 1968 Parvin agreed to sell out to Delbert Coleman with Sidney Korshak acting as intermediary (and getting a $500,000 finder's fee for the transaction). At the end of 1968, while the sale went through, Coleman and Korshak succeeded in artificially boosting the Parvin-Dohrman stock from $35 to $141 a share with the aid of financial impresarios like Bernie Cornfield of Investors' Overseas Services (IOS). After the inevitable collapse, Korshak and Coleman pocketed their profits and Parvin-Dohrman changed its name to Recrion (Fried, 1980: 282–286).

At this point, we run into the brilliant young businessman Allen Glick. In the early 1970s, Glick set up his own company, Argent, in Las Vegas and began raising a series of large loans from the Teamsters' Pension Fund. By 1976 Glick owed the Teamsters about $146 million. In 1973 this largesse enabled him to take over all the shares of Recrion and become a major gambling magnate in Nevada, but it was scarcely a good investment. Under Glick's management, the Stardust tried too hard at the skimming game. Some $3.5 million was skimmed from its slot machines between 1974 and 1976—a scale which was regarded as much too blatant by Argent's entertainment director, Chicago-based gambler Frank "Lefty" Rosenthal. By 1979, the Nevada Gaming Commission ordered Glick to sell—which he did, to friends of Moe Dalitz. He sold for a $2 million down payment, the assumption of $92 million in debts, and another $66 million to be paid from the casino's earnings by 1991. Presumably, Lansky was behind at least some of this skullduggery—but by this stage, he was extremely adept at hiding his hand.

The Move to Florida

Organized crime's move into Florida came at least as early as the western migration. Al Capone himself was one of the first to see possibilities in Florida for gambling and tourism. By the 1930s, mob money was moving into real estate and into ventures like Tropical Park Race Track in Coral Gables (a joint New York-Chicago operation), and especially Lansky's Colonial Inn. The development of Miami Beach coincided with that of Las Vegas. For instance, in the 1940s, the Wofford Hotel in Miami was the Florida base for both Lansky and Costello; and the proprietor, Tatum Wofford, was friendly with rising stars Richard Nixon and Bebe Rebozo. Rebozo himself was close to the Cleveland syndicate. By the 1950s, organized crime had a well developed role in Miami hotels like the Sands and the Grand. By the 1980s, some estimates claimed that roughly half of Miami Beach hotels were connected to mob money through Lansky or associates like Lansburgh and Yiddy Bloom (Moldea, 1978: 105–107).

Florida also provided an extremely valuable banking structure that could be used by organized criminals from all parts of the country. This was unraveled (at least in part) by investigations surrounding the Watergate affair of the 1970s. For example, the scandal of Nixon's "Winter White House" revealed some interesting connections concerning the "Keyes Realty Company." This company was named in the Kefauver hearings for its role as intermediary in bribes between organized crime and Dade County political officials. In the 1940s, it played a major role in developing Miami gambling. In 1948 this company transferred a Key Biscayne property to ANSAN, "a shadowy Cuban investment group" in which syndicate money was allegedly involved. This linked the Cuban *ancien regime* (such as Jose Aleman) with Batista and Luciano allies. Later, control of this real estate passed to two new groups: the Teamster's Union Pension Fund and Lansky's Miami National Bank. In 1967 this land passed to Nixon and Bebe Rebozo at bargain rates. One of the Watergate burglars, a Cuban exile, was a vice president of Keyes Realty.

The Miami National Bank is an interesting case study in itself. In 1958, it was taken over for the Teamsters, using Lou Poller as a front. Poller specialized in laundering money, and, not surprisingly, he owed his primary loyalty to Lansky. Organized crime money now reemerged in the form of real estate, apartment buildings, hotels, motels, and mobile home companies. The Teamsters acquired this bank through Arthur Desser, another link between Hoffa and Lansky, and it was Desser who made the 1967 Key Biscayne real estate deal with Nixon and Rebozo (Cook and Carmichael; Scott et al., 1976: 356–358; Hinckle and Turner, 1981).

By the 1970s, a "subculture of banks in southern Florida" was linked by "interlocking directorates and major investors" (Fried, 1980: 141). Besides the Miami National, there were the Bank of Miami Beach, International Bank of Miami, the Key Biscayne Bank, and Southeast First. Federal prosecutors linked Southeast First to the intelligence community and especially to the 1976 murder of Chilean exile Orlando Letelier.

Cuba

Cuba represented the first major international venture of organized crime (Messick, 1967; 1973; Blakey and Billings, 1981: 228–232; Hinckle and Turner, 1981). Lansky had acquired the Hotel Nacional in Havana as early as 1937, and this gave his friends a foundation on which to build after Batista's coup of 1952. Casinos now appeared rapidly—Lansky's Havana Riviera, run by the Cellini brothers; the Havana Hilton; the San Souci; the Capri; the Commodore; the Tropicana. At the Nacional, Cleveland money was the key investment, but the operator was Jake Lansky, and in each case there were massive opportunities for skimming. Castro's revolution came as a disaster for American crime, but Lansky's circle of investors was already on the lookout for opportunities further afield.

The Banks

At least by the 1950s, organized crime was learning the importance of clean money; no longer could gangsters depend on the loyal silence of bankers as in the bootlegging days. Lansky learned the techniques of laundering profits, especially through Swiss numbered accounts. Nig Rosen used such Swiss bank accounts for his heroin "connection" in the 1950s. Soon, Lansky and his associates established their own banks. Malnik established the Bank of World Commerce in Nassau. Mob money flowed into the Bahamas before passing to Tibor Rosenbaum's International Credit Bank in Switzerland. Then, it could return to the United States for reinvestment. At every stage in these operations, we find familiar faces: the Bank of World Commerce was headed by John Pullman, and investors included Ed Levinson. In turn, Levinson and Siegelbaum were active in other Swiss "laundry shops," such as the Exchange Bank of Geneva. These banks could provide a clean base for further ventures. For instance, it was Rosenbaum's bank which supported Cornfeld's IOS. Again, the Overseas Investors Corporation gave Robert Vesco his opportunity to plunder a fortune. Both the Vesco and Rosenbaum ventures collapsed by the 1970s (Raw et al., 1971; Fried, 1980: 276–286; Clark and Tighe, 1975; Hutchinson, 1974; Messick, 1969: 201–209).

The Bahamas

Summarizing the complex saga of gambling in the Bahamas is no easy task. Briefly in the 1950s, the success of Lansky's ventures in Cuba led to attempts to establish similar gambling enterprises elsewhere. The front men for the Lansky enterprise, Wallace Groves and Louis Chesler, attempted to develop a "freeport" in the Bahamas; and in the early 1960s Lansky interests were established at the Freeport Monte Carlo casino. This casino was managed by two of Lansky's longest-established gambling technicians, Dino and Eddie Cellini (Mahon, 1980).

Also in the late 1950s, Huntingdon Hartford was attempting to establish a casino at Hog Island—promptly rechristened "Paradise Island." However, he found considerable difficulty in getting a gambling license from the governmental minister, Sir Stafford Sands. At this point Alvin Malnik entered the picture. Malnik made a very tempting offer: Paradise Island would be bought out by a firm called Mary Carter Paint, and Lansky would see to obtaining a gambling license. The dating of this deal in the early 1960s was important; obviously, Lansky was seeking another Caribbean haven to replace Castro's Cuba. He brought with him old gambling partners like Max Courtney, "Trigger Mike" Coppola, Frank Ritter, and the Cellini brothers.

From the mid-1960s, events happened rapidly; in 1966 Hartford and his adviser, Seymour Alter, sold Paradise Island to Mary Carter Paint. In 1967 the Paradise Island casino opened with a glittering assembly of guests—including Richard Nixon as the official "greeter," and in 1968 Mary Carter Paint changed its name to "Resorts International." However, the pressure was also intensifying, especially after the dominant conservative political party, the "Bay Street Boys," was defeated in the 1967 election. Lansky involvement in the casino was blatant, represented as it was by the presence of Dino and Eddie Cellini—both veterans of gambling operations in Kentucky and Cuba. In the United States, the Organized Crime Strike Force of the Justice Department was appalled by the Lansky operation and began to release information about it to the media. However, it was the Watergate affair which led to the greatest embarrassments. It was suggested that Resorts International had been linked to Bebe Rebozo, that Resorts and Robert Vesco had been laundering Nixon campaign money, and that Seymour Alter had been the bagman for Vesco, Rebozo, and Resorts. Clouds were gathering over Paradise Island but not sufficiently to prevent Resorts International from acquiring a gambling license in New Jersey (Mahon, 1980; Cook and Carmichael).

Tax Havens

Organized crime learned long ago that it was useful to register companies and place investments in foreign nations with fairly lenient laws on the transfer of money. Examples include Switzerland, Liechtenstein, the Bahamas, Panama, the Cayman Islands, and the Netherlands Antilles.

The Industrialized World

Organized crime money has flowed freely into Canada—pornography syndicate money through Morton Goss in Toronto and Lansky's money through John Pullman. Also, Canada's convenience for drug importation has made cities like Montreal ripe for organized crime. Britain has proved an equally tempting target since the legalization of gambling there in 1960. Lansky, the Cellinis, Angelo Bruno, and others all made exploratory journeys there in the 1960s. The British government closed casinos because of alleged organized crime involvement—the Colony Club in 1966, and *Penthouse* magazine's interests in 1971. British gangsters like the Krays also tried to link up with U.S. colleagues—apparently both Bruno and Lansky. In England as in Holland, Reuben Sturman has made major incursions into the pornography trade (Blum and Gerth, 1978). When Australia was discussing the legalization of gambling in the mid-1970s, the Bally corporation attempted to gain a foothold, but extensive connections with Dino Cellini and Gerry Catena led to their exclusion (Blum and Gerth, 1978). Bally was much more successful in its ventures in Sweden (Block and Chambliss, 1981: 135–142).

South America

In Latin America we find the most consistent pattern, hardly surprising if we look at the prosperous cities frequented by Americans in the 1930s and 1940s—Havana, Rio, Buenos Aires. In addition to Cuba, there is clear evidence of organized crime involvement in a number of other countries, including Mexico. In the National Lottery scandal of 1947–1949, Mexican senators were bought by mob money. Also, there is an interesting connection through Gulf and Western Corporation to Mexican operations. In 1970 the Illinois Racing Commission found that Gulf and Western was a partner with Philip Levin (a Gulf and Western director) in the Acapulco Towers Hotel. This hotel was run by Moe Morton, who in 1969 entertained an impressive guest list there: (1) from Miami: Lansky; (2) from Las Vegas: Dean Shendel, Moe Dalitz, Hyman Segal; (3) from Montreal: Tony Roma; and, (4) from Chicago: Sydney Korshak and Delbert Coleman. In 1970, Acapulco was the center for another meeting involving Lansky, Levin, Korshak, and Newton Mandell of Gulf and Western (Gulf and Western was also associated with Michele Sindona, the Italian banker whose collapse in the late 1970s caused major damage to the Vatican's finances) (Lernoux, 1980: 240). Gulf and Western was also the corporation that U.S. military intervention in 1965 brought to a dominant role in the small Dominican Republic, where it enjoys the rights of a feudal barony. It is also widely active, for instance, in Brazil. In Honduras, leading army officers were involved with organized crime in making the country a bridge for the cocaine traffic. Guatemalan government officials provided Carlos Marcello with phony nationality papers after his expulsion from the United States by the Kennedy Justice Department. Both Costa Rica and Nicaragua were CIA fiefdoms in the 1950s and 1960s and were heavily involved in anti-Castro plots. Those CIA ventures involved dabbling in organized crime, primarily through Marcello and Trafficante. Dictators like Stroessner (Paraguay) and the Somozas were easy targets for organized crime blandishments. Lansky's South American drug trade was coordinated by August Ricord from Argentina (Chambliss, 1978: 165).

Fascination with Lansky-related enterprises can blind us to the achievements of others who shared both his humble origins and his later achievements. Mere association with a Lansky corporation should not lead us to believe that an individual is a Lansky creation, much less a front.

Moe Dalitz

In a FBI wiretap, the New Jersey gangster "Gyp" De Carlo remarked, "There's only two Jews recognized in the whole country today. That's Meyer and . . . Moe Dalitz." We have already discussed Dalitz' role in the "Cleveland Four" and his move into Las Vegas, especially his involvement at the Stardust and the Desert Inn. However, in the mid-1960s, income tax trouble and heat from the Casino Control Commission forced him to sell his enterprises. With the help of a large Teamster Union loan ($57 million between 1964 and 1972), Dalitz established an extremely posh country club at La Costa, north of San Diego.

We have already discussed the consequences of his sale of the Stardust to Parvin-Dohrman, but in 1979 an old associate of his bought back these casinos after the departure of Allen Glick. The club at La Costa presents interesting questions. Many have seen it as a Mob social club. Like Lansky, Dalitz has proceeded from the bootlegging underworld to very substantial prosperity. In 1980 a *Forbes* article estimated his wealth in the $100–150 million bracket, second only to Lansky among the alumni of organized crime. It also cited his extremely healthy investment portfolio—including Detroit Steel and the Rock Island Railroad (Cook and Carmichael).

The Teamsters and the Dorfmans

Anyone studying organized crime will have frequent call to look at the activities of the Teamsters' Central States Pension Fund. This fund—it passed the billion dollar mark in 1972—has served as an organized crime bank. It has largely financed the development of Las Vegas and of gambling and leisure in Florida and California; it financed the La Costa Country Club and the "Cove Associates" deal; it finances real estate deals and played a large role in the deals that resulted in removing President Nixon from office. From the 1950s to the 1970s, this fund was largely directed by Paul Dorfman and his stepson, Allen. Let us trace the progression of events by which this vast fortune passed into the hands of men accessible to organized crime interests.

In the 1930s, the teamsters secured their position by providing employers with a tame and amenable alternative to the radical CIO and the Communists. From the early 1930s, the leadership was closely tied to gangsters—especially in Detroit; but by the late 1940s, Jimmy Hoffa had consummated the organized crime–Teamster Union alliance. Hoffa's former mistress became friendly with Moe Dalitz, and this contact gave Hoffa a whole series of Mob friends—the Pressers in Cleveland and the Chicago mob. From the latter, Hoffa became close to Paul Dorfman, an associate of Anthony ("Big Tuna") Accardo. Dorfman had a distinguished record in the Capone mob as a labor racketeer. In the 1920s and 1930s, he had led the corrupt Chicago Wastehandlers Union after the murder of a predecessor (a murder allegedly carried out by Jack Ruby) (Moldea, 1978: 49–50, 55–58, 86–88, 141–49; Demaris, 1981: 321–326, 342, 378, 402).

In 1951 the Teamsters set up the Central States Health and Welfare Fund, the insurance portion of which was run through a company managed by Paul's inexperienced stepson, Allen Dorfman (born 1923). Allen learned quickly. He guided the investments both of the Teamsters and of Hoffa personally. They moved into oil, stocks, and especially real estate—one unusually corrupt deal involved the Sun Valley retirement community, a deal which would later result in legal trouble for Hoffa. In 1955 the union established a new Central States South Eastern and South Western Pension Fund, run almost entirely by the Dorfmans.

Allen did extremely well. His own Union Casualty Agency had now become a substantial conglomerate. It owned insurance companies, oil interests, and slum housing; it held real estate—even a resort in the Virgin Islands. From the 1950s, the alliance with Lou Poller's Miami National Bank gave the Dorfmans a "laundry" akin to Lansky's. The move into the Sunbelt was reflected by friendship with Dave Yaras and through him with Carlos Marcello and Santo Trafficante. Allen Dorfman was a man of great importance, close to the Chicago and Cleveland syndicates, to Las Vegas and all the varied interests the Teamsters had funded. Allen himself was succeeded in the Teamsters by Alvin Baron as "Asset Manager." Who had benefited from the Dorfmans' largesse? When the old trustees relinquished their control of the Central States Pension Fund in 1976, the chief recipients were familiar faces (Cook and Carmichael): Allen Glick—$140 million, Morris Shenker—$135 million, Moe Dalitz—$93 million, and Alvin Malnik—$20 million.

Ed Levinson

Ed Levinson was born in Chicago and operated as a gambler in Detroit, Miami, and quasi-"open cities." In 1952 he joined the mob migration to Nevada. He bought into the Sands, then the Flamingo, and later the Fremont with the help of a Teamster loan, and he began a sizable skim operation of between one and two million dollars a year in the early 1960s. Meanwhile his brother Louis kept a foothold in the Cleveland syndicate's territory of northern Kentucky (Messick, 1969: 348–362; Mollenhoff, 1973: 104, 114–116; 187–189).

Levinson was extremely well-connected both with the legitimate and the criminal worlds. "Above ground" his connections were so good as to secure access to secret FBI wiretaps while he contributed generously to Nevada politicians at all levels of government. In the underworld, he was close to Lansky faithfuls like Doc Stacher and Benjamin Siegelbaum while he participated in operations of the Bank of World Commerce and the Exchange Bank of Geneva.

In 1962 the IRS began a large-scale investigation of Las Vegas "skimming," resulting in 1967 convictions. Levinson was fined a token sum, but his notoriety was primarily due to a 1963 link with wayward politician Bobby Baker (Mollenhoff, 1973). In short, like Dalitz, Levinson seems to be another example of the rise from organized crime to corporate business.

Reuben Sturman

Sturman is a figure of considerable wealth and influence, whom frequent reports have linked to organized crime. This does not necessarily mean that he was himself a criminal—though his pornography trade floated on the margins of legality, and he was convicted on both RICO and tax charges in the late 1980s. Nor does it mean that he is in any sense a servant of organized crime. He is merely an interesting example of the sort of rich and powerful figure who is extremely hard to fit into traditional models of organized crime. By contrast, he can easily be reconciled with theories that emphasize the coordinating role of capital and finance.

Sturman was born in 1924. By the late 1970s, he owned perhaps 800 retail pornography stores in the United States, often through very complex patterns of concealed ownership. In England, he worked in close collaboration with local organized criminals like the Holloway family, a well-established pornography group. On the European continent, his chief foothold was through a firm called Intex Nederland, a key distributor of pornographic videos. A subsidiary of Intex is Video-Rama, which distributed pornographic videos throughout Europe and to the extremely lucrative Middle Eastern market of Cairo, Beirut, Kuwait City, and Riyadh. Firms like Intex, Video-Rama, and their associated companies (like First Columbus Trust) are registered in the Netherlands Antilles, a territory whose laws of business secrecy make the Swiss look ostentatious (Pennsylvania Crime Commission, 1980: 118–121). In the Miporn investigation (1977–1980), the FBI found Sturman associated with mobsters like Robert DiBernardo and Teddy Gaswirth (Pennsylvania Crime Commission, 1980: 118).

Was Lansky the only operator on his scale, or were there others? If so, how many? It's difficult to say. We can only indicate briefly that there seem to be others much less publicized, whose command of wealth is awesome. For instance, there is no doubt that when Doc Stacher fled to Israel, he retired a rich man (worth at least $100 million). John Pullman may well have accumulated the same sort of fortune over the years. Did these men act as independent financiers? It seems that these are vital questions to answer in order to appreciate the nature and scale of organized crime.

Certainly the continuation of such massive criminal money-moving operations in contemporary American society is obvious. The great Savings and Loan collapses of the 1980s represent only the most recent example of high-level business-governmental-mob collaboration.

ORGANIZED CRIME, THE CIA AND THE SAVINGS AND LOAN SCANDAL

The savings and loan scandal of the 1980s has been depicted in myriad ways. To some, it is "the greatest . . . scandal in American history" (Thomas, 1991: 30). To others it is the single greatest case of fraud in the history of crime (*Seattle Times*, June 11, 1991). Some analysts see it as the natural result of the ethos of greed promulgated by the Reagan administration (Simon and Eitzen, 1993: 50). All of these depictions of the S & L scandal contain elements of truth, but to a large degree the savings and loan scandal was simply business as usual. What was unusual about it was not that it happened, or who was involved, but that it was so blatant and coarse a criminal act that exposure became inevitable. With its exposure, three basic but usually ignored "truths" about organized crime were once again demonstrated with startlingly clarity:

1. There is precious little difference between the people society designates as respectable and law abiding and the people society castigates as hoodlums and thugs.
2. The world of corporate finance and corporate capital is as criminogenic and probably more criminogenic than any poverty-wracked slum neighborhood.
3. The distinctions drawn between business, politics, and organized crime are at best artificial and in reality irrelevant. Rather than being dysfunctions, corporate crime, white-collar crime, organized crime, and political corruption are mainstays of American political-economic life.

It is not our intent to discuss the unethical and even illegal business practices of the failed savings and loans and their governmental collaborators. Our interest is in the savings and loans as living, breathing organisms that fused criminal corporations and organized crime into a single entity. Let us begin by quickly summarizing the most blatant examples of collaboration between financial institutions and the mob.

Palmer National Bank

The Washington, D.C.-based Palmer National Bank was founded in 1983 on the basis of a $2.8 million loan from Herman K. Beebe to Harvey D. McLean, Jr. McLean was a Shreveport Louisiana businessman who owned Paris (Texas) Savings and Loan. Herman Beebe played a key role in the savings and loan scandal. *Houston Post* reporter Pete Brewton linked Beebe to a dozen failed S & Ls, and Stephen Pizzo, Mary Fricker, and Paul Muolo, in their investigation of the S & L fiasco, called Beebe's banks "potentially the most powerful and corrupt banking network ever seen in the U.S." Altogether, Herman Beebe controlled, directly or indirectly, at least 55 banks and 29 S & Ls in eight states. What is particularly interesting about Beebe's participation in these banks and savings and loans is his unique background. Herman Beebe served nine months in federal prison for bank fraud and was a known financier for New Orleans-based organized crime figures, including Vincent and Carlos Marcello (Bainerman, 1992: 277–278; Brewton, 1993: 170–179).

Harvey McLean's partner in the Palmer National Bank was Stefan Halper. Halper had served as George Bush's foreign policy director during the 1980 presidential primaries. During the general election campaign, Halper was in charge of a highly secretive operations center, consisting of Halper and several ex-CIA operatives who kept close tabs on Jimmy Carter's foreign policy activities, particularly Carter's attempt to free U.S. hostages in Iran. Halper was later linked both to the "Debategate" scandal, in which it is alleged that Carter's briefing papers for his debates with Ronald Reagan were stolen, and with "The October Surprise," in which it is alleged that representatives of the Reagan campaign tried to thwart U.S. efforts to free the Iranian hostages until after the presidential election. Halper also set up a legal defense fund for Oliver North.

During the Iran-Contra Affair, Palmer National was the bank of record for the National Endowment for the Preservation of Liberty, a front group run by Oliver North and Carl "Spitz" Channell, which was used to send money and weapons to the contras.

Indian Springs Bank

Another bank with clear connections to the CIA and organized crime was the Indian Springs Bank of Kansas City, Kansas (Bainerman, 1992: 279–280; Brewton, 1993: 197–200). The fourth largest stockholder in Indian Springs was Iranian expatriate Farhad Azima, who was also the owner of an air charter company called Global International Air. The Indian Springs bank had made several unsecured loans to Global International Air, totaling $600,000 in violation of the bank's $349,000 borrower limit. In 1983 Global International filed for bankruptcy, and Indian Springs followed suit in 1984. The president of Indiana Springs was killed in 1983 in a car fire that started in the vehicle's back seat and was regarded by law enforcement officials as of suspicious origin.

Global International Air was part of Oliver North's logistical network that shipped arms for the U.S. government on several occasions, including a shipment of 23 tons of TOW missiles to Iran by Race Aviation, another company owned by Azima. Pete Brewton, in his investigation of the Indian Springs bank collapse, was told that FBI had not followed up on Indian Springs because the CIA informed them that Azima was "off limits" (*Houston Post*, February 8, 1990). Similarly the assistant U.S. Attorney handling the Indian Springs investigation was told to "back off from a key figure in the collapse because he had ties to the CIA."

Azima did indeed have ties to the CIA. His relationship with the agency goes back to the late 1970s, when he supplied air and logistical support to EATSCO (Egyptian American Transport and Services Corporation), a company owned by former CIA agents Thomas Clines, Theodore Shackley, and Richard Secord. EATSCO was prominently involved in the activities of former CIA agent Edwin Wilson, who shipped arms illegally to Libya. Azima was also closely tied to the Republican party. He had contributed $81,000 to the Reagan campaign.

Global International also had other unsavory connections. In 1981, Global International made a payment to organized crime figure Anthony Russo, a convicted felon with a record that included conspiracy, bribery, and prostitution charges. Russo was the lawyer of Kansas City organized crime figures, an employee of Indian Springs, and a member of the board of Global International. Russo later explained that the money had been used to escort Liberian dictator Samuel Doe on a "goodwill trip" to the United States.

Global International's planes based in Miami were maintained by Southern Air Transport, another CIA proprietary company. According to Franck Van Geyso, an employee of Global International, pilots for Global International ferried arms into South and Central America and returned to Florida with drugs. Indian Springs also made a loan of $400,000 to Morris Shenker, owner of the Dunes Hotel in Las Vegas, former attorney for Jimmy Hoffa, and close associate of Nick Civella and other Kansas City organized crime figures. At the time the loan to Shenker was made, he, Civella, and other Kansas City mobsters were under indictment for skimming $280,000 from Las Vegas' Tropicana Casino.

Vision Banc Savings

In March, 1986, Robert L. Corson purchased the Kleberg County Savings and Loan of Kingsville, Texas for $6 million and changed its name to Vision Banc Savings (Bainerman, 1992: 280–81; Brewton, 1993: 333–51). Harris County, Texas, judge Jon Lindsey vouched for Corson's character in order to gain permission from state regulators for the bank purchase. Lindsey was the chairman of the Bush campaign in 1988 in Harris County and later received a $10,000 campaign contribution and a free trip to Las Vegas from Corson (*Houston Post*, February 11, 1990).

Robert L. Corson was well known to Federal law enforcement agents, who classified him as a "known money launderer" and a "mule for the agency," meaning that he moved large amounts of cash from country to country. When Corson purchased Vision Banc, it had assets in excess of $70 million. Within four months it was bankrupt. Vision Banc engaged in a number of questionable deals under Corson leadership, but none more so than its $20 million loan to Miami Lawyer Lawrence Freeman to finance a real estate deal (*Houston Post*, February 4, 1990). Freeman was a convicted money launderer who had cleaned dirty money for Jack Devoe's Bahamas-to-Florida cocaine smuggling syndicate and for Santo Trafficante's Florida-based organized crime syndicate. Freeman was a law partner of CIA operative and Bay of Pigs paymaster Paul Helliwell. Corson, in a separate Florida real estate venture costing $200 million, was indicted on a series of charges.

Hill Financial Savings

Vision Banc was not the only financial institution involved in Freeman's Florida land deals. Hill Financial Savings of Red Hill, Pennsylvania, put in an additional $80 million (Brewton, 1993: 346–48). The Florida land deals were only one of a series of bad investments by Hill Financial, which led to its collapse. The failure of Hill Financial alone cost the U.S. treasury $1.9 billion.

Sunshine State Bank

The cast of characters involved with the Sunshine State Bank of Miami included spies, White House operatives, and organized criminals (Bainerman, 1992: 281; Brewton, 1993: 310–12, 320–23). The owner of the Sunshine State Bank, Ray Corona, was convicted in 1987 of racketeering, conspiracy, and mail fraud. Corona purchased Sunshine in 1978 with $1.1 million in drug trafficking profits supplied by Jose Antonio "Tony" Fernandez, who was subsequently indicted on charges of smuggling 1.5 million pounds of marijuana into the United States.

Among Corona's customers and business associates were Leonard Pelullo, Steve Samos, and Guillermo Hernandez-Cartaya. Pelullo was a well-known associate of organized crime figures in Philadelphia who had attempted to use S & L money to broker a major purchase of an Atlantic City Casino as a mob frontman. Pelullo was charged with fraud for his activities at American Savings in California. Steve Samos was a convicted drug trafficker who helped Corona to set up Sunshine State Bank as a drug-money laundry. Samos also helped set up front companies that funneled money and weapons to the Contras. Guillermo Hernandez-Cartaya was a veteran CIA operative who had played a key role in the Bay of Pigs of invasion. He also had a long career as a money launderer in the Caribbean and in Texas on behalf of both the CIA and major drug trafficking syndicates.

Mario Renda, Lender to the Mob

Mario Renda was a Long Island money broker who brokered deposits to various savings and loans in return for their agreement to loan money to phony companies (Brewton, 1993: 45–7; 188–90; Pizzo et al. 1989: 466–71). Renda and his associates received finders fees of 2 to 6 percent on the loans, most of which went to individuals with strong organized crime connections who subsequently defaulted on them. Renda brokered deals to 160 Savings and Loans throughout the country, 104 of which eventually failed. Renda was convicted of diverting $16 million from an S & L and for tax fraud.

Renda also served CIA and National Security Council interests as a money broker helping arrange for the laundering of drug money through various savings and loans on behalf of the CIA. He then obtained loans from the same S & Ls, which were funneled to the Contras. An organized crime-related stockbroker, a drug pilot, and Renda were all convicted in the drug money laundering case.

Full-Service Banking

All told at least twenty-two of the failed S & Ls can be tied to joint money laundering ventures by the CIA and organized crime figures (Pizzo, et al., 1989: 466–71). If the savings and loan scandals of the 1980s reveal anything, they demonstrate what has often been stated as a maxim in organized crime research: corruption linking government, business, and syndicates is the reality of the day-to-day organization of crime. Investigations of organized crime in the United States, Europe, and Asia have all uncovered organized crime networks operating with virtual immunity from law enforcement and prosecution. Chambliss' study of organized crime in Seattle exposed a syndicate that involved participation by a former governor of the state, the county prosecutor, the police chief, the sheriff, at least 50 law enforcement officers, leading business people (including contractors, realtors, banks, and corporation executives), and, of course, a supporting cast of drug pushers, pimps, gamblers, and racketeers (Chambliss, 1988). The Chambliss study is not the exception but the rule. Other sociological inquires in Detroit, Texas, Pennsylvania, New Jersey, and New York have all revealed similar patterns (Albini, 1971; Block, 1983; Block and Chambliss, 1981; Block and Scarpitti, 1985; Jenkins and Potter, 1989; 1986; Potter and Jenkins, 1985; Potter, 1994).

Organized and White-Collar Crime

"Organized crimes" exhibit many of the same the same characteristics of "white-collar crimes." In fact, Dwight Smith, Jr. has argued that organized crime "represents, in virtually every instance, an extension of a legitimate market spectrum into areas normally proscribed. Their separate strengths derive from the same fundamental considerations that govern entrepreneurship in the legitimate marketplace: a necessity to maintain and extend one's share of the market" (Smith, 1978: 164).

Organized crime represents a series of reciprocal relationships and services uniting criminals, clients, and "persons of respectability." Organized crime has as its most important function the task of providing a bridge between the covert world of organized crime and the overt world of legitimate business, finance, and politics. This reciprocal relationship, uniting what Alan Block has called the "underworld" and the "upperworld," is the primary task of an organized crime syndicate.

The relationship between organized crime and business is both functional and necessary to the continued existence and efficient operation of organized crime. Organized crime has grown into a huge business in the United States and is an integral part of the political economy. Enormous amounts of illegitimate money are passed annually into socially acceptable endeavors. An elaborate corporate and financial structure is now tied to organized crime. The existence of that structure renders much of the utility of social constructs such as "white-collar" and "organized crime" irrelevant.

References

Albini, J. L. 1971. *The American Mafia: Genesis of a Legend.* New York: Appleton-Century-Crofts.

Bainerman, J. 1992. *The Crimes of a President.* New York: S.P.I. Books.

Baxter, B. 1982. *Alienation and Inauthenticity.* London: Routledge, Kegan Paul.

Bernstein, B. 1976. The road to Watergate and beyond: The growth and abuse of executive authority since 1940. *Law and Contemporary Problems* 40: 57–86.

Blair, J. 1976. *The Control of Oil.* New York: Random House.

Blakey, G. R., and R. N. Billings. 1981. *The Plot to Kill the President.* New York: Times Books.

Block, A. 1983. *East Side-West Side: Organizing Crime in New York, 1930–1950.* New Brunswick, NJ: Transaction.

Block, A., and T. Bernard. 1988. Crime in the waste oil industry. *Deviant Behavior* 9: 113–129.

Block, A., and Chambliss, W. J. 1981. *Organizing Crime.* New York: Elsevier.

Block, A., and F. Scarpitti. 1985. *Poisoning for Profit: The Mafia and Toxic Waste in America.* New York: William Morrow.

Blum, H., and J. Gerth. 1978. The mob gambles on Atlantic City. *New York Times Magazine* (February 15).

Brewton, P. 1992. *The Mafia, CIA & George Bush*, New York: S.P.I. Books.

Chambliss, W. J. 1988. *On the Take: From Petty Crooks to Presidents.* Bloomington: Indiana University Press.

Clarke, T., and J. Tigue. 1975. *Dirty Money.* New York: Simon and Schuster.

Clinard, M., and P. Yeager. 1980. *Corporate Crime.* New York: Free Press.

Coleman, J. 1989. *The Criminal Elite: The Sociology of White Collar Crime*, 2nd ed. New York: St. Martin's Press.

Cook, J., and J. Carmichael. 1980. The invisible enterprise. *Forbes* 126, issues 7–11.

Cressey, D. 1969. *Theft of the Nation.* New York: Harper & Row.

Demaris, Ovid. 1981. *The Last Mafioso.* New York: Bantam.

———. 1986. *The Boardwalk Jungle.* New York: Bantam.

Ermann, M., and R. Lundman (eds). 1978. *Corporate and Governmental Deviance: Problems in Organizational Behavior in Contemporary Society.* New York: Oxford University Press.

Etzioni, A. 1968. Basic human needs, alienation, and inauthenticity. *American Sociological Review* 33: 870–884.

———. 1969. Man and society: The inauthentic condition. *Human Relations* 22: 325–332.

Fried, A. 1980. *The Rise and Fall of the Jewish Gangster in America.* New York: Holt, Rinehart and Winston.

Hammer, Richard. 1975. *Playboy's Illustrated History of Organized Crime.* Chicago: Playboy Press.

Hinckle, W., and W. Turner. 1981. *The Fish Is Red—The Story of the Secret War Against Castro.* New York: Harper and Row.

Hutchinson, J. 1970. *Imperfect Union: A History of Corruption in American Trade Unions.* New York: Dutton.

Jenkins, P., and G. W. Potter. 1986. Organized crime in London: A comparative perspective. *Corruption and Reform* 1(2): 165–187.

Katz, J. 1979. Legality and equality: Plea bargaining in the prosecution of white-collar and common crimes. *Law and Society Review* 13 (Winter): 431–459.

King, R. 1975. Gambling and crime. In L. Kaplan and D. Kessler (eds.) *An Economic Analysis of Crime.* Springfield, IL: Charles C. Thomas.

Kwitny, J. 1979. *Vicious Circles: The Mafia in the Marketplace.* New York: Norton.

Lernoux, Penny. 1984. *In Banks We Trust.* Garden City, NY: Anchor Press.

Levi, M. 1984. Phantom capitalists. In W. Chambliss (ed.) *Criminal Law in Action.* New York: John Wiley & Sons, 136–148.

Mahon, Gigi. 1980. *The Company That Bought the Broadwalk.* New York: Random House.

Messick, Hank. 1967. *The Silent Syndicate.* New York: Macmillan.

———. 1969. *Secret File.* New York: Macmillan.

———. 1973. *Lansky.* New York: Berkeley.

Mokhiber, R. 1985. Triple damages. *New York Times* (September 14): 23.

Moldea, D. E. 1978. *The Hoffa Wars: Teamsters, Rebels, Politicians and the Mob.* New York: Paddington.

Mollenhoff, Clark R. 1972. *Strike Force: Organized Crime and the Government.* Englewood Cliffs, NJ: Prentice-Hall.

Pearce, F. 1976. *Crimes of the Powerful.* London: Pluto Press.

Pennsylvania Crime Commission 1980. *A Decade of Organized Crime.* St. David's: Commonwealth of Pennsylvania.

Pizzo, S., M. Fricker, and P. Muolo 1989. *Inside Job.* New York: McGraw-Hill.

Pontell, H., and K. Calavita. 1993. The savings and loan industry. In M. Tonry and A. Reiss (eds.) *Beyond the Law.* Chicago: University of Chicago Press, 203–246.

Pontell, H., S. Rosoff, and E. Goode. 1990. White-collar crime. In E. Goode, *Deviant Behavior.* 3rd ed. Englewood Cliffs, NJ: Prentice-Hall.

Potter, G. W. 1994. *Criminal Organizations.* Prospect Heights, IL: Waveland Press.

Presthus, R. 1978. *The Organizational Society,* rev. ed. New York: St. Martin's Press.

Raw, C., B. Page, and G. Hodgson. 1971. *Do You Sincerely Want To Be Rich?* New York: Viking.

Reuter, P. 1987. *Racketeering in Legitimate Industries: A Study in The Economics of Intimidation.* Santa Monica, CA: Rand.

Reid, E. 1969. *The Grim Reapers.* New York: Bantam.

Scott, P. et al. 1976. *The Assassinations.* New York: Random House.

Seeman, M. 1966. Status and identity: The problem of inauthenticity. *Pacific Sociological Review* 9: 67–73.

Simon D., and S. Eitzen. 1993. *Elite Deviance.* Boston: Allyn and Bacon.

Smith, D. C., Jr. 1978. Organized crime and entrepreneurship. *International Journal of Criminology and Penology* 6.

———. 1980. Paragons, pariahs, and pirates: A spectrum-based theory of enterprise. *Crime and Delinquency,* 26.

Sutherland, E. 1940. White collar criminality. *American Sociological Review* 5: 1–12.

Thomas, M. 1991. The greatest American shambles. *New York Review of Books* (January 30): 30.

Turk, A. 1981. Organizational deviance and political policing. *Criminology* 19: 231–250.

Wellford, H. 1972. *Sowing the Wind: A Report from Ralph Nader's Center for Study of Responsive Law.* New York: Grossman.

◂ PART II ▸

Forms of White-Collar Crime

Each of the forms of white-collar crime examined in the articles contained in this section is encouraged by the free-enterprise system of capitalism, which emphasizes fierce competition and concentrates on profit. Many are facilitated by technological developments such as the computer. "Respectable" people commit these crimes in the course of their occupations; these people are often experts in their field and are shielded from outsiders. If the crimes are detected, they may not be reported, sometimes because of who commits the crimes and sometimes to protect the reputation of the organization that employed them.

In many cases, there is a "legal lag." The law may take years to define the illegality of the actions of white-collar criminals. Even when offenses are finally outlawed, the regulatory agencies set up to enforce the new laws are often influenced by the very people they are supposed to be policing. The regulators have the same backgrounds as the offenders, identify with them, and often move from the regulatory agency to employment in the companies subject to regulation. The regulatory agencies are almost always underfunded. When they do act, they are often under great political pressure to "deregulate."

Most criminologists insist that white-collar crime is a more serious threat than street crime. It injures and kills many more people than are harmed by all other forms of violent crime, and it eats away at society from within—destroying the basic trust upon which society depends. As the previous articles in the first part of this volume show, there is considerable argument about the exact definition of white-collar crime.

Sometimes the best approach to definition is to examine examples of the phenomenon to be defined. In the first article of this section, Gary Green argues that embezzlement may not be a white-collar offense in the original meaning of the term, for although it is generally committed in the course of one's occupation, it does not usually involve high-status offenders. Of course, Green's objection poses less of a problem if we simply describe white-collar offenders as "respectable" rather than insisting that only offenders of extremely high status can be white-collar criminals. The element of deception is central to many conceptions of white-collar crime, and one needs only to be respectable to be trusted. This is probably why Sutherland (1940) cited embezzlement as an example of white-collar crime when he first introduced the term. Sketching the history of the laws defining embezzlement, Green makes it a clear example of violation of trust. Green explores some of the explanations that have been offered in an effort to explain why people embezzle. Is it a matter of low self-control? Can it be traced to their associates? Or is it largely a question of opportunity?

In their examination of the largest set of white-collar crimes ever uncovered, Kitty Calavita and Henry Pontell maintain that the growth of finance capitalism has replaced industrial capitalism and set the stage for "collective embezzlement" or "looting" of organizations as a way of life. Where corporate crime in the industrial economy (e.g., price fixing) tends to enrich the corporation at the expense of consumers or competitors, the white-collar crimes of the savings and loan industry tended to damage everyone concerned, often even destroying the financial institution itself. Where the economic system sets the stage for traditional white-collar crime, the government may be the major facilitator. As finance capitalism was going into high gear in the 1980s, a new ideological movement insisted that the free enterprise system works best when least regulated by government. "Deregulation" became the new watchword. The Federal Home Loan Bank Board (FHLBB) was charged with regulating the savings and loan industry, but it was also charged with promoting it. Enforcing regulations could be seen as contrary to the goal of promotion or even as interference with growth and development.

Calavita and Pontell argue that the basic contradiction is inherent in the structure of finance capitalism, which produces almost nothing. It is a "casino economy." The white-collar crimes that characterized the saving and loan business represented a pattern of reckless, illegal gambling, most of it with other people's money. For the savings and loan business, the results of "deregulation" included a pattern of unlawful risk-taking and collective embezzlement ("robbing your own bank" with "buying sprees," "excessive compensation," "land flips," or "daisy chains"), which were then followed by a pattern of illegally "covering up" the crimes.

To keep the faith of investors and allow the stock market to function, laws restrict insiders' ability to trade based on information that is confidential or not available to the general public. Elizabeth Szockyj's article presents an excellent example of some of the difficulties involved in prosecuting white-collar crime cases involving insider trading. The major decision in many white-collar crime cases is whether to prosecute in criminal court or through civil proceedings. Most cases of insider trading are handled in civil proceedings, but the government was under some pressure to prosecute and win at least a token criminal case because of the extensive damage to public faith in the stock exchange. As Szockyj points out, the civil suit in this case reveals some of the motivations of both the offenders and the prosecutors for seeking a settlement in civil court rather than moving forward with a prosecution in criminal court. At the same time, Szockyj's case is interesting in that one defendant was actually prosecuted in a criminal trial. Despite the fact that the prosecutor felt confident of winning, the defendant was acquitted. The criminal case reveals the various points of law necessary to prove insider trading to the satisfaction of a jury and provides a glimpse into the minds of jurors as they weigh guilt in such a case, where the defendant, as in most white-collar crime cases, is respectable, middle-class, and resembles the "next door neighbor."

Financial crimes come in many forms. Jeffrey Doocy, David Shichor, Dale Secrest and Gilbert Geis take us into the world of telemarketing fraud. We learn many of the common techniques, including how telemarketers "psych themselves up" to make effective calls and the sense of power they experience as they defraud the suckers they call "mooches." As the article points out, there are about 140,000 telemarketing firms in the United States, with about 10 percent believed to engage in fraudulent activities. The authors describe the images that the fraudster tries to project and the scripts used to prepare the performer for various responses offered by the "mooch."

One of the most interesting features of this article is the insight it gives us into the backgrounds of telemarketing fraudsters themselves. Mostly young, recent transplants to the region from which they make their calls, they tend to be in their mid-thirties, to have held few jobs for much more than one year, and to be relatively "marginalized middle-class persons." Apparently these are the backgrounds that provide the most motivated and effective telemarketing fraudsters. More than half had already had a criminal action filed against them in the past.

Some have said that the computer is to the white-collar criminal what the gun was to the highway robber. David Carter and Andra Bannister document the rapid increase of computer-related crime in recent years, with the most rapid increase coming after 1995 when Internet growth suddenly exploded. Computers may be the target of white-collar crime or a tool to commit a crime. White-collar crime is on the increase in part because the computer provides new opportunities for easier commission of traditional crimes such as embezzlement and newer crimes such as computer harassment or cyberstalking. The authors highlight the need for a more uniform reporting system to provide accurate figures on the incidence and distribution of computer-related crime. As with other forms of white-collar crime, this will require uniform definitions and guidelines to calculate losses. They point to the need for development of "new law and policy" as well as the need to address issues of security, prevention, investigation, prosecution, and damage recovery.

Carter and Bannister examine the motivations of offenders, the socialization patterns by which they mutually influence one another, and the possibility that prolonged interaction via computer, without face-to-face contact with other people, might change social values and attitudes, thus contributing to deviance and criminal activity. "Cyberpunks" such as "hackers," "crackers," and "phreakers," for example, tend to be young, male products of a culture where attacking computer systems has been defined as a recreational or educational activity indicating cleverness and expertise rather than a criminal offense. The authors speculate that these offenders might be dominated by "egocentricity" and an atmosphere of "anarchy."

White-collar crime goes beyond property crimes; in fact, white-collar crimes injure and kill many more people than does street crime. The fact that the victim is usually injured or killed at a distance rather than in a face-to-face confrontation does not make the injury or death any less serious, nor does the fact that there was "nothing personal" about it. The primary motive is profit. The white-collar offender injures or kills from willful negligence rather than from any malice against the victim.

The health care industry offers many examples of such white-collar crime. Approximately 400,000 patients are victims of mistakes or misdiagnoses each year, with more than 10 percent suspected to be the result of negligence. John Liederbach, Francis Cullen, Jody Sundt, and Gilbert Geis insist on using the term "violence" to describe the cases they examine. As they point out, the decision whether to use this term or some milder term such as "negligence" is a decision that affects how we see the reality of what is happening.

The cases described in this article are only the tip of the iceberg. The authors indicate that most of the prosecutions would not have occurred if the following conditions had not existed: the injury or death was very dramatic; it occurred very shortly after the violence; it involved "fringe" physicians operating outside the respectable setting of a hospital (a significant number of whom had a history of professional misconduct); and it featured very sympathetic victims and took place in situations where the profit motive was exceptionally blatant.

In the subsequent piece on fraud control in the health care industry, Malcolm Sparrow points out that losses to fraud and abuse may exceed 10 percent of annual health care spending, or $100 billion per year. Fraud control is a challenging job. Detection systems are very weak. Only a tiny proportion of fraud is discovered. In fact, the person reporting the fraud often is punished in some way for bringing a problem to the attention of management it did not want to admit existed.

Law enforcement has traditionally taken a reactive rather than a proactive position. Only recently has more attention been directed toward detecting crimes that are not being reported or working to prevent them from occurring in the first place. Sparrow notes that the respectability of the health care industry shields it from suspicion and that the lack of public sympathy for insurance companies or "big government" makes programs such as Medicare or Medicaid ripe for fraud. Fraud control suffers from a problem common to all prevention efforts: success is measured by what did not happen, and the boss may not be impressed. Even when a strong fraud control system is developed, it has to keep adapting. Management is usually overly optimistic and does not want to invest in the effort needed to keep ahead of potential offenders. The strength of any fraud control system depends on deterrence, and this depends on the potential fraudster's estimate of the chances of getting caught, the probability of being convicted if caught, and the severity of the punishment that might result. In the case of white-collar crimes in general, and fraud in particular, all of these are very low. This crime does pay.

Sparrow also notes that there is a fine line between "bending" and "breaking" the law. Many in government, business, and the professions have had occasion to "bend" the law. To condemn those who break the law might call into question their own tendencies to bend it. The lack of a clear distinction between terms such as "fraud" and "abuse" also makes it more difficult to measure the extent of the problem and gives an excuse to anyone who does not want to deal with it.

Although safety laws were passed by the mid-nineteenth century, factories remained dangerous places, and workers had little protection. Within the past century, occupational hazards to health and safety have increased with the proliferation of many dangerous substances in the workplace. Obvious injuries such as a broken leg are easier to detect and remedy than long-term effects of dangerous workplace chemicals or substances such as asbestos. Current estimates indicate that about one worker in every six dies of an occupationally related disease.

Nancy Frank argues that the current emphasis on administrative regulation needs to be replaced by a stronger stand against long-term occupational diseases. As she notes, problems in developing new health regulations are both technical and political. Technical issues revolve around estimating the health risks associated with various workplace dangers, estimating costs of reducing the risks, and estimating the health and economic benefits that would result. Political problems are even more complicated. Employers want voluntary standards without government regulation while workers want government regulation to make workplaces safer.

Charged with enforcing the Occupational Safety and Health Act, the Occupational Safety and Health Administration (OSHA) was soon pressured to rely on voluntary compliance. Tort law, which involves civil action for injury caused by wrongful conduct, has been somewhat successful in obtaining compensation for workers injured due to employer negligence. However, it has been ineffective in cases involving long-tern health hazards. Even when workers eventually became aware of health risks, it was difficult to prove that particular diseases contracted years later resulted from the hazards on the job—and even harder to prove that the employer was negligent. Frank suggests that the law be used as a series of "checks and balances" with severe criminal penalties invoked where serious illness or death results from reckless disregard for the health and welfare of the workers.

New forms of white-collar crime are being invented every day. Alan Block and Thomas Bernard provide a good case study showing how the decline in the re-refining industry was accompanied by an expansion in the recycling of waste oil for use as heating fuel, opening criminal opportunities to "cocktail" toxic wastes and sell them as fuel oil or to do "midnight dumping." They also show how enforcement can be blocked, pointing out the ineffectiveness of the Environmental Protection Agency (EPA).

Harry Brill argues that corrupt practices by government agencies such as OSHA or the EPA are routine. Charged with enforcing the law, many of these agencies refuse to act. As Brill stresses, when failure to act results in injury or death, it is a criminal offense. Brill describes many ways in which OSHA ignores its legal obligations to enforce the law and how it is aided and abetted by the courts, which tend to side with business. At the same time, everyone concerned is good at giving the illusion of doing the job or finding excuses for not doing it.

Jurg Gerber and Eric Fritsch examine white-collar crime and the government from a different angle. They examine the questionable relationships between a government agency, NASA, and its various subcontractors. Central to their article is that contractors often experience cost overruns, miss completion deadlines, and sometimes provide inferior products. NASA's complicity in these problems is of most concern. It seems that NASA does little when such problems occur, and these same contractors continue to be used, even after problems occur. It would seem that such activities have become a "common business practice" that results in substantial loss to the taxpayer. Moreover, such questionable business practices commonly occur in other federal bureaucracies, especially the Department of Defense. Gerber and Fritsch also discuss how newspapers can be used to investigate white-collar crime and other crime problems. Essentially, newspapers provide an excellent chronicle of events and can supplement other data sources, allowing researchers to conduct a more precise evaluation of events. This methodology should be used more frequently in the study of white-collar crime.

The articles in this section provide only a few examples of the many forms taken by white-collar crime. In every case, the offenders are protected by their respectability. Their crimes are hidden behind a web of deceit. As we will see in Part III, the criminal justice system faces major problems in investigating, prosecuting and punishing white-collar criminals.

5

White-Collar Crime and the Study of Embezzlement

Gary S. Green

Embezzlement involves the theft of entrusted property. Jerome Hall finds it recorded as early as Aristotle's *Politics*, which alluded to embezzlement by road commissioners and other officials.[1] Embezzlement in English case law originated in 1473 in the Carrier's case, which broke jurisprudential ground by declaring as criminal an agent who stole goods placed in his care. Prior to Carrier's, no trespass of the goods—the essential element of larceny—could be shown in a theft-after-trust because the goods were considered to be in the legal possession of the thief. The first embezzlement statute was passed in 1529. Embezzlement laws initially included trust theft from specific victims—for example, a servant's master, banks, the military, or the post office—and then evolved into the modern general definition of wrongful conversion of entrusted property.[2]

Edwin Sutherland referred to embezzlement as an example of a white-collar crime when he first employed that phrase more than fifty years ago in reference to offenses committed by persons of

Reprinted from *The Annals of the American Academy of Political and Social Science*, 525 (January 1993): 95–106.

high social prestige in the course of their occupation.[3] Sutherland's examples of embezzlement were atypical, however, in that they included only high-dollar crimes committed by business executives. By using embezzlement in this way, Sutherland seems to have created a rather exotic image of the crime among criminologists, one that is inconsistent with its quotidian character. The present article will address the problems encountered in the modern study of embezzlement as trust violation, particularly as they touch upon Sutherland's ideas about white-collar crime.

The Heterogeneity of Embezzlement Labels

Embezzlement is a crime of specific intent in which a person fraudulently misappropriates or misapplies something that has been legally entrusted to that person but which he or she does not own, thereby usurping the legal owner's control. Although virtually any property, including money, goods, animals, and trade secrets, can be embezzled, determining exactly what constitutes embezzlement is sometimes difficult.

Embezzlement is essentially fungible with the offense of criminal conversion, for both are defined in terms of theft-after-trust. Criminal conversion is often an essential element of embezzlement, and some jurisdictions have only conversion statutes by which to punish embezzlers. If any difference exists between the offenses of embezzlement and conversion, it is that in an embezzlement the thief usually holds a fiduciary relationship to the victim, such as trustee, guardian, agent, or employee. Persons charged with embezzlement need not hold such a relationship, however, and persons charged with criminal conversion may indeed meet the requirements of a fiduciary. To complicate matters further, embezzlement is usually differentiated from fraud according to the exact point at which the intent to steal was present. If the intent occurred prior to possession of the property stolen, then the offense usually constitutes fraud rather than embezzlement. Yet, many persons have been convicted of embezzlement even though they formed the intent to steal before gaining possession of whatever was peculated. And, of course, larceny is a lesser offense compared to embezzlement, although necessarily included in it. In short, the legal labels attached to the theft-after-trust crimes are often a function of criminal justice system discretion and legal constraints.

Donald Cressey, in his research on the social psychology of embezzlement, initially attempted to interview prisoners specifically convicted of embezzlement. But he soon discarded this legal category because he found that some persons convicted of embezzlement had intended to steal prior to entering the role in which they committed theft and that they therefore were more accurately defrauders. He also found that many persons who were charged with crimes other than embezzlement had accepted in good faith the role in which they committed theft. Cressey identified 502 inmates at three prisons who had been convicted of a crime that might meet the criterion of the after-trust in good faith. He then pared this group he believed best met that criterion, and he called them "criminal violators of financial trust."[4] The factors leading to Cressey's abandonment of the legal label of embezzlement demonstrate the problems associated with that designation when it is employed without careful discrimination.

Equating Embezzlement and White-Collar Crime

These heterogeneous labelings of embezzlement crimes show that the offense category does not necessarily coincide with Sutherland's original conception of white-collar crime. Generically, embezzlement includes many persons who do not meet the criteria for a white-collar criminal either in terms of high social status or to occupational position. It also tends to ignore high-status persons who violate occupational trust but to whom nonembezzlement labels are attached. In explaining the "white-collar" portion of his term, Sutherland stated that he referred "principally to business managers and executives in the sense in which [the term] was used by a president of General Motors who wrote *An Autobiography of a White-Collar Worker.*"[5] Sutherland considered social status and respectability to be independent of economic wealth.[6] But it is significant that Cressey found that, as a group, his trust violators could not be considered white-collar criminals because they lacked the requirement of social prestige.[7] Similarly, Dorothy Zeitz, who studied female embezzlers using Cressey's case-study method, did not find that the women could be characterized as having high social status.[8] To their credit, Cressey and Zeitz never referred to their trust violators as white-collar offenders. Some criminologists have redefined Sutherland's original conception of white-collar crime[9] so that in several case studies of embezzlement it is declared that "[white-collar crimes are] economic offenses committed through the use of fraud, deception, or collusion."[10] This clearly misses both of Sutherland's definitive points about white-collar crime, namely, that they are committed (1) by persons of high social status and (2) in the course of their occupation. What has happened, then, is that these revisionist scholars reconcile embezzlement and white-collar crime not by the inherent characteristics of the offense or its offenders, but rather by changing the original idea of white-collar crime. A case in point is Daly, who uses this redefinition in her study of federal "white-collar" offenders. She reports that while about 95 percent of the 201 bank embezzlers she studied used their occupational role to commit their theft, less than a third were in professional or managerial positions when they embezzled.[11]

Perhaps Sutherland's most telling statement about white-collar crime is that it is "organized crime."[12] He believed this because white-collar crime involves formal and informal pro-criminal agreements within and across various industries and professions. Formal organization is inherent in offenses that are collusive. Bribery, price fixing, bid rigging, industrial espionage, and physician fee splitting are examples of formally organized illegalities. Such crimes are accomplished through "gentlemen's agreements, pools, . . . and cartels."[13] Other kinds of offenses that do not require collusion may also have elements of white-collar formal organization, such as some insider trading and bank fraud crimes. White-collar criminals are also formally organized "for the control of legislation selection of administrators, and restriction of appropriations for the enforcement of laws which may affect themselves."[14] In other words, white-collar criminals purposefully and in concert use their economic and political influence to deflect criminal definitions from their illegal behaviors.

Sutherland discussed "informal" organization as well, referring to business moralities that run counter to the law.[15] Entire industries and professions—or major segments of them—are often characterized by beliefs that are in legal conflict with the larger social systems in which they operate. Thus, without any formal organization or agreement among its members, professions and industries nevertheless can be tacitly encouraged to carry out criminal behaviors. My inference from Sutherland's writing is that his litmus test for informal criminal organization is the extent that "the businessman who violates the laws which are designed to regulate business does not customarily lose status among his business associates."[16]

Embezzlement, on the contrary, is unlike the other white-collar offenses Sutherland discussed because it lacks criminal organization. The legal definition of embezzlement does not require conspiracy, which is necessary in other inherently collusive crimes. Daly reported that about four of five embezzlers acted alone.[17] Nor are occupational embezzlers as a group formally organized to avoid criminal labels. When those incriminated escape arrest, it is most likely because of the victim's unwillingness to prosecute, not because of any formal organization among embezzlers. Embezzlement is also not "informally organized," for it can hardly be said that the crime is promoted by widespread business beliefs that encourage it. Sutherland did not have embezzlement in mind when he discussed informal criminal organization, since he was referring to offenses that do not victimize one's employing organization.

If anything, embezzlement seems most associated not with offenders but with organized white-collar victims. Hall cogently demonstrates that the Carrier's Case was closely tied to the interests of that era's emerging merchant-based capitalism.[18] Sutherland, too, noted a high degree of victim organization when he referred to embezzlement as one of the most "foolish" of white-collar crimes because offenders are often relatively powerless compared to their victims.[19] The other white-collar offenders about whom he wrote—primarily corporations—typically were more powerful than the consumers, competitors, inventors, and employees they victimized. Sutherland thus seems to have been ambivalent about whether embezzlement truly fit his conception of white-collar crime. It is the cavalier usages of the term "white-collar crime," including atypical references by Sutherland himself, that have been responsible for the generally erroneous belief by some criminologists that embezzlement ipso facto represents a white-collar crime.

Use of Aggregated Embezzlement Data

The primary source on the extent and characteristics of embezzlement in the United States is the Uniform Crime Reports (UCR), compiled annually by the Federal Bureau of Investigation from data submitted by state and local police departments.[20] Embezzlement is classified as a Type II, or nonindex, offense and is reported only in terms of persons arrested for offenses that conform to the UCR definition of embezzlement. That generic definition includes theft-after-trust crimes: "Misappropriation or mis-application of money or property entrusted to one's care, custody, or control." As such, the category contains embezzlers and criminal converters, regardless of their social prestige or whether their crimes occurred in the course of their employment. In many cases, trust violation arrests are coded as "embezzlement" without regard to whether the offender first took possession of the stolen property in good faith. Thus the arrestee category runs the gamut from the person who stole a rented piece of lawn equipment, without ever having intended to return it, to the corporate executive who embezzled a large sum of money.

Because the UCR category for embezzlement includes all types of trust violators, it is inappropriate for scholars to represent it as indicating relative involvement in white-collar crime according to age, gender, and race.[21] Not only do UCR embezzlement arrestees comprise offenders other than white-collar ones, but they may not even be representative of differential involvement in trust violation generally. There are many factors that render these recording rates inconstant.

Thorsten Sellin once wrote that "the value of criminal statistics as a basis for the measurement of criminality . . . decreases as the procedures take us farther away from the offense itself."[22] Arrests are two steps removed from the offense itself. (1) The police must discover embezzlements and (2) discovered embezzlers must be arrested. Police are largely dependent upon victims to report offenses to them. Victims may know that they have been done in by an embezzlement but may be unaware of who is responsible. Even if victims know a thief's identity, they may choose to handle the episode through informal channels, such as restitution or job termination, and this response may be differentially invoked according to the offender's characteristics.

If the police are notified of an embezzlement and an arrest warrant is issued, the authorities still may not be able to locate the offender, and the rates for those escaping arrest probably vary according to age, gender, and race. These possible inequities in the rates of discovery and arrest could easily cause counts to be unrepresentative of the true nature of the offense.[23] Without any independent corroboration that UCR embezzlement arrestee data closely parallel the relevant universe, their use can be precarious and can be inappropriate for determining involvement in white-collar crime.

The Explanation of Embezzlement

The two approaches by which embezzlers have been differentiated here are (1) whether the intention to steal was present after or before the goods were accessed—good and bad faith, respectively—and (2) whether the access to stolen items was based upon an occupational role. While explanations are needed for all offenders to address the subject comprehensively, the following discussion centers on good-faith occupational trust violators, since they are the focus of existing explanations of trust violation, probably because of the earlier tendency to equate embezzlement and white-collar crime.

The platitudinous cause of good-faith occupational embezzlement is "wine, women, wagering."[24] Yet, as Cressey pointed out, these are motivations to steal, not explanations for stealing. Cressey noted that when "'people tell you why they did [something, this] does not give you explanations of why they did it.'"[25] In searching for a fresh approach through the use of analytic induction, Cressey revamped hypotheses until he reached a four-step process that he believed explained the crimes of all of his 133 offenders: (1) there exists an unshareable financial problem, a problem that the offender is ashamed or afraid to share with others and for which legitimate sources of money are unavailable; (2) embezzlement is seen as a means for solving the problem; (3) the offender possesses the technical knowledge to carry out the theft; and (4) the criminal behavior is neutralized to be acceptable or to reflect general irresponsibility of the offender—for example, the money was borrowed rather than stolen, the victim mistreated the offender and deserved to be victimized, the money belonged to the offender anyway, the offender had personal problems.[26]

There are at least two problems with Cressey's methodology, as Karl Schuessler has pointed out.[27] First, it is based upon incarcerated offenders only (recall Sellin's statement). Second, after arriving at his analytically induced four-step process—rather than using the more straightforward method of strict hypothesis testing—Cressey may well have forced his interpretations to fit his theme. Cressey was probably aware of this potential bias when he granted that there is "no positive answer" to the question of whether he "neglected or unwittingly distorted" negative cases.[28]

Later students have come across many instances of embezzlement that do not fit Cressey's sequential process. Regarding the unshareable financial problem, Gwynn Nettler, Michael Benson, and Dorothy Zeitz all found that such a circumstance was not a universal precondition to the offense. For men, a taste for a more affluent life-style—that is, greed—also proved to be a major factor.[29] For the women studied by Zeitz, stealing was seen as a way of meeting the basic needs of their families or of retaining or regaining the affections of a husband.[30] Daly found the needs of self and family as well as greed to be among the motives of both male and female embezzlers.[31]

Thirty years after his original research, Cressey concluded that while the unshareable problem was important, it was "not critical," and it was the neutralization of the criminal nature of the behavior that was his most salient finding.[32] Yet Benson reports that his subjects admitted freely that they were aware that what they were doing was criminal and that they did not feel any need to neutralize.[33] Zeitz also found that her female embezzlers did not have to justify their behavior; they simply were driven by their expectations, learned since childhood, of the proper role of mothers, wives, daughters, and lovers.[34] Given these negative cases, Cressey may have erred in assuming that the excuses given by his subjects to avoid feelings of guilt occurred prior to their thefts. Instead, they may have been rationalizations that emerged afterward to repress feelings of guilt. Benson alludes to this type of subconscious post factum rationalization in his conclusion that the embezzlers he studied chose later to view their offense as a single "aberration" in otherwise law-abiding life histories.[35]

Two other theories, differential association and propensity-event, deserve mention because, unlike Cressey's attempt to explain embezzlement specifically, these theories purport to describe factors characteristic of criminality generally. Sutherland's differential association, briefly stated, hypothesizes that crime is a function of learned moralities and that the extent to which persons learn values that favor a criminal act over those that disfavor it will be the extent to which they will commit an offense. The principal source of this learning is significant others.[36] Cressey initially attempted to ascertain whether differential association explained embezzlement.[37] The effort was understandable because Sutherland, his mentor, had labeled embezzlement a "white-collar crime" and had insisted that differential association was the most plausible explanation for all white-collar crime.[38] While Cressey abandoned differential association early in his study as a root cause of embezzlement, he did report that his findings provided indirect support for the theory.

Cressey points out that in the vast majority of cases he studied, at some time prior to the crime the individuals believed there existed certain situations in which trust violation was acceptable. When subjects applied these situations to their personal circumstances, trust was violated. Further, the neutralization aspect of Cressey's process is consistent with the theory of differential association in that there was a gradual erosion of the subjects' morality, culminating in the justification for embezzlement, assuming that the excuses were not post factum impressions. While Cressey's offenders did not associate with persons who directly influenced their decisions to embezzle, there was some evidence that through contacts with others, they came to believe that some business offenses were merely technical violations rather than morally wrong.[39]

Cressey's reconciliation of his findings with differential association does not strictly coincide with the postulates of that theory but is nevertheless loosely consistent. In her discussion of the relevance of differential association to female embezzlers, Zeitz still emphasized the dominance of personal expectations of role fulfillment rather than contact with alternative moralities, but she did find that in several cases there was evidence of outside influences that modified personal values.[40]

Michael Gottfredson and Travis Hirschi's propensity-event theory, on the contrary, dismisses the basic thesis of differential association, which assumes that crime is caused by culturally induced motives. Briefly stated, "propensity" in the Gottfredson and Hirschi theory refers to the extent that people differ in their self-control. Individuals with the lowest levels of self-control commit the most crime, and this is independent of the type of offender, such as white-collar or street criminal, male or female, young or old. Symptoms associated with low self-control are "risk-taking," or a quest for exciting and dangerous behavior; "simplicity," or an avoidance of difficult tasks; "low frustration tolerance"; "physicality," or a desire for physical rather than mental activity; "immediate gratification," or impulsivity, more concern with immediate than future pleasures; and "self-centeredness"—looking out for oneself first or tending to blame oneself last. Self-control is a function of socialization, and one's degree of self-control is said to be relatively constant from adolescence through adulthood.

"Event" relates to the circumstances surrounding a potential criminal episode, specifically the opportunity to commit a crime in a given situation and the associated perception of the certainty, severity, and celerity of punishment for it. When there exist low self-control, ample opportunity, and a minimal perception of punishability, propensity-event predicts that crime is very likely to be committed. The absence of any one of the three conditions nullifies this prediction.[41]

The Gottfredson and Hirschi theory has been indirectly tested on a macro level in the area of trust violation by its originators.[42] They found that the distribution of embezzlement arrestees by gender, race, and age, variables that supposedly reflect different degrees of self-control, was similar to distributions for other crimes. This macro-level test might be seen as rather vague because it did not differentiate between embezzlers and nonembezzlers as a function of self-control, holding opportunity and perceived punishment constant. The test has been criticized on other grounds as well,[43] and more detailed, micro-level examinations of the theory in the area of trust violation are in order. If the idea of propensity event is going to be useful, it must explain trust violation, since trust violation in many cases epitomizes simplicity because people merely have to take property that is already in their possession.

Propensity-event appears particularly promising in the area of trust violation because an a priori inference can be made that embezzlers have low self-control. "Wine, women, and wagering," debt-ridden finances, and greed clearly are symptomatic of immediate gratification and self-centeredness. Another symptom of self-centeredness is the tendency to blame oneself last, which characterizes the variety of justifications and mitigations claimed by embezzlers, independent of whether these explanations arise before or after the crime. Impulsivity can be seen in the fact that many embezzlers' decisions to steal are not planned earlier but are impulsive acts.

Regarding "event," the opportunity to embezzle must, of course, be present. For the other component of "event" —perceived punishability—both Cressey and Zeitz indicate that many of their embezzlers saw little likelihood of punishment, especially in terms of its celerity. Many offenders hid their thefts for extended periods of time. Others intended to replace the stolen money. Some of the embezzlers in both studies thought they could avoid or delay punishment by absconding, were their thefts discovered.

There is further indirect support for the Gottfredson and Hirschi theory as an explanation for embezzlement. Because the theory assumes that embezzlers have low self-control and that this condition is relatively stable over time, "embezzlers will turn out to have been involved in other crimes as well."[44] One recent study analyzed state criminal records for the 229 persons arrested for embezzlement in Georgia during 1982.[45] For only a third—76—of the subjects was their 1982 embezzlement their sole criminal arrest when their offense histories were generated in 1990. The remainder—153—had between 2 and 42 arrests associated with criminal episodes; four-fifths, or 122, had an additional arrest for a theft crime—23 had more than one embezzlement arrest—and about one of three had an additional arrest for a violent crime (35 percent) or drunken driving (29 percent). The average number of criminal arrests for the 153 multiple offenders was 6.6; the median was 4. Gottfredson and Hirschi appear to be mostly correct in their assertion that embezzlers' offending is not singular.

◂ Conclusion ▸

The criminal violation of trust is a heterogeneous offense category because it includes acts that are chargeable under numerous criminal statutes, including embezzlement, criminal conversion, fraud, and larceny. Because trust violators who are charged with embezzlement include good-faith and bad-faith offenders, persons who commit theft both occupationally and otherwise, and persons of varying social prestige, the offense category is not in line with the original meaning of white-collar crime. Further, because centralized data sources on embezzlers include this hodgepodge of violators, those sources are inappropriate for the study of white-collar crime.

Even though cases of embezzlement by persons of high status in the course of their occupation may technically fit Sutherland's definition of "white-collar crime," these cases nevertheless are atypical of white-collar crime because of the absence of criminal organization. Given this, if criminologists still want to study trust violation as white-collar crime, they must be careful to include only cases that strictly conform to the original definition, ignoring the legal charge under which the offender comes before the criminal justice system. Such an approach will yield limited numbers. On the other hand, because of the problems determining whether an offender is of high social status, it may be more prudent to study job-related trust violation as a form of occupational crime. This approach highlights the source of opportunity for trust violation, allows for its differential distribution, and is not muddied by the concept of white-collar crime.[46]

Occupational relatedness need not be a determinative factor in criminological explanation because similarities may exist between trust violators who commit offenses both occupationally and non-occupationally. To arrive at the most comprehensive explanations for trust violations, attempts should be made to reconcile with existing theory offenders who commit their crimes under both good-faith and bad-faith conditions.

◂ Notes ▸

[1] Jerome Hall, *Theft, Law, and Society* (Indianapolis, IN: Bobbs-Merrill, 1952), p. 36.

[2] Ibid., pp. 1–40.

[3] See Edwin H. Sutherland, "White-Collar Criminality," *American Sociological Review*, 6:1–12 (Feb. 1940); idem, "Crime and Business," *The Annals of the American Academy of Political and Social Science*, 217:112–18 (Sept. 1941); idem, *White Collar Crime* (New York: Holt, Rinehart & Winston, 1961), pp. 13, 154, 231, 252–53; idem, *White Collar Crime: The Uncut Version* (New Haven, CT: Yale University Press, 1983), pp. 9, 153, 154, 237–38.

[4] Donald R. Cressey, *Other People's Money* (Glencoe, IL: Free Press, 1953), chap. 1. See also idem, "Criminal Violation of Financial Trust," *American Sociological Review*, 15:738–43 (Dec. 1950); idem, "Criminological Research and the Definition of Crimes," *American Journal of Sociology*, 56:546–51 (May 1951).

[5] Sutherland, *White Collar Crime*, p. 9.

[6] Ibid. See also idem, "White-Collar Criminality"; idem, "Crime and Business."

[7] Cressey, *Other People's Money*, p. 184, n. 9.

[8] Dorothy Zeitz, *Women Who Embezzle or Defraud* (New York: Praeger, 1981).

[9] See, for example, Herbert Edelhertz, *The Nature, Impact, and Prosecution of White-Collar Crime* (Washington, DC: Government Printing Office, 1970), p. 3; James W. Coleman, *The Criminal Elite* (New York: St. Martin's Press, 1985), p. 5; Albert Biderman and Albert Reiss, Jr., *Data Sources on White-Collar Law-Breaking* (Washington, DC: Government Printing Office, 1980), p. xxviii. The Biderman and Reiss monograph is the truest to Sutherland's original focus.

[10] See Susan Shapiro, *Thinking about White-Collar Crime: Matters of Conceptualization and Research* (Washington, DC: Government Printing Office, 1980). At least three studies employ this redefinition to classify embezzlers as white-collar criminals: Michael L. Benson, "Denying the Guilty Mind: Accounting for Involvement in White-Collar Crime," *Criminology*, 23:585–607 (Nov. 1985); Kathleen Daly, "Gender and Varieties of White-Collar Crime," ibid., 27:769–93 (Nov. 1989); Stanton Wheeler, David Weisburd, and Nancy Bode, "Sentencing the White-Collar Offender: Rhetoric and Reality." *American Sociological Review*, vol. 47 (Oct. 1982). It should be noted that Wheeler et al. purposely used a definition of white-collar crime that did not contain social prestige in order to use prestige to explain sanctioning.

[11] Daly, "Gender and Varieties of White-Collar Crime," p. 777. Using the same data set as Daly, Weisburd et al. could classify only 47— 23.4 percent—of the 201 embezzlers as white-collar criminals using Sutherland's two criteria of social respectability and occupational role. See David Weisburd et al., *Crimes of the Middle Classes* (New Haven, CT: Yale University Press, 1991), p. 178.

[12] Sutherland, *White Collar Crime*, chap. 13.

[13] Ibid., p. 220.

[14] Ibid.

[15] Ibid., p. 221.

[16] Ibid., p. 219.

[17] Daly, "Gender and Varieties of White-Collar Crime," p. 783.

[18] Hall, *Theft, Law, and Society*, pp. 14–33.

[19] Sutherland, *White Collar Crime*, p. 231.

[20] See, for example, U.S., Department of Justice, Federal Bureau of Investigation, *Crime in the United States* (Washington, DC: Government Printing Office, 1990). In the UCR, conversion offenses and embezzlement offenses share the same uniform offense code range, 2701–99.

[21] See, for example, Freda Adler, *Sisters in Crime* (New York: McGraw-Hill, 1975), pp. 16, 156, 252; Travis Hirschi and Michael Gottfredson, "Causes of White-Collar Crime," *Criminology*, 27:949–74 (Nov. 1987); Michael Gottfredson and Travis Hirschi, A *General Theory of Crime* (Stanford, CA: Stanford University Press, 1900), chap. 9. These writers have similarly been faulted for using UCR data on fraud and forgery arrestees as measures of white-collar criminals because those categories also contain mundane offenses, such as writing bad checks and credit card fraud. See Darrell Steffensmeier, "On the Causes of 'White-Collar' Crime," *Criminology*, 27:345–58 (May 1989).

[22] Thorsten Sellin, "The Significance of Records of Crime," *Law Quarterly Review*, 67:490 (1951).

[23] An exception is national bank embezzlement arrestees, who probably do reflect national bank embezzlers. Although they are not routinely included in the UCR, regular required audits will expose them, and, furthermore, it is a crime not to report them to the authorities—nonreporting is considered abetting the offense.

[24] Cressey used this term in *Other People's Money*, p. 154. Coleman describes it as "slow horses and fast women," in *Criminal Elite*, p. 81. See also "bookies, babes, and booze" in Herbert Bloch and Gilbert Geis, *Man, Crime, and Society* (New York: Random House, 1962), p. 336. In today's world, one would hope that these authors would be aware that these are sexist comments; in truth, of course, it is not the women who are responsible for the embezzlement but the men who chase them. Regarding the term "embezzlement," Bloch and Geis trace it to the French *bezzle*, which means "drink to excess, gluttonage, revel, waste in riot and plunder." Ibid.

[25] John Laub, "Interview with Donald Cressey," in *Criminology in the Making*, ed. John Laub (Boston: Northeastern University Press, 1983), p. 139.

[26] Cressey, *Other People's Money*, chap. 1; see also idem, "Criminal Violation of Financial Trust."

[27] Karl Schuessler, "Review [of *Other People's Money*]," *American Journal of Sociology*, 49:604 (May 1954).

[28] Cressey, *Other People's Money*, p. 156.

[29] Gwynn Nettler, "Embezzlement without Problems," *British Journal of Criminology*, 14:70–77 (Jan. 1974); Benson, "Denying the Guilty Mind," p. 595.

[30] Zeitz, *Women Who Embezzle or Defraud*, chap. 6.

[31] Daly, "Gender and Varieties of White-Collar Crime," p. 785.

[32] Laub, "Interview with Donald Cressey," p. 138.

[33] Benson, "Denying the Guilty Mind," p. 595.

[34] Zeitz, *Women Who Embezzle or Defraud*, chap. 6.

[35] Benson, "Denying the Guilty Mind," p. 595. Carl Klockars refers to this kind of justification as a "metaphor of the ledger," that is, that an individual perceives many more good behaviors than bad ones in his or her personal deportment account. See Carl B. Klockars, *The Professional Fence* (New York: Free Press, 1974), pp. 151–61.

[36] See Edwin H. Sutherland and Donald R. Cressey, *Principles of Criminology*, 9th ed. (Philadelphia: J. B. Lippincott, 1974), chap. 4, or any other edition of this textbook.

[37] Donald R. Cressey, "Foreword," in Sutherland, *White Collar Crime*, p. xii.

[38] Sutherland, "White-Collar Criminality"; idem, *White Collar Crime*, chap. 14.

[39] Cressey, *Other People's Money*, pp. 147–51.

[40] Zeitz, *Women Who Embezzle or Defraud*, pp. 71–72.

[41] Gottfredson and Hirschi, *General Theory of Crime*, chap. 5.

[42] Ibid., chap. 9; Hirschi and Gottfredson, "Causes of White-Collar Crime."

[43] See Steffensmeier, "On the Causes of 'White-Collar' Crime." Steffensmeier's major criticism is that, contrary to the arguments by Hirschi and Gottfredson, the distribution of embezzlers according to race, gender, and age does not parallel those distributions for other crimes. For a rejoinder, see Travis Hirschi and Michael Gottfredson, "The Significance of White-Collar Crime for a General Theory of Crime," *Criminology*, 27:359–71 (May 1989).

[44] Gottfredson and Hirschi, *General Theory of Crime*, p. 40.

[45] Gary S. Green, "An Analysis of Embezzlers' Arrest Records" (Paper delivered at the annual meeting of the American Society of Criminology, San Francisco, Nov. 1991).

[46] For a more detailed discussion of the benefits of treating occupations as simply opportunities for crime, see Gary S. Green, *Occupational Crime* (Chicago: Nelson-Hall, 1990), chap. 1.

◂ 6 ▸

"Heads I Win, Tails You Lose"

Deregulation, Crime, and Crisis in the Savings and Loan Industry

Kitty Calavita
Henry N. Pontell

In the winter of 1989, reports of the biggest set of white-collar crimes ever uncovered hit the news. According to the reports, some savings and loan operators across the United States had brought their institutions to financial ruin while pocketing untold millions of dollars in personal profits, passing the tab on to the American taxpayer.

The savings and loan crisis provides an important opportunity for the study of white-collar crime. First is its mere size. Official estimates of the cost of the rescue effort to bail out insolvent savings and loans are placed at $200 billion over the next decade, and range from $300 billion to $473 billion by the year 2021[1] Government reports suggest that criminal activity was a central factor in 70 to 80% of these insolvencies.[2] Second, the case brings into sharp relief the mechanisms of the production and reproduction of white-collar crime and the role of the state in those processes.

Reprinted from *Crime & Delinquency* 36(3): 309–341.

This article investigates the factors facilitating savings and loan crime and traces the responses of regulators and other state officials to evidence of this crime over time. Drawing on a wide variety of sources, including General Accounting Office (GAO) reports, Congressional Hearings and debates, and media accounts, the study highlights the central role played by deregulation in the generation of thrift fraud. In this respect it confirms the conclusions of previous analyses of white-collar crime that emphasize the pressures associated with competition as important causal factors.[3] More important, however, it is argued that the advance of finance capitalism has set the context for what is called here "collective embezzlement" or "looting," the examination of which may lead to a more precise understanding of how various types of business crime are generated within distinct economic structures.

The article is organized as follows. First, a brief overview of the savings and loan system and the current crisis in the industry is provided as background for the discussion of thrift fraud. Next, three types of crime that permeate the savings and loan industry are identified and their respective causal and facilitating factors are discussed. The article then examines the regulation and enforcement process, focusing on the ideological, political, and structural forces that have constrained regulators and have contributed to the epidemic of crime in the industry. Finally, it concludes with a discussion of the possibility that the structure of finance capitalism, as distinct from the industrial capitalism upon which most previous analyses of white-collar crime have been based, both provides the incentives and opportunities for new types of white-collar crime and inhibits the state from responding effectively.

◂ Descriptive Background ▸

Underpinnings of the Crisis

The federally insured savings and loan system was established in the early 1930s, both to promote the construction of new homes during the depression and to protect financial institutions against the kind of devastation that followed the panic of 1929. The Federal Home Loan Bank Act of 1932 (USC 1421 *et. seq.*) established the Federal Home Loan Bank Board (FHLBB) whose purpose was to create a reserve credit system to ensure the availability of mortgage money for home financing and to oversee federally chartered savings and loans. Two years later, the second principal building block of the modern savings and loan industry was put in place when the National Housing Act of 1934 (USC 1724 *et. seq.*) created the Federal Savings and Loan Insurance Corporation (FSLIC) to insure deposits in savings and loan institutions.

The FHLBB has been (until the 1989 reform, to be discussed later) the primary regulatory agency responsible for federally chartered savings and loans. It is an independent executive agency made up of a Chair and two members appointed by the President. This agency oversees 12 regional Home Loan Banks that serve as the conduit to the individual savings and loan institutions that comprise the industry. It is the function of these regional district banks to provide a pool of funds for their member institutions at below market rates, in order to disburse loans and cover withdrawals. In 1985, the FHLBB delegated to the district banks the task of examining and supervising the savings and loans within their regional jurisdiction. Thus, although the FHLBB is formally responsible for promulgating and enforcing regulations, agents of the district banks oversee the thrifts' operations and have discretion to initiate corrective measures and/or to notify the Bank Board of savings and loan misconduct. As will be shown, this dual role of the district banks and the Bank Board to both promote *and* regulate the savings and loan industry is a potentially critical factor in explaining their curiously complacent response to ongoing indications of fraud in the industry.

The National Housing Act of 1934 provided for federal insurance on savings and loan deposits through the FSLIC, also under the jurisdiction of the FHLBB. In exchange for this protection, thrifts were regulated both geographically and in terms of the kinds of loans they could make, essentially being confined to the issuance of home loans within fifty miles of their home office. The 1960s brought a gradual loosening of these restraints—for example extending the geographical area in which savings and loans could do business and slowly expanding their lending powers—yet did not significantly alter the protection/regulation formula.

A confluence of economic factors in the 1970s radically changed both the fortunes of the savings and loan industry and ultimately the parameters within which they were to operate. Most important, "stagflation" hit the savings and loan industry particularly hard, as the "double whammy" of high interest rates and slow growth squeezed the industry at both ends. Locked into relatively low-interest fixed mortgages from previous eras, limited by regulation to pay no more than 5.5% interest on new deposits, and with inflation at 13.3% by 1979, the industry suffered steep losses. Not surprisingly, thrifts found it difficult to attract new money when inflation outpaced the meager 5.5% return on deposits. Even worse, the new Money Market Mutual Funds allowed middle-income investors to buy shares in large denomination securities at high money market rates, triggering "disintermediation," the euphemism for massive withdrawals from savings and loans.

In 1979, Paul Volker, head of the Federal Reserve Board, tightened the money supply in an effort to break the back of inflation, sending the interest rate up to its highest levels in this century, and ultimately contributing to a serious recession. Faced with defaults and foreclosures resulting from the recession, combined with increasing competition from high-yield investments given the new hikes in the interest rate, savings and loans were doomed. The net worth of the industry fell from $16.7 billion in 1972 to a *negative* net worth of $17.5 billion in 1980, with 85% of the country's savings and loans losing money.[4]

Deregulation: The Cure that Killed

Coinciding with these economic forces, a new ideological movement was afoot. Since the early 1970s, policymakers had been considering significantly loosening the restraints on savings and loans so that they could compete more equitably for new money and invest in more lucrative ventures. However, it was not until the deregulatory fervor of the early Reagan administration that this strategy gained political acceptance as a solution to the rapidly escalating savings and loan crisis. Throwing caution to the wind and armed with the brashness born of overconfidence, the deregulators undid most of the regulatory infrastructure that had kept the thrift industry together for four decades.

The conviction of deregulators was that the free enterprise system works best if left alone, unhampered by perhaps well-meaning but ultimately counterproductive government regulations. The bind in which the savings and loan industry found itself seemed to confirm the theory that government regulations imposed an unfair handicap in the competitive process. The answer then was to return the industry to what these policymakers saw as the self-regulating mechanisms of the free market. In 1980, the Depository Institutions Deregulation and Monetary Control Act (DIDMCA; P.L. 96-221) began to do just that, phasing out restrictions on interest rates paid by savings and loans. It is important to point out, however, that the move to the free market model was incomplete and accompanied by a decisive move in the *opposite* direction. For, at the same time that the law unleashed savings and loans to compete for new money, it bolstered the federal protection accorded these "private enterprise" institutions, increasing FSLIC insurance from a maximum of $40,000 to $100,000 per deposit.[5]

The 1980 law was followed by devastating losses in the industry. In the first place, it triggered an even more pronounced "negative rate spread." Savings and loans did attract more new money at the higher interest rates they could now offer, but the discrepancy between the high rates they had to pay to attract short-term deposits and the low rates at which they had invested in long-term home mortgages widened. The law's primary effect was to precipitate larger losses on more money.

When these deregulatory measures did not work, Congress prescribed more of the same. In 1982, the Garn-St. Germain Depository Institutions Act (P.L. 97-320) did away with the differential between permissible interest rates for commercial banks and savings and loans, and accelerated the phase-out of the ceiling on interest rates initiated in the 1980 law. Probably more important, it dramatically expanded the investment powers of savings and loans, moving them farther and farther away from their traditional role as a provider of home mortgages. They were now authorized to increase their consumer loans, up to a total of 30% of their assets; make commercial, corporate or business loans; and invest in nonresidential real estate worth up to 40% of their total assets. Furthermore, the Garn-St. Germain Act allowed thrifts to provide 100% financing, requiring no down payment from the borrower, in an apparent effort to attract new business to the desperate industry.

Industry regulators soon joined Congress in the deregulation. In 1980, regulators removed the 5% limit on "brokered deposits," allowing thrifts access to unprecedented amounts of cash. Brokered deposits were placed by middlemen who aggregated individual investments that were deposited as "jumbo" certificates of deposit (CDs). Since the maximum insured deposit was $100,000, these brokered deposits were packaged as $100,000 CDs, on which the investors could command high interest rates. So attractive was this system to all concerned—brokers who made hefty commissions, investors who received high interest for their money, and thrift operators who now had almost unlimited access to funds—that between 1982 and 1984, brokered deposits as a percentage of total assets increased 400%.[6] These brokered deposits turned out to be a critical factor both in creating pressure to engage in misconduct and in providing unprecedented opportunities for fraud.

In 1982, regulators dropped the requirement that thrifts have at least 400 stockholders, with no one owning more than 25% of the stock, opening the door for a single entrepreneur to own and operate a federally insured savings and loan. Furthermore, single investors could now start thrifts with noncash assets, such as land or real estate. Presumably hoping that the move would halt the dying off of savings and loans as innovative entrepreneurs bought them up, the deregulators seemed unaware of the disastrous potential of virtually unlimited new charters in the vulnerable industry.

The deregulatory process was complicated and accelerated by the fact that federal and state systems of regulation coexisted and not infrequently overlapped. State-chartered thrifts were regulated by state regulatory agencies and governed by their regulations, but could be insured by FSLIC if they paid the insurance premiums, which most did. (By 1986, 92.6% of the country's savings and loans—holding 98.5% of the industry's assets—were insured by FSLIC.)[7] This dual structure, which had operated smoothly for almost fifty years, had disastrous consequences within the context of federal deregulation. Because the funding for state regulatory agencies was provided in large part from "member" institutions, state agencies that were perceived by savings and loans as more rigorous or enforcement-oriented than the federal system risked losing their funding. The experience of the California Department of Savings and Loan serves as a good example of the effect of the regulatory competition that resulted.

Beginning in 1975, the California Department of Savings and Loan had been staffed by no-nonsense regulators who imposed strict rules and tolerated little deviation. The California thrift industry complained bitterly, and when federal regulations were relaxed in 1980, they switched en masse to federal charters.[8] With the exodus, the California Department lost over half of its funding and more than half of its staff. In July 1978, the California agency had 172 full-time examiners; by 1983, the number of examiners had shrunk to 55.[9]

It seemed that California policymakers had learned the hard way that if the state's Department of Savings and Loan was to survive (and if California state politicians were to continue to have access to the industry's lobbying dollars), they had to make it more likable. On January 1, 1983, the Nolan Bill (Cal. Stats. 1983c. 1091) passed with only one dissenting vote, making it possible for almost anyone to charter a new savings and loan, and virtually eliminating any limitations on investment powers. Similar state legislation around the country followed the federal initiative, as state legislatures and regulators deregulated for their survival. Some states—Texas, for example—already had thrift guidelines that were even more lax than the new federal regulations, but those that did not quickly enacted "me-too" legislation.[10]

At the same time as this deregulation zeal gained momentum, Congress passed a Joint Current Resolution in 1982, putting the full credit of the U.S. government behind the savings and loan industry. Although by law (12 USC 1435), the federal government is not obligated to rescue the FSLIC to cover insured deposits, Congress acted with this joint resolution to appease the fears of depositors. Once again, the free market deregulators had applied their principles selectively, setting in place the ultimately fatal formula of deregulation and protective insurance.

Losses continued to mount. In 1982, the FSLIC spent over $2.4 billion to close or merge insolvent savings and loans, and by 1986 the federal insurance agency was itself insolvent.[11] As the number of insolvent and ailing thrifts climbed, the FSLIC, knowing that its resources were inadequate to cope with the financial disaster, began to slow the pace of closures. Hoping against hope that windfall profits or an innovative buyer might reverse the decline of these institutions, the fateful decision compounded the crisis. In 1988, the FSLIC closed or sold 220 defunct savings and loans, and 300 other insolvent institutions were waiting in the wings.[12] In the first six months of 1988, the industry lost an unprecedented $7.5 billion.[13]

Major Forms of Thrift Crime and Their Causal Structure

In 1987, the Federal Home Loan Bank Board referred 6,205 savings and loan cases to the Justice Department for possible criminal prosecution, and an additional 5,114 cases were referred in 1988 (testimony before the Senate Committee on Banking, Housing and Urban Affairs).[14] It has been estimated that crime or misconduct played a significant role in 80% of the insolvent savings and loans destined to be bailed out by the U.S. government.[15] A GAO study of 26 of the nation's most costly thrift failures found evidence of "numerous and sometimes blatant violations of laws and regulations" in every one of the thrifts in the sample.[16] Furthermore, the GAO concluded that criminal activity was the central ingredient in the collapse of all of these institutions. By October, 1988, the FSLIC had sued the officers or directors of 51 failed thrifts for misconduct and estimated that these cases alone had cost the government over $8 billion.[17]

The Federal Home Loan Bank Board, in a report to Congress in 1988 defined fraud as it relates to the savings and loan industry:

> Individuals in a position of trust in the institution or closely affiliated with it have, in general terms, breached their fiduciary duties; traded on inside information; usurped opportunities or profits; engaged in self-dealing; or otherwise used the institution for personal advantage. Specific examples of insider abuse include loans to insiders in excess of that allowed by regulation; high-risk speculative ventures; payment of exorbitant dividends at times when the institution is at or near insolvency; payment from institution funds for personal vacations, automobiles, clothing, and art; payment of unwarranted commis-

> sions and fees to companies owned by a shareholder; payment of "consulting fees" to insiders or their companies; use of insiders' companies for association business; and putting friends and relatives on the payroll of the institutions.[18]

The varieties and possible permutations of criminal activity perpetrated by thrift operators are seemingly endless. By and large, however, fraud in the savings and loan industry falls into three general categories, classified here as "unlawful risktaking," "looting," and "covering up." Although these categories of fraud are analytically distinct in their makeup and in terms of the incentives, pressures, and facilitating factors that produce them, in practice they are often found as interacting parts of the same complex money machine.

Unlawful Risk-Taking

The GAO, in its study of 26 insolvent savings and loans, found that "All of the 26 failed thrifts made nontraditional, higher-risk investments and in doing so . . . violated laws and regulations and engaged in unsafe practices."[19] Deregulation made it legal for thrifts to invest in "nontraditional, higher-risk" activities, but regulations and laws were often broken in the process, either by extending these investment activities beyond permissible levels or by compounding the level of risk by, for example, inadequate marketability studies or poor supervision of loan disbursements. In order to explain the prevalence of this unlawful risk-taking, it is important to understand the new deregulated environment in which it was taking place, the pressures that this environment exerted, and the opportunities that it accorded. Two related thrift activities—brokered deposits and Acquisition, Development, and Construction (ADC) loans—were an integral part of this environment and will serve as good examples of both the incentive to commit fraud and the disastrous consequences for the industry.

The deregulation of savings and loans' investment powers unleashed an escalating competitive process in which brokered deposits were a key ingredient. Overnight, ailing savings and loans could obtain huge amounts of cash to stave off their impending insolvency. But the miracle drug had a downside. Like a narcotic, the more these institutions took in brokered deposits, the more they depended on them, and the more they were willing to, and had to, pay to get them. As brokerage firms shopped across the country for the best return on their money, thrifts had to offer ever-higher interest rates to attract them. And, like a drug, the most desperate institutions needed the most and paid the highest interest rates. In a perverse contortion of the theory of the survival of the fittest to which the free market deregulators subscribed (and tenaciously clung in spite of all the contrary evidence), in this environment it was the weakest thrifts that grew the fastest.

By 1984, Edwin Gray, Chair of the FHLBB, was so alarmed over the rate of growth of brokered deposits that he attempted unsuccessfully to reregulate the handling of these accounts.[20] Referred to in the business as "hot money," brokered deposits often entail huge sums, at high rates for the short term—not infrequently passing through an institution in twenty-four hours, then moving on to the next highest bidder. Institutions whose survival depends on such jumbo deposits are clearly vulnerable to the effects of unexpected withdrawals. But the problems associated with brokered deposits go far beyond this simple vulnerability factor.

The FHLBB today claims that "a large influx of brokered savings" is an "abuse flag," in recognition of the high probability of misconduct related to dependence on these deposits.[21] Given the addictive quality of brokered deposits and the high cost of obtaining them, it should not be surprising that they are associated with what is called here "unlawful risk-taking." Not only do the large cash infusions facilitate risky speculative ventures, but conversely and more importantly, long-shot investments with the potential for high payoff are undertaken by desperate institutions to offset the costs of high-interest deposits.

Among the most popular of the high-risk strategies used in conjunction with brokered deposits are Acquisition, Development, and Construction (ADC) loans. The power of federally chartered savings and loans to invest in commercial real estate projects was expanded with the deregulation of 1982, so that thrifts could invest up to 40% of their total assets in such ventures. Increasingly, high-risk loans were made to developers to acquire and develop projects for commercial use, more than tripling such loans between 1980 and 1986.[22] As long as high-risk ADC loans remained within the 40% limit stipulated by federal regulation, they did not, by themselves, constitute misconduct. The problem was that, given the competitive pressure exerted on thrifts by the new deregulation and the proliferation of high-interest brokered deposits that it triggered, some thrifts exceeded the federal ceiling on ADC loans and/or committed misconduct in handling them.

Because these high-risk loans have the potential (although are unlikely) to be very profitable in the long run, and because they provide a desperately needed cash flow in the short run (in the form of "points" paid up front), they are an extremely attractive source of investment for the brokered money to which faltering savings and loans increasingly turned in the early and mid-1980s. But it was the "no-risk," federally insured, nature of these "high-risk" investments that ensured their proliferation and abuse. For, should developers default on these loans, they suffered no personal liability, and deposits were protected by FSLIC insurance. William Black, the San Francisco regional counsel for the newly created Office of Thrift Supervision, referring to the enormous cash flow generated by such loans, observed that "it was as simple as 'ADC.'"[23] The short-term and long-term potential of these ADC loans, in combination with their low risk for the investor, triggered a scramble among savings and loans to enter the world of speculative development (particularly in Texas and other states where no ceiling existed for ADC lending).

The scramble was often accompanied by inadequate marketability studies of project potential, violations of the loans-to-one-borrower limitations, and other such regulatory misconduct. The GAO concluded that of the 26 failed institutions it examined, 19 engaged in ADC lending, and two-thirds of these performed either no marketability studies or inadequate studies, in violation of federal regulations.[24]

In some cases, thrift operators dropped any pretense of caution. Tyrell Barker, owner and operator of State Savings and Loan in Texas, who has since pleaded guilty to misapplication of bank funds, told speculators in Dallas in the early 1980s, "You bring the dirt, I bring the money. We Split 50–50."[25] When one Barker-backed speculator was asked how he determined which property to buy, he replied flippantly "Wherever my dog lifts his leg I buy that rock and all the acreage around it." So common are such arrangements that they have come to be known colloquially in the industry as "cash-for-dirt" loans. With the caution of a state official and the clarity of overdue hindsight, the U.S. Attorney for the Central District of California described the motive: "It appears that there have been institutions . . . that have been sufficiently desperate for income in the competitive arena for loan money that they have become less conscious and vigilant than one would like."[26]

The House Committee on Government Operations concludes that in some cases "normally honest bankers (including thrift insiders) have resorted to fraud or unsafe and unsound practices in efforts to save a battered institution. In those cases an incentive existed to turn an unhealthy financial institution around by garnering more deposits and then making even more speculative investments hoping to 'make it big.'"[27] The Commissioner of the California Department of Savings and Loan described the pressure to engage in fraud in the competitive environment dominated by brokered deposits: "If you have got a lot of money, high-cost money pushing you, and you have to make profits, you have to put it out awful fast."[28] FHLBB Chair M. Danny Wall described the bind of thrift operators on a "slippery slope of a failing institution trying to save probably their institution first and trying to save themselves and their career."[29] But, the words of an unidentified witness best summed up the formula that produced an epidemic of unlawful risk-taking in the thrift industry: "If you put temptation and the opportunity and the need in the same place you are asking for trouble."[30]

Deregulation was heralded by its advocates as a free market solution to the competitive handicap placed on thrifts by restraints on their investment powers and interest rates. But the "cure" turned out to be worse than the disease. Deregulation itself triggered an ever-escalating competition for deposits, and pressed some thrift operators into high-risk, often unlawful, loan arrangements. Dennis Fitzpatrick, Chair of Beverly Hills Savings and Loan in the early 1980s, told the Congressional Committee investigating wrongdoing at the thrift whose insolvency cost the FSLIC almost $1 billion (apparently with no irony intended), "We could not survive if we continued to do business in the traditional fashion."[31]

As deregulation lifted the ceiling on interest rates and intensified competition, it provided a primary incentive for fraud, and by opening up investment powers, it provided the opportunity; by simultaneously deviating from the free market model upon which these moves were ostensibly based, and increasing the level of protective FSLIC insurance, would-be "deregulators" added the irresistible force of temptation.

In many respects, the factors that generate this unlawful risk-taking are similar to those highlighted in other analyses of white-collar crime. Most obviously, Sutherland, Farberman, Geis, Hagan, and others, have cited the importance of the force of competition in the profit-making enterprise as a major incentive to commit corporate crime.[32] According to these analyses, the corporate criminal violates laws and regulations in the pursuit of the maximization of profits within the context of a competitive economy. Thus executives at Ford Motor Company in the 1970s decided to design and build the Pinto with a defective rear assembly, in spite of their knowledge that even minor rear-end collisions would cause death, injury, and burned vehicles. Spending the $11 per vehicle that it would cost to correct the defect, they reasoned, would cut into profits and impair their competitive position.[33] At about the same time, the president of General Motors explained his refusal to use safety glass in Chevrolets: "You can say perhaps that I am selfish, but business is selfish. We are not a charitable institution—we are trying to make a profit for our stockholders."[34] How similar is the refrain of a Houston savings and loan consultant and developer, explaining regulatory violations in the thrift industry: "If you didn't do it, you weren't just stupid—you weren't behaving as a prudent businessman, which is the ground rule.

You owed it to your partners, to your stockholders, to maximize profits. Everybody else was doing it."[35]

In addition, the opportunity structure has been cited as a facilitating factor in the commission of corporate crime. Some analyses, for example, have emphasized the ease with which these crimes can be committed as complementary to the profit motive in the production of such crime.[36] The infamous electrical company conspiracy of the 1940s and 1950s, in which employees of the heavy electrical manufacturing industry engaged in price-fixing, is exemplary.[37] Clearly, the reduction of competition and the maximization of profits were the motives for the price-fixing, but the relatively small number of very large companies such as General Electric and their domination of the industry (in a sense, the relative lack of competition) provided the opportunity structure for, and facilitated, the criminal conspiracy.

But the unlawful risk-taking in the savings and loan industry described here is distinct from such corporate crimes in a number of very important ways. Probably most fundamental is the way in which the savings and loan industry itself resembles the gambling casinos that they financed so heavily in the early 1980s. Whereas corporate crime in the industrial economy virtually automatically "pays off" in increased profits and long-term liquidity for the company, unlawful risk-taking in the thrift industry is a gamble—and one with very bad odds. It should not be surprising, then, that unlike more traditional corporate crimes in the manufacturing sector, these financial crimes often result in the bankruptcy of the firm.

Furthermore, although the logic of the economic structure (i.e., the inexorable drive for profits in a competitive economy) is primarily responsible for traditional corporate crime, in the case of thrift crime, the state itself has in large part set in place the generating components, in the form of deregulation, enhanced competition, and cushioned losses. The following discussion of "collective embezzlement"—a crime unique to the economic structure of finance capitalism—underscores the opportunities and temptations that this peculiar mix of deregulation and protectionism produces, the seemingly endless variety of scams devised to capitalize on it, and the havoc that it unleashes on the thrift industry.

Collective Embezzlement

In its report on crime and fraud in financial institutions, the House Committee on Government Operations concluded, "Usual internal controls do not work in this instance."[38] Elaborating, the Committee quoted the Commissioner of the California Department of Savings and Loans: "We built thick vaults; we have cameras; we have time clocks on the vaults; we have dual control—all these controls were to protect against somebody stealing the cash. Well, you can steal far more money, and take it out the back door. *The best way to rob a bank is to own one.*"[39]

"Collective embezzlement," also called here "looting," refers to the siphoning off of funds from a savings and loan institution for personal gain, at the expense of the institution itself *and with the implicit or explicit sanction of its management.* This "robbing of one's own bank" is estimated to be the single most costly category of crime in the thrift industry, having precipitated a significant number of the thrift insolvencies to date.[40] In characteristic understatement, the GAO reports that of the 26 insolvencies it studied, "almost all of the 26 failed thrifts made transactions that were not in the thrift's best interest. Rather, the transactions often personally benefited directors, officers, and other related parties."[41]

In discussing various forms of white-collar lawbreaking, Sutherland noted that "the ordinary case of embezzlement is a crime by a single individual in a subordinate position against a strong corporation."[42] Cressey, in his landmark study, *Other People's Money,* developed an explanatory model of the behavior of the lone white-collar embezzler, stealing from his or her employer.[43] Traditionally, then, embezzlement has been considered an isolated act of individual employees.[44] The "collective embezzlement" described here is a relatively new form of corporate crime that has yet to be closely studied. Previous analyses have differentiated between corporate crime (in which fraud is engaged in *by* the corporation *for* the corporation) and embezzlement (in which crime is committed *against* the corporation), but the "collective embezzlement" discussed here is a hybrid—perhaps "crime *by* the corporation *against* the corporation."

In some cases, thrift embezzlement takes the form of "buying sprees,"[45] in which thrift operators and others with inside access to thrift funds purchase luxury goods and services and charge them to the institution. Examples abound. When Erwin Hansen took over Centennial Savings and Loan in California at the end of 1980, one of the industry's most expensive shopping sprees began. "Erv" Hansen threw a Centennial-funded, $148,000 Christmas party for 500 friends and invited guests that included a 10-course sitdown dinner, roving minstrels, court jesters, and pantomimes. Hansen and his companion Beverly Haines, a senior officer at Centennial, traveled extensively around the world in the thrift's private airplanes, purchased antique furniture at the thrift's expense, and "renovated" an old house in the California countryside at a cost of over $1 million, equipping it with a gourmet chef at an annual cost of $48,000. A fleet of luxury cars was put at the disposal of Centennial personnel, and the thrift's offices were adorned with art from around the world.[46] Hansen died before he could be formally charged, but Haines was convicted of having embezzled $2.8 million. Centennial's inevitable insolvency cost the FSLIC an estimated $160 million.[47]

Don Dixon similarly operated Vernon Savings and Loan in Texas as if it were his own personal slush fund. He and his wife Dana divided their time between a luxury ski resort in the Rocky Mountains and a $1 million beach house north of San Diego, commuting on one of two Vernon jets that cost the thrift $100,000 apiece to operate. They went on luxury vacations across Europe, in one case running up a bill of $22,000, paid for with Vernon funds. Dixon bought a 112-foot yacht for $2.6 million, with which he wooed Congressmen and regulators on extravagant boating parties. In March, 1987, Vernon Savings and Loan was declared insolvent; it was estimated that the Vernon debacle would cost FSLIC $1.3 billion. Regulators argued in court that Dixon and others connected with Vernon had "wrongly extracted" up to $40 million from the thrift's coffers.[48]

Other more subtle forms of collective embezzlement include a variety of schemes to obtain "excessive compensation" for the institution's directors and officers. As defined by the General Accounting Office, "compensation includes salaries as well as bonuses, dividend payments, and perquisites for executives." Although a federal regulation limits permissible compensation for thrift personnel to that which is "reasonable and commensurate with their duties and responsibilities," the GAO found instances of excessive compensation in 17 of the 26 failed thrifts they studied.[49]

At one thrift, the chairman of the board of directors resigned his formal position in January 1985, whereupon he arranged a "services agreement" with the institution to carry on all his previous responsibilities. According to this agreement, he was to be paid $326,000 plus a percentage of profits in the form of a bonus. Six months later, the thrift paid him a bonus of $500,000 in "special employee compensation," even though it reported a loss of approximately $23 million during the course of 1985.[50]

The most widespread techniques of looting discovered thus far, however, involve an array of "special deals." For example, in "nominee loan" schemes,[51] a "straw borrower" outside of the thrift obtains a loan for a third person, who is usually affiliated with the thrift from which the loan is received. Such nominee loans are a popular device for disguising violations of the regulation which limits unsecured commercial loans to "affiliated persons" to $100,000. Don Dixon, of Vernon, was particularly adept at this, setting up an intricate network of at least 30 subsidiary companies for the express purpose of making illegal loans to himself.

A related system for violating the loans-to-affiliated-persons regulation is "reciprocal loan arrangements."[52] Hearings before the House Subcommittee on Commerce, Consumer, and Monetary Affairs in 1987 described four investigations in Wyoming that "revealed a pattern of complex activities . . . [which] include reciprocal loans in which the insiders from one bank authorize loans to the insiders of another bank in return for similar loans."[53] The scam resulted in losses to taxpayers of $26 million when the loans defaulted and the institutions failed.

So-called "land flips" use real estate deals as the mechanism for looting.[54] Land flips are defined as "transfers of land between related parties to fraudulently inflate the value of the land. The land is used as collateral for loans based on the inflated or fraudulent valuation. Loan amounts typically greatly exceed the actual value of the land."[55] Hansen of Centennial Savings and Loan, his friend and high financier Sid Shah, and Dutch investor Neik Sandmann, regularly used this technique to mutual advantage. According to reporters Pizzo et al., the three "flipped" one property worth $50,000 back and forth in the early 1980s until it reached the inflated value of $487,000, upon which they received a loan from Atlas Savings, the "sucker" institution of choice for Hansen.[56]

Similarly, loan broker J. William Oldenburg bought a piece of property in Richmond, California, in 1979 for $874,000. Two years later, after a number of "flips," he had the land appraised at $83.5 *million*. After buying State Savings and Loans in Salt Lake City for $10.5 million, he sold the property to the newly acquired thrift for $55 million.[57] In 1985, the ill-fated thrift went under, leaving the FSLIC responsible for $416 million in outstanding deposits.

"Linked financing," or "daisy chains" as they are known in the industry, is perhaps the most subtle and complex of the "special deals" used for embezzling. Linked financing is "the practice of depositing money into a financial institution with the understanding that the financial institution will make a loan conditioned upon receipt of the deposits."[58] It often involves large brokered deposits, made by a deposit broker who then receives a generous loan from the bank or thrift for his business. The brokers can then default on their loans, essentially obtaining free cash (these are called "drag loans," because the borrower simply drags away the loan, with no intention of repayment); middlemen obtain a generous "finder's fee"; and thrift operators record hefty deposits and inflated assets, which spell extra bonuses and dividends for thrift executives.

Looting is not confined to inside operators of thrifts. More often than not, the scheme requires intricate partnerships with those outside the industry, usually in real estate or loan brokerage.[59] In some cases the outsiders themselves initiate the fraud by identifying weak thrifts as "easy targets" that are "ripe for the plucking."[60] In one infamous deal, loan broker Charles J. Bazarian, Jr., engaged in fraudulent real estate transactions that contributed to the insolvency of two large California thrifts—Consolidated Savings Bank of Irvine and American Diversified Savings Bank of Costa Mesa. According to charges brought against Bazarian, in one instance he borrowed more than $9.5 million from Consolidated, putting close to $5 million of it into a partnership in which the owner of the thrift, Robert Ferrante, had a direct interest. The same year, Bazarian arranged a reciprocal transaction with American Diversified in which the thrift bought $15 million of "worthless" investor notes from Bazarian's brokerage firm, in exchange for Bazarian's purchase of $3.85 million in promissory notes and two pieces of real estate from the thrift. When federal regulators finally closed the two thrifts, together they registered close to $200 million in losses.[61]

"Daisy chains," "dead cows for dead horses," "land flips," "cash for trash," "cash for dirt," "kissing the paper," "white knights"—their playful jargon reflects the make-believe, candy-store mentality of this new breed of white-collar criminal and belies the devastating consequences of their actions. In Arkansas, where one-third of all thrifts have collapsed since 1986, taking with them $4 billion in deposits (a sum which is more than the state's annual budget), local residents have developed a jargon of their own. "S&L" they say, stands for "Squander and Liquidate."[62]

As looters were shoplifting goods and pilfering cash out the back door of thrifts, more shady characters were being welcomed in the front door. Increasingly, the word spread that deregulation of thrifts had offered up a money machine to the unscrupulous. At the federal level, new charters, which had averaged 45 a year in the 1970s, shot up to an average of 96 per year in the 1980s.[63] In states such as Texas and California where regulations were especially lax, the number of new charters increased even more sharply. In California, 235 applications for new thrift charters were received by the California Department of Savings and Loan in a little over a year between 1982 and 1984, and most were quickly granted.[64]

Summarizing the looting epidemic, the House Committee on Government Operations lamented the opportunities opened up for the con artist: "We have even got organized crime types taking a look at thinly capitalized institutions which are candidates for takeover and then using [various specified fraud schemes] . . . to create a paper financial asset which they can pull the plug on after a year-and-a-half or two, and leave the FDIC or FSLIC, i.e., the taxpayers, holding the bag."[65]

Deregulation and subsequent intense competition had produced the incentive for those on the "slippery slope of a failing institution" to try to save that institution via unlawful, but in the end not very "risky," risk-taking. As deregulation had thus opened the doors to gambling risk-free with depositors' money, it simultaneously opened them to crooks and swindlers whose intention was to embezzle funds. Not infrequently, the gamblers and swindlers were the same people. Whether the motive was to keep the doors open for further sport, or to get in and out with as much of the pot as possible, the game was the same: "Heads I win. Tails you lose."

Covering Up

As savings and loans teetered on the brink of bankruptcy, broken by negligent loan practices on one hand and outright looting on the other, their operators struggled to hide both the insolvency and the fraud through a manipulation of their books and records. This "covering up" was, and is, perhaps the most widespread criminal activity of thrift operators. Of the alleged 179 violations of criminal law reported in the 26 failed thrifts that the GAO studied, 42 were for such covering-up activity, constituting the largest single category of fraud.[66] Furthermore, every one of the 26 failed thrifts had been cited by regulatory examiners for "deficiencies in accounting."[67]

In some cases, the cover-up comes in the guise of deals similar to those discussed above—the difference being that the primary purpose of the transactions is to produce a misleading picture of the institution's state of health. Most important, thrifts are required to have on hand a specific amount of capital, as well as a given capital-to-assets ratio; when they fail to meet these standards, they are subject to enforcement actions. U.S. Attorney Anton R. Valukas describes a number of cover-up deals and the motivation for them:

> In the prosecuted cases of Manning Savings and Loan, American Heritage Savings and Loan of Bloomingdale and First Suburban Bank of Maywood, when the loans ("nominee loans") became non-performing the assets were taken back into the institution, again sold at inflated prices to straw purchasers, financed by the institution, in order to inflate the net worth of the bank or savings and loan. The clear purpose was to keep the federal regulatory agencies . . . at bay by maintaining a net worth above the trigger point for forced reorganization or liquidation.[68]

In some cases, deals can be arranged that include a built-in cover-up. For example, in cases of risky insider or reciprocal loans, a reserve account can be included in the original loan to be used to pay for the first few months (or years) of interest. Thus if a real estate developer, or for that matter a straw borrower, wants to borrow $500,000, he can be extended $750,000, putting the additional $250,000 into a special account from which the interest payments can be drawn. The effect is to make a loan appear current whether or not the real estate project has failed or was phony in the first place.

Probably most common, however, is simply adjusting the books to shield the thrift from regulatory action. At one savings and loan studied by the GAO, three irreconcilable sets of records were kept—two on two different computer systems and one manually.[69] At another, $21 million of income was reported in the last few days of 1985 in transactions that were either fabricated or fraudulent, allowing the thrift to report a net worth of $9 million, rather than its actual worth of negative $12 million.[70] Noting the prevalence of such cover-up devices, the president of one savings and loan testified in Congressional hearings that, "instead of attempting to remedy the problems which were so apparent, they [industry operatives] spent all of their efforts in proposing intricate schemes which . . . would appear to aid in maintaining the equity at a proper level."[71]

Having perpetrated fraud and brought their institutions to ruin, thrift operators had to cover their tracks, both to protect themselves from prosecution and to keep their money machine running. Ironically, they were aided and, some would say, encouraged in their efforts by the same agencies from which they were presumably hiding. The Federal Home Loan Bank Board set in place a number of bookkeeping strategies during the deregulatory period that simultaneously provided the industry with the tools to juggle their books to present themselves in the best possible light, and implicitly relayed the message that in trying to keep afloat, "anything goes."

Most important, in 1981 the FHLBB devised and encouraged the use of new accounting procedures known as "regulatory accounting procedures" (RAP). The new procedures entailed a complex formula that allowed for the understating of assets and the overstating of capital.[72] The sole purpose of the new RAP techniques was to inflate an institution's capital-to-assets ratio, thereby bolstering its image of financial health, and warding off reorganization, which the FSLIC increasingly could not afford. Not only did the procedures supply the industry with a "gray area" within which they could commit fraud with little chance of detection, but it sent the message that the Bank Board itself promoted deceptive bookkeeping.

In addition, the Bank Board in the early 1980s sent a more general message that it condoned discretionary reporting by thrifts. The GAO, for example, cites the Board's failure to provide appropriate guidelines for recording ADC transactions until 1985, thereby implicitly encouraging accounting treatments that inflated thrifts' net worth. ADC transactions can be classified as loans or investments; "Thus, a thrift could possibly forestall regulatory action by using whichever classification resulted in the most favorable portrayal of its financial condition."[73] Nonetheless, the Bank Board issued no guidelines for the recording of these important transactions. One district bank official who sought advice from the Board as to how these transactions should be reported "was told that the Bank Board was not going to act on this issue."[74]

Deregulation, based on a free market model of capitalism, had provided the economic pressure and the opportunity for thrift operators and their partners to make a fortune fast. But the free market model was by no means uniformly applied. As deregulators busily dismantled restrictions on thrifts, protections were not only left intact, but were increased, providing a risk-free environment for the white-collar heist of the century. In the following section, we address the question asked pointedly by one of the most prolific of thrift embezzlers, Charles Bazarian: "So where were the regulators?"[75]

Savings and Loan Enforcement
Ideology, Networks of Influence, and Structural Factors

Deregulation Ideology and Limited Resources

According to the House Committee on Government Operations "serious deficiencies" exist in the way the federal banking regulators and the Justice Department have handled fraud in the banking and thrift industry.[76] The Committee Report points out that in the early 1980s, many thrifts were able to avoid timely examination altogether,[77] and that those that were found to be violating the law, were treated too leniently to offer any deterrence.[78] The Committee faults the "graduated response" strategy of enforcement, describing the system as follows:

> An agency uncovers abuse and issues a directive or letter; the abuse continues and becomes worse, and the agency then issues a MOU [Memorandum of Understanding] or a supervisory agreement; and then, as the situation worsens, the agency issues one or more supervisory directives, and possibly a C&D [Cease and Desist] order or removal [of management], but by then the institution is failing. This committee specifically criticized this practice in its 1984 report. With certain exceptions, the agencies' approach has not changed.[79]

Both the House Committee and the GAO report a general lack of "formal enforcement actions" against even the most serious offenders. One GAO study[80] examined 424 "Significant Supervisory Cases," that is, thrifts that both have serious internal control problems and are in imminent danger of insolvency, and found that formal actions had been taken by regulators in fewer than 50% of the cases; in most of these cases the formal actions involved placing the thrift into receivership after it had become insolvent. Another GAO report[81] concludes that "numerous safety and soundness problems" had been documented by examiners in 26 of the nation's most costly insolvencies over the course of five years or more. Despite the examiners' notes that these thrifts required "urgent and decisive corrective measures," in most cases nothing substantive was done before it was too late.[82] The House Committee on Government Operations[83] reports that enforcement actions, which they had argued in a 1984 report[84] were already too rare to constitute a deterrent, declined further after 1986.

Not only did thrift fraud go relatively undetected by regulators, and was generally not dealt with through formal actions, but those offenders who were prosecuted typically received lenient sentences. According to the report of the House Committee cited above, "The message to culpable insiders and outsiders is: 'Crime does pay.'"[85] Every U.S. Attorney who testified before the Committee complained of the light sentences handed down in financial fraud cases. The U.S. Attorney for Southern California reported that in his district since January 1986, 60% of the convictions under the bank fraud statutes have brought sentences of probation; 10% received less than a year in custody; and fewer than 5% of the defendants were given five years or more in prison.[86] The House Subcommittee on Commerce, Consumer, and Monetary Affairs conducted its own examination of the sentences of 38 serious offenders in 28 thrifts and found that 16 received probation, and that only 8 of these were ordered to pay significant restitution.[87] As one U.S. Attorney put it, responding to such lenience, "If someone had walked in the door of the bank with a note saying this is a robbery . . . and walked out with $1500, 1 dare say he would have received 5 to 10 years in prison.[88]

The lack of meaningful enforcement in the savings and loan industry in the 1980s is partly the result of ideological imperatives in the deregulatory era. In the first place, deregulators believed wholeheartedly in the intrinsically healthy nature of intense competition and in the healing power of entrepreneurial innovation. Regulators themselves had invented and encouraged the use of Regulatory Accounting Procedures that would camouflage thrifts' actual state of declining health. The perpetrators of thrift fraud were, in a sense, only carrying this message of the deregulators to an extreme. Second, having deregulated the thrift industry, policymakers and industry regulators were undoubtedly reluctant to intervene while the new deregulated thrift environment was presumably working its magic and revitalizing the industry. If a few thrift operators were getting carried away, and their institutions were on the brink of insolvency, this was merely a transitional period on the road to a reinvigorated industry.

Related to these ideological imperatives of deregulation, inadequate resources compounded the problem. The size of the examination staff of the FHLBB remained constant for almost 20 years, despite dramatic increases in workload. In 1966, when the total assets of thrift institutions were $133.8 billion, FHLBB had a field examination staff of 755 persons; by 1985, when total assets had soared to $1 trillion, the examination staff stood at 747. The House Committee on Government Operations remarks on this shortage of inspectors: "No one questions that this contributed to untimely detection of misconduct in numerous institutions which subsequently failed."[89]

Despite repeated requests by the FHLBB for budget increases commensurate with the growth of the industry, the Office of Management and Budget (OMB) was determined to maintain existing low levels of funding in the first half of the 1980s. Citing OMB's "disdain for the examination process," the former deputy director of the FSLIC told the House Subcommittee on Commerce, Consumer, and Monetary Affairs that OMB budgetary policies were directly responsible for the lack of supervision in the thrift industry.[90] In July 1985, the FHLBB decentralized its examination process in the quasi-independent FHL District Banks, thereby taking it outside the budgetary control of OMB. As a result, the examination staff doubled in two years.[91]

Networks of Influence

The increase in budget and enforcement personnel after 1985 proved insufficient to offset the impact of political influence and favor-trading that dictated against strict enforcement. A revolving door between the state and federal regulatory agencies and the thrift industry itself provides one dimension of these networks of influence. For example, it is commonly understood that the U.S. League of Savings Associations, a powerful lobbying group of thrift executives, had virtual veto power on the nomination of the head of the FHLBB, and that members of the regulatory board are drawn almost entirely from the industry itself.[92] Richard Pratt, head of the FHLBB at the time, in a moment of candor told his subordinates at an agency conference that the Bank Board was "perhaps too closely allied to the industry that it regulates."[93] At the lower levels, it is not uncommon for thrifts to woo examiners and regulators with job offers in the industry.[94] Journalists Pizzo et al. put it bluntly, describing the strategy of "Erv" Hansen, owner and embezzler of Centennial Savings and Loan: "Hansen had his own way of appeasing regulators. He'd hire them." Hansen, for example, hired Pat Connolly, former deputy commissioner of the California Department of Savings and Loan, making him an executive vice president of the thrift and doubling his $40,000 a year government salary.[95]

In one of the most infamous cases of personal intrigue in the savings and loan crisis, it has been charged that M. Danny Wall, head of the FHLBB at the time, met personally with Charles Keating, owner of Lincoln Savings and Loan, and intervened on behalf of Keating to ward off FHLBB regulators in the San Francisco district who were investigating the thrift.[96] Wall managed to move the investigation from the San Francisco office to Washington and to delay closure of the insolvent thrift for two years—a delay that is estimated to have cost the FSLIC insurance fund $2 billion.[97] Once the investigation had been moved to Washington, according to Congressional testimony, Rosemary Stewart, head of the enforcement office in Washington, signed a "memo of understanding" with Lincoln. This "understanding" was bitterly referred to by examiners in the San Francisco office as "Rosemary's Baby," because it essentially permitted Lincoln to continue its high risk-taking and misconduct for a full year before it was finally closed.[98]

Similar networks of influence have been documented between members of Congress and the thrift industry, with significant repercussions on enforcement. For example, just before the Lincoln case was moved to Washington, five U.S. Senators (Cranston, Glenn, DeConcini, McCain, and Riegle) who had received campaign and other contributions from Charles Keating, called San Francisco regulators to Washington to discuss their prolonged examination of Lincoln.[99] According to a racketeering lawsuit brought against accountants in the Lincoln case, the intervention of the Senators "protracted the examination process and afforded [operators] additional time in which to exacerbate their frauds."[100]

In other well-publicized cases, former House speaker Jim Wright and former Democratic Whip Tony Coelho have been linked to the savings and loan industry in Texas, intervening on behalf of Dixon's Vernon Savings and Loan, and attempting to devise more "flexible" regulatory policies.[101] Republicans are by no means exempt from the maneuverings. According to one report, the Republican National Committee put together an exclusive group of high financiers and named them the "Team 100." A prominent member of this group, and one who donated heavily to the Bush campaign in 1988, was Texas billionaire Trammel Crow. Crow has managed the Texas real estate repossessed by the FSLIC for years. As thrift failures have increased, Crow and other members of the "Team" have been offered the insolvent S&Ls at bargain-basement prices, suggesting a link between thrift failures in Texas and the financial fortunes of the Republicans' "Team 100."[102]

Structural Conflicts and Enforcement

Besides these networks of personal influence and corruption, more general structural forces sabotaged regulation. According to the GAO, a "basic structural flaw" permeated the FHLB system. This structural flaw consisted of the complex division of labor and overlapping responsibilities of thrift regulators and, related to this, the "conflicting responsibilities for promoting the thrift industry while at the same time regulating and insuring it."[103] Prior to the reform of 1989, the FHLB regulatory system included the following layers: the 12 district banks' examiners, to whom primary field-level responsibility was delegated in 1985; the Office of Regulatory Activity (ORA), established in 1986 to oversee these district bank examiners; the Office of Enforcement (OE) within the central FHLBB in Washington, DC, to whom the district examiners made recommendations for formal enforcement actions; the three-member Federal Home Loan Bank Board itself; and, finally, the FSLIC, which had ultimate responsibility for liquidating or reorganizing insolvent thrifts.

In addition to the potential for overlapping responsibilities inherent in this system, the structural problems were twofold. First, the FSLIC, which insured the thrifts and had to pay the tab for insolvencies, had no legal authority to monitor or supervise the institutions and had to receive approval from the Bank Board before it could take any final action. Making matters worse, a "fundamental conflict" existed in the Bank Board and district banks' "roles in both promoting and regulating the industry."[104] The Bank Board was responsible for chartering new thrifts and promoting the general welfare of the savings and loan system, yet at the same time was the main thrift regulator. The district banks, whose field examiners had to uncover any potential problems or misconduct, had as their primary role the provision of banking services to the member institutions and depended on these institutions for their livelihood. The thrift industry executives who made up the vast majority of district bank board members[105] were the personal embodiment of this symbiotic relationship between the district banks and the thrift industry that they were supposed to regulate. Previous analyses have used the concept of "captive agencies" to refer to regulatory agencies that are subordinate to, and cater to, the industries they are charged with regulating.[106] The dual functions of the FHLBB effectively *institutionalized* the "captive agency" syndrome.

But there are other, even more fundamental, structural problems. First, not only was the FSLIC dependent on the Bank Board for approval for its actions, but the insurers faced a catch-22 situation: The worse the crisis in the thrift industry, the less likely it was that the FSLIC could respond. This dilemma has plagued the insurers for years, but by the mid-1980s it paralyzed them. By 1986, the FSLIC itself was insolvent (its liabilities exceeded its assets by an estimated $3 billion to $7 billion), drained of its resources by the epidemic of thrift failures.[107]

Throughout the 1980s, the FHLBB had extended "forbearance" to ailing thrifts, forestalling their closure or reorganization, "either because it believed the thrift to be capable of recovery" in the new deregulated environment, or "because the regulators desired to postpone using insurance fund reserves."[108] When the fund itself became insolvent in 1986, forbearance became a matter of necessity. As the FSLIC stopped closing insolvent thrifts, not only did the final costs escalate, but fraud—which in many cases had contributed to the insolvency in the first place—went undeterred. With nothing to lose, careless risk-taking and looting permeated the brain-dead institutions until they were finally, mercifully, put out of their misery.

Finally, and perhaps most importantly, a contradiction inherent in the structure of finance capitalism underlies the inability of regulators to respond effectively to the widespread fraud in the thrift industry. Clues as to the nature of this contradiction occasionally surface in government reports on the crisis. For example, the U.S. Attorney for the Southern District of Texas testified before the House Subcommittee on Commerce, Consumer, and Monetary Affairs that "the public's faith in the security and integrity of their banking institutions is considered so vital to the continued viability of the banking system that Congress has promulgated laws to prevent people from even starting rumors about a bank's solvency or insolvency."[109] Although the official concluded from this that the state must act quickly to deter crime and restore public confidence in the banking system, quite a different conclusion could be drawn. In fact, the House Committee on Government Operations reports that "Although every other Federal regulatory agency discloses final enforcement actions, the banking agencies continue to refuse to routinely disclose the existence or a summary of final civil enforcement orders taken against individuals or institutions."[110] The FHLBB argument against the "adverse publicity" that such disclosure would generate is that it would damage public confidence in the institution, worsening its condition. The Committee points out that this reluctance of the agency to act decisively and openly, in the interest of protecting the banking industry, has exacerbated thrift misconduct.[111]

An essential characteristic of finance capitalism is that its product is illusory—based on collectively agreed upon, but fundamentally arbitrary, values and shared faith. In this context, the "market" works so long as all of the players agree to pretend. Alan Webber, managing editor of the Harvard Business Review, points to this make-believe quality of our "soap-bubble" economy and explains, "That's why the slightest whiff of smoke can so easily spook the crowd to rush for the exits."[112] The banking industry is a clear and simple example of the importance of the collective agreement to have faith, since its success, indeed its very survival, depends on our illusion that banks in fact can pay off their debts (our deposits). Any "whiff of smoke" to the contrary sets off a run on the bank. For the regulator caught between sending up this smoke and shattering the collective illusion, or ignoring fraud and insolvency, the name of the game may be "Heads I Lose, Tails You Win."

◂ Discussion ▸

The House Committee on Government Operations summed up the testimony of senior Justice Department officials on the topic of bank fraud, reporting "(a) that financial institution fraud has reached epidemic proportions, [and] (b) that the number of criminal cases is increasing at an alarming rate."[113] Federal Bureau of Investigation figures reveal that Financial Institution Fraud and Embezzlement (FIF & E) cases make up 45.2% of all white-collar crime convictions or pretrial diversions, and that more than 80% of these involve insider fraud.[114]

The argument presented here has been that the epidemic of financial fraud in the thrift industry can be traced in large part to state policies and related ideologies of the 1980s that set in place a formula of deregulation and protectionism that unleashed unprecedented incentives and supplied tempting opportunities to commit fraud. Furthermore, it has been shown that the economic structure of the deregulated and protected thrift industry has generated a new breed of white-collar crime, called here "collective embezzlement," in which the systematic embezzlement of company funds is *company policy.*

But a more general point is implicit in this analysis: Both this new hybrid of white-collar crime—crime by the corporation against the corporation—and the role of the state in its generation and proliferation, are products of a new economic structure. French economist and Nobel prize winner, Maurice Allais, has called finance capitalism in the United States a "casino" economy.[115] Profits in this economy are made from speculative ventures designed to bring windfall profits from having placed a clever bet. In contrast to industrial capitalism where profits are dependent on the production and sale of goods and services, profits in finance capitalism increasingly come, as one commentator has put it, from "fiddling with money."[116] Corporate takeovers, currency trading, loan swaps, land speculation, futures trading—these are the "means of production" of finance capitalism. Only one thing is missing: Nothing is being produced but capital gains.

Maurice Allais underlines the magnitude of this shift from an economy based on the circulation of goods to one circulating money itself, by pointing out that "more than $400 billion is exchanged every day on the foreign exchange markets, while the flow of commercial transactions is only about $12 billion."[117] Nothing epitomizes the new financial era like the junk bond. The irony of its name should not be lost. The device transforms debt into wealth, and "junk" into "one of the greatest fortunes in Wall Street history."[118]

The advent of finance capitalism has clearly created new opportunities for fraud, because the amount that can be reaped from financial crime is confined only to the limits of one's imagination. Furthermore, as we have seen, state policies in the form of deregulation multiplied the opportunities in the savings and loan industry. But there is a way in which the new economic structure more generally encourages fraud, or at least fails to discourage it. A number of analysts have delineated the constraints placed on entrepreneurs in industrial or manufacturing capitalism, focusing on the contradiction between the simultaneous need to maximize surplus value and to minimize labor unrest and other forms of economic and political instability.[119] Weinstein, for example, explains Progressivism in the early 20th century as the product of capitalists' pressing need for stability dictated by long-term investments in the costly infrastructure of capitalist production versus the potential instability of an escalating class struggle.[120] Industrial capitalism clearly presents incentives and opportunities for serious crime, as several generations of students of white-collar crime have documented. Nonetheless, these corporate criminals are generally pressed into crime to *advance* their corporation and are constrained by a vested interest in its long-term survival. By contrast, perpetrators of financial fraud in the thrift industry and throughout the "casino" economy have little to lose by their reckless behavior. With no long-term investment in the infrastructure of production and no labor relations (since there are no workers in this "production" process) to inhibit them, the casino capitalists' main concern is to get in and out of the "house" with as much of the pot as possible. The effect of their crimes on the health of the casino, or even its long-term survival, are unimportant to these financial gamblers. Not surprisingly, then, the repercussions of these crimes, unlike more traditional white-collar crimes, have the potential to extend far beyond their direct costs to wreak havoc throughout the economy.

The structure of finance capitalism not only has contributed to the unprecedented proportions and far-reaching consequences of savings and loan and other financial fraud, but has limited the state's ability to respond to it effectively. One reason for this paralysis of the state in treating thrift fraud has to do with outdated assumptions and ideologies that were the product of industrial capitalism, but which are anachronistic in the new economic environment. Most important is the notion that individual profit-making activity is intrinsically beneficial to the general economy, and that the spillover will eventually "trickle down" to the public at large in the form of increased jobs, better wages, and an overall improved standard of living. Thus, in 20th century America, it became a truism that "What's good for General Motors is good for the country." There was a certain, albeit limited, logic to this trickle-down axiom within the framework of early 20th century capitalism. State actions calculated to provide conditions favorable to capital accumulation, while exacting brutal sacrifices from workers, at least had the *potential* to pay a return on those sacrifices in the form of an expanded economy. Given the right conditions (a strong and active labor movement being a central one), trickle-down theory could, and sometimes did, work.

This trickle-down ideology born of industrial capitalism has had direct implications for the treatment of corporate crime. Policymakers and regulators have reasoned that an overly punitive approach to corporate crime is counterproductive if it cuts into profits or discourages aggressive business practices. Theorists of the state have thus noted a structural contradiction between the need of the capitalist state to encourage the maximization of profits versus the threat to profit maximization entailed in, for example, the rigorous enforcement of occupational safety and health standards.[121]

But the logic of finance capitalism is such that capital gains based on speculative ventures are, at best, irrelevant to the welfare of the general population. Unlike the production of goods and services, "fiddling with" money produces few new jobs and no consumer goods. Policies based on outdated assumptions about the intrinsically beneficial nature of entrepreneurial activity tend to exacerbate the situation. Thus, for example, deregulation—rooted in notions of the inherent desirability of profit maximization—

within the context of the new casino economy not only did not solve the thrift crisis, but compounded it by condoning fraud as simply aggressive business practices that would eventually stimulate recovery. In the case of savings and loans, the abstract theory of "trickle down" yielded the harsh reality of "trickle up," as taxpayers foot the bill for the casino extravaganza.

As policymakers are mired in the old ideologies of a past era, a new contradiction adds to the paralysis. As we have seen, a fundamental contradiction between profit maximization and enforcement of standards and regulations permeates industrial capitalism and limits the state's ability to respond to corporate crime. The logic of finance capitalism contains its own set of contradictions, with even more disastrous consequences. The new economy is built on "soap-bubbles" and illusion, where prosperity is based on debt, and the collective agreement to ignore the emperor's nakedness not only staves off collapse but is the very motor that drives the economy. In this context, the role of the state is not to establish optimal conditions for productive activity, as it was in industrial capitalism, but to shore up the illusion and minimize the potential for panic. Thus it makes sense that the same deregulators who dismantled all restrictions on the savings and loan industry in the name of the free market deviated so dramatically from their own convictions and *increased* deposit insurance. The contradiction underlying the thrift debacle, then, is that the casino economy is based on illusion but that that illusion must be preserved at all costs. As losses were covered by federal insurance, and regulators were discouraged from publicizing fraud and insolvencies, the state response to the thrift crisis and financial fraud inevitably contained within it the seeds of its own destruction.

The future is likely to bring more of the same, because the savings and loan reform act passed by Congress in August, 1989, leaves untouched the major causal factors in both the thrift crisis and the crime that contributed to it. The Financial Institutions Reform, Recovery, and Enforcement Act of 1989 (FIRREA), among other things, raises the capital-to-assets ratio required of thrifts, reorganizes the regulatory apparatus by creating a new Office of Thrift Supervision, and sets up the Resolution Trust Corporation to manage and sell an estimated $500 billion worth of assets from failed thrifts. However, the deregulation and protectionism that in the early 1980s provided the unprecedented incentives and opportunities for white-collar crime in the thrift industry, and the underlying contradictions upon which these policies were based, remain fundamentally unchanged. Having been bailed out with huge subsidies from taxpayers and their coffers replenished, the savings and loan casino is once again open and ready for business.

NOTES

1 U.S. Congress, House Comm. on Ways and Means, "Budget Implications and Current Tax Rules Relating to Troubled Savings and Loan Institutions," *Hearings*, February 22, March 2, and March 15, 1989, p. 20; U.S. Congress, Senate Comm. on Banking, Housing and Urban Affairs, "Problems of the Federal Savings and Loan Insurance Corporation (FSLIC)," *Hearings*, March 3, 7–10, 1989, p. 9.

2 U.S. General Accounting Office [GAO], "Thrift Failures. Costly Failures Resulted from Regulatory Violations and Unsafe Practices," *Report to the Congress*, 1989; U.S. Congress, House Comm. on Government Operations, "Combatting Fraud, Abuse, and Misconduct in the Nation's Financial Institutions," *Report* (100–1088), 1988, p. 51.

3 Edwin H. Sutherland, *White Collar Crime*. New York: Dryden, 1949; Harvey Farberman, "A Crimogenic Market Structure: The Automobile Industry," *Sociological Quarterly*, 16 (1975):438–457; Stanton Wheeler and Mitchell Rothman, "The Organization as Weapon in White Collar Crime," *Michigan Law Review*, 80 (1982):1403–1426.

4 Stephen Pizzo, Mary Fricker, and Paul Muolo, *Inside Job: The Looting of America's Savings and Loan*. New York: McGraw-Hill, 1989, p. 11.

5 This change, which some critics argue is the single most expensive mistake in the "deregulatory" series, was made in the absence of Congressional hearings on the subject and with very little debate. Apparently a concession to the U.S. League of Savings Institutions, one of the most powerful lobbying groups in Washington, one House staff person reported later that "It was almost an afterthought" (quoted in Pizzo et al., p. 11).

6 GAO, "Thrift Industry Restructuring and the Net Worth Certificate Program," *Report to Congress*, 1985, p. 7.

7 Federal Home Loan Bank System, *A Guide to the Federal Home Loan Bank System*. Washington, DC: Federal Home Loan Bank System Publishing, 1987, p. 11.

8 U.S. Congress, House Comm. on Government Operations, Subcomm. on Commerce, Consumer, and Monetary Affairs, "Fraud and Abuse by Insiders, Borrowers, and Appraisers in the California Thrift Industry," *Hearings*, June 13,1987, pp. 12–13.

9 U.S. Congress, House, *op. cit.*, 1988, p. 62.

10 GAO, "Failed Thrifts. Internal Control Weaknesses Create an Environment Conducive to Fraud, Insider Abuse and Related Unsafe Practices," *Statement of the Assistant Comptroller General to House Judiciary Committee*, 1989, p. 25.

11 U.S. Congress, House Comm. on Banking, Finance and Urban Affairs, Subcommittee on Financial Institutions Supervision, Regulation and Insurance, "Financial Institutions, Reform, Recovery, and Enforcement Act of 1989 (H.R. 1278)," *Hearings*, March 8, 9, 14, 1989, p. 286.

12 GAO, "Failed Thrifts," *op. cit.*, p. 2.

13 Ned Eichler, *The Thrift Debacle*. Berkeley: University of California Press, 1989, p.119.

14 GAO, "Failed Thrifts," *op. cit.*, p. 11.

15 U.S. Congress, House, 1988, *op. cit.*, p. 51.

16 GAO, "Thrift Failures," *op. cit.*, pp. 51, 2.

17 U.S. Congress, House, 1988, *op. cit.*, pp. 4–5.

18 GAO, "Thrift Failures," *op. cit.*, p. 22.

19 *Ibid.*, p. 17.

20 According to Pizzo et al., pp. 77–83, the U.S. League of Savings, Treasury Secretary Donald Regan, and a coalition of powerful brokerage firms led by Merrill Lynch, reportedly stymied the effort and successfully discredited Gray as a pessimist and a naysayer.

21 U.S. Congress, House, 1988, *op. cit.*, p. 41.

22 U.S. Congress, House, "Fraud and Abuse by Insiders," *op. cit.*, p. 265.

23 *Los Angeles Times*, October 28, 1989b, p. D1.

24 GAO, "Thrift Failures," *op. cit.*, p. 27; as reported in GAO, "Failed Thrifts," *op. cit.*, p. 23. The overbuilding that resulted from ADC lending practices has been cited as a critical failure in the collapse of the commercial real estate market in areas where the activity is concentrated. Although the decline in oil prices was in part responsible for the real estate glut in Texas, the excess supply resulting from the logic of ADC lending compounded the crisis.

25 Pizzo et al., *op. cit.*, p. 191.

26 U.S. Congress, House, "Fraud and Abuse by Insiders," *op. cit., p.* 334.

27 U.S. Congress, House, 1988, *op. cit.*, p. 34.

28 U.S. Congress, House, "Fraud and Abuse by Insiders," *op. cit.*, p. 13.

29 U.S. Congress, House, 1988, *op. cit.*, p. 46.

30 U.S. Congress, House, "Fraud and Abuse by Insiders," *op. cit.*, p. 9.

31 Eichler, *op. cit.*, p. 108.

32 Sutherland, *op. cit.;* Farberman, *op. cit.;* Gilbert Geis, "The Heavy Electrical Equipment Antitrust Cases of 1961." In Marshall Clinard and Richard Quinney, eds., *Criminal Behavior Systems: A Typology*. New York: Holt, Rinehart & Winston, 1967, pp. 140–151; John Hagan, *Modern Criminology, Crime, Criminal Behavior, and Its Control.* New York: McGraw-Hill, 1985.

33 Mark Dowie, "Pinto Madness." In Jerome Skolnick and Elliot Currie, eds., *Crisis in American Institutions.* 4th ed. Boston: Little, Brown, 1979, pp. 26–34.

34 Morton Mintz and Jerry Cohen, *Power, Inc.: Public and Private Rulers and How to Make Them Accountable.* New York: Viking, 1976, p. 110.

35 Curtis J. Lang, "Blue Sky and Big Bucks," *Southern Exposure,* 17 (1989):21.

36 Wheeler and Rothman, *op. cit.*

37 Geis, *op. cit.*

38 U.S. Congress, House, 1988, *op. cit.*, p. 34.

39 *Ibid.* (emphasis in original).

40 *Ibid.*, p. 41; GAO, "Thrift Failures," *op. cit.*, p. 19.

41 GAO, *Ibid.*

42 Edwin Sutherland, *White Collar Crime: The Uncut Version.* New Haven: Yale University Press, 1983, p. 231.

43 Donald Cressey, *Other People's Money: A Study of the Social Psychology of Embezzlement.* Glencoe, IL: The Free Press, 1953.

44 In Sherman's terms, such embezzlement constitutes deviance *in* an organization, as distinguished from deviance *by* an organization, such as the corporate price-fixing discussed above (see Lawrence Sherman, *Scandal and Reform.* Berkeley: University of California Press, 1978).

45 Pizzo et al., *op. cit.*, p. 36.

46 *Ibid.*, pp. 25–37; GAO, "Thrift Failures," *op. cit.*, p. 22.

47 U.S. Congress, House, 1988, *op. cit.*, p. 38.

48 Pizzo et al., *op. cit.*, p. 193.

[49] GAO, "Thrift Failures," *op. cit.*, p. 21.
[50] *Ibid.*
[51] U.S. Congress, House, 1988, *op. cit.*, p. 41.
[52] *Ibid.*
[53] U.S. Congress, House Comm. on Government Operations, Subcomm. on Commerce, Consumer, and Monetary Affairs, "Adequacy of Federal Efforts to Combat Fraud, Abuse, and Misconduct in Federally Insured Financial Institutions," *Hearings*, November 19, 1987, pp. 79–80, 129–130.
[54] U.S. Congress, House, 1988, *op. cit.*, p. 41.
[55] *Ibid.*, p. 42.
[56] Pizzo et al., *op. cit.*, p. 46.
[57] *Ibid.*, p. 177; U.S. Congress, House, 1988, *op. cit.*, pp. 180–181.
[58] U.S. Congress, *Ibid.*, p. 42.
[59] U.S. Congress, House, "Fraud and Abuse by Insiders," *op. cit.*, p. 332.
[60] U.S. Congress, House, 1988, *op. cit.*, p. 12.
[61] *Los Angeles Times*, September 19, 1989, pp. A3, A23; Bazarian has also been accused of siphoning money off of two housing projects of the Department of Housing and Urban Development (HUD), thus providing a human link between two of the biggest scandals of the 1980s—corruption at HUD and the savings and loan debacle.
[62] Eric Bates, "Outrage in Little Rock," *Southern Exposure*, 17 (1989):16–18.
[63] Federal Home Loan Bank Board, *Savings & Home Financing Source Book.* Washington, DC: Federal Home Loan Bank Board, 1987, p. A29.
[64] U.S. Congress, House, "Fraud and Abuse by Insiders," *op. cit.*, p. 18.
[65] U.S. Congress, House, 1988, *op. cit.*, pp. 5–6.
[66] GAO, "Thrift Failures," *op. cit.*, p. 51.
[67] *Ibid.*, p. 40.
[68] U.S. Congress, House, "Adequacy of Federal Efforts," *op. cit.*, pp. 99–100.
[69] GAO, "Thrift Failures," *op. cit.*, p. 41.
[70] *Ibid.*, pp. 44–45.
[71] U.S. Congress, House, "Fraud and Abuse by Insiders," *op. cit.*, p. 546.
[72] Eichler, *op. cit.*, pp. 72, 77.
[73] GAO, "Thrift Failures," *op. cit.*, p. 42.
[74] *Ibid.*
[75] Pizzo et al., *op. cit.*, p. 14.
[76] U.S. Congress, House, 1988, *op. cit.*, p. 8.
[77] *Ibid.*, p. 69.
[78] *Ibid.*, pp. 16, 34–39.
[79] *Ibid.*, p. 16.
[80] GAO, "Troubled Thrifts. Bank Board Use of Enforcement Actions," *Briefing Report*, 1989.
[81] GAO, "Thrift Failures," *op. cit.*, p. 4.
[82] GAO, "Troubled Thrifts," *op. cit.*, p. 4.
[83] U.S. Congress, House, 1988, *op. cit.*, pp. 75–77.
[84] U.S. Congress, House Comm. on Government Operations, "Federal Response to Criminal Misconduct and Insider Abuse in the Nation's Financial Institutions," *Report* (98-1137), 1984.
[85] U.S. Congress, House, 1988, *op. cit.*, p. 35.
[86] *Ibid.*, p. 36.
[87] U.S. Congress, House, "Adequacy of Federal Efforts," *op. cit.*, pp. 982–1014.
[88] *Ibid.*, pp. 110–111.

89 U.S. Congress, House, 1988, *op. cit.*, p. 69.
90 U.S. Congress, House, "Fraud and Abuse by Insiders," *op. cit.*, p. 175.
91 U.S. Congress, House, 1988, *op. cit.*, p. 15.
92 Eichler, *op. cit.*, p. 131.
93 Richard T. Pratt, "Perspective of the Chairman." Paper presented at the Eighth Annual Conference of the Federal Home Loan Bank Board, San Francisco, December 1982, p. 46.
94 See, *Los Angeles Times*, September 1, 1989, sec. 4, p. 1.
95 Pizzo et al., *op. cit.*, p. 47.
96 *Los Angeles Times*, October 21, 1989, p. D1; *Los Angeles Times*, October 25, 1989, p. D2.
97 *Ibid.*, October 25, p. D2.
98 *Ibid.*, October 27, 1989, pp. A1, A31.
99 A memorandum of notes of the meeting is quoted in Pizzo et al., *op. cit.*, pp. 392–404.
100 *Los Angeles Times*, September 21, 1989, sec. 4, p. 3.
101 *U.S. News and World Report*, June 12, 1989, pp. 21–22.
102 Lang, *op. cit.*, p. 24.
103 GAO, "Failed Thrifts," *op. cit.*, p. 80.
104 *Ibid.*
105 *Ibid.*, *p.* 81.
106 Theodore Lowi, *The End of Liberalism.* New York: Norton, 1969; Francis E. Rourke, *Bureaucracy, Politics, and Public Policy.* Boston: Little, Brown, 1969.
107 GAO, "Thrift Industry. Forbearance for Troubled Institutions, 1982–1986." *Briefing Report*, 1987, p. 3.
108 *Ibid.*, p. 1.
109 U.S. Congress, House, "Adequacy of Federal Efforts," 1987, *op. cit.*, p. 126.
110 U.S. Congress, House, 1988, *op. cit.*, p. 17.
111 *Ibid.*
112 *Los Angeles Times*, October 18, 1989, p. B7.
113 U.S. Congress, House, 1988, *op. cit.*, p. 5.
114 U.S. Congress, House, "Adequacy of Federal Efforts," pp. 991–992, 592–593.
115 *Los Angeles Times*, October 26, 1989, p. D1.
116 *Ibid.*, October 4, 1989, sec. 2, p. 7.
117 *Ibid.*, October 26, *op. cit.*
118 James Grant, "Michael Milken, Meet Sewell Avery," *Forbes* (October 23, 1989):60–64.
119 Ralph Miliband, *The State in Capitalist Society.* New York: Basic Books, 1969; James Weinstein, *The Corporate Ideal in the Liberal State, 1900–1919.* Boston: Beacon, 1968; Robert H. Wiebe, *The Search for Order, 1877–1920.* New York: Hill and Wang, 1967.
120 Weinstein, *op. cit.*
121 Daniel M. Berman, *Death on the Job, Occupational Health and Safety Struggles in the United States.* New York: Monthly Review Press, 1978; Patrick Donnelly, "The Origins of the Occupational Safety and Health Act of 1970," *Social Problems*, 30 (1982):13–25; Lisa Stearns, "Fact and Fiction of a Model Enforcement Bureaucracy: The Labor Inspectorate of Sweden," *British Journal of Law and Society*, 6 (1979):1–23.

‹ 7 ›

Insider Trading

The SEC Meets Carl Karcher

Elizabeth Szockyj

Corporate officers and major shareholders are restricted as to when and on what grounds they may trade company stock, but insider trading is not illegal in the United States. On the contrary, allowing officers and directors of corporations to own and to deal in stock in their company is supported in order to reward past performance and to supply an incentive for future profitability. What is illegal is when an insider trades on information that is confidential or not available to the general public, such as advance knowledge regarding a new product or unanticipated profits or losses. Trading on nonpublic information, or tipping other people who then trade, is said to undermine "the fair and honest operation of our securities markets."[1]

In 1988, the California office of the Securities and Exchange Commission (SEC) filed a civil insider trading action against Donald Karcher, the president, and Carl Karcher, the founder of Carl Karcher Enterprises (CKE), a fast-food chain, and against 13 members of the Karcher family. Before the case was over, the head

Reprinted from the *Annals of the American Academy of Political and Social Science*, 525 (January 1993): 46–58.

of the CKE accounting department, Alvin DeShano, was prosecuted criminally by the Department of Justice for alleged illegal insider trades. After much publicity, negotiation, and expense, the Karcher family members settled with the SEC. DeShano was acquitted of criminal charges by a jury whose members felt uncomfortable convicting him on the basis of entirely circumstantial evidence.

Both the civil and criminal nature of insider trading are illustrated in this case. The civil suit reveals the motivations, on the part of all parties, for pursuing a settlement, the most frequent method of disposal of insider trading cases. By not forcing the defendants to admit to committing the offense, that is, by allowing them to settle without admitting or denying guilt, the SEC is able to assess penalties that the court might deny, while the defendants may be better off financially and emotionally by avoiding possible higher fines, additional legal fees, disruption to the corporate functioning, psychological stress, and potential adverse publicity.

The criminal trial in this case depicts the subtleties of a jury trial for a white-collar offense. The jury's shift from an initial stance favoring guilt to an acquittal of the defendant reveals the dynamics of the jury deliberation process, particularly when a respectable defendant is being tried. The uncertainty of proving criminal intent based on circumstantial evidence has haunted attempts to prosecute insider traders. Set in a time when insider trading had became a household word and when penalties from the newly passed Insider Trading Sanctions Act of 1984 (ITSA) could be applied, the Karcher case takes the reader from the circumstances surrounding suspect securities trades to the discovery of possible illegality and then to a final resolution.

Discovery of Suspicious Trades

Aroused by unusual trading activity, the computer in the Washington offices of the National Association of Securities Dealers (NASD) red-flagged shares trading in Carl Karcher Enterprises, Inc. Heavy selling of stock on 22 October 1984 resulted in a fourfold increase in volume from the previous day, with a jump from 21,250 to 107,620 shares. On 23 October the volume rose to 182,000 shares after CKE released its startling profit expectations, under the wire service headline "Carl Karcher Said Third Quarter Net Could Be Off by 50%." NASD, now alerted, surveyed the brokers involved in the trades to determine the individuals who had bought and sold CKE stock. By January 1985, NASD, whose suspicions of illegal insider trading appeared confirmed, turned its findings over to the SEC for further investigation and possible official action.[2]

The stock under scrutiny was fairly new to the over-the-counter market. The company, CKE, had gone public in 1982 after decades of nurturing by its founder, Carl Karcher. From his humble beginnings in Los Angeles in 1941, with a small hot dog stand purchased for $326, Carl Karcher had watched his investment grow into a chain of 449 restaurants spanning four states.[3]

Precursors to the 1984 News Release

As the three-and-a-half-year SEC investigation progressed, the events of the days prior to the news release regarding the drop in CKE earnings were revealed. Due to some poor business ventures, primarily an ill-fated national expansion attempt, as well as a slump in the Los Angeles fast-food industry following the 1984 summer Olympics, the CKE earnings for the fiscal period ending 5 October 1984 were approximately 83 percent lower than for the same period the previous year, as stated in the SEC charges; the Department of Justice estimated the decline at 65 percent. These reduced period-nine earnings had a strong impact on CKE earnings for the third quarter ending 2 November 1984.

DeShano, the director of general accounting for the corporation, received the preliminary report for period nine on Friday, 12 October. Between that Friday and Tuesday, 16 October, DeShano, the controller, and staff members adjusted and corrected the information in the report. On 16 and 17 October the final report was distributed to the CKE executives. Donald Karcher, the president of the corporation, was notified in Europe of the period-nine results. Not only were the results devastating news for the company, but Donald was scheduled to speak at a conference on 23 October and there were certain to be questions regarding the economic status of CKE. At a meeting of company executives on Saturday, 20 October, it was decided that in lieu of releasing the customary report of earnings in November, a special press notice would be issued just prior to Donald Karcher's speaking engagement. CKE had never before made a midquarter announcement. The release was transmitted Tuesday morning, 23 October, over the Dow Jones newswire. That day the CKE stock opened at 21½, declined to a low of 16½, and closed at 17¼.

In a flurry of activity before the time of the press release, stocks and debentures were sold by several of Carl Karcher's children, relatives of Donald Karcher, and Alvin DeShano. Sales by the Karcher family members accounted for 27.5 percent of the total trading volume of CKE common stock for 22 October 1984.[4] It was these trades, which occurred after the preliminary report but before the press release, that were of concern to the SEC; it was during this time that nonpublic information that would affect the price of the stock was in the hands of Donald and Carl Karcher.

THE SEC INDICTMENT

Insider trading was at this time a well-known priority for the SEC. With increased sanctions for insider trading legislated just months before by the ITSA, the SEC was moving full-steam ahead. On the East Coast, the agency made media headlines in 1984 and 1985 with insider trading charges against Paul Thayer, the Deputy Secretary of Defense to President Reagan, and against *Wall Street Journal* reporter R. Foster Winans.

In 1984, when Irving Einhorn arrived in Los Angeles to head the regional SEC office, he found the branch "in an embarrassing state of disarray."[5] What the office needed was the successful prosecution of a major securities-fraud case. With the Karcher case, the office was guaranteed national exposure. Because of the sheer number of possible defendants—16 in all—this was the largest insider trading case the Los Angeles SEC had encountered.

After countless interviews with CKE officials, traders, and family members, and after tracing telephone conversations and stock reports, the SEC announced, on 14 April 1988, three and a half years after the relevant events, its charges against a number of Karcher family members and the CKE accountant. According to the SEC, Carl Karcher and his wife, Margaret,[6] had conveyed information regarding the impending decline in profits to three daughters, a son, and two sons-in-law. Karcher had assumed the role of advising his children in their financial affairs; and all the children charged were heavily in debt from stock margin accounts.[7] Donald Karcher and his wife, Dorothy, were also charged with relaying confidential information to four relatives.

The complaint claimed that the 10 relatives avoided a total of $310,000 in losses by trading on the confidential information before the public announcement of 23 October. Neither Donald nor Carl Karcher was accused of selling CKE stock himself, only of tipping the others.

Finally, both the accountant, Alvin DeShano, and Carl Karcher's son and vice president of manufacturing and distribution, Carl Leo Karcher, were said to have been aware of the drastic decline in earnings because of their position. DeShano was accused of selling all of his 1725 shares of CKE stock, thereby avoiding losses of $9367—the Department of Justice estimated this sum at $7107—while it was alleged that Carl Leo Karcher avoided approximately an $8000 loss through his sale of stock.

In the complaint, the SEC sought, for all defendants, a permanent injunction from engaging in insider trading violations. For those guilty of trading illegally, disgorgement of the avoided loss, to be paid to the stockholders defrauded, and fines up to triple the amount disgorged—in accordance with the ITSA—were requested. The individuals charged with passing the information would be responsible for damages up to triple the amount of the losses avoided by those they allegedly tipped. Under these stipulations, Carl Karcher would be required to pay close to $1 million in fines.

◂ A Determination of Guilt ▸

Carl Leo Karcher, a vice president of the company at the time in question, was aware of the period-nine report by virtue of his position. At the monthly meeting of company officers, he was startled to see the drastic period-nine drop in earnings and the dismal third-quarter profit expectations. Two days later, Carl Leo instructed his broker to sell 75 debentures. He hoped to reduce his $836,000 debt to his brokerage firm, thereby avoiding a margin call.

In testimony before the SEC, Carl Leo stated that after he had made the phone call to his broker, the chief financial officer for CKE warned him not to sell the debentures until after the public announcement on the third-quarter earnings. Upon receiving this information, Carl Leo canceled his order, but 50 debentures already had been sold. He did not attempt to reacquire these debentures. Within an hour after the earnings news release, he sold another 50 debentures.

The SEC charged Carl Leo with trading on inside information to avoid potential losses estimated at $8000. During testimony before the SEC, Carl Leo admitted to receiving and acting on the confidential earnings information, stating that at the time he believed that as long as he was selling at a loss, this act would not be considered insider trading. Carl Leo explained, "I had a legal right to sell the debentures because the sale would result in a loss to me."[8]

With this evidence in hand, the SEC asked that Carl Leo be found guilty and fined without a trial. Carl Leo proved to be the only defendant to admit to using the inside information to trade. In the summary proceedings that took place on 12 September 1988, the defense argued that Karcher had not intended to defraud, deceive, or manipulate but had simply made a mistake. Los Angeles Federal Court Judge Edward Rafeedie found that there was enough evidence without a trial to convict the former vice president of insider trading. Carl Leo's personal knowledge of the law was not relevant to his guilt.[9]

Armed with the ITSA, which allows civil penalties of up to three times the amount gained or avoided, the SEC requested that Carl Leo pay $10,500, including interest, for the losses that he avoided, plus up to $34,500 in civil penalties. The judge granted the $10,500 disgorgement and enjoined Carl Leo from committing future securities violations, but he refused to impose the treble penalty. Judge Rafeedie felt that the provision should be used for "a more egregious case." He continued, "This involved a single trade [and] is not the type of case that has been in the headlines involving . . . secret transactions [referring to the Levine-Boesky-Siegel insider trading cases]."[10]

The Carl Leo Karcher case, one of the first that attempted to use the triple-damages provision in the ITSA, dealt a blow to SEC enforcement ambitions.[11] Ironically, the standard SEC settlement incorporates a civil penalty equal to the profit obtained or loss avoided, which is more stringent than the civil court sentence handed down in the Carl Leo case. This is contrary to the normal plea-bargaining assumption that one will receive a more lenient sentence by waiving the trial alternative. As discussed later in this article, the remainder of the Karchers settled with the SEC by agreeing to pay a penalty equal to the amount disgorged.

◂ The DeShano Trial ▸

The only criminal charge in the Karcher episode was laid in March of 1989 against the head accountant, Alvin DeShano. This was a case where the link between the confidential period-nine report and the sale of CKE stock was direct. Since neither Carl nor Donald Karcher sold his own stock, the government would have to show that the brothers first had access to the nonpublic report and then relayed the information to their families and that thereafter the relatives charged sold the stock based on that knowledge. In the accountant's case, the government did not have the difficult task of proving the middle step.

A long-time employee of CKE, DeShano, who turned 55 during the course of the trial, was depicted as an unsophisticated investor, an honest man whose major fault was that he procrastinated. The defense claimed that DeShano had intended to sell the stock long before the preliminary ninth-period report was compiled but never quite got around to doing so.

Held in Los Angeles federal court from 23 May to the final jury verdict on 5 June 1989, the DeShano criminal trial demonstrated the difficulty of litigating insider trading cases. For the defense, there was the presupposition of guilt in the jurors' minds to be overcome. For the prosecution, a case based on circumstantial evidence is always risky.

The judge's instruction to the jury had explicated the elements that constitute insider trading. Essentially, the jurors were required to find, beyond a reasonable doubt, that the defendant (1) was a corporate insider, (2) was in possession of nonpublic material information, (3) used and relied on that information, and (4) intended to defraud. It was primarily the third and fourth elements that led the jurors to reach a verdict of not guilty.

When DeShano took the stand, he denied that he sold his stock because of the unfavorable preliminary report; instead, he claimed that he had intended to sell weeks before but had procrastinated. It was argued by the defense that DeShano was a numbers cruncher; he was not in a position to step back and view the entire picture, nor was he able to forecast the drastic decline in the stock price from the limited information he possessed. One of the jurors countered this position with his own analysis of the situation:

> My argument against that was . . . that he could have almost done it in his head. You can look at your checkbook and you don't have to run it all the way through to know that you've got a lot less money than you had a month ago at this time, not right to the dollar amount, but you know.[12]

In his summation to the jury, the defense attorney, David Wiechert, explained that the case is "as complicated as the human mind. You have to determine what he [DeShano] was thinking when he sold his stock."[13] The jury took this advice to heart.

One of the jurors, who originally had voted for guilt, reflected:

> I relented only because one of the elements that the judge had instructed us on, as a prerequisite for a guilty finding, was something that couldn't possibly be reached. It was asking us for a smoking gun and there was no such thing possible. . . . In the instructions to the jury, Judge Tashima pointed out that we would have to conclude he [DeShano] had used it [the preliminary report] in his decision to sell. And, of course, that's an impossibility. I mean how can we presuppose what went on in his mind?[14]

The same juror later added, "The last element, of course, was that he did in fact use it in determining whether to sell his stock. And that was the one that stopped everybody, because, like I say, you can't delve into the man's mind."[15]

The consensus appeared to be that the circumstantial evidence presented was not sufficient to judge that DeShano had a guilty mind. Another juror stated, "Nobody saw him [DeShano]. Nobody knew what he was thinking. That's what broke the jurors down."[16] The acquittal, my interviews indicated, was the result of the jury's inability to determine positively that DeShano was aware of the drastic fiscal implications of the preliminary report and that he used this information in his decision to sell.

This ambivalence on the part of the jury is significant particularly in light of a statement made by the judge in *Herman and MacLean v. Huddleston:*

> The proof . . . required in fraud cases is often a matter of inference from circumstantial evidence. If anything, the difficulty of proving the defendant's state of mind supports a lower standard of proof [lower than a preponderance of the evidence]. In any event, we have noted elsewhere that circumstantial evidence can be more than sufficient.[17]

This and other court decisions allow intent to be liberally inferred from the circumstantial evidence presented,[18] but the jury in the DeShano case chose not to do so.

Often, nonlegal characteristics of the offender, such as socioeconomic status, moral character, and severity of the possible sentence, may induce juror sympathy and leniency. The finding on whether socioeconomic status has an effect on juror judgment is inconclusive,[19] however, juror responses indicate that DeShano's class was noted. One juror described the defendant's appearance in court as follows: "[DeShano] was well presented, [a] calm, serene individual. . . . He was likable. Both he and his wife presented themselves as a very nice mid-aged couple. I think that impressed everybody."[20]

The moral character of the defendant also was raised by the jurors in the interviews. Studies have found that a defendant's emotional demeanor is influential in a judgment of conviction; those who suffer or appear remorseful may be treated more leniently.[21] An example of this sentiment was expressed by a juror who stated, "I think justice being done in this world, if it ever is, I think it was done in this case because I really think that Al DeShano is the kind of person that suffered . . . over this thing."[22] Moreover, at least one juror may have had sympathy for the defendant because he could picture himself in a similar situation. One of the jurors, commenting on the attitude of another juror, explained, "He made it look like it was okay for [DeShano] to do that because he was a white-collar worker and he might do it, too. He might have done it."[23]

Finally, the five-year maximum prison term that DeShano possibly faced may have swayed some individuals. Krupa has shown that jurors are less likely to convict where the prosecutoral evidence was weak, the prescribed punishment severe, and the final sentence outside of their control.[24] A juror commented:

> We talked about that in the jury room . . . what would they do to him in a case like this. We couldn't possibly see a prison sentence, for instance. I think perhaps that may have been uppermost in the minds of some of those who were [for] not guilty in the beginning, who just couldn't see [giving him] a strong life-changing kind of punishment [that would cause a] loss of a job and all the rest of it. I think they were thinking more along the lines of the punishment situation.[25]

The jury was able to justify its decision to acquit based on the evidence presented. They did not feel the prosecutor established beyond a reasonable doubt that DeShano used the information in the preliminary report in his decision to sell the stock. Yet, factored into the conversion toward an acquittal were several extralegal variables: the socioeconomic status of the defendant, his demeanor at the trial, and the length of the potential prison sentence.

Motivations for Prosecuting DeShano

There are several factors the SEC considers before it decides to pursue a case. In her analysis of SEC docket investigations, Shapiro lists the following elements, among others: (1) recurrence of the offense, (2) recency, (3) nature of the offense, (4) amount of money involved, (5) culpability, and (6) strength of evidence. Shapiro found that the prior record of investigated offenders was unrelated to the likelihood of SEC prosecution.[26] The Karcher case exemplifies these findings; the extent of the illegal activity, the total of 16 persons charged, and the sum of money involved, $314,000, amounted to sufficient reason for the SEC to devote three years of resource-intensive labor to the case. An added incentive was the publicity that the Karcher name guaranteed.

The SEC generally refers cases to the Department of Justice for consideration of criminal charges. Such was the situation with DeShano. He was the only individual in the case not connected to the Karcher family by blood or marriage. There was no denial that DeShano had access to the confidential preliminary report and that he had read it. Einhorn, the regional administrator of the SEC, stated that DeShano "had the books in front of him and he acted on that information. The rest who traded are either tippees or tippers, and they aren't company employees."[27] DeShano himself perceived the strength of the case against him, stating, "They [the SEC] thought that it would be a good lead case because it was different. They thought because I actually sold they had more [of an] ability to prove that I was guilty."[28] But he also added that both he and the Karchers felt "all along that I was being used as a scapegoat to get to them [the Karchers]. . . . No one knows me, but they sure know his [Carl Karcher's] name."[29] The defense counsel, a former assistant U.S. attorney, reflecting on why the Department of Justice brought the criminal case against DeShano, stated, "They wanted to bring an insider trading case. It's a high priority. There haven't been many in the office."[30]

When taken on its own merit, out of the context of the Karcher family trades, the DeShano case appeared petty and inconsequential. Here was a man who was depicted by witnesses as honest and loyal, who, by all appearances, had never traded on inside information before, and whose loss avoided amounted to only $7107. Small cases such as this may be advantageous from a deterrence standpoint, conveying the message to the community that the district attorney will prosecute small-time offenders. But, as one of DeShano's defense attorneys remarked,

> if you want to use that as a goal of the prosecution, the deterrence aspect, then you've got to pick a case that's a strong case because if you lose it then you may have the opposite effect. The word may go out that you can't even win the little one.[31]

The jurors did not view this case as particularly strong; there was no eyewitness testimony as to DeShano's intent. They could only infer it from the circumstantial evidence presented in court. A juror remarked:

> It was a case that I wondered why the government brought in the first place. . . . I think everybody should be prosecuted . . . [when there is] sufficient evidence to bring a case. But I don't think that, in this case for instance, they were wisely using the taxpayers' money to bring this case unless they had something more to go on than they did.[32]

The Department of Justice believed it had a strong case. Circumstantial evidence, such as that presented in this case, had been sufficient in the past to return a guilty finding. DeShano was an insider who sold stock after he received the preliminary report. But, when there is only circumstantial evidence, the jury must infer the thought process of the defendant based solely on the timing of the stock trade and the information he had available. Although arguably the strongest case, taken by itself, out of the context of the Karcher family trades, the DeShano trade appeared insignificant. In light of the blatant abuse of inside information by individuals such as Boesky, the case against DeShano made the jury question the prudence of the government's decision to prosecute.

◂ Settlements with the SEC ▸

The Karcher family civil trial was set for May of 1989. Numerous defense motions had been filed, including one to have the case dismissed and another to try each Karcher separately. The motions served to tie up SEC resources and undoubtedly enriched the Karcher attorneys. As the trial date approached, two of the three lawyers of the SEC's litigation department were devoting their full attention to the case. But there was no trial.

Donald Karcher and those he allegedly tipped settled the civil charges with the SEC in February of 1989. The six defendants agreed to pay a total of $187,560 to settle their portion of the case. This included disgorgement of the loss avoided by those trading, with fines of the same amount, and a fine of $62,520 for Donald and his wife: All the defendants consented to an injunction from future securities violations.

The cases against the other Karchers were based primarily on circumstantial evidence: Carl had talked with his children during this time frame and they all sold their securities around the same time. An SEC lawyer later stated, after an unsuccessful defense motion to dismiss charges against the family, "They've never been able to explain what it was that triggered those sales. It's a little too much to believe that they coincidentally all decided to dump their stock on the same weekend."[33] The Karcher children claimed that they had personal financial reasons for selling more than $1 million worth of stock in the days before the announcement.

On 2 May 1989, the day the Karcher trial was to begin and more than a year after the complaint had been first filed by the SEC, headway was being made toward a settlement. Wes Howell, Carl Karcher's attorney, explained:

> The money we're talking about is not going to make an enormous amount of difference [to Karcher]. [But] he was seeing his whole family being swept up. . . . He was seeing his company, with all of the principal executives, being subpoenaed. . . . And I couldn't promise him that he'd win.[34]

Before the SEC settlement could be completed, however, Karcher wanted assurance that the Department of Justice would not later file criminal charges. In July, the final settlement was reached, and it was formalized in August 1989. Karcher and the remaining family members neither admitted nor denied guilt. The stipulations in the consent agreement included an injunction from violating the insider trading regulations, disgorgement from the tippees of a total of $332,122 in profit, in addition to fines totaling the same amount, and $332,122 in fines for Carl Karcher. An SEC attorney pointed out that this settlement was fairly standard for insider trading cases.[35]

A *Los Angeles Times* interview with Karcher's attorney, Thomas Holliday, revealed that, "by settling the case, Karcher chose to avoid both the emotional and financial costs of a trial. . . .'We had a winnable case,' Holliday said, 'but the monetary cost, in terms of lawyers and personal impact on the family, far outweighed the desire to win' at trial."[36]

Alvin DeShano formally settled the SEC civil charges against him in August of 1989. While neither admitting nor denying guilt, he agreed to an injunction against future insider trading infractions and consented to a disgorgement of $12,386, the amount he saved, plus interest, by selling the stock, in addition to a fine for the same amount.

◂ Conclusion ▸

The Karcher case study sheds light on the difficulties encountered when prosecuting either a civil or criminal white-collar crime. It was through the computer surveillance program at NASD that the Karcher trades were initially discovered. The case was then turned over to the SEC, which decided to investigate and file a complaint against those involved. Proactive market surveillance is one of the most frequently used insider trading detection techniques, but, at the same time, it has the greatest inaccuracy rate.[37] Approximately 0.6 percent of the initial inquiries made by self-regulatory organizations, such as the New York Stock Exchange or NASD, into anomalies detected by their surveillance strategies were referred to the SEC for the fiscal years 1985 and 1986. Of these 468 insider trading referrals, only 45, approximately 10 percent, resulted in SEC enforcement actions.[38] The Karcher case was one of the few that made it to the final stage of the process.

As affluent, prominent members of the community, the Karchers were able to engage the SEC in numerous pretrial motions. In the end, Carl Karcher was not prosecuted criminally, and, like most white-collar defendants, agreed to the sentence without admitting or denying guilt. By settling the case, both the SEC and the defendants avoided the time-consuming, resource-draining alternative of a trial. Yet, because of the reluctance of the trial judge in the Carl Leo Karcher case to use the treble penalties available under the ITSA, the defendants who settled with the SEC were financially penalized to a greater extent than the only defendant sentenced by the court.

The criminal prosecution of DeShano, in which his stock sale was examined by itself and not in the context of the other Karcher trades, appears trivial and insignificant when compared to more heinous criminal offenses. Ordinarily, though, a theft of approximately $7000 by a street criminal would be considered egregious. The average loss from robbery in 1987, for instance, was $447, with only 6 percent of the completed robberies involving property valued at more than $1000.[39]

Unlike a bank robbery, however, where the offense is not debated, the prosecutor in insider trading cases must prove that an offense was indeed committed. The complexities of the definition of the offense and the reliance on circumstantial evidence are common problems that prosecutors of white-collar crime must overcome. What looked like the strongest case for the government resulted in a not-guilty finding, leaving jurors questioning the wisdom of allocating resources to the prosecution of this offense.

◂ NOTES ▸

1 U.S. Congress, House Committee on Energy and Commerce, *Insider Trading and Securities Fraud Enforcement Act* of 1988, Report no. 100-910, 100th Congress, 2d Sess., 1988, p. 8.

2 Eric Shine, "A Little Bell Set Carl Karcher Probe in Motion," *Los Angeles Times*, April 15, 1985.

3 Mary Ann Galante, "Karcher: Cloudy Chapter in Horatio Alger Success Story," *Los Angeles Times*, April 15, 1988.

4 Gary G. Lynch et al., "Recent SEC Enforcement Developments." In *Insider Trading, Fraud, and Fiduciary Duty under the Federal Securities Laws*. Washington, DC: American Law Institute, American Bar Association, 1 (1989):508.

5 David A. Vise and Steve Coll, *Eagle on the Street*. New York: Charles Scribner's Sons, 1991, p. 260.

6 Charges against Margaret Karcher were dropped in March 1989.

7 A margin account allows investors to buy securities on credit as long as they maintain a minimum amount of equity in their account. If the securities in the account drop in value, the brokerage firm may request that the investor provide more equity; this is known as a margin call.

8 Declaration of Carl Leo Karcher to the Securities and Exchange Commission, filed August 9, 1988, para. 5.

9 Mary Ann Galante, "Judge Rules Karcher Son Violated Stock Sale Laws," *Los Angeles Times*, September 13, 1988.

10 *Ibid.*

11 Theodore A. Levine, Arthur F. Mathews, and W. Hardy Callcott, "Current Legal Developments Affecting Insider Trading Enforcement Actions and Litigation 1988–1989," *Insider Trading, Fraud, and Fiduciary Duty*, 1 (1989):5.

12 Personal interview with juror.
13 *Ibid.*
14 *Ibid.*
15 *Ibid.*
16 *Ibid.*
17 459 U.S. 3759 384 (1983).
18 See John W. Bagby, "The Evolving Controversy over Insider Trading," *American Business Law Journal*, 24 (1986):571, 606–607.
19 Francis C. Dane and Lawrence S. Wrightsman, "Effects of Defendants' and Victims' Characteristics on Jurors' Verdicts." In Norbett L. Kerr and Robert M. Bray, eds., *The Psychology of the Courtroom*. New York: Academic Press, 1982.
20 Personal interview with juror.
21 Dane and Wrightsman, *op. cit.*
22 Personal interview with juror.
23 *Ibid.*
24 Martin F. Kaplan, "Cognitive Processes in the Individual Juror." In Kerr and Bray, *The Psychology of the Courtroom, op. cit.*
25 Personal interview with a juror.
26 Susan P. Shapiro, *Wayward Capitalists: Target of the Securities and Exchange Commission*. New Haven, CT: Yale University Press, 1984.
27 Mary Ann Galante, "Carl's Jr. Chief Accountant Charged with Stock Fraud," *Los Angeles Times*, February 17, 1989.
28 Personal interview with Alvin DeShano.
29 *Ibid.*
30 Personal interview with one of DeShano's defense attorneys.
31 *Ibid.*
32 Personal interview with a juror.
33 David Greenwald, "Karcher Denies Telling His Children to Sell Their Stock," *Orange County Register*, March 21, 1989.
34 Mary Ann Galante, "Tentative Settlement in Suit against Karchers," *Los Angeles Times*, March 21,1989.
35 Personal interview with an SEC attorney.
36 Mary Ann Galante, "Karchers Settle Insider-Trading Case with Fine," *Los Angeles Times*, July 25, 1989.
37 Shapiro, *op. cit.*
38 U.S. General Accounting Office, *Securities Regulations: Efforts to Detect, Investigate, and Deter Insider Trading*. Washington, DC: General Accounting Office, 1988.
39 U.S. Department of Justice, Bureau of Justice Statistics, *Special Report: Robbery Victims*. Washington, DC: Department of Justice, April 1987.

8

Telemarketing Fraud

Who Are the Tricksters and What Makes Them Trick?

Jeffrey H. Doocy
David Shichor
Dale K. Sechrest
Gilbert Geis

Telemarketing fraud constitutes a business transaction that is proscribed by the criminal law because the seller has overstepped what have been legislatively and judicially established as acceptable limits of merchandizing truthfulness. Permissible selling rules today are more restrictive than they were in earlier times. A seventeenth-century English judge, for instance, was taken aback when asked to decide so obvious a question as whether B should be punished because he took advantage of the credulity of A. Of course not, he ruled.[1]

Telemarketing fraud differs only in degree from legitimate telemarketing salesmanship, and other sales practices in which high-

Reprinted from *Security Journal* 14:3 (2001). Perpetuity Press publishes the *Security Journal*, and can be contacted at P.O. Box 376, Leicester LE2 1UP, UK, email info@perpetuitypress.co.uk, phone + 44 116 221 7778.

pressure tactics that prey upon human weakness abound.[2] It is a crime to categorically promise persons at the other end of a telephone line that they will receive a 33 percent annual return after they invest in your oil drilling enterprise if you have no legitimate basis for specifying that level of gain. The offense is particularly egregious, of course, if the oil well or a site for it does not exist. Essential to making the transaction an offense is the buyer's reliance upon false information as a basis for the purchase. For a sales pitch to meet the law's requirements, a potential customer should be informed about all the material facts concerning the product and its purveyors that might influence him or her not to part with money. It is not a crime, however, if you subtly suggest that unspecified wealth (and the marvelous sequelae that accompany it) await the person who hops upon the investment train before its imminent departure from the station. It is often subtlety compared to outright lies that marks the dividing line between an acceptable and a criminal marketing pitch.

Determination of criminality in telemarketing schemes is somewhat complicated by the common-law doctrine of mens rea, that insists—though with ever-expanding exceptions—that to be guilty of a crime one must have a guilty mind; that is, in our context, the perpetrator must be aware that the sales tactic is deceptive. This requirement can make it difficult to secure criminal convictions, though it is a rare telemarketing fraudster who remains unaware for very long, if at all, that lies are being fed to the person being hustled by phone.

As evidence of their awareness that they are complicit in an illegal enterprise, scammers (who sometimes refer to themselves as "wallet surgeons") will on occasion adopt aliases, so that if there is a callback complaint the customer can be told that the person being sought no longer works there. In fact, an experienced seller, in a procedure dubbed "the recovery room," may say that the salesperson was fired because he was mishandling transactions, and that for a certain sum the person who has answered the phone will be able to make it up to the customer for previous losses.

If as a symbolic anodyne gesture the company pays out a slight return on investment, top-notch salespersons strive to have that sum reinvested. "Not one person who invested with me over twenty years—and people invested millions and millions of dollars—ever saw a return on their money," a veteran salesperson told an interviewer. "If they ever got their initial investment back, I'd convince them to put it into something else."[3]

Almost invariably, it should be noted, it is a sales*man* who is doing the lying, though women, who typically do the clerical work for the scammers, will sometimes also be prosecuted if they were actively and knowingly compliant in the swindles.

Aliases are also employed to transmute ethnic-appearing names into blander Anglo forms. In one such case, Steven Samuel Weinstein became "Steven West," Debra Horowitz announced herself as "Debra Hall," and Edward Gottlieb was "Ed Graham."[4] Besides providing camouflage, the adopted names clearly attempt to neutralize resistance based, in this case, on possible antisemitic prejudices among potential investors.

This article seeks to fill gaps in criminological scholarship by focusing on persons who engage in telemarketing fraud. There is a considerable literature that offers advice, particularly to older people, on how to protect themselves from being gulled.[5] Portraits of the victims of such frauds are also relatively abundant,[6] but very little is known about the tactics and the traits of those who engage in telemarketing fraud, beyond an excellent monograph by Stevenson,[7] who partly financed his graduate studies by working for nine years in both legitimate and outlaw telemarketing organizations on the U.S. east coast. Stevenson's work tends toward the experiential, and he too points out that there is not much research literature on telemarketing fraudsters.[8] Our aim is to build upon the foundation Stevenson lays by looking more intently and systematically at those engaged in the trade, in terms of matters such as demographics and work style, and tying these findings to related social science axioms and theories, particularly those in the realm of white-collar crime and confidence games.

Our eclectic approach derives its scientific justification from a chapter in a classic book on research methods by Webb et al.[9] In its entirety, the chapter reads:

> We must use all available weapons of attack, face our problems realistically, and not retreat to the land of fashionable sterility, learn to sweat over our data with an admixture of judgment and intuitive imagination, and accept the usefulness of particular data even when the level of analysis for them is markedly below that for other data in the empirical area.

The victim's active involvement distinguishes telemarketing fraud from street crimes such as burglary and robbery, offenses in which the victim is either absent or passive and unwilling. Rape, like most street offenses (though not statutory rape), also has a nonconsenting victim, though seduction for purposes of sexual intercourse is, within specified and wide limits, permissible and in some respects resembles telemarketing tactics. The telemarketing fraudster can have his way with the victim only if the victim agrees. As has been observed of this form of fraud: "In the great majority of cases, we are confronted with crimes which require affirmative acts of cooperation by victims before the fraud can be completed."[10]

The offense can be seen as a clash of wills, with the perpetrator seeking by various ruses to impose his/her definition of the situation upon a person, almost invariably a total stranger, who has become entangled in a relationship that is not face-to-face and that has rarely been anticipated. On the other hand, since the prospective victim (or "mooch" or sometimes "mullet" in telemarketing fraud language) is in his/her own home a false sense of security may exist.

◂ BACKGROUND ▸

Confidence games of diverse sorts have been with us since history has been recorded. In American literature, Herman Melville's allegorical novel, *The Confidence Man* (1857) tells of scammers who operate on a Mississippi steamboat, trying to interest passengers in such fictitious entities as the "Seminole Widow and Orphan Asylum," the "Protean Easy Chair," and the "Samaritan Pain Dissuader."[11] Similarly, O. Henry, who had served prison time for embezzlement, wrote about fellow inmates, such as Andy who "grifted a dollar whenever he saw one that had a surplus look about it." Andy, Henry writes, "used to devise schemes of money-making so fraudulent and high-financial they wouldn't have been allowed in the by-laws of a railroad."[12] In the criminological literature, the classic work was done by a linguist, who focused not only on the argot of swindlers but also on the details of their tactics.[13] More recently, Dornstein has described the "swoop and squat" schemes that arose soon after the advent of automobiles.[14]

Illegal telemarketing sales pitches come under the general category of fraud, which has been succinctly defined as "the art of deception for gain."[15] Nonetheless, the law does not specifically say what is fraudulent behavior. One judge noted, rather pedantically, that the law "does not define fraud; it needs no definition, it is as old as falsehood and as venerable as human ingenuity."[16] The elements of telemarketing fraud have been defined by the U.S. Department of Justice as a "plan, program, promotion, or campaign that is conducted to induce purchases of goods or services, or participation in a contest or sweepstakes, by use of one or more interstate telephone calls initiated . . . by a person who is conducting the plan, program, or campaign . . ."[17]

Most illegal schemes rely on the mails to collect funds from purchasers of their product, which for purposes of prosecution brings them under the federal mail fraud statute, the nation's oldest consumer protection law.[18] Mail fraud has recently been expanded in the United States to cover not only the postal service but also private systems such as UPS and FedEx.[19] (Use of the mails is usually essential in that most schemes operate interstate, since their victims are likely to contact local authorities who will be handcuffed from taking effective action against a far-distant operation.) Besides, a handful of states now ban the use of couriers to pick up checks at victims' houses.

There are an estimated 140,000 telemarketing firms in the United States and they generate higher annual sales than magazines, yellow pages, radio, television, and direct-mail advertising.[20] About 10 percent of telemarketers are believed to engage in fraudulent activities (American Association of Retired Persons, 1998).[21] Americans are said to lose about $40 billion a year to the fraudulent organizations, though only one in 10,000 victims are believed to report their loss to the authorities, often because they are too embarrassed at having been duped.[22]

Telemarketers are different from other salespersons in the sense that they do not have a face-to-face contact with their prospective customers, only a "voice-to-voice" contact. Telemarketing is also different from mail order sales, because it does establish a personal contact, albeit not a visual one. In a previous article by three of the present authors, the victims of an investment fraud scheme conducted through telemarketing reported that the most decisive point in their investing was the persuasiveness of the telemarketer.[23] It is easier for telemarketers than for traditional con men to defraud their victims because the former do not have to worry about their appearance and can easily alter their voices and use other ways of tricking their potential victims.[24] In addition, it may be easier for salespersons to make fraudulent claims and statements, and to use bold tactics, if they are not facing their "marks." Finally, it is easier to reach large numbers of potential victims through the telephone than by personal contact.

◂ Working the Scam ▸

Goffman has suggested that any social establishment may be studied profitably from the point of view of "impression management."[25] In telemarketing scams, using his terminology, we have "performers" who "present to an audience a given definition of a situation." Goffman points out that there is often a back room where the performance is orchestrated and a front room where it is put into action. For telemarketing fraud the staging protocol is almost invariably reversed: the performance is scripted in comfortable offices while the work is performed in cluttered cell-like rooms.

In another classic contribution, Goffman discussed "cooling the mark out," that is, getting aggrieved customers to accept their fate with some degree of equanimity—or, at least, not to report to the authorities what has befallen them.[26] This, too, is an important consideration in telemarketing schemes. Given the number of victims, however, it is generally impossible to calm all of them effectively, so that hit-and-run tactics will typically be substituted; that is, after operating for a while, a scam will take on a new identity and relocate to new quarters.

To be successful, a telemarketer typically requires verbal skills and an ability to improvise, though the basic pitch and the recommended responses to customer questions are often provided to the sales staff by those who direct the scam. Typical are the canned responses that were part of a haul seized by one of the authors during a raid on a telescam operation. An excerpt from the script book conveys the nature of the process:

> If the customer says, "I don't like doing business over the phone," the following response is recommended: "If doing business over the phone is difficult for you, I can certainly empathize with you. It is difficult for me as well. However, business lives on the phone. If it is a national and international business, millions of dollars are transacted daily by phone. I know for a fact that there are literally thousands of investors, much like yourself, who are making between $50,000 and $100,000 from business consummated over the phone. A $20,000 investment is not a lot of money and it can't hurt you financially. So I'm asking you to give me just one percent of your confidence and the opportunity to earn the other 99 percent. Let me prove to you what I can do for you and base all future activity on the results I get for you. Fair enough?"[27]

Similarly, an undercover agent working a case in New York told a court that he had surreptitiously taped the following training talk by a manager to members of his sales force:

> You tell them, "I've been trying to get you all week. Listen, I've got some good news." Don't give them a chance to say, "Well, I've been home." Create the urgency. "We're wrapping up the promotion this evening, we need to know tonight." You have to be tough with these people on the phone; you cannot have any compassion for these people whatsoever.

The manager scolded his workers in a way that made the victims appear to be the traducers: "You still put up with the same bullshit excuses from these people," he said. "You shouldn't, there's no reason to."[28]

Scripted material provides responses to virtually any resistance the customer might put up. If a mooch says that he needs to talk to his wife, he is told that he is undoubtedly more knowledgeable about such things than she is, that he got where he is today by being decisive, not weak. If he objects that he is putting his money on an unknown thing, he is reminded that at one time McDonalds, Microsoft, and other winners also were unknowns. The salesperson says that he/she seeks only to make solid purchases on behalf of his/her customers so that they will give him repeat business.[29]

In many respects successful sales talents are similar to those of the successful actor: an ability to convince others that you are what you truly are not, and to have them believe that the lines you speak are truths. In fact, southern California scammers sometimes hire out-of-work actors to staff their phone lines. Actors are also more readily able to play multiple parts, such as the floor manager or the director, when they pretend that they must first secure permission to make a particular sale. Like missionaries who seek to proselytize people who are otherwise-inclined theologically, telemarketers have to win over persons who almost invariably are initially hostile and suspicious. Perhaps it was not altogether chance that a person interviewed by the present authors, the manager of a telemarketing scam, told us that his ambition as a young man had been to enter the ministry.

Salespersons also sometimes carefully frame what they say so that customers cannot later use their words to prove them dishonest. One veteran telemarketing cheater notes that he never tells customers they can sell the stock being offered because he knows they cannot: "You just tell him he can liquidate. Sell means you need a buyer, but what the hell does liquidate mean? Liquefy it or what?"[30]

Usually, the salespersons (called "yaks" in the trade) are ingratiating and smooth. With women they will employ a considerable number of "dears" in their sales pitch. One 81-year-old woman, swindled out of thousands of dollars, remembers being told that she couldn't be a day over 45. A salesperson "almost always takes on an image of a caring child," one enforcement officer says. "That is very tantalizing to older people."[31] To older folks, salespeople are likely to say "sir" or "ma'am" and "please" and "thank you."

At times, salespeople, if they sense that it might prove effective, can turn mean, particularly when they sense that older people are not up to direct confrontations. They will belabor the selfishness of a prospective customer who by not participating is depriving grandchildren of an adequate inheritance. One telemarketer of a phony product is reported to have told a nonparticipating customer that he would regret his failure to buy for the remainder of his life.

There are a number of job advantages attached to telemarketing from what are called "boiler rooms," a term first used in the 1920s when stock swindles were literally operated from phone lines placed in basements.[32] In return for a six-hour day on the phone, some salespersons can average $30,000 a week, plus cash bonuses known as "spills."[33] In the "Two Daves" scheme (see below) that was the particular focus of the present authors' work, it was said that the sellers got to keep between 30 and 40 percent of the income they generated. If you have the sales talent it matters not what your credentials look like when you seek a telemarketing job. For another thing, the work atmosphere is notably tolerant, usually marked by irregular working hours, a wide variety of dress styles, and, often, some offbeat worldviews and personalities. Salespeople tend to come and go, their departures triggered by inadequate sales records and/or dissatisfaction with the demands of the role. Job performance is readily measurable, though various management maneuvers can enhance or frustrate selling success. Managers, for instance, often know which lists are likely to produce the most buyers and they can assign those lists to favorites, while giving a much tougher roster to those newcomers or those they want to jettison from the sales force.[34]

Salespeople typically work for forty minutes and then take twenty minutes off. The ambiance of some operations has been described in the following terms: Inside the boiler room the din is ear-numbing. Hyped-up salespeople often pace back and forth, speaking intensely into the telephones while a tape deck booms out disco. A bell rings every time a sale is made. None of this commotion is audible to the customers because boiler-room phones are equipped with "confidencers"—devices that screen out background noise.[35]

A favorite disco tune is Billy Joel's *Easy Money*, which contains the line: "Someone's got a fortune they're begging me to take." Inventive sellers may create sound effects, first developed in radio broadcasting, that they feed into the phone. They will beat on staplers to duplicate the noise of a teletype machine, or place their head inside a drawer and tell the customer that they are calling from inside the company vault.[36]

The "Two Daves" Telemarketing Enterprise

The telemarketing operation that we will scrutinize was known as the "Two Daves" line of business because of the similar first names of both principals. In 1985, the California Department of Corporations (DOC) had investigated a number of operations spawned by David Kane (a third Dave). A federal civil suit had resulted in the closure of Kane's operations, but many of his salespeople subsequently established similar kinds of scams, which relied on lists of potential investors that Kane had purchased.

The two leading breakaway salesmen were David H. Bryant and David C. Knight. Within a year, the DOC issued Desist and Refrain Orders and obtained a Permanent Injunction against Bryant and Knight and their company, Parker Bryant, Inc., barring them from selling securities in California. Nonetheless, complaints about the company and its offshoots continued to accumulate. Four years later—in 1990—a corollary investigation found that shares in oil and gas limited and/or general partnerships had been sold nationwide by ten aligned organizations, twenty securities broker-dealer firms, and 187 separate investment programs, all under the control of the two Daves. The companies had made about 12,000 unlawful sales to about 9,000 persons and collected between $150 and $200 million. Customers received an average return of ten cents on every dollar invested. The DOC report noted the failure of the earlier restraining order and suggested that only a criminal conviction would be likely bring the operation to an end.

It was pointed out that leases acquired with funds raised by the companies were not retained by them but were assigned to other entities owned by Bryant and Knight, and monies were commingled in these diverse firms. Investors were of course kept in ignorance of the fact that not only California but also Oregon, New Mexico, Arizona, and Iowa had issued cease and desist orders against the companies, and that innumerable lawsuits had been filed against the owners and various of their businesses.

Early in 1991, the DOC filed a civil suit, *The People v. Parker-Bryant* against the two Daves.[37] The state was awarded a judgment of $212 million against Bryant and co-owners in the civil trial, the largest award granted in a California gas and oil swindle.

But the criminal case had rattled about long enough for the statute of limitations to preclude the filing of either state or federal charges. As the case was finally being prepared to go forward, the accountant who was scheduled to testify for the state died, and the authorities felt unable to go ahead without his testimony.

In July of 1997, the California Supreme Court turned down Bryant's petition for review of the civil judgment still outstanding against him. Earlier, the court of appeal had held that the judgment was properly decided and had rejected Bryant's and his colleagues' contention that they were denied due process because frozen funds were not released to pay for their defense and because the trial had proceeded despite their filing for bankruptcy.[38]

The adverse finding hardly put an end to Bryant's telemarketing career. Two years later, the DOC was back in court seeking the appointment of a receiver to try to recover assets from Performance Development, Inc., a multimillion dollar enterprise that had raised $58 million from about 2,000 California investors by telling them that it was purchasing the right to collect debts owed to financial institutions at basement prices, and that it could make fine profits by recovering the face value of these debts. The company, run by Bryant's cousin, did reasonably well, buying debts owed to credit card companies for about 1 percent of their face value and collecting about 11 percent of the total. But it was not returning the profits to investors. Bryant, who was never mentioned in the company's literature or sales pitch, was nonetheless responsible for negotiations with some persons who owed money to the firm. He used the name of David Welsh, a not uninteresting pseudonym given his past record.

The receiver named by the court had served with some success in a similar role in the Parker-Bryant imbroglio. In that case (according to the DOC petition), he had had to contend with difficult, obstructive personalities who had hidden assets, concealed and commingled millions of dollars, and defrauded thousands of investors.

The case against Performance Development later took an odd twist when the state, in the words of a newspaper report, "dropped their case . . . and agreed to walk away from a legal morass."[39] Performance Development's founder called the decision a vindication and said that he would seek to remove the company from control of the bankruptcy trustee. The state said that it had stepped aside because it had achieved its purpose by drying up new investments in Performance Development and that the matter could better be dealt with by the federal bankruptcy court. For his part, the owner planned to resume sales as soon as possible, saying that he was certain he could in time adequately compensate investors.

Modus Operandi

Potential investors in companies operated by the two Daves were told that what was being offered were "great deals that could not fail" and "risk-free investments." Their names had been secured from list-compiling firms that identify persons believed to have disposable income. Potential customers routinely were cold-called. The sellers were fueled by an awareness that theirs was a statistical enterprise: like baseball batters, they would succeed only in a relatively small percentage of cases. They much preferred customers who would hang up or abruptly terminate the interchange to those, called "strokers," who would string them along and waste time that could be used to hook a real sucker. The general estimate is that about two or three persons out of one hundred will fall for the scam. Those possible buyers who showed interest were told to hurry, to make up their minds quickly because others desired to get in on this attractive deal and there was only limited room on the bandwagon.

In most cases, nonetheless, no attempt was made on the initial call to obtain money. The salesperson sought primarily to determine whether potential customers were in a financial position to participate in the scheme. If so, they were sent elegant promotional materials that were prominently labeled: “Confidential Private Placement.” If the customer wanted to check with others, he/she was referred to a “singer,” an accomplice masquerading as a satisfied customer. There were nonetheless some persons—called “lay-downs”—who could be hooked on the first try.

Before hanging up, the broker would tell potential customers to write down questions about the material that they were being sent: these would be discussed during a later telephone conversation. The second call generally came about a week later, the prospect having been given time to read the offering brochure. The sales pitch typically involved a friendly mix of warm greetings and contrived small talk, followed by a rundown, one example of which could be about some “great acreage” sitting on the top of “huge oil reserves.” During the latter days of the scheme, investors who claimed that they did not have sufficient money to partake were referred to Manufacturer’s Hanover, a bank that was willing to make loans to persons with adequate collateral and whose cooperation provided the scam with considerable credibility.[40] The telemarketers would indicate that the loan could be repaid readily with the early dividends ($11 for every dollar paid in) from the investment.

Then came the closer: “Most of my clients have been taking five to ten units, but of course I leave that up to you. Can you handle five units, or would you want to consider a stronger position?” The salesperson him/herself was most often mentioned as the most compelling single reason for the investment.

Methodology

Further details about telemarketing scamming derive from an analysis of the characteristics and backgrounds of 162 salespersons (out of a total sales force of about 300), most of whom (83 percent) worked for six or more months during the period from 1984 to mid-1991 for one of the various incarnations of the two Daves’ oil and gas telemarketing schemes. Those we focused on had each generated more than $250,00 in gross sales during the period that the companies operated. As such, they represented the higher producers of this group of 300 telemarketers. Their records were available because California requires telemarketing salespersons to be registered and bonded. Illegitimate schemes find this requirement useful: being able to tell customers that they are registered with the state sends a (false) message that they are legitimate.

We gathered information about the background of the salespersons involved with the business operated by the “two Daves” from the Central Registration Depository (CRD), maintained since 1981 by the National Association of Securities Dealers (NASD). Recovering the data from this source was at times a frustrating challenge: indeed, the NASD is said currently to be spending millions of dollars to expand and, hopefully, to upgrade the information on the CRD. Many different persons and agencies reported information, which was placed onto the computer with varying degrees of thoroughness and, at times, with apparently arguable accuracy. So we were severely challenged to make sense of what was available to us. The information that we ultimately compiled, while clearly not meticulously exact, offers a basis for what we see as important insights into practitioners of telemarketing fraud.

The data with which we worked also included, for the 162 persons we had selected, their age, gender, the number of positions they had held, and the months they had stayed on each job. The average number of jobs for each subject was computed by dividing the total of jobs held by the number of possible working years since the age of 18.

We also calculated the number and type of alleged violations of the law charged against the salespersons and the sanctions imposed. The 46 offenses found in the records were placed into one of three categories: (a) drug/alcohol; (b) crimes; and (c) trading offenses, including bankruptcy. The very last, of course, is not a violation of the law, but in California at least it is often a tactic used to avoid the consequences of reckless money management.

Drug offenses were in nine categories, including marijuana possession, driving under the influence of drugs, and possession of drugs for sale. The crime roster also covered nine illegal acts, such as grand theft, rape, robbery, and assault with a deadly weapon. There were 61 separate trading offenses; the most common were misrepresentation, sale of unregistered securities, and working without a license.

Major limitations of the study were the problems of working with existing records and our inability to get an adequate response to a mail survey of these individuals. The number of interviews obtained was also quite small, although we feel that the responses were representative of this group of telemarketing scammers.

Findings

We had known that salespersons involved in the schemes of the "two Daves" tended to be young recent transplants to southern California. They were paid a certain percentage of their sales totals, so that there was little to be lost by those in charge in taking on as large a number of employees as they could accommodate. Those who did not work out were rapidly terminated. Many of the salespersons were recruited by David Bryant, a recovering alcoholic, who met them at Alcoholics Anonymous meetings. Our record search uncovered the following information:

Age and Work History Age was computed for the subjects based on the midpoint of the scam period, which was mid-July 1988; the period of the scam was about 1984 to 1992. Age by gender is shown in Table 1 below: 154 (95.1 percent) were males and eight were females, a ratio that may eventually rise with increases in the proportion of women in higher-paying jobs. The mean age of the group was 34.6 years. The women tended to be somewhat older, with a mean age of 38 compared to 34.4 for the men.[41]

The study population seemed to be extraordinarily mobile vocationally. For all subjects, the average number of jobs held since age 18 was 12.9, with a median of 13. The average amount of time spent on any job was little more than a year—14.6 months.

The remainder of our review of the records seconded Stevenson's conclusion that the dialers were marginalized middle-class persons: "[O]ffice workers who are more comfortable with a cup of coffee and a tall tale than a lunch pail and a few quick beers."[42]

Other jobs that they had held generally involved lower-echelon positions in places that typically provide the worker with a cubicle and protection from outdoor weather cycles.

Table 1:
Age and Gender of Subjects (*n*=162)

	Age		
	Up to 33	**34 or Older**	**Total**
Male count	84	70	154
% within gender	54.5%	45.5%	100.0%
% within age	96.6%	93.3%	95.1%
Female count	3	5	8
% within gender	37.5%	62.5%	100.0%
% within age	3.4%	6.7%	4.9%
Total count	87	75	162
% within gender	53.7%	46.3%	100.0%
% within age	100.0%	100.0%	100.0%

Offense History A total of 349 different infractions was recorded for the group of salespersons we were studying. Of the 162 persons, 93 (57.4 percent) had had at least one action filed against them in their adult lifetime, while 69 had clean records in the state Department of Corporations files. The average for the 93 persons with actions against them was 3.75 offenses each (2.15 per person for the total 162 person sample). The three-category breakdown of offenses by members of our sample is shown in Table 2.

Table 2:
Types of Offenses (for 162 individuals)

	Frequency	Valid Percent	Cumulative Percent
Drugs/Alcohol	34	16.4	16.4
Criminal Offense	28	13.5	30.0
Trading Offense	145	70.0	100.0
Total	207	100.0	

The 211 actions taken in response to the offenses recorded varied considerably. In 13 percent of the cases there was some kind of settlement, though the records provide no indication of its nature. In 11 percent of the cases the charges were dropped, while 10 percent resulted in a fine, probation, community service, or some combination of these outcomes. In only four cases (1.9 percent) was there a restitution order. Cease and desist orders were issued to individuals in 8 percent of the cases. There were six cases (2.8 percent) involving criminal convictions. An additional 14 cases involved jail or prison time, though the records do not contain sufficient information about the charge that resulted in these penalties.

There were no statistically significant differences between the men and the (rather few) women in the sample on offense history. Nor, unexpectedly, were there significant differences in terms of age; that is, older members of the group did not show greater involvement in criminal activity. The older subjects, however, had a tendency to be involved in trading violations as opposed to violations in the other two categories.

The High Novelist Doris Lessing provides a significant clue to the dynamics that drive many telemarketing salespersons. She notes, regarding a con man who sought to exploit her, that: "His strength was—and I could feel just how powerful that strength was—this terrible, compelling anxiety that he should be able to force someone under his will . . .

It was almost as if he were pleading silently, in the moment when he was tricking a victim: Please let me trick you; please let me cheat you; I've got to, it's essential for me."[43] Friedrich Nietzsche also offered a classic statement of the dynamics of interpersonal power struggles that involve deception:

> In all great deceivers a remarkable process is at work, to which they owe their power. In the very act of deception with all its preparations . . . amid the whole effective scenario they are overcome by their belief in themselves; and it is this belief which then speaks so miraculously, so possessively, to their audience . . . For men believe in the truth of all that is seen to be firmly believed.[44]

To succeed, an organization must motivate those who work for it to buy into its ethos, whether they are involved in a legal or a criminal enterprise. As Cohen has observed: "Any organization must justify to its own members its claim upon them for loyalty, discipline, effort and sacrifice." It must also obtain acceptance, Cohen adds, "of the internal ordering of the enterprise, including the division of labor, authority, status, and distribution of rewards."[45]

In telemarketing fraud, the rainbow of high financial rewards is a considerable inducement to buy into the rules and tactics of the operation. The nature of the business—its challenge—also has strong appeal to many salespersons. The ability to impose one's will upon another person—and to obtain a measurable financial award for doing so—is highlighted in many of the reports of illegal telemarketing practices. During a training session for new employees, David Bryant put into words his ecstatic reaction to selling success:

> When I make a sale, it's like woooo. I'm like . . . Yes! I got addicted to it. I have to have it. It's like . . . more exciting than anything! To know that the money was on the table and it was a battle of wills and I won! Yeah! I backed the guy down. He woke up that day not expecting a call from me. The furtherest thing from his mind was to get into fucking oil and gas.

This will to power also contains a strong infusion of aggression and relies on metaphors of physical violence, as Bryant illustrates in this excerpt from a lecture to the newcomers on his sales force: "And to know that I made him do it!" he says. "That I got a hold of him and just ripped his thyroid out . . .[46]

Enforcement officials told us that sellers often have mirrors in the cubicles in which they work. They are told to look into the mirror and see the face of a hotshot salesperson. Sometimes there will be a motto on the wall, such as: "Each No gets me closer to the Yes

I want." Boiler room owners and managers—and Dave Bryant often did this—may put large bills on a bulletin board and say that the next sale or the highest total sales for the day will qualify for this extra reward. Often the sales people have to stand up when they consummate a transaction, so that the boss can note them and they can take pleasure in the achievement.[47]

Field Interview

Only one telemarketing executive of the many dozens we contacted by mail agreed to be interviewed. We presume that his operation was characteristic of many like it, though it clearly was up-scale in terms of the elegance of the southern California high-rise office building setting in which he and his colleagues dealt with a few customers face-to-face. The telephoning action was located elsewhere in the building and our several requests to observe it were deflected with the amiable comment that it would not really be worth our time.

The person we spoke to was a colleague of the one who had agreed to meet with us. Our man had gone home sick, with what we were told was a chronic stomach problem. The man we talked with was born in the Midwest and is now in his mid-30s. He had gone to junior college and then to a Bible college; his goal, never realized, had been to be a missionary in China. He was smooth, radiated self-confidence, and adroitly controlled our discussion.

When he moved to California, he got a job doing construction sales but did not like the constant car travel. His entry into telemarketing was with a company selling currency options, but he found the management "tyrannical" and the site "not a fun place to work." He said, "they were always pushing the upside" (that is, accentuating profits while ignoring increased risks). A major problem was that there were no repeat customers, since all but 5 percent of the investors lost their money. Those who ran the business, he told us, got ulcers; so did those who worked for them. He did not mention the psychosomatic reactions of customers who lost a great deal of money dealing with his company.

He had worked with the firm where he was presently employed as a "registered principal" for the past dozen or so years, and now mixed a small amount of sales work with management chores, including responsibility for locating lists of potential customers. Typically, a list sold for 50 cents for each name on it. His company markets limited partnerships, and investors must be "accredited" to put up $1 million, though the company was said to be organizing a program that would allow for an investment of one-quarter that amount. Almost all sales are made by telephone, a "more productive" approach. He prefers female customers, especially widows, because "they need the money." Persons with higher education levels who are employed are also good bets because they have more funds to invest. The most difficult customers, he indicated, were "Asians under 30."

The company uses an auto-dialer that has the capability to call 15,000 numbers daily. Each salesperson has a bank of four working phones. If by chance the telephoner gets two simultaneous answers, the machine automatically hangs up on one. They do not bother to redial persons who fail to answer or responses from answering machines. They are looking for a "live person." Optimal calling times to businesses are right before or after lunch; for CEOs right after five o'clock; for retirees from four to seven o'clock.

Of some 300 to 400 calls, there will be about 100 contacts "if you're lucky." Of those who answer the telephone, 60 to 70 percent are in no way interested, and half of the remainder are "not qualified." About ten will be sent information by mail. Perhaps there will be one sale in a cohort of this size.

We were told by the subject that he would not employ a person he does not trust: "If he lied to get a deal, he will do it again." The worst part of the job, he told us, was "work stress" that comes "when you know that what you're doing is right, you're doing it correctly, and nothing is happening." Why would this be happen? "It just does," he answered. These sorts of frustrations "submarine" (his invented verb) some salespeople out of the business.

No hint was conveyed that what he was doing might not be altogether legitimate; indeed, by word and appearance he conveyed the assured appearance of a most respectable entrepreneur. He granted that there were outliers in the business who violated the law and said that "better training procedures" were necessary to rein them in. He thought the government was a poor monitor of the industry: they do some things correctly, but outsiders like us "couldn't imagine some of the rules they make."

Not long after our interview the firm went into bankruptcy, and both he and the man we had the original appointment with became part of a new endeavor working out of the same offices. This too went bottom-up, and at this time both men are working in San Diego, rather far from their homes to the north, for a firm operated by a man trained in telemarketing sales by David Bryant.

Survey Results

Part of our research plan was to obtain questionnaire responses and interview information from a couple dozen salespersons who worked for the two Daves. This intention collapsed, however, when one of the authors, perhaps less zealously committed to the dictates of research than he was to the practice of honesty (especially on a probe that dealt with dishonesty), insisted that we had to put into the covering letter of our questionnaire that we had picked this person because he/she was a member of a company that had been the object of a civil suit. Unfortunately, we had also unthinkingly sent the questionnaires out with a covering letter on university Department of Criminal Justice stationery—much too obvious a warning signal about the nature of our quest.

Not surprisingly, of the 95 questionnaires we mailed, only three were returned completed. We had four others that were done during the pretest with persons known to be involved in oil and gas scams. Only two persons agreed to interviews, one of whom backed out when the time for our meeting came closer. On the telephone earlier, he had told us that he was very interested in talking about "the bad things in the industry." The results of the remaining interview are reported in the previous section.

That we could obtain only eight questionnaires for analysis was undoubtedly also a consequence of the targeted subjects' fear of either civil or criminal actions and their reluctance to talk about the shady aspects of their business. And, unfortunately, four of these had to be the pretests and one a phone interview, although we did not feel these significantly affected the responses.

Because of the low response rate, questionnaire answers were difficult to aggregate meaningfully. We will therefore confine ourselves to portraying items about which there was considerable consensus, and will offer individual comments that seem to shed additional light on our subject.

The eight respondents averaged about ten years in telemarketing, most working with investment programs. Four had spent at least four years in supervisory positions. All were white males; seven were married, their median age was 38.5, and six of them claimed a BA degree or better. Only one indicated that he would like a child of his to work in telemarketing, although three others said they "probably" would like that. Three quarters expressed strong or very strong religious beliefs.

Almost all said they relied primarily on telephone rather than personal closings. Reasons provided for why they were in telemarketing were the potential income, the excitement or challenge, flexible hours, and benefits and perks, such as bonuses and trips awarded to top producers.

While almost half of the respondents indicated that the work made them "nervous," the majority claimed that they enjoyed telephone sales. Two respondents said that they had left the industry, one because of illegal operations within the "syndicate" he had worked for and the other because of "tyrannical" bosses.

About half of the respondents maintained that they "believed in the product" they were selling and the same percentage said that they were "confident [they could] sell any product to any person." About the same percentage indicated that they believed that "regulations are important to the industry," although there were few suggestions about what form such regulations might take. Seven of the eight respondents replied that they had never "worked for a broker-dealer firm that encouraged you to misrepresent the program in order to make a sale." Given the evidence we had, this seemed an obvious falsehood.

When asked to whom they preferred to sell, they primarily indicated white males in the 30- to 59-year age range who lived in the suburbs and were college-educated. Our interpretation is that they favored targets who presumably had disposable income and might be persuaded to define the investment as a "smart" move. They said that the most difficult targets were women, Asians, and people under 30 with less than a college education who lived in the central city.

The respondents were evenly divided regarding their belief that their success was related to the state of the economy.

Job stress was not tied by more than a few respondents to any particular concern, except for the pressure to close a deal. Other stress factors noted were getting started each day, being motivated, the absence of positive feedback when doing well, and lack of credibility. A larger sample might show more differentiation among these items.

Significantly, half the respondents did not reply to our question about "the image of telephone sales in the eyes of the general public", and the half that did answer saw that image as negative to very negative.

Most said that they did not employ a particular script to make sales, but rather than they mixed scripted material with "winging it," noting that each call had a different quality. Several respondents accepted our open-ended invitation to comment on the industry, though they did so rather cryptically:

> My observation of the securities business as a proprietor and broker was that regulations . . . forced brokerage firms to maintain operating expenses and small profits.

The more responsive salesperson noted that telemarketing is one of the highest paying jobs for those who are good at it. He also shared two vignettes with us:

> When I was a couple of weeks new in phone sales I closed an oil and gas deal, but the client asked me first, how long have you been working in oil and gas? I told him to hold on a minute, I had another call. My supervisor asked me, how long have you been driving? I said for 15 years. He said, then you've been working with oil and gas for 15 years, haven't you?

The other story also related to when he was a beginner in the business:

> I was selling a test well (highly risky) program. The client said it was too risky for his blood. My supervisor told me to tell him that this is a step out well (conservative risk). After the client bought the package I went back to my supervisor to better understand the program. I told him I understood this program to be a highly risky test well. He said, don't worry about it, this is a step out well. Then he winked at me, and said, step out on a limb!

◂ CONCLUSION ▸

Our examination of the world of telemarketing fraud shows that the earnings to be made represent the primary driving force behind the work, though there appears to be a considerable element of what Katz depicted as the "sneaky thrill" involved in outsmarting others, particularly others who are rich and well-educated, and that such a thrill can be "independent of material gains."[48]

Beyond its congruence with some of Katz's ideas our review of telemarketing scamming and its practitioners at best fits awkwardly with criminological typologies of offenses and offenders. White-collar crime, classically defined "approximately" as "a crime committed by a person of respectability and high social status in the course of his occupation,[49] is typically taken to involve managers and executives and others in positions of power who abuse that power.

Salespersons in operations run by the two Daves do not comfortably fall under the traditional white-collar crime definition, though they self-evidently come within the revisionist categorization of the Yale school that establishes a category labeled "crimes of the middle class" and places into it violators of a specified roster of federal offenses, including mail fraud.[50] The heterogeneity of those embraced by such a definition, however, precludes any attempt to understand their actions by any but the most amorphous kind of theoretical construct.

More recently, Calavita et al. have interpreted the savings and loan scandals in terms of what they label "collective embezzlement."[51] Such offenses involved bank executives signing over to themselves large amounts of the institution's holdings. But these companies at one point were legitimate businesses, a trait not characteristic of the telescam operations.

Edelhertz referred to the kinds of schemes practiced by salespersons such as those we have studied as "white collar crime as business."[52] Such schemes involve "stealing by deception by individuals (or "rings") who have no continuing institutional position and whose major purpose from the outset is to bilk people of money."[53] The best insights into our subject probably can be found in the rather slim literature on confidence games. Big-con operations, so solidly researched by Maurer[54] seem to have faded from the scene, though quicker and dirtier short cons, such as the pigeon drop, occasionally are mentioned in a few of the newspapers. Their elements generally are depicted; interpretation almost invariably is absent.

Comparing salesmen engaged in fraudulent activities to conmen, Blum noted that the confidence thief commits "theft by guile in a person-to-person relationship," while the salesperson's approach is more impersonal. The confidence man usually provides no material objects for his victim's money, Blum observes, whereas the telemarketer may deliver a product, albeit not the one desired.[55] It is arguable whether these items truly distinguish our study population from the ideal types established by Blum, since very little of any value to the customer resulted from the telemarketing exchange. There undoubtedly is a need for what might be labeled "a continuum of crookedness" that differentiates scams in terms of major characteristics of their operations.

From a criminological viewpoint, we see telescamming as an inventive offshoot of legitimate enterprise, perhaps best understood in terms of capitalist social structure that encourages the accumulation of money by any tactic but imposes a penalty if the effort is illegal and, of course, if it is discovered, often a very unlikely outcome. Telescamming brings together two Gs: guile and what unflatteringly is often labeled as victim greed. Such greed, it seems to us, is also a cultural given, the quest for a deal, for something that will improve one's condition. It is not truly greed, however, that appears to differentiate victims from nonvictims but rather the victims' careless risk taking.

The fact that our analysis shows little difference in the offense patterns of telemarketing salespersons in terms of age may indicate that those with a heavier roster of violations and crimes drop out, leaving the field as the years go by to those with less serious abusive records. Or, of course, it may be that the newcomers display poorer law-abiding records than those who have preceded them into the field.

Key to any interpretation focused on cultural imperatives is the doctrine of *caveat emptor*, stressing an ethos of individualism. The ethos grew out of Puritan religious doctrine and seventeenth-century political philosophy.[56] The emphasis on individualism means that persons are responsible for their decisions; if they are careless and make a wrong move, it is their fault alone. Hamilton describes sarcastically how the doctrine of *caveat emptor* entered into English and American legal and business tradition: "[N]ot until the nineteenth century did judges discover that *caveat emptor* sharpened wits, taught self-reliance, made a man—an economic man—out of the buyer, and served well its two masters, business and the public."[57]

To date, virtually all public policy has focused on making persons who are targeted by telemarketing scams—particularly older persons—aware of the tactics involved in them. A more valuable approach could be to drive the purveyors of telescam ruses out of business by tightening licensing requirements, beefing up enforcement personnel, and imposing tougher penalties for those engaged in the business.

The American Association of Retired Persons labels telephone scams perpetrated against the elderly "electronic mugging,"[58] but, as we have seen, the analogy is inexact because victims are being done in not by force but by allowing themselves to be talked into something that disadvantages them. This is not to say that they are to be blamed—though they often blame themselves[59]—but only that telescamming is not a street offense even though the losses and emotional suffering that it produces may be as or more severe.

Special protection is now offered to persons over the age of 55 in the nature of a five-year additional penalty for telemarketers who target more than ten of them (Title 18, ss. 2325–7). This kind of "special-group legislation," akin to the outlawing of so-called "hate crimes," seems to us more a political gesture than an acceptable doctrine for a democracy where all people should be treated equally unless there are inordinately compelling reasons to single out a particular group for aid.

It is important to emphasize that telescammers often have rather unsavory records, but nonetheless continue to be authorized by the state to engage in sales, often in a way that duplicates their earlier violations. It is characteristic that state associations that monitor professional groups are reluctant to abrogate the right of lawyers, doctors, and similar folk, despite some strikingly nefarious actions on their part.[60] It is often pointed out, in defense of leniency, that professionals have trained long and hard to achieve their status, that what they do, if done legally, benefits society; and that it would therefore be unduly cruel to take away their right to earn a livelihood and to be useful.

Such a defense, weak as it may be, hardly applies very forcefully to telemarketing. To be successful at telemarketing requires very little training, and it is likely that its practitioners could rather readily locate legitimate occupational outlets for whatever skills they might have that make them successful scammers.

Enforcement agencies, after they succeed in closing up a telescam operation, are often unable to recover much of the money that was derived from the phony pitches. Often such agencies spend a good deal of their time and resources acting as collection agencies. Perhaps the most promising tactic might be to mount the kind of campaigns of reintegrative shaming that some jurisdictions, particularly in New Zealand and Australia,[61] have used to bring offenders into conformity, to try to impress on them the harm they have done to the persons they have victimized and yet to treat them so that they do not find themselves isolated from support that might set them on another and law-abiding vocational path.

In doing research on telemarketing scammers, there are new directions to be taken. With the rise of the Internet, their techniques have shifted to this new medium, which has been addressed in a presidential initiative as a national priority.[62] This has set the U.S. Department of Justice in motion to gather more information, increase training for law enforcement personnel, and establish the Internet Fraud Complaint Center, with the National White Collar Crime Center. Also, there are increased efforts to coordinate Internet fraud prosecution at all levels of government and to provide support and advice regarding prosecutions. Finally, public education has become a priority at all levels of government. All of these areas, especially prevention and the impact of these new schemes on victims, are subjects that require additional research.

◂ NOTES ▸

1 Mannheim, H. (1946). *Criminal Justice and Social Reconstruction.* London: Routledge and Kegan Paul; Pollock, F. and Maitland, F. W. (1909). *The History of English Law.* Boston, MA: Little, Brown.

2 Note the high-pressure sales tactics employed in the life insurance business (as described for instance in Swafford, J. [1996]. *Charles Ives: A Life with Music.* New York: Norton), but keep in mind that in these cases the sellers generally believe that the customers are doing themselves and their families a service in buying protection for them. For a fascinating vignette of a salesman who prospered mightily by being scrupulously honest, see Singer, I. B. (1998). *Shadows on the Hudson.* Trans. J. Sherman. New York: Farrar, Straus, Giroux, pp. 194–95: "Grein did no fast talking or exaggerating; he advised potential buyers of all the dangers associated with the stock market. He repeated the words of David Hume: the fact that until now the sun has always risen is no proof that it will rise again tomorrow . . . He even assembled a string of facts about firms which year after year had shown themselves to be as firm as rock yet which had suddenly gone bankrupt. [He had] a perpetual fear of leading people into error and harming them."

3 Kristof, K. M. (1997). Groups Band Together to Crack Down on Telemarketing Fraud. *Los Angeles Times*, 19 January, p. 2.

4 *United States v Weinstein* (1992). Complaint, Case 9103302 (E.D.N.Y.).

[5] See for instance Office for Victims of Crime (1998). *Telemarketing Fraud Prevention: Public Awareness and Training Activities.* Washington, DC: US Department of Justice.

[6] Levi, M. and Pithouse, A. (2000). White Collar Crime and Its Victims: The Social and Media Construction of Business Fraud. New York: Oxford University Press; Shover, N., Fox, G. L. and Mills, M. (1994). Long-Term Consequences of Victimization by White-Collar Crime. *Justice Quarterly.* Vol. 11, pp. 301–24; Spalek, B. (1999). Exploring the Impact of Financial Crime: A Study Looking into the Effects of the Maxwell Scandal upon the Maxwell Pensioners. *International Journal of Victimology.* Vol. 6, pp. 213–30; Titus, R. M., Heinzelman, F. and Boyle, J. M. (1995). Victimization of Persons by Fraud. *Crime and Delinquency.* Vol. 41, pp. 54–72.

[7] Stevenson, R. J. (1998). *The Boiler Room and Other Telephone Sales Scams.* Urbana: University of Illinois Press.

[8] Ibid, p. 213.

[9] Webb, E. J., Campbell, D. T., Schwartz, R. D., Sechrest, L., and Grove, J. B. (1981). *Nonreactive Measures in the Social Sciences.* Boston, MA: Houghton Mifflin, p. 329.

[10] Edelhertz, H. (1970). *The Nature, Impact and Prosecution of White-Collar Crime.* Washington, DC: National Institute for Law Enforcement and Criminal Justice, p. 16.

[11] Wright, N. (1952). The Confidence Man of Melville and Cooper. *American Quarterly,* Vol. 4, pp. 266–8.

[12] Porter, W. S. ("O. Henry") (1960). *Complete Works.* New York: Doubleday, p. 127.

[13] Maurer, D. (1949). *The Big Con.* Indianapolis, IN: Bobbs-Merrill.

[14] Dornstein, K. (1996). *Accidentally on Purpose: The Making of a Personal Injury Underworld in America.* New York: St. Martin's Press.

[15] Zervos, K. (1992). Responding to Fraud in the 1990s. In Grabosky, P. N. (ed.) *Complex Commercial Fraud.* Canberra: Australian Institute of Criminology, p. 199.

[16] *Weiss v United States* (1941), p. 681.

[17] U.S. Department of Justice (1995). *Attorney General Guidelines for Victim and Witness Assistance.* 18 USC Section 2325 (1)(A)(B). Washington, DC: U.S. Department of Justice.

[18] Coffee, J. C., Jr. (1983). Metastasis of Mail Fraud: The Continuing Story of the "Evolution" of a White-Collar Crime. *American Criminal Law Review.* Vol. 21, pp. 1–37; Zingale, M. (1999). Fashioning a Victim Standard in Mail and Wire Fraud: Ordinarily Prudent Person or Monumentally Credulous Gull? *Columbia Law Review.* Vol. 99, pp. 795–832.

[19] Title 14, U.S. Code s. 1341 ff.

[20] Hakstian, A. R., Scratchley, L. S., McLeod, A. A., Tweed, R. G. and Siddarth, S. (1997). Selection of Telemarketing Employees by Standardized Assessment. *Psychology & Marketing.* Vol. 714, pp. 703–26.

[21] American Association of Retired Persons (1998). *Consumer Fraud: Telemarketing.* Washington, DC: AARP.

[22] O'Hanlon, K. (1997). Let the Pesky Telemarketer Down Easy. *Los Angeles Times,* 6 October, p. ED7.

[23] Shichor, D., Doocy, J. H. and Geis, G. (1996). Anger, Disappointment and Disgust: Reactions of Victims of a Telephone Investment Scam. In Sumner, C., Israel, M., O'Connell, M. and Sarre, R. (eds.), *International Victimology: Selected Papers from the 8th International Symposium.* Canberra: Australian Institute of Criminology.

24 See Stevenson, op. cit.
25 Goffman, E. (1959). *The Presentation of Self in Everyday Life.* Garden City, NY: Doubleday Anchor, p. 238.
26 Goffman, E. (1952). On Cooling the Mark Out: Some Aspects of Adaptation to Failure. *Psychiatry.* Vol. 15, pp. 451–62.
27 A letter to the *New York Times* tells the story of a new telemarketing salesman who was befuddled when he was first confronted by someone claiming never to do business over the phone. He thought about it for a while, then asked: "Don't you ever order a pizza?" See Magill, M. (1998). Manhattan Diary. In Nemy, E. (ed.). *New York Times,* 19 April, p. 40.
28 *United States v Bulla* (1989). Affidavit for Search Warrant and Complaint, Case 809-0431M (EDNY), p. 6.
29 See further Schulte, F. (1995). *Fleeced! Telemarketing Rip-Offs and How to Avoid Them.* Amherst, NY: Prometheus, pp. 343–47.
30 Francis, D. (1988). Contrepreneurs. Toronto: Macmillan of Canada, p. 22.
31 Emshwiller, J. R. (1995). Having Lost Many Thousands to Con Artists, Elderly Widow Tells Cautionary Tale. *Wall Street Journal,* 20 September, p. C4.
32 Smythe, H. B. (1994). Fighting Telemarketing Scams. *Hastings Communications and Entertainment Law Journal.* Vol. 17, pp. 347–81.
33 Harris, M. (1983). America's Capital of Fraud. *Money.* November, pp. 225–38.
34 Stevenson, op. cit.
35 Harris, op. cit, p. 236.
36 Holcomb. B. (1986). Inside the Boiler Room: How Some Scam Artists Steal Millions on the Phone. *New York,* 4 August, pp. 39–42.
37 *The People v Parker-Bryant* (1991). BC027461.
38 *The People v Parker Bryant, Inc.* (1997). Cal. Lexis 4242 (9 July).
39 Sanders, E. (1999). State Drops Lawsuit Affecting 2,000 Investors. *Los Angeles Times,* 16 September, pp. C1, C3.
40 Weisz, B. M., Ziff, H. E., Wilde, E. C. and Inman, M. H. (1992). Gas, Lies and Computer Tape: The Saga of Dave and Dave. Report to the American/Allied Trustee. Los Angeles: Inman, Weisz, and Steinberg.
41 In 1999, undercover federal agents, posing as distributors of a (non-existent) computerized automatic dialing service, gained entry into a host of San Diego telemarketing scam operating rooms and charged 90 persons with felonies. The average age of these persons was 32.8 years.
42 Stevenson, op. cit, p. 208.
43 Lessing, D. (1963). *In Pursuit of the English.* New York: Simon and Schuster, p. 53.
44 Nietzsche, F. W. (1919). *Human, All Too Human: A Book for Free Spirits.* Trans. A. Harvey. Chicago: C. H. Kerr, p. 52.
45 Cohen, A. (1977). The Concept of Criminal Organization. *British Journal of Criminology.* Vol. 17, p. 109.
46 Goldman, S. (1995). The Two Daves. *California Lawyer.* February, p. 45; see also Shover, N. (1996). *Great Pretenders: Pursuits and Careers of Persistent Thieves.* Boulder, CO: Westview; Katz, J. (1988). *Seductions of Crime: More and Sensual Attractions of Doing Evil.* New York: Basic Books.
47 Biegelman, M. (1998). Personal interview, 22 September.
48 Katz, op. cit, p. 52.
49 Sutherland, E. H. (1939). *White Collar Crime.* New York: Dryden, p. 9.
50 Weisburd, D. S., Wheeler, S., Waring, E. and Bode, N. (1991) *Crimes of the Middle Classes: White-Collar Offenders in the Federal Courts.* New Haven: Yale University Press.

51 Calavita, K., Pontell, H. N. and Tillman, R. (1997). *Big Money Crime: Fraud and Politics in the Savings and Loan Crisis.* Berkeley: University of California Press.

52 Edelhertz, H. (1983). "White-Collar and Professional Crime." American Behavioral Scientist. Vol. 27, p. 116.

53 Moore, M. H. (1980). Notes Towards a National Strategy to Deal with White-Collar Crime. In Edelhertz, H. and Rogovin, C. H. (eds.), *A National Strategy for Containing White-Collar Crime.* Lexington, MA: Lexington Books, p. 42.

54 Maurer, op. cit.

55 Blum, R. H. (1972). *Deceivers and Deceived.* Springfield, IL: Thomas, p. 12.

56 Bellah, R., Madsen, G. R., Sullivan, W. M. and Tipton, S. M. (1985). *Habits of the Heart: Individualism and Commitment in American Life.* New York: Macmillan.

57 Hamilton, W. H. (1931) The Ancient Maxim of Caveat Emptor. *Yale Law Journal.* Vol. 40, p. 1186.

58 Ostrow, T. and Perry, T. (1995). U.S. Targets Telemarketing Fraud Against the Elderly. *Los Angeles Times,* 8 December, pp. A1, A23.

59 Sechrest, D. K., Shichor, D., Doocy, J. H., and Geis, G. (1998). Women's Response to a Telemarketing Scam. *Women and Criminal Justice.* Vol. 10, pp. 75–89.

60 Jesilow, P., Pontell, H. N. and Geis, G. (1993). *Prescription for Profit: How Doctors Defraud Medicaid.* Berkeley: University of California Press.

61 Braithewaite, J. (1989). *Crime, Shame and Reintegration.* Cambridge: Cambridge University Press.

62 U.S. Department of Justice (1999). *Office of Justice Program News.* Washington, DC: U.S. Department of Justice. At *http://www.ojp.usdoj.gov/ovc/infores/99/99006.ht*

‹ 9 ›

Computer-related Crime

David Carter
Andra J. Bannister

Computer-related crime has increased dramatically in recent years. Indeed, both the character and nature of these offenses and their frequency of occurrence has changed notably since about 1995, when the Internet experienced explosive growth (c.f., Parker, 1999). How much computer crime is occurring? It is simply unknown. Not only is there significant inconsistency in defining computer crime offenses, there has been no organized attempt to collect offense data.

Computer crimes are not necessarily considered white-collar crimes, but computers are increasingly being used as an instrument to commit white-collar crime and an assortment of other criminal offenses. There is an upswing in the frequency with which computers are being used in occupational crimes where employees, customers, and others are committing fraud and other offenses against corporations. The bulk of the law-enforcement establishment in the United States is ill prepared to investigate or otherwise deal with computer crime. Thus, it is important to examine computer crimes in the context of white-collar crime.

Offenses vary in character from clear criminality (e.g., theft, fraud, or destruction of data files) to acts where criminal culpabil-

Prepared by David Carter and Andra J. Bannister especially for *Readings in White-Collar Crime.*

ity is less clear, such as violations of privacy (e.g., unauthorized access to credit reports or medical records). Similarly, types of criminal behavior by computer users also vary (e.g., pornography, extortion, fraud, false advertising, cyberstalking, or gambling).

This is complicated by the global character of networking offenses—transactions and behavioral interactions that can occur between people worldwide, from their homes, with no scrutiny by immigration, customs, or other government entity. The gravity of the problem is illustrated by the Computer Crime and Intellectual Property Section of the U.S. Department of Justice, which estimates cybercrime costs as high as $10 billion annually (Williams, 1999).

Since data are not collected to document the nature, trends, and extent of computer crime, it is difficult to develop a true image of the problem. Unobtrusive measures and anecdotes, however, can provide insights that may be extrapolated. The importance of such an exercise has both theoretical and pragmatic implications. Theoretically, computer criminals may represent a unique taxonomy of criminality that prompts provocative questions: Could socialization via computer networks where individuals have no direct social contact—perhaps not even interacting by speaking—contribute to deviance? To what extent does interaction with stimulus through a computer network, void of human interaction, realign attitudes, values and beliefs of an individual? Are individuals who are defined as computer "criminals" inappropriately labeled, since the law has not completely resolved criminal and ethical issues associated with computer crime? This last question is particularly relevant when one considers the distinction between "hackers" and "crackers," as will be discussed later in the chapter. Pragmatically, there is a growing need to collect useable data in order to formulate law and policy related to cybercriminality. Prevention programs and resource allocation for investigation and prosecution are not possible without data that provide insights into the character and extent of the crime problem.

What Is Computer Crime?

Since computer crimes can vary widely, a single definition—beyond criminal behavior wherein a computer is involved—is insufficient. Rather, it is more accurate to describe computer crime based on the different, albeit overlapping, methods by which a computer is involved in (or associated with) criminal acts.

- **The computer as the target.** In these cases, the intent of the offender is either (1) to take information from the computer's memory or (2) to damage intentionally application programs, information, or data files. These offenses are defined by unauthorized access to stored memory by either a network incursion (i.e., hacking/cracking), a violation of trust (i.e., an employee or otherwise authorized user violates the conditions of access to the computer); or unauthorized direct access to the computer. *Intentional* theft or damage is a necessary criterion for inclusion in this category. Offenses may include theft or sabotage of intellectual property, theft of marketing information, sabotage of software applications or data files, or the unlawful access to or tampering with personal, business, or government records.

One area that has experienced notable growth since the rapid expansion of networking is referred to as *hactivism*—the practice of hacking into a Web site of a person, group, government, organization, or business for political or ideological reasons. The intent of the incursion is typically to deface a Web page, disrupt the Web site's function, incur repair expenses for the Web site owner; and/or articulate an opposing viewpoint. For example, animal rights activists have hacked Web pages of research organizations and businesses that use animals for product testing.

- **The computer as an agent.** In these cases, the processes of the computer are used to facilitate the crime. Crimes may include frauds from use of ATM cards and accounts, theft of money through "round-off" schemes on interest calculations or currency conversions, credit card fraud, fraud from transactions in the computer, or telecommunications fraud.
- **The computer as incidental to other crimes.** These are circumstances where the computer is not essential to the crime, but the technology is being used to facilitate the crime more easily. Crimes may include: money laundering, pornography distribution, facilitation of pedophilia, counterfeiting, embezzlement, book making, and even murder.
- **Crimes associated with the prevalence of computers.** Just as computers may be targets and instrumentalities, computers and related technologies may also be crime commodities. The crime may be committed without a computer; however, the advent of the personal computer has produced new crime targets. Crimes may include: software piracy and counterfeit, copyright violations of software, counterfeit equipment, and black market trafficking of stolen computer memory, processors, peripherals, and software.
- **Networking malfeasance.** This type of offense is committed explicitly as a result of the communications and access

afforded by networking. It includes a wide array of behaviors, including some that are "improper" but not criminal, per se, (e.g., privacy violations) and others at the opposite end of the continuum that may be considered as crimes against persons. Examples include: harassment; defamation of an individual or an organization via networking messages; use of a computer's access and dissemination abilities as a threat; use of the computer in con games, cyberstalking, or criminal inducement (i.e., pedophiles, illegal gambling, inciting hate crimes); and the unauthorized access to a computer system, including the viewing of files just to "explore" the system (sometimes referred to as "walking through a computer"). In some cases, there may be a criminal violation—depending on the nature of the information accessed and the criminal law in the jurisdiction where the incident occurred—but in many cases this will most likely be a civil matter.

◂ Literature Review ▸

The professional literature on computer crime is comparatively limited, particularly with regard to sociobehavioral aspects of cybercrime. Despite the growing body of information, there is virtually no scientific exploration of the varieties and trends of computer crime such as can be found with predatory crime, burglaries, and drug-related offenses.

A Developmental Perspective

Since the introduction of the microcomputers on the public market in the late 1970s, the access to and the volume of personal computing grew. Technological development of memory capacity, processing speed, software capabilities, and remote communications (i.e., networking) increased geometrically. Similarly, there a was rapid integration of computing, telecommunications, multimedia, and information archiving technologies. With the public embrace of the Internet and its staggering growth since 1995, the need for network security has become obvious. Certainly there were some early efforts in exploring the idea of computer crime and recognition of it as a criminal problem. However, these inquiries were groundbreaking yet limited, just as was the technology.

One of the earliest publications on computer crime was by Parker (1979), discussing the possibility of and potential for cybercriminality. In the late 1970s and early 1980s the Bureau of Justice Statistics focused on the topic through a series of publications that included an overview of computer crime issues (BJS, 1979), computer security (BJS, 1980), and crimes related to electronic fund transfers (BJS, 1982). These monographs centered on the potential for cybercriminality and considered issues of law, investigation, case development, and possible criminal strategies. In what was a groundbreaking arena of research, many of the methodologies still have applications to operational aspects of security and crime control. Yet, the reports contained very limited documentation of actual criminality and did not discuss cybercriminals, per se.

During this time period networking capabilities became increasingly available to the public. Although some aspects of network-related issues were discussed, in reality networking was in its infancy and posed no real threat at the time. Most computers were still batch-processing mainframes; interactive computers were just appearing on the market but were too expensive for widespread use. Virtually everything that was learned about technological issues in this early foray has changed significantly as a result of microcomputers and their diverse applications.

In the 1980s a few more publications emerged on this topic, predominantly dealing with logistical issues associated with computer-related criminality. Several publications discussed methods to prevent computer crimes (Bequai, 1983; Cooper, 1984, Roache, 1986; Carroll, 1987; Gallery, 1987; and Arkin, 1988). Others explored practices for effectively investigating and prosecuting computer crime cases (Thackery, 1985; Rostoker and Rines, 1986; Arkin, 1988; Consor, et al, 1988; Holinger, et al., 1988; and Conly, 1989).

McEwen (1989) addressed the need for dedicated computer crime units, while Bequai (1987) offered a classification for computer crimes, which is largely dated as a result of the significant changes in computing capabilities (such as digital imaging) and networking. Kusserow (1983) documented cases of computer-related fraud occurring in government agencies (nearly all of which were cases of trust violations), and Landreth (1985) discussed the capabilities of hackers in the early days of bitnet (the Internet "predecessor").

A whole industry has emerged, generating many publications and products directed at various aspects of computer security. Firewalls, encryption systems, operations security, virtual private networks (VPNs), physical security, access controls, and biometric security developments are some of the issues explored. Nearly all of the publications employ the same format, namely, the description of security issues, a presentation of options for solution, and the technological procedural alternatives for each potential solution. However, *behavioral approaches* concerning these problems and trends are virtually nonexistent. One exception is Icove, et. al., (1995) who comprehensively focus on security and investigation but also offer some interesting insights about criminal motivations and behavior patterns. Moreover, the behavioral implications provide some guidance based on a limited number of observations and investigations rather than a scientific study of trends or patterns.

Most recently, publications about cybercrime are often found in the popular press. Case studies such as *The Cuckoo's Egg* (Stoll, 1988) and *Takedown* (Shimomura, 1996) look at specific cases of network incursion. Stoll documents the case of a computer hacker from Germany who penetrated a wide range of U.S. academic and military computers seeking information to steal and sell on the global national security market. Shimomura describes the investigation, arrest, and prosecution of Kevin Mitnik, perhaps the most well-known of all hackers, who spent five years in federal prison for computer crime violations and was released in early 2000. Both publications provide interesting and unique insights about the capacity to commit cybercrimes as well as the difficulty of investigating these offenses. However, as case studies they offer introspection about specific offenders, not generalization about trends in cybercriminality.

A great deal of effort continues to be dedicated to all forms of computer security, ranging from firewalls to encryption to access control to virus prevention, because of growing problems in hacking/cracking and the use of malicious software. Interestingly, the computer security industry has grown rapidly without fully understanding the nature of cybercrimes and criminals. The effects of this rapid change are that cybercrime, per se, largely has been ignored—by both policymakers and the research community.

Cyber Victimization

According to Parker, the lack of attention historically paid to computer crime is no accident. "In 1970, a number of researchers concluded that the problem was merely a small part of the effect of technology on society and not worthy of specific explicit research" (1989:5). However, Parker went on to note that "the increase in substantial losses associated with intentional acts involving computers proved the fallacy of this view" (Parker, 1989:5). The irony is that Parker's observations were made a decade ago, yet there has been no substantial progress in understanding and addressing the problem from criminological perspectives. Furthermore, when Parker's early observations were made, most computing was the province of big business, government, and academe. Today, personal computing has changed the entire face of the computer industry and computer use.

While there is some debate about who poses the greatest risk as a cybercriminal, the fact remains that anyone who has computing skills may pose a criminal threat (Carter and Katz, 1999). In the mid-

1980s Van Duyn observed that "insiders pose a far greater threat to the organization's computer security than outside 'electronic invaders' possibly could" (1985:4). His reasoning was that "insiders are familiar with their employers' data processing operations and the type of data each system and application is storing and processing" and therefore know exactly where to look for information. Certainly this logic still has merit. However, the emergence of networking, expansive growth of easily adapted databases integrated with web pages, and user-friendly protocols are changing this balance.

Van Duyn (1985) goes on to observe that the vulnerability of an organization from within is the most dangerous and poses the most serious threat. A number of more recent studies support this conclusion. In fact, "one study estimated that 90% of economic computer crimes were committed by employees of the victimized companies" (U.N. Commission on Crime and Criminal Justice, 1995). A more recent study conducted in North America and Europe found that 73 percent of the risk to computer security was from internal sources while only 23 percent was attributable to external sources (U.N. Commission on Crime and Criminal Justice, 1995). Unlike "outsiders" attempting to break into a system, "insiders" oftentimes are more easily able to circumvent safeguards, therefore reducing their chances of being detected. Moreover, if an employee has authorized access to the information but chooses to steal or destroy it, detection is even more difficult.

Consistent with evidence that "insiders" pose the greatest threat to computer security, Parker (1989) cites several factors that alone or in conjunction with others help to create an atmosphere conducive to computer crime within organizations. The first factor is the youth of employees who are likely to become perpetrators. He notes that it is not youth, in and of itself, which translates into a generation of computer criminals. However, "younger people in data processing occupations tend to have received their education in universities and colleges where attacking computer systems has become common and is sometimes condoned as an educational activity" (Parker, 1989:39).

In accordance with differential association theory, vulnerability erupts from "groups of people working together and mutually encouraging and stimulating one another to engage in unauthorized acts that escalate into serious crimes" (Parker, 1989:39). The potential for one-upmanship becomes magnified as the acts escalate in risk and sophistication.

The Changing Character of Cybervictimization

While these studies provide important insights, the reader is cautioned to consider the social and technological changes that have occurred since those early works. Terms such as "explosive," "staggering," and "unprecedented" are not overstatements for describing the growth of networking, the technological evolution, and the social adaptation to computing technology in the last few years.[1]

From a descriptive perspective, Barrett (1997) offers insights about the wide range of cybercriminality. He provides an insightful foundation about the capacity of computers to be used as criminal instruments as well as instruments of warfare. Interestingly, the dynamics and processes are virtually the same, hence the integrated discussion of criminality and national security is becoming an increasingly prevalent theme in the literature. In many ways, inferences from the National Infrastructure Protection Center <www.fbi.gov/nipc/nipc.htm> can be made that cybercrime and cyberwarfare are on parallel tracks. This is reinforced by the January 1999 experience of simultaneous attacks on United States Defense Department computer systems originating in Russia. Similar tactics were used by Russian organized crime groups against banks (Sinuraya, 1999).

The extent and nature of computer crime appears to be on a rapidly ascending curve. A study conducted by the American Bar Association in 1987 found that of the 300 corporations and government agencies surveyed, 72 (24 percent) claimed to have been the victim of a computer-related crime in the 12 months prior to the survey (ABA, 1987). The estimated losses from these crimes ranged from $145 million to $730 million over the one-year period. This broad range is illustrative of the problem in estimating losses. Not only is it difficult to identify and document these crimes, but it is even more difficult to place a monetary value on losses such as that of intellectual property wherein the actual value may not be known for months or years.

Two years later, the Florida Department of Law Enforcement (FDLE) surveyed 898 public and private sector organizations that conducted business by computer. Of the 403 (44.9 percent) respondents, 25 percent reported they had been victimized by computer criminals (FDLE, 1989). The Florida study found embezzlement of funds by employees to be a major source of the crimes; however, no attempt to estimate losses was made because, according to one of the researchers interviewed, "losses would have been nothing more than a guess."

In perhaps one of the most comprehensive studies, conducted in 1991, a survey was done of 3,000 Virtual Address Extension (VAX) sites in Canada, Europe, and the United States to assess computer security threats and crimes. The results show that 72 percent of the respondents reported a security incident occurring within the previous 12 months. Out of this figure, 43 percent reported that the incident was criminal in nature (U.N. Commission on Crime and Criminal Justice, 1995). By far, the greatest security threats came from employees or people who had access to the computers, suggesting that threats of computer crime generally come from employees, just like much of the theft in retail businesses. However, a number of external security breeches from hackers telephoning into the systems or accessing via networks were also reported. The ABA and FDLE studies scarcely even mentioned this "external threat" and gave little attention to it as a growing problem. This is not surprising, however, since networking in the late 1980s was predominantly used by the military, academics, and researchers. Access was comparatively limited and networking technology was both more expensive and more cumbersome. However, the 1991 United Nations study suggested that external threats via remote access became a problem that would grow in the years to come.

The data from Carter and Katz (1998) show a trend of victimization that increased significantly over previous studies, with 98.5 percent of the respondents reporting they had been victimized—43.3 percent reported being victimized more than twenty-five times. While these numbers seem dramatic, security professionals with whom these results were discussed stated they were surprised at the frequency of admitted victimization, not actual victimization. One respondent stated, "Do we know the national or even local scope of the computer crime threat? Probably not; but it has to be higher than anyone wants to admit."

The 1998 joint survey by the FBI and Computer Security Institute found that for the third year in a row corporate security directors reported an increase of computer system penetration by outsiders. This represented a 20 percent increase of successful system incursions since 1996 (Computer Security Institute, 1999). Collectively, these data provide empirical support for the anecdotal evidence: Not only is unauthorized access to and theft from computer systems increasing, but the number of system incursions committed by "outsiders" is increasing, as well.

Although hacking and thefts are the best-documented offenses, other forms of cybercriminality are emerging. Fraud through investment Web sites, theft of identity, and theft of telecommunications services are all examples of expanding areas of criminality (see FBI, 1999; Public Information Research Group, 1999). Nor is cybercrime limited to crimes against property. A recent initiative by the U.S. Department of Justice explored the problem of cyberstalking, noting the rapidly increasing nature of the problem, which is aggravated by the increasing amount of personal information available on the Internet (U.S. Department of

Justice, 1999). While largely anecdotal information has been collected on these crimes, little is known about offense patterns and offender characteristics.

Offenders

As mentioned previously, research shows that the most common perpetrators are employees. However, as noted in the FBI/Computer Security Institute research, the proportion of computer-related crimes via network incursions are clearly on the rise. With respect to "inside" perpetrators the primary threat comes from full-time employees, followed by part-time and "outsource" employees. Computer hackers finish a close third—a finding that was expected, since there appears to be a correlation between theft and access to computers (Heffernan, 1995). However, the important dynamic to recognize is that "access" is changing dramatically in tandem with networking capabilities.

Sterling emphasized this point in his book, *The Hacker Crackdown.* As an investigative writer, he explored elements of the hacker culture and the potential impact of these "cyberpunks" (1992:146). His work described the impact hackers/crackers can have on issues related to crime, infringement of civil liberties, cybervandalism, and creating chaos.[2] Professor Dorothy Denning of Georgetown University has also studied hackers, mostly through observations of their hacking accomplishments and via e-mail communications. Her initial work (Denning, 1990) suggested that hackers were "explorers" from whom we could learn about computer security and networking behavior. However, after further study she observed:

> Hackers justify their illegal or unethical actions by appealing to the First Amendment and by claiming that the vulnerabilities they find need to be widely exposed lest they be exploited by "real criminals" or "malicious hackers." In fact, information disseminated through hacker publications and bulletin boards has frequently been used to commit serious crimes, with losses sometimes reaching millions of dollars. Hackers do not acknowledge the value of information to those that produce it (even while jealously guarding access to some of their own files), using the hacker ethic that "all information should be free" as a convenient rationale for disseminating whatever they please. . . . I do not have a solution to the hacker problem, but I no longer recommend working closely with hackers towards one. I doubt that many hackers have any serious interest in seeing their attacks successfully thwarted, as it would destroy a "game" they enjoy. (Denning, 1995:1–2)

Money and intellectual property have been stolen, corporate operations have been impeded, and jobs have been lost as a result of computer crime. As Joyce and Barrett observe, there are strong political and financial incentives to commit computer crimes (1999:28). Information systems in government and business alike have been compromised, and it has been fortunate that more damage has not been done.

Researchers must explore the problems in greater detail to learn the criminal etiology of this growing group of offenders, their methodologies, and motivations. Decision makers must react to this emerging body of knowledge by developing policies, methodologies, and regulations to detect and investigate incursions, prosecute the perpetrators, and vigilantly prevent future crimes. In the race against cybercrime our institutions have already fallen behind the criminals; at this point the question is not whether we can catch up, but whether we can keep the gap from widening.

◂ The Impact of Computer Crime ▸

Cybercrime represents a wide array of behaviors, ranging from theft to cyberstalking to counterfeiting. Despite these wide variances, the greatest impact of computer crime falls within the broad parameters of crimes against property. As in the case of "traditional" crimes against property, monetary loss is often a barometer used to determine criminal justice priorities and the allocation of resources.

There are many anecdotes describing individual losses from computer crime. The most sensational cases are in the news, with trade publications reporting a wide array of offenses. How representative are these anecdotes? Are losses downplayed by companies to minimize bad publicity or overplayed to take advantage of insurance or for other strategic reasons? Are the reports of victimization representative of the types of computer crime that are actually occurring or are the reports skewed, showing victimization of only certain types of offenses or reflecting only certain industries? Should indirect losses or anticipated losses be calculated into an assessment of the crimes' impact? At this point, there are simply no clear answers to these questions.

Sikellis (1999) extrapolated the data from the FBI/CSI annual computer crime survey and estimated annual "losses related to computer crimes in the U.S. alone now total over $10 billion a year." That same survey (Computer Security Institute, 1999) reports losses such as the average loss from theft of proprietary information is over $1.2 million, and the average loss from data or network sabotage is over $1.1 million.

The reliability of such data is inherently questionable, not because of impropriety but because of the lack of uniform definitions of behaviors and uniform methods of accountability. Assessing the economic impact of any crime is difficult, at best. Estimates are based on a wide range of variables: discovery of the loss, extrapolation of indirect losses, valid reporting of direct losses, operational definitions of where the offense occurred, and the time frame during which losses were incurred as a result of the crime. Currently, there is not a reliable system for documenting cyberoffenses.[3]

With a uniform computer-crime reporting system, operational definitions can specify the types of incidents that could be classified as a "computer crime," regardless of a specific jurisdiction's statutes. For example, one jurisdiction may define the theft of a computer as a computer crime. Another jurisdiction may define an offense as a computer crime only when a computer is used to steal information from a network. Uniform definitions would resolve different interpretations so that agencies and consumers of the data can understand the parameters of cybercrime data. Similarly, guidelines can be developed for the calculation of losses. While subjectivity is inevitable for estimating losses of indirect costs or loss of potential income, methodological guidelines will nonetheless introduce some controls as well as perspective.

All of these factors complicate the ability to articulate the impact of computer crime. The problem is further compounded by the tendency to view cybercrime one dimensionally. Estimating computer crime losses involves differentiating types of crimes and assessing a variety of factors, such as:

- Internet fraud
- Theft via computer
- Piracy of software
- Royalty losses from copyrighted materials placed on the Internet without permission for downloading (e.g., music, documents, video, software)
- Intellectual property losses by trying to:

  detect intellectual property that has been stolen and place an accurate and fair value on the loss

  estimate losses of future income as a result of the theft
- Expenses, including time/labor, software maintenance, and/or equipment repairs associated with:

  hacked Web pages

  server intrusions

  malicious software

- Telecommunications losses either as a theft of service or "piggy backing" a telecommunications system for remote or long-distance networking
- Theft of computer equipment
- Theft of information/data that has a dynamic value (such as a credit card or billing account number)

This returns to the original question: What is the impact of computer crime? There are direct monetary losses, indirect monetary losses, and the trauma of victimization, but at this point estimating these losses is futile. Currently, the best approach would be to analyze reported computer crime cases and record the estimated losses and impact (i.e., indirect losses). Collectively this would provide an intuitive picture of cybercrime that could serve as a point of reference until a uniform system is developed.

Piracy and counterfeiting are areas where some of the best estimates exist on the impact of computer crime. The United States Customs Service predicted that copyright violations and counterfeiting on a global basis were going to dwarf every other type of crime in the coming years. It is estimated that U.S. companies lose $200 billion a year to all types of piracy and counterfeiting of goods. Globally, software piracy alone is estimated to cost the industry $11 billion, with 38 percent of the 615 million new software installations being illegal copies. These data represent the proverbial tip of the iceberg.

For appropriate allocation of resources and crime-control strategies, a formal system to report and document cybercrime comprehensively and uniformly needs to be developed. The challenge is daunting.

Computer Hacking

Hackers have had a huge impact on computer crime since the overwhelming growth of networking. Consequently, it is useful to understand characteristics of the hacking culture. As in the case of any subcultural description, the characteristics described below are normative and, in some cases, intrinsic. While there will always be exceptions, as a general rule several clearly defined cultural elements emerge.

Several critical definitions will provide a foundation for understanding the hacker culture. According to the on-line "new hacker's dictionary," a hacker is a person who enjoys exploring the details of programmable systems and how to stretch their capabilities, as opposed to most users who prefer to learn only the minimum necessary. Hackers have a great deal of expertise and knowledge about computer systems and software capacity. They use their skills for solving computing problems, identifying security holes, and "pushing" systems beyond their intended use or design. Within this technoculture hackers maintain that they neither violate privacy nor take the property of another or disrupt systems. Dann and Dozois take a simpler approach by stating, "Just about everyone knows what a hacker is, at least in the most commonly accepted sense: someone who illicitly intrudes in computer systems by stealth and manipulates those systems to his own ends, for his own purposes" (1996:xii). Taylor simply defines it as "an attempt to make use of any technology in an original, unorthodox, and inventive way" (1999:15).

A cracker is one who breaks the security of a computer system to explore private files, download information, and/or disrupt the intended operation and use of a computer system. Contrary to widespread belief, this does not usually involve some ingenious application or insightful brilliance, but rather persistence and the dogged repetition of techniques that exploit common weaknesses in the security of target systems.

While many hackers and crackers tend to insist that these two terms are distinct from each other, the media and the general culture use the terms synonymously. Indeed, on Web sites that have been defaced by system intruders, it is common to see statements such as "you've been hacked" (rather than "you've been cracked"). As a result, I will use the terms "hackers" and "crackers" interchangeably, largely for purposes of readability.

Another important player in the technoculture is the "phreaker," who has developed the knowledge and expertise to crack telecommunications systems. This practice has increased significantly over a very short time due to the growth of digital telecommunications networks and the use of computers in voice mail and as telecommunications switches.

The basis for concern lies in the integrated characteristics of the hacker culture and the development of criminal enterprises. Many active computer crackers belong to groups that share common interests. That interest may be in using certain types of computers, cracking specific types of systems, supporting a specific cause—such as opposition to government controls on the Internet. Alternatively, hackers may belong to a self-selected group that feels their hacking skills are greater than those of others, and they hack into challenging systems as a demonstration of their abilities. In furtherance of their common interest, they share techniques and may even agree on a specific plan to accomplish their hacking goals.

Generally, these groups are informal, with "membership" varying a great deal; a relative few appear to be more formally structured with an explicit goal. For example, the group "Masters of Downloading" hacked a number of United States government Web sites to demonstrate their skills. Another group known as "United Loan Gunmen" (ULG) have been credited with breaking into the Web sites of Nasdaq, the American Stock Exchange, C-SPAN, the American Broadcasting Company, and the Associated Press (Security Wire Digest, 1999). The FBI has also reported that for several months a number of hacker groups have been using coordinated scans and probes of Web sites (FBI, 1999). Among those were attacks on multiple government sites, which were penetrated and changed in the same day. The salient point to note is that there are a wide range of these groups, some of which are operating with common purpose and success in penetrating security barriers.

A number of personal and cultural characteristics emerge within the hacker culture. They tend to be young (teens to late twenties), male, and intelligent. The brazen nature of attacks on systems and the practice of leaving condescending or insulting comments indicate both arrogance and elitism. The elitism is further demonstrated by egocentricity based on attitudes toward other people who do not have the same level of computer skills.

The hacker ethic, "all information should be free," suggests little or no self-responsibility for actions related to computer incursions. Indeed, some comments of hackers suggest it is the system administrator's fault if a system is hacked because the administrator should have employed better security to prevent a successful incursion. Conversely, hackers appear to be hypocritical because they have little tolerance for those who criticize them.

A tone of anarchy permeates the language and culture of hackers, with most of their contempt directed toward government attempts at regulating the Internet, at businesses capitalizing on the Internet for e-commerce, and at casual users or Internet "surfers." Hackers clearly have a great deal of patience and tenacity. Most successful system incursions are products of substantial time investment, attacking a system to identify weaknesses and circumvent security barriers.

Finally, crackers are collectors of information. When a system is successfully penetrated, they tend to download information as evidence of their success and frequently share this information with friends and others in their hacking collective. Typically the information is used only as an electronic trophy of a successful incursion. Kevin Mitnik, an icon of the hacker culture, had thousands of telecommunications billing codes, electronic identification numbers, valid credit card numbers with documentation information, and assorted forms of intellectual property stored on his hard drive when finally arrested. Generally, it does not appear Mitnik converted this information for personal use or monetary gain but maintained it as evidence of his successful incursions.

Conclusions and Recommendations

Organizations—public and private alike—must be made aware of the realistic threat posed by technology-related abuses and its impact on both crime and national security. One of the greatest challenges in this process is the willingness of organizations and people to be aware of changing criminal trends and to devote resources to address emerging problems.

As part of this change process, new law and policy must be developed. Policy should include regular development of both strategic and tactical intelligence as related to the integrated criminal and national security threats posed by computer crime and its evolution. Similarly, there must be a body of both civil and criminal law developed that expressly addresses the unique elements of cybercrime, including the issues of transnational criminality and the ambiguities of attaching value to information and intellectual property.

In addition, effective policy must address security, prevention, investigation, prosecution, and damage recovery of electronic property. There must also be a new standard of personnel development to ensure that employees have necessary skills to deal with computer and technology-related crime. Informed employees should have knowledge of security issues, processes, and practices; be trained in investigative techniques; and have the capacity to perform forensic analysis of electronic evidence.

Global crime issues require global strategies. In this regard, it would be advisable to have a transnational working group of police; national security; and relevant commerce, security and regulatory groups to help guide efforts in the prevention, investigation, and prosecution of computer-related crime. With the furious pace of technological development and the global growth of e-commerce, networked computers are rapidly becoming as commonly used as the telephone. There is a need for empirical data collection and analysis on computer criminality to define the problem, map trends, and understand the characteristics of the offenses and offenders. While exploration of hardware and software system protection is important, as is operational security of computers, research must go further. Defining behaviorally-based prevention, exploring the cybercrime equivalent of crime "hot spots," developing a catalog of "best practices" for investigation and prosecution of computer crime, and researching crime control methodologies in a fashion similar to predatory crime are all strategies on which emerging research must focus.

NOTES

[1] Computer manufacturers are now making powerful yet inexpensive computers designed specifically for easy and quick Internet access, making it available to even wider segments of society.

[2] Interestingly, the publication of his book led to retaliation against Mr. Sterling by various hackers, including threatening to alter his credit report and electronically changing his home telephone into a payphone.

[3] The *National Center for Computer Crime Data* (1222-17th Avenue; Santa Cruz, CA 95062-4457) is a private entity that documents cybercrime. Reports are voluntary and there appear to be no controls for validity and reliability. While the center can provide anecdotal evidence, there are significant methodological problems that limit any form of meaningful analysis or generalization of trends.

REFERENCES

American Bar Association. (1987). *Report on Computer Crime.* Chicago, IL: American Bar Association.

Arkin, S. (ed.) (1988). *Prevention and Prosecution of Computer and High Technology Crime.* Oakland, CA: Matthew Bender.

Barrett, N. (1997). *Digital Crime.* London: Kogan Page.

Bequai, A. (1983). *How to Prevent Computer Crime.* New York: John Wiley and Sons.

Bequai, A. (1987). *Technocrimes.* Lexington, MA: D.C. Heath and Company.

Bureau of Justice Statistics. (1979). *Computer Crime: Criminal Justice Resource Manual.* Washington, DC: U.S. Department of Justice.

Bureau of Justice Statistics. (1980). *Computer Security Techniques.* Washington, DC: U.S. Department of Justice.

Bureau of Justice Statistics. (1982). *Electronic Fund Transfer Systems and Crime.* Washington, DC: U.S. Department of Justice.

Carroll, J. M. (1987). *Computer Security.* Boston: Butterworth Publishing.

Carter, D. L. (1992). *Emerging Trends in Espionage.* Monterey, CA: PERSERC, Office of Naval Research, U.S. Department of Defense.

Carter, D. L. and Katz, A. J. (1998). "Computer Crime Victimization: An Assessment of Criminality in Cyberspace." *Police Research Quarterly,* 1.

Carter, D. L. and Katz, A. J. (1999). "Computer Applications by International Organized Crime Groups." In L. Moriarity and D. L. Carter (eds.), *Criminal Justice Technology in the 21st Century.* Springfield, IL: Charles C. Thomas, Publisher.

Computer Security Institute. (1999). *Issues and Trends: 1999 CSI/FBI Computer Crime and Security Survey.* San Francisco: Computer Security Institute.

Conly, C. H. (1989). *Organizing for Computer Crime Investigation and Prosecution.* Cambridge, MA: Abt Associates.

Conser, J. A., et al. (1988). "Investigating Computer-Related Crimes Involving Small Computer Systems." In M. Palmiotto (ed.), *Critical Issues in Computer Investigations*, 2d ed. Cincinnati: Anderson Publishing Company.

Cooper, J. A. (1984). *Computer Security Technology.* Lexington, MA: D.C. Heath and Company.

Dann, J. and Dozois, G. (1996). *Hackers.* New York: Ace Books.

Denning, D. (1990). "Concerning Hackers Who Break into Computer Systems." Paper presented at the National Computer Security Conference, Washington, DC.

Denning, D. (1995). Postscript to "Concerning Hackers Who Break into Computer Systems." Available: www.cosc.georgetown.edu/~denning/hackers/Hackers-Postscript.txt.

Federal Bureau of Investigation, (1999). *CyberNotes*, 3:1–13.

Florida Department of Law Enforcement. (1989). *Computer Crime in Florida.* An unpublished report prepared by the Florida Department of Law Enforcement, Tallahassee, Florida.

Gallery, S. (1987) (ed.). *Computer Security.* Boston: Butterworth Publishing Company.

Heffernan, R. (1995). *Securing Proprietary Information (SPI) Committee of the American Society of Industrial Security.* Committee presentation at the ASIS Annual Meeting, New Orleans, LA, September 12, 1995.

Hollinger, R. C., et al. (1988). "The Process of Criminalization: The Case of Computer Crime Laws." *Criminology*, 26(1): 101.

Icove, D. et al. (1995). *Computer Crime: A Crimefighter's Handbook.* Sebastopol, CA: O'Reilly & Associates, Inc.

Information Security. (January 2000). *By the Numbers*, p. 12.

Joyce, M. A. and S. Barrett. (June 1999). "The Evolution of the Computer Hacker's Motives." *The Police Chief*, pp. 28–32.

Kusserow, R. P. (1983). *Computer-Related Fraud and Abuse in U.S. Government Agencies.* Washington, DC: U.S. Department of Health and Human Services.

Landreth, B. (1985). *Out of the Inner Circle: A Hacker's Guide to Computer Security.* Bellevue, WA: Microsoft Press.

McEwen, T. (1989). *Dedicated Computer Crime Units.* Washington, DC: National Institute of Justice.

Parker, D. (1979). *Crime by Computer.* New York: Charles Scribner and Sons.

Parker, D. (1989). *Fighting Computer Crime.* New York: Charles Scribner and Sons.

Parker, D. (1999). *Fighting Computer Crime: A New Framework for the Protection of Information.* New York: John Wiley and Sons.

Public Interest Research Group. (1999). *Identity Theft II: Return to the Consumer X-Files.* PIRG Report. Available: www.igc.org/pirg/consumer/xfiles/index.htm

Roache, J. Y. (1986). "Computer Crime Deterrence." *American Journal of Criminal Law*, 13(2): 391.

Rostoker M. and R. Rines. (1986). Computer Jurisprudence. New York: Oceana Publications.

Shimomura, Tsutomu. (1996). *Takedown.* New York: Hyperion Books.

Security Wire Digest. (1999). Vol. 1, No. 6. Available: www.infosecuritymag.com/newsletter

Sikellis, R. (1999). *Guarding Against High Technology Crimes.* DSFX, International. Available: www.dsfx.com/html/hi_tech.html

Sinuraya, T. (June 1999). "The Cyber Crime Problem Increases." *Crime and Justice International,* pp. 1–10, 32.

Sterling, D. (1992). *The Hacker Crackdown.* New York: Bantam Books.

Stoll, C. (1988). *The Cuckoo's Egg.* New York: Bantam Books.

Taylor, P. A. (1999). *Hackers: Crime in the Digital Sublime.* New York: Routledge.

Thackery, G. (1985). "Problems of Computer Evidence." In *The Practical Prosecutor,* Vol. 2. Houston, TX: National College of District Attorneys.

U.N. Commission on Crime and Criminal Justice. (1995). *United Nations Manual on the Prevention and Control of Computer-Related Crime.* New York: United Nations.

U.S. Department of Justice. (1999). *Cyberstalking: A New Challenge for Law Enforcement and Industry.* A report to the Vice-President. Available: www.usdoj.gov/ag/cyberstalkingreport.htm

Van Duyn, J. (1985). *The Human Factor in Computer Crime.* Princeton, NJ: Petrocelli Books, Inc.

Williams, W. (1999). "The National Cyberterrorism Training Partnership." *The Informant,* 25(3): 7–11.

10

The Criminalization of Physician Violence

Social Control in Transformation?

John Liederbach
Francis T. Cullen
Jody L. Sundt
Gilbert Geis

Acts of violence by physicians during their professional practice clash with their traditionally esteemed status in the American social system. In the 1940s, the National Opinion Research Center presented a list of 90 occupations to a representative national sample of 2,900 persons. Physicians finished in a tie for second place with state governors and were surpassed only by U.S. Supreme Court justices (National Opinion Research Center 1941). More recently, a Gallup poll found doctors outpacing the clergy, college professors, and business executives among occupations designated "very prestigious" (Rosoff 1987). Even so, a stream of

Liederbach, John, et al. "The Criminalization of Physician Violence: Social Control in Transformation?" *Justice Quarterly*, 18(1): 141–170. Reprinted with permission of the Academy of Criminal Justice Sciences.

patients' horror stories now pours from the popular media: the wrong leg is amputated from a Tampa man; a New York newborn dies after an HMO-mandated one-day hospital stay; a Dallas surgeon removes a healthy right lung while leaving a cancerous left lung; and an eight-year old Colorado boy dies during minor surgery when the anesthesiologist falls asleep ("D.A. to stay on Death Case Against Doctor" 1995; Rosoff, Pontell, and Tillman 1998; Susman 1995).

These anecdotal accounts of physician wrongdoing are reinforced by research noting a high incidence of inept diagnoses and inexpert treatment by doctors, a large number of medical malpractice claims, and heavy punitive damages awarded against physicians. Some 400,000 patients are said to be victims of negligent mistakes or misdiagnoses each year ("Patients, Doctors, Lawyers: Medical Injury, Malpractice Litigation, & Patient Compensation" 1990). A Harvard researcher estimates that 180,000 patients die every year, at least in part because of medical mistakes, "the equivalent of three jumbo jet crashes every two days" (Susman 1995). The National Academy of Sciences recently ranked medical errors as the fifth leading cause of death in America, ahead of breast cancer, highway accidents, and AIDS (Weiss 1999). Each year, 10 of every 100 physicians are sued for malpractice; the resulting judgments exceed $1.5 billion ("Report of the Task Force on Medical Liability & Malpractice" 1987). Although some of the cases certainly could be won by the doctors or their insurance companies if they chose to absorb the cost of litigation, those who bring suits undoubtedly are a relatively small portion of the total number of patients with winnable cases. Indeed, according to one estimate, actual victims of medical malfeasance outnumber claimants by seven to one (Brennan 1991).

How many of these medical tragedies represent negligence on the part of doctors? A recent Department of Justice study found punitive damages awarded in 13 percent of the medical malpractice claims in their sample (Bensel and Goldberg 1996). Punitive damages indicate that at least a portion of behavior by physicians represents truly egregious conduct, a clear failure to provide the degree of care mandated by law and professional requirements. Many, if not most, of the other malpractice awards undoubtedly also are based on acts that could be regarded, under criminal codes, as a form of assault; some acts reach the level of negligent manslaughter.

Nonetheless, despite the realities of patient victimization, physician violence historically has not been treated as a crime. Physicians' traditional immunity from criminal prosecution stems in part from victims' preference for civil sanctions because doctors make inviting targets for civil suits. First, their income and assets render them well worth pursuing to obtain financial redress (Jesilow, Pontell, and Geis 1993). Second, malpractice insurance provides "deep pockets" as a source of monetary compensation. Unless the act is especially horrifying, victims typically are less interested in obtaining penal justice and revenge than in securing financial satisfaction.

Physicians' immunity from criminal prosecution also has been a product of their professional ethos. First, physicians' commitment to the patient's best interests, professed in the Hippocratic oath, surrounds them with an aura of altruism that serves as a "protective cloak" (Jesilow et al. 1993). Charges of intentionally harmful patient care can be difficult to justify when juxtaposed with the physicians' caring professional persona.

Second, physicians have been insulated from criminal processes by the personal, trusting nature of the doctor-patient relationship and by the patients' lack of a sophisticated understanding of the intricacies of medical treatments. These conditions have created a pattern of "deference" to doctors (Bucy 1989:858), a pattern defined generally by the critic Frank Kermode (1995:213) as a "tendency to irrational and premature compliance with the expectations of anybody who assumes the right to demand it." As a result, the trusting patient may fail to hold a truly negligent doctor accountable.

Finally, an incompetent medical act can be camouflaged by the profession's long-standing desire for self-regulation. Peer-oriented sanctions substitute for criminal prosecution, providing a veneer of professional accountability. The recent striking increase in disciplinary actions by state medical boards demonstrates the profession's continuing recourse to peer-oriented sanctions, and may reasonably be viewed as an attempt to keep more formidable forces from closely monitoring waywardness in their practice of medicine (Bensel and Goldberg 1996).

Despite the existence of these traditional barriers, physicians' continued immunity from criminal prosecution appears to be uncertain. During the past two decades we have witnessed a broad movement against other forms of white-collar violence, resulting in the criminal prosecution of offenses such as occupational safety violations and the manufacture of dangerous consumer products (Geis, Meier, and Salinger 1995). In addition, the physician's protective professional environment has been compromised dramatically by the advent of managed care and the intrusion of corporate and governmental economic interests into the practice of medicine (McKinlay and Stoeckle 1988).

In this context, our research explores the present state of physicians' immunity to criminal prosecution. Specifically we investigate whether (and, if so, to what extent) acts of violence by doctors during the course of their professional practice are being subjected to criminal sanctions. As a prelude to this analysis, we consider several factors suggesting that physician violence may become increasingly vulnerable to prosecution.

First, however, we must add a warning that was prompted by a reviewer's legitimate concern. The reviewer objected to our use of the term violence to characterize acts in which the physical harm is not intended. In doing so, we have imposed our definition of reality on "physician malfeasance," a decision in which (stated the reviewer) we succumbed to the temptation to be "politically correct (and inflammatory)." Although the central point of our research is not affected by this criticism—that is, that physicians now are being prosecuted for violent crimes—readers persuaded by this reasoning are free to view our work as focusing on the criminalization of physician "negligence," "wrongdoing," or "decision making."

Although we see the merits in this position, we retained the term violence for two reasons. First, the use of this term is not idiosyncratic. Rather (as the reviewer also noted), it links our work to a broader tradition within the study of white-collar illegality (see, for example, Cullen, Maakestad, and Cavender 1987; Frank and Lynch 1992; Hills 1987; Kramer 1992; also see Ross 1907). In this approach, the actions of white-collar and corporate offenders are conceptualized as "violent" when the behavior involved is physically injurious. Whether such conduct is criminally violent hinges on whether the offender is potentially punishable under the criminal law. In the case of physicians who harm patients because of excessive negligence, we are comfortable in calling their acts "violent."

Second, as critical criminologists have long argued (see, for example, Schwendinger and Schwendinger 1975), the decision not to use terms such as violence is itself a decision to socially construct one reality over another. Legal terms such as negligence have the advantage of sounding neutral. Even so, they risk truncating reality because they portray physician misconduct as lacking "true intent" even when such actions in fact may involve substantial choice and responsibility (or, as the rational choice theorists point out, self-interested behavior). More important, such language inadvertently sanitizes the conduct under investigation by directing attention away from the fact that we are focusing on a situation in which people are injured and die.

Physicians' Increasing Vulnerability to Criminal Liability

Although doctors have evaded prosecution for victimizing patients, their criminal sanctioning for other offenses indicates that they are not fully immune from criminal liability. Those who commit violent offenses that are unrelated to their medical role, such as assault or murder, appear to enjoy no special protection from criminal prosecution (Hall 1995; McKnight 1996). Offenses relating to the dispensing of illegal narcotics and other controlled substances always have been treated severely (Musto 1973). In earlier days as well, doctors' involvement in abortions, if discovered, was likely to lead to a criminal charge (Howell 1969).

More important, a number of recent developments have increased the likelihood that doctors will come before a criminal court for other violations that potentially have been the subject of penal prosecution, but never actually were. The advent of government-financed programs such as Medicare and Medicaid involved the practice of medicine with concerns about fiscal oversight by non-medical authorities regarding the manner in which taxpayers' funds were being spent. This development in turn created a cadre of investigators who developed specialized competence in dealing with fraudulent billing practices and other medical misbehavior (Jesilow, Pontell, and Geis 1985). Investigators began in the 1970s to criminally prosecute Medicaid providers, usually those engaged in the most egregious practices. Sometimes these cases included physicians involved in financial schemes that resulted in physical harm to patients. Although such cases could be viewed as a form of "violence," it is equally instructive that prosecutors continued to use fraud statutes rather than violent crime laws to convict doctors. One especially horrific case, for example, involved the prosecution of a California ophthalmologist who performed cataract surgery on patients with healthy eyes solely to collect the Medicaid fee (Pontell, Geis, and Jesilow 1985). Even though these medically unnecessary procedures "blinded a lot of people," the doctor eventually was convicted and was sentenced only for fraud (Pontell, Geis, and Jesilow 1985:1–1; Welkos 1984).

In a related area, nursing homes also have become the target of state and federal investigations regarding inhumane conditions and overcharging (Rosoff et al. 1998). Just five months after opening, one New York facility came under investigation for charges of patient abuse (Rosoff et al. 1998). Extreme cases of patient neglect have resulted in the prosecution of nursing home administrators in Wisconsin and Texas for reckless homicide and criminal neglect (Schudson, Onellion, and Hochstedler 1984).

Some evidence, then, suggests that the criminal law is beginning to penetrate the medical domain; the key issue, however, remains whether the criminal liability of physicians will extend to patient victimization and will be prosecuted explicitly as violent crime. There are several reasons to expect the criminal law to expand into the control of physician violence. One factor that may increase physicians' vulnerability is the broad societal movement against other forms of white-collar violence. In recent decades, this movement has produced criminal prosecutions in corporate cases traditionally viewed as civil matters, including matters of workplace injuries and death (Benson and Cullen 1998; Dutzman 1990), environmental pollution (Addison and Mack 1991; Cohen and Shapiro 1995), and (though to a lesser extent) the marketing of dangerous consumer products (Bonner and Forman 1993; Geis et al. 1995). These legal attacks on corporate violence suggest a changing ideological context in which the criminalization of physician violence seems more likely.

Cultural Changes

A number of cultural changes appear to be influencing this movement. First, public trust in society's elite groups has declined since the social turmoil of the 1960s and 1970s. The erosion of confidence in big business and the emergence of anti-business sentiments has created a cultural climate more conducive to the criminal prosecution of corporate violence (Cullen et al. 1987). A recent national survey of prosecutors found that more than 40 percent were or had been involved in cases regarding unsafe workplaces or environmental crimes (Benson and Cullen 1998). This legal response suggests that professional groups (including doctors, whose occupation remains prestigious) may no longer enjoy the degree of trust that traditionally protected them from legal attacks.

In addition to this erosion in public confidence, there is evidence that citizens are growing increasingly intolerant of being exposed to risks to their physical health and general well-being (Evans, Cullen, and Dubeck 1993; Friedman 1985). Previously acceptable business practices, such as the failure to provide safe workplace conditions, now are viewed as unacceptably hazardous. In this more vigilant climate, elite crimes are perceived not as accidents or situations that must be passively tolerated but as grounds for criminal prosecutions.

Finally, the struggles for social and political equality that began in the 1960s have sensitized the public to historical disparities in the legal response to white-collar and street crimes, and have fostered a growing commitment to equal treatment under the law (Evans et al. 1993). The increased criminalization of corporate violence in the 1970s and 1980s reflected these public expectations regarding the need for equitable sanctioning of both poor and rich offenders (Cullen et al. 1987).

Health Maintenance Organizations

The cultural changes reflected in the broad movement against white-collar violence provide one possible avenue to the criminalization of physician violence. A second consideration that may heighten physicians' vulnerability to prosecution relates to the envelopment of medical practice into a network of health maintenance organizations (HMOs). Health care has become increasingly "corporatized"; these large-scale bureaucracies have gained wider control over the practice of medicine (McKinlay and Stoeckle 1988). Doctors and patients have been replaced by "providers" and "enrollees" in the new managed care environment. Physicians now must divide their loyalties between the patient and the organization, and the patient is fast assuming a secondary role. For their part, doctors report diminished gratification from relationships with patients, and they see patients as more critical, more adversarial, and less strongly committed to long-term attachments (Stoeckle 1989). Corporatization seems to have whittled away doctors' autonomy and has depersonalized the doctor-patient relationship that traditionally helped to insulate doctors from criticism and criminal prosecution.

Corporatization may influence the imposition of criminal sanctions more directly. Research suggests that the public is more willing to sanction corporate offenders as an entity than individual actors; corporate offenses are viewed as more deserving of harsh civil and criminal penalties (Frank et al. 1989; Hans and Ermann 1989). Public disdain for corporatized medicine apparently has reached a fever pitch, fueling congressional debates and calls for a "patient's bill of rights" (Kilborn 1998). The physician-employee of an impersonal corporation appears more vulnerable to criminal prosecution than did the trusted family doctor of the past.

Corporatization also ties the medical enterprise more clearly to money. HMOs employ a variety of procedures designed to increase physicians' economic productivity, including incentives to reduce costs, limiting access to specialized care, and mandatory case reviews by nonphysicians (Wrightson 1990). The use of financial incentives by some HMOs significantly alters physicians' treatment decisions (Hillman, Pauley, and Kerstein 1989). The RAND Health Insurance Experiment found HMO care to be associated with reduced costs, lower patient satisfaction, and poorer health status among low-income enrollees (Wagner and Bledsoe 1990; Ware et al. 1986).

When the profit motive begins to compete with the physician's commitment to care, public attitudes regarding the meaning of adverse outcomes may be redefined. For example, corporations that have been found to balance dollars against the cost of human lives have been vulnerable to prosecution (Swiggert and Farrell 1980). Patient victimizations seen as the product of deliberate business decisions also may be defined as criminal. One Texas HMO recently chose to pay a $5.35 million settlement rather than answering in court to charges of profit-driven care ("Kaiser Settles Texas Malpractice Case for $5.35 Million" 1998).

The Role of Prosecutors

A third consideration pertaining to physicians' increasing vulnerability is the role of prosecutors and their willingness to initiate criminal charges against doctors. Studies of prosecutors indicate that the decision to file criminal charges is influenced by the perceived strength of traditional systems of control (Benson and Cullen 1998; Benson, Cullen, and Maakestad 1990). Prosecutors seem more likely to file criminal charges in corporate cases when "regulatory agencies fail to act," or when they believe that corporate offenses have "escaped appropriate penalty" (Benson et al. 1990:364).

Prosecutors' perceptions regarding the strength of traditional systems of control are not formed in a vacuum. In the case of physician violence, recent legislative actions may work to lessen the perceived strength of traditional control systems. States have moved to curb the cost and frequency of civil malpractice litigation by limiting damage awards, emphasizing alternatives to jury trials, and shortening statutes of limitations connected to malpractice claims ("Report of the Task Force on Medical Liability & Malpractice" 1987). These legislative actions, which weaken the force of civil sanctions, may prompt prosecutors to fill the void by employing the criminal law to punish cases of physician violence.

In summary, we have identified several factors that we believe signal a change in the social control of physician violence. The signposts include both broad cultural forces and changes within the field of medicine that seem to threaten the doctor's traditional protection from prosecution. We turn now to the core of our research, in which we explore cases involving the criminal prosecution of doctors for violent patient victimization. We argue that these cases represent a transformation in the social control of physician violence—perhaps still in its beginning stages but potentially profound in its implications—from the exclusive use of civil and peer-initiated sanctions to the emergence of the criminal sanction.

◂ METHODS ▸

We sought to locate cases in which physicians had been criminally prosecuted for acts committed while delivering services to patients. Our objective was to locate cases of criminal prosecution for acts that traditionally have been subject to civil or professional sanctions. One information source was the Lexis-Nexis on-line information database. Lexis-Nexis provides full-text and bibliographic access to publications representing law, government, news, business, and medicine. Lexis-Nexis accesses wire service dispatches, newspapers, periodicals, television news transcripts, and legal or government documents. We performed additional on-line searches using Westlaw, the computer-assisted legal research service offered by West Publishing Company.

Results from these searches are limited in at least two respects. First, the amount of information concerning each case depends in part on the amount of coverage provided by newspapers, periodicals, and law journals. Second, on-line information resources offer data for only a limited time span. The Lexis-Nexis database contains Lexis legal information from 1973 to the present; Nexis supplies news data beginning in 1979.

In addition, we searched for relevant cases in the Public Citizen Health Research Group's *16,638 Questionable Doctors Disciplined by State and Federal Governments* (Wolfe et al. 1998). This database contains case information on doctors disciplined from 1987 through 1996 by the medical boards of all 50 states and the District of Columbia, by the U.S. Department of Health and Human Services, by the Drug Enforcement Administration, and by the Food and Drug Administration. We searched all case entries listing "criminal conviction or plea of guilty, nolo contendere, or no contest to a crime." These listings included case information on 1,861 doctors and 2,545 disciplinary actions. The Public Citizen Health Research Group currently maintains the only publicly available national database of disciplinary actions taken against individual doctors.

One weakness of this database, however, is that the amount of information on each case varies by state and depends on the record-keeping system of each state's medical board. In addition, criminal convictions against doctors for which no board action was taken are not listed. Further, some states do not list the specific criminal offenses related to the disciplinary actions; thus it is sometimes difficult to discern whether a criminal conviction was related to a physician's medical practice.

We made contact with the American Medical Association's Center for Health Policy Research for further records of criminal cases against physicians. We also searched white-collar and occupational crime texts for material on physician violence (see especially Green 1997). Because we cannot be certain that we secured information about every relevant case, our data set, if anything, would underestimate the behavior of concern to us.

◂ Results ▸

Our search revealed 15 cases in which physicians were prosecuted for violent crimes for conduct undertaken in the course of a medical practice. These cases included 19 individual doctors as well as one criminally suspect HMO. In keeping with the thesis that the prosecution of physicians for violent crime is a recent occurrence, we discovered no relevant cases before 1986. Most instructive, perhaps, eight of the cases occurred during the last five years; five of these prosecutions originated in the period beginning in 1998. Although the search identified only a few cases, their very existence indicates that physician violence no longer remains entirely beyond the reach of the criminal law.

Below we offer a brief description of each case, including the factual background, the criminal charge(s), and the results of the prosecution (if they are available). Then we examine the cases in terms of a number of common characteristics that are associated with the criminal prosecutions and thus may have prompted them.

Descriptions of Cases

United States v. Billig (1986). Cmdr. Donald Billig, former chief heart surgeon at Bethesda Naval Hospital, was charged with involuntary manslaughter and negligent homicide in the deaths of five patients during surgery (Engelberg 1986). Prosecutors contended that the deaths resulted from Billig's "blunders, mistakes, and arrogance," including torn aortas and the misidentification of coronary veins as arteries ("Navy Surgeon Convicted" 1986; Van Grunsven 1997). Testimony revealed that Billig was nearly blind in one eye from a tennis injury, and that he defied orders to perform surgery only under supervision (Engelberg 1986). Billig originally was convicted in three of the five deaths and was sentenced to four years in prison (Spolar 1988). He became the first Navy doctor to be convicted of manslaughter stemming from a medical procedure ("Navy Surgeon Convicted, Faces Prison in Death of Three

Patients" 1986). A Navy appeals court later overturned his conviction on the grounds that Billig did not bear primary responsibility for the deaths (Van Grunsven 1997).

Utah v. Warden (1988). Obstetrician David Warden was charged with negligent homicide in the death of a premature infant he delivered in the home of 18-year-old Joanne Young, the mother (Van Grunsven 1997). Warden's negligence resulted from his failure to perform a sonogram to confirm Young's due date, his judgment that Young was a suitable candidate for in-home delivery, and his abject failure to provide follow-up care immediately after the birth (Van Grunsven 1997). The infant died the morning after delivery from respiratory distress related to the premature delivery. Warden had left Young's home only 40 minutes after the delivery, while the baby was still experiencing difficulty breathing. He was unavailable while his patient and her mother attempted to contact him when the baby's hands and feet "turned a deeper shade of blue" during the night (Van Grunsven 1997:26). Although Warden's initial prosecution ended in a mistrial, he was later convicted as charged in a second trial (Van Grunsven 1997).

California v. Kapen (1988). Anesthesiologist Harold Kapen's gross negligence and incompetence contributed to the death of a seven-week-old baby during emergency surgery ("Probation in Baby's Death" 1988; Wolfe et al. 1998). Kapen pleaded guilty to involuntary manslaughter before trial and was sentenced to two years of unsupervised probation on the condition that he no longer practice medicine ("Probation in Baby's Death" 1988).

California v. Klvana (1989). Obstetrician Milos Klvana's failure to recommend hospital deliveries for women involved in high-risk pregnancies led to his prosecution on nine counts of second-degree murder. The case originated with the untimely death of infant Jason Friel (Omstad 1986). The mother's labor was premature, and the case was complicated by her diabetic condition.

Ignoring these danger signs, Klvana proceeded with the difficult delivery in his private clinic. The baby was born listless and pale; nonetheless, Klvana sent the mother and child home four hours later. The infant died 14 hours after birth because his undeveloped lungs were unable to support his breathing. A subsequent investigation uncovered eight other infant deaths related to Klvana's penchant for risky out-of-hospital deliveries. Prosecutors equated his behavior with that of a drunk driver: they acknowledged that he had no criminal intent, but maintained that the unnecessary risks he imposed on patients constituted "implied malice" (Munder 1987). Klvana was convicted and sentenced to 53 years to life in prison. He was the first physician in the country to be convicted of murder due to poor care (Van Grunsven 1997).

Oklahoma v. Reynolds (1990). Dr. Joe Reynolds was convicted of second-degree manslaughter in the death of a patient (his wife), who died during liposuction surgery performed in Reynolds' private office (Wolfe et al. 1998; "Oklahoma" 1990). The doctor was "not accused of deliberately killing his wife. Instead he (was) accused of acting with such criminal recklessness that he caused her death" (Clay 1991). Further, defense attorneys for Reynolds highlighted the path breaking nature of the charges, arguing that they had seen "no reported case in Oklahoma where a licensed physician (had) ever been charged, much less convicted, of second-degree murder involving the death of a patient during surgery" (Clay 1991).

People v. Einaugler (1993). Dr. Gerald Einaugler was charged with reckless endangerment and willful violation of health codes because he was slow to hospitalize an elderly nursing home patient (Crane 1994). Alida Lamour was a blind 72-year-old woman in extremely poor health when she was admitted to Brooklyn's Interfaith Nursing Home. During her prior two-month hospitalization for kidney failure, doctors had inserted a catheter into her abdomen to permit dialysis treatment. In his initial examination, Einaugler mistakenly identified the dialysis catheter as a feeding tube. The patient subsequently was fed through the catheter for two days. After she died four days later from chemical peritonitis that had developed from the feedings, Einaugler altered the medical records (Cohen and Shapiro 1995). When a grand jury refused to indict him for manslaughter, the prosecutor brought the lesser charge of reckless endangerment and failure to obey the health code because Einaugler had been tardy in transferring the patient to the hospital after recognizing his error in regard to the catheter. Einaugler was convicted and sentenced to one year in prison (Green 1997). The sentence later was commuted to 52 days ("Doctor in Negligence Case Has Sentence Eased" 1997).

People v. Hyatt (1993). Dr. Abu Hyatt's dangerous and illegal abortion practices led to his criminal prosecution. In one instance, he ordered patient Marie Moise to leave his office midway through an abortion procedure when she refused his demand for an additional $500. He left a portion of the fetus inside the patient. In a second case, Hyatt failed to complete an illegal third-trimester abortion successfully. Patient Rosa Rodriquez and the baby both survived, though the baby lost an arm during the procedure (Ambramovsky 1995). Hyatt was charged with assault and with performing an illegal abortion. After his indictment, 30 other former patients came forward to complain of injuries they said were caused by his negligence. The "Butcher of Avenue A" was convicted and received a prison term of 29 years (Abramovsky 1995).

Wisconsin v. The Chem-Bio Corporation (1995). The Chem-Bio Corporation provided laboratory services to the Family Health Plan, an HMO. Criminal charges stemmed from the lab's repeated failure to detect abnormalities in HMO enrollee Karin Smith's pap smears (DeBlieu 1996). Smith saw her HMO doctor 15 times and underwent three Pap smear tests in an attempt to discover the cause of her chronic vaginal bleeding. In each instance, Chem-Bio reported normal test results. Still faced with chronic bleeding after three years of diagnostic tests, Smith sought treatment elsewhere. The tests were repeated, and advanced cervical cancer was detected. Smith would have had a 90 to 95 percent chance for total recovery if the HMO lab had detected the cancer earlier. Instead the advanced stage of the disease led to her death.

A criminal inquest recommended that Smith's doctor be prosecuted criminally, but the district attorney elected to pursue Chem-Bio on a charge of reckless homicide. The prosecutor characterized the company as a cost-cutting enterprise that encouraged sloppy diagnoses by paying technicians per slide. "The Family Death Plan," as the company was dubbed, was convicted of reckless manslaughter for Smith's death as well as the death of Delores Geary under similar circumstances ("Pap Smear Death Draws $20,000 Fine" 1996). Chem-Bio was fined $10,000 for each death, the maximum penalty permitted by law.

People v. Benjamin (1995). Dr. David Benjamin was charged with second-degree murder after his abortion procedure resulted in the death of patient Guadalupe Negron (Holloway 1995): he was the first doctor ever to be charged in New York State with murder involving the death of a patient during a medical procedure (Cohen and Shapiro 1995:4). Benjamin had miscalculated the length of Negron's pregnancy because he failed to perform a sonogram. He estimated the age of the fetus at 13 weeks and began a suction procedure more appropriate for first-trimester pregnancies. Negron was actually 19 weeks pregnant, and the size of her fetus prevented removal by suction. A three-inch tear in the patient's uterus resulted, and she bled to death in Benjamin's recovery room while he attended to a second abortion in an adjacent office (Holloway 1995).

The trial connected Negron's death to the inappropriate abortion procedure. Benjamin also was charged with failure to summon paramedics to the scene promptly, with trying to cover up his mistake by telling paramedics that his patient had suffered a heart attack and with suppressing her medical records. On conviction, Benjamin received a prison sentence of 25 years to life.

Colorado v. Verbrugge (1996). Anesthesiologist Joseph Verbrugge was charged with reckless manslaughter in connection with the death of eight-year-old Richard Leonard during ear surgery (Lindsay

1996). The case was the first in Colorado to involve criminal charges against a physician in the death of a patient (Lindsay 1997). The normally routine procedure went awry when the boy's heart rate jumped significantly after Verbrugge administered the anesthetic. During the surgery, the patient's breathing became irregular and his temperature soared to 107 degrees. Prosecutors contended that Verbrugge failed to react to those danger signs because he had fallen asleep during the operation. The patient died after three hours in surgery: his reaction to the anesthesia had increased the level of carbon monoxide in his blood to four times the normal level.

Verbrugge denied that he had fallen asleep during this operation, but admitted to sleeping during four previous surgeries (Lewis 1996). The defense charged that the death was attributable solely to a rare condition that produced the reaction to the anesthetic. The jury was deadlocked on a manslaughter charge, but convicted Verbrugge for criminal negligence ("Anesthesiologist Accused of Dozing in Surgery Found Negligent" 1996). The Colorado Court of Appeals later overturned the conviction because the prosecutor failed to file charges within 18 months of the boy's death (Ensslin 1999).

California v. Schug (1998). Emergency room physician Wolfgang Schug was charged and indicted for second-degree murder in the death of 11-month-old Cody Burrows (Dolan 1998). The child had been taken to rural Redbud Community Hospital because he was dehydrated and vomiting. Schug diagnosed the problem as an ear infection and prescribed antibiotics (Van Grunsven 1997). Cody's parents returned to Redbud two days later, when the boy's symptoms returned. Prosecution witnesses contended that Schug waited too long to insert an intravenous feeding tube and failed to summon on-call help when he realized that the patient was in grave danger (Van Grunsven 1997). He also did not call for an ambulance or helicopter to transport the patient; thus Cody's parents were forced to drive one hour and 20 minutes to the nearest pediatric hospital (Van Grunsven 1997). The boy died the next day from conditions stemming from the initial ear infection; medical experts, however, provided conflicting testimony as to Schug's culpability. Schug was acquitted when the judge ruled that prosecutors had failed to present substantial evidence of criminal conduct (Dolan 1998).

California v. Falconi (1998). Guillermo Falconi's sloppy surgical skills turned a routine cosmetic operation into a fatal ordeal for patient Barbara Rojas. Falconi removed excess fat tissue from Rojas's arms during an in-home operation. The Brazilian-trained surgeon offered Rojas a reduced fee, but he concealed the fact that he was not licensed in the United States (Dirmann 1997). The operation was marked by Falconi's incompetence and unprofessional demeanor. He never sterilized the bed before operating. He had to be reminded to wash his hands by the patient's 14-year-old daughter. The excess fat tissue was discarded in a grocery bag. The patient bled continuously after the surgery and lost consciousness. She died three weeks later from multiple organ failure due to extreme blood loss (Dirmann 1998). Falconi was convicted of second-degree murder, disposing illegally of hazardous waste, and practicing medicine unlawfully. He faces a mandatory sentence of 15 years to life in prison.

California v. Steir (1998). Dr. Bruce Saul Steir was charged with second-degree murder after patient Sharon Hamptlon bled to death following an abortion. Prosecutors contend that Steir discharged Hamptlon after he knowingly perforated her uterus during the procedure (Smith 1998). The case has been stayed pending a review by the California Supreme Court. Steir alleges that the prosecution amounts to unconstitutional discrimination and is a politically motivated attempt to limit access to abortion ("No Hearing on March 3 for Dr. Bruce Steir" 1999).

Polk (PA) Medical Center Cases (1999). Polk Center is Pennsylvania's largest state-operated medical facility for the mentally handicapped ("One Doctor is Cleared in PA Case" 1999). Prosecutors originally charged six doctors who worked at the facility with an array of offenses including involuntary manslaughter, reckless endangerment, patient neglect, and abuse. Dr. Cesar Miranda and Dr. Hyunchel Shin were both charged with manslaughter for neglecting three patients so grievously that they died (Roddy and Hernan 1999). The remaining physicians faced assault charges for using sutures and surgical staples to close patients' wounds without anesthetic (Roddy and Hernan 1999). Charges against Dr. Shin have since been dropped for lack of evidence ("One Doctor Is Cleared in PA Case" 1999).

Arizona v. Biskind (1999). Dr. John Biskind was charged and indicted with manslaughter in the case of a woman who bled to death from a punctured uterus following an abortion procedure (Steckner and Snyder 1999). Charges are pending.

Analyzing the Cases

In addition to investigating the emergence of doctors' criminal prosecutions, we explored whether the cases we uncovered had common characteristics or were largely idiosyncratic, thus indicating that the prosecutions were more random than patterned events. This analysis of cases must be viewed as suggestive—as a basis for future research—for at least two reasons. First, we cannot disentangle whether the characteristics we discern show that certain doctors are more vulnerable to prosecution or are more deeply involved in medical violence—or both. Most observers of white-collar crime suggest that such offenses are only the "tip of the iceberg." If this is also true of physicians' acts of criminal violence, then the data may be seen as revealing, at least in part, which doctors are more vulnerable to prosecution.

Second, and in a related vein, we do not have a data set (nor does anyone else) that would include all cases of physician violence which have been discovered and brought to prosecutors' attention. If we had such data, it would be possible to examine, controlling for the nature of the misconduct in question, which physician characteristics were related to differential prosecution. Again, without such data, we present our analysis as suggestive.

In distilling the cases for potential commonality, we looked for characteristics that emerged in the course of the analysis (e.g., location where medical services were provided, history of previous sanctions, lack of insurance, victims' vulnerability, physician's gender). We also used the previous literature on white-collar crime prosecutions to inform our assessment. In this latter regard, the research suggests that characteristics of the offense and the offender can affect the likelihood of a prosecution.

First, the factual and legal complexities of some white-collar crimes have been associated with a decreased willingness to file criminal charges (Benson et al. 1990). Cases involving complex fact patterns require extensive investigation and specialized expertise. Local prosecutors often have resources inadequate for prosecuting highly technical cases effectively (Benson et al. 1990).

Second, the incidence of criminal prosecutions against other white-collar offenders increases significantly with greater offense seriousness (Shapiro 1985). Cases involving particularly severe physical harm to victims appear to provoke the strongest response from prosecutors (Benson and Cullen 1998).

Third, criminal prosecutions can be legitimized if the offender can be shown to be a "rational calculator" who places profit above human lives, much like a "street criminal" (Cullen et al. 1987).

Fourth, vulnerability to criminal prosecution also may be related to certain physician attributes. Research indicates that physicians punished for Medicaid violations typically do not represent the mainstream. They often practice in poor inner-city communities, where low fees may encourage and rationalize illegal procedures (Pontell, Jesilow, Geis, and O'Brien 1985).

In Table 1 we display details of the cases in terms of a number of common characteristics that tended to mark the prosecutions. These are represented in the second through the last columns. If a characteristic is present, an X is placed in the row designating the case. An O indicates that the characteristic is absent; an M (for "missing") means that the relevant information was not recoverable from the sources available to us. We discern several patterns, some more pronounced than others.

Table 1:
Case Characteristics of Physician Prosecutions

Case	Year	Serious Harm	"Fringe" Doctor	Profit-Driven Care	Simple Facts	Out of Hospital	Previous Sanctions	Lack of Insurance	
United States v. Billig	1986	X	O	O	O	O	X		
Utah v. Warden	1988	X	M	M	X	X	M		
California v. Kapen	1988	X	O	O	O	O	O		
California v. Klvana	1989	X	X	X	X	X	X	X	X
Oklahoma v. Reynolds	1990	X	M	O	M	X	M		
People v. Einaugler	1993	O	M	O	X	X	O		
People v. Hyatt	1993	X	X	X	X	X	M		
Wisconsin v. Chem-Bio	1995	X	O	X	X	X	O		
People v. Benjamin	1995	X	X	X	X	X	X	X	X
Colorado v. Verbrugge	1996	X	M	O	X	O	X	O	X
California v. Schug	1998	X	M	O	O	O	O		
California v. Falconi	1998	X	X	X	X	X	O		
California v. Steir	1998	X	M	O	X	X	X		
Polk Med. Ctr. Cases (PA)	1999	X	X	O	X	X	M		
Arizona v. Biskind	1999	X	M	X	X	X	O		
Total		14	5	6	11	11	5		

X=present
O=not present
M=missing from case information

To begin, all but one of the cases clearly involved serious physical harm to patients. Thus, in 13 of the prosecutions, the patient died. For example, the Klvana, Warden, and Kapen cases rested on infant deaths; the Benjamin, Steir, and Biskind cases involved women who died after abortion procedures. Further, in the Hyatt case, an infant suffered a severed arm during an illegal abortion. The Einaugler case may be the only episode not associated with serious patient harm, even though a patient's demise triggered the prosecution. The death of Einaugler's elderly patient was never linked clearly to the doctor's actions because of her grave prior condition and the absence of an official autopsy (Crane 1994). The reduced charges brought against Einaugler contrast with the allegations in the other cases: assault, manslaughter, reckless homicide, and murder.

It also appears that "fringe" or marginal doctors, most notably those trained abroad, may be particularly susceptible to prosecution. In five of the eight cases where we discerned this characteristic, the physician was coded as a "fringe" doctor. Dr. Klvana received his medical training in Czechoslovakia (Omstad 1986); Dr. Hyatt graduated from the Calcutta Medical School (Kocieniewski 1993); Dr. Falconi was trained in South America; and Dr. Benjamin was an Iranian immigrant (Abramovsky 1995). In addition, Abu Hyatt and David Benjamin practiced in low-income Hispanic communities and advertised in the same Spanish-language newspapers. Further, those who were charged in the Polk Medical Center cases were employed in a "low-status" position: civil service doctors working in Pennsylvania's largest state-operated medical facility for the mentally handicapped ("Six Doctors Charged in Abuse of the Mentally Retarded" 1999). Although precise information is unavailable, the names of at least some of the physicians charged suggest that they probably were foreign-born. In contrast, Dr. Billig supervised the Navy's Cardiothoracic Surgery Department, Dr. Kapen was an anesthesiologist in a regular hospital, and the doctors who worked for the HMO involved in the Chem-Bio case represented mainstream American medicine.

Six of the cases show evidence of profit-driven care. For example, the case against Chem-Bio's laboratory linked screening errors to the lab's cost-cutting method of operation. From a larger perspective, the case illustrates clearly the "quality care versus cost containment" debate that has accompanied the HMO movement. The Hyatt case, which was precipitated by the doctor's demand for money in the middle of a medical procedure, is a prime example of profit-driven treatment. Dr. Falconi offered reduced fees because he was not licensed in the United States. In the Benjamin case, the $650 charge was well above the norm (Garcilazo and Merrill 1995); in addition, Benjamin's rapid exit from the recovery room to deal with another patient caused prosecutors to characterize his clinic as an "abortion mill." Similarly, economic concerns apparently influenced the poor care apparent in the Biskind abortion case (Steckner and Snyder 1999). Dr. Klvana's preference for home deliveries also apparently was influenced by economic motives, though the fact that his staff privileges at four area hospitals had been withdrawn also figured in the situation.

Cases involving simple fact patterns seem to be attractive candidates for criminal prosecution. As shown in Table 1, 11 of the 15 cases contain factual scenarios that are easily understood. A dialysis catheter is mistaken for a feeding tube; a doctor allegedly falls asleep during an operation; an unattended patient bleeds to death in a recovery room. Yet these rather straightforward scenarios were rendered considerably more judicially complicated when issues relating to criminal culpability were introduced. Einaugler's defense attorney argued successfully that the feeding tube error did not cause the patient's death. Prosecutors in the Kapen case accepted a plea bargain because they were uncertain whether they could prove criminal intent in court. Similarly, in the Verbrugge case, the patient's rare genetic condition had to be considered in the question of the physician's guilt.

Eleven of the 15 cases involve victimizations that resulted from procedures performed outside the typical hospital setting. The Chem-Bio case involved a medical lab, the Einaugler case a nursing home, and the Polk case a state-operated mental institution. The Benjamin, Hyatt, Steir, and Biskind cases all stemmed from abortions performed in private clinics. The Falconi, Warden, and Reynolds cases involved in-home procedures. The high-risk deliveries in the Klvana case occurred either in Klvana's private office or at the victims' homes. While prosecutors focused on the risks associated with out-of-hospital procedures, Klvana's defense attorneys characterized the case solely as a means of discouraging less costly alternatives to expensive hospital deliveries.

Doctors had a history of professional misconduct in at least five of the cases. Klvana and Verbrugge had lost staff privileges at several hospitals before their criminal cases. In 1978, Klvana was convicted on 26 counts of illegally prescribing controlled substances (Klunder 1987). Benjamin was investigated repeatedly in the mid-1980s by the New York Department of Health. In 1986, the state medical review board convicted him on 38 counts of negligence and suspended his license for three months (Abramovsky 1995). Prior professional sanctions also influenced an additional common characteristic: at least five of the doctors were unable to obtain malpractice insurance before their criminal misconduct because of their checkered professional careers. Eight of the 15 cases include either past professional sanctions or the absence of malpractice insurance, indicating the prior failure of traditional systems of control with these physicians. This factor is related to the use of criminal sanctions against other types of white-collar offenders (Benson and Cullen 1998; Benson et al. 1990).

The patients, or victims, in 11 of the cases share certain attributes that prosecutors could use to promote an image of vulnerability and a need for protection. Victims in the Klvana, Warden, Kapen, and Schug cases were helpless infants; the victim in the Einaugler case was a blind 72-year-old female; the Polk residents were mentally handicapped. Similarly, the Verbrugge case involved the death of an 8-year-old boy. In the Benjamin, Hyatt, Steir, and Biskind cases, pregnant females were victims. Notably, only two of the cases involved adult male victims. This situation suggests the possible existence of a "chivalry effect," whereby prosecutors become increasingly willing to initiate criminal prosecutions in cases in which the victims reflect traditional perceptions of vulnerability. All 15 of the cases involved male physicians. The image of vulnerability projected by infants, females, and the elderly may be more pronounced in the presence of adult male victimizers.

In summary, the cases in which physicians have been prosecuted for violence stemming from their clinical practices have involved male doctors and serious harm to patients. They also tend to be marked by the provision of services outside a hospital, to be offenses in which the facts are "simple" or understandable, and to be instances in which the victim is vulnerable. These cases also tend, although less strongly, to be characterized by the prosecution of "fringe" doctors, by the delivery of medical care that appeared to be profit-driven, and by the physicians' history of professional misconduct and/or lack of malpractice insurance.

◂ Discussion ▸

"Criminal" violence is not merely an objective event but also a socially constructed reality. Objective harms—even egregious harms—can exist for years without being defined and treated as a crime deserving prosecution. Indeed, critics from E. A. Ross (1907) to a host of contemporary commentators have illuminated how the violence perpetrated by white-collar elites escapes attention and is not brought within the reach of the criminal law. They have shown that the street is not the only venue for violence; physically harmful business practices also exact enormous costs. The critics' goal has been to socially construct white-collar misconduct as "criminal" and to define misconduct that harms people as "violence" (see, for example, Cullen et al. 1987; Frank and Lynch 1992; Hills 1987; Kramer 1992; Mokhiber 1989).

Criminologists often reveal the barriers that inhibit the portrayal of white-collar harm as violent crime. Those with the wherewithal can play a significant role in the shaping of laws; also, many acts seem too technical and their perpetrators too far above the common herd to be subjected to the glare and humiliation of a public criminal trial (Sutherland 1949). The news media focus disproportionately on violent street crime and often neglect the costs of white-collar crime (see, for example, Lynch, Nalla, and Miller 1989; Wright, Cullen, and Blankenship 1995).

Even so, important strides have been made in redefining white-collar misconduct as criminal. The emerging official movement against white-collar crime has made the prosecution of white-collar offenders an unexceptional event (Benson and Cullen 1998; Weisburd et al. 1991; Wheeler, Mann, and Sarat 1988; also see Mann 1985). Although only a small fraction of elite criminals are detected, the sight of white-collar offenders—whether embezzlers, inside traders, perpetrators of fraudulent business schemes, or politicians accused of corruption—standing before the court and sitting behind bars no longer shocks nor necessarily earns front-page newspaper headlines. Violent white-collar crimes are prosecuted with some regularity, especially in urban areas and in jurisdictions where district attorneys have established special units to deal with such offenses (Benson and Cullen 1998; also see Cullen et al. 1987).

Closer to our purposes, physicians are not immune from prosecution for criminal acts such as Medicaid/Medicare fraud, inappropriate prescription of drugs, and sexual assault of patients (Green 1997; Jesilow et al. 1993). Central to our analysis, however, is the question of whether violence that physicians exact *in the course of their medical practice* has been brought within the reach of the criminal law. Although it is a daunting task to determine how much potentially criminal physician violence occurs, certainly the phenomenon exists (Green 1997). Historically such violence has been hidden due to the secrecy accorded to medical procedures or has been handled by other mechanisms of social control such as civil suits or professional sanctions. When we initiated this project, however, we anticipated that physicians' invincibility to prosecution for violent medical practices would be penetrated.

Two general factors seemed to indicate that attempts would be made to socially construct doctors' malpractice as "violent crime." First, it appeared plausible that the general attempt to criminalize white-collar violence—mostly the physically harmful behavior of corporations (Cullen et al. 1987)—eventually would spread to cover violence by individual professionals such as doctors. Second, changes affecting the medical profession and the delivery of services seemed likely to increase the possibility of a transformation in the way in which physicians' behavior is controlled.

As reported, our search for cases uncovered 15 instances in which physician violence resulted in criminal prosecution. One might argue that 15 cases are inconsequential when compared with the numerous instances of physician violence that escape prosecution. One also can note that most of the prosecutions focused on doctors whose social status, past record of questionable medical practice, and/or egregious behavior made them vulnerable (or "easy") targets for legal attack. In the meantime, more systematic, hidden malpractice by high-status physicians in high-status hospitals apparently remains beyond prosecutorial scrutiny. In this light, the small number of prosecutions might be seen merely as symbolic gestures that will have no substantive impact on the medical profession.[1]

An alternative view merits consideration, however: these 15 cases may represent an unprecedented breakthrough in the social control of doctors. They show that the very practice of medicine no longer lies beyond the reach of the criminal law. In the not-too-distant past, the presence of prosecutors investigating after a death and blaming a doctor for a patient's demise would have been virtually unthinkable. Pathbreaking cases, however, are important because they make the unthinkable "thinkable": they help to socially construct a new reality. Even though the initial prosecutions have focused on the most vulnerable doctors, whose criminal liability is established most easily, future cases may push the boundaries of physicians' liability up the status hierarchy and into complex domains where guilt is more difficult to prove.

Indeed, although still in a developing stage, there is some evidence that when white-collar prosecutions are initiated, social status may be associated *positively* with the severity of criminal sanctioning (see, for example, Wheeler, Weisburd, and Bode 1982; but also see Benson and Walker 1988). Rosoff (1989) refers to this phenomenon as "status liability"; he furnishes evidence from a vignette study showing that, for serious offenses (homicides not related to medical practice), respondents allocate harsher verdicts to physicians with higher-status specialties. Similar results are revealed by vignette research focusing on misconduct by psychologists and on civil sanctioning. Thus Shaw and Skolnick (1996) report that an offender's status may lessen the harshness of respondents' judgments in cases that are unrelated to their professional role (in this instance, an assault), but increase harshness when the act is related to professional practice (an altercation in the office with a patient).

More generally, it is instructive that all of the 15 cases identified in our search *have occurred since 1986, including eight in the last five years.* No evidence from any source that we have encountered shows that any cases appeared before the mid-1980s (see Van Grunsven 1997). Indeed, in a comment on the recent trend toward holding physicians criminally negligent for medical practices, the American Medical Association observed that "a decade ago . . . it would have been unheard of for a doctor to be in criminal court" (Snyder 1998:Al). This convergence of prosecutions in a specific period thus suggests that we are witnessing not a blip on the radar screen but the beginning of a trend that has the potential to grow stronger.

As we noted in the introduction, the social transformation of medicine may erode the very conditions that historically have afforded physicians protection from criminal sanctions. In particular, as long-term one-to-one doctor-patient relationships become less prevalent and as profit increasingly constrains decisions on the delivery of medical services, patients' trust in doctors—especially when things go badly in a medical treatment or procedure—will decline and the ability to view doctors as criminals will increase. The care of patients is unlikely to be reduced fully to a mere business transaction like any other business transaction; yet the movement of medicine in that direction makes it possible to construct the reality that a physician, like a business executive, has placed profits or convenience over human lives. Such a narrative, which suggests amoral calculation or at least indefensible neglect, invites the attribution of criminal liability (Cullen et al. 1987; Kramer 1992; Swiggert and Farrell 1980; also see Vaughan 1997).

Perhaps most important, such a context makes prosecutions more likely because they can amass political capital for district attorneys. Even if the action is largely symbolic, hauling a doctor who has "murdered" a patient into court has the potential to bring publicity to a prosecutor; there is little risk of arousing the antagonism of voters, who no longer have strong ties of allegiance to the "family doctor." Thus, insofar as juries now may be prepared to convict such offenders, high-profile cases can be won and careers can be advanced in ways that previously did not exist (Van Grunsven 1997:50).

Indeed, the American Medical Association (AMA) has begun to recognize—and worry about—the emergence of a movement to criminalize physicians' clinical misconduct. In 1995 the AMA created a specific policy opposing what it termed "the current trend toward the criminalization of malpractice" (AMA Policy H-160.946). AMA resolutions enacted in 1998 addressed the subject further. These resolutions not only describe criminal prosecutions as "becoming a very serious problem" (AMA Resolution 224), but also express the profession's "opposition to the criminalization of health care decision-making" (AMA Resolution 227). The AMA's latest resolution on the topic actually calls for the "*de*-criminalization of medical decisions" (AMA Resolution 245; emphasis added). The AMA's *American Medical News* also has addressed the issue recently in feature articles (Prager 1998) and editorials ("Clinical Not Criminal" 1998). Currently the organization is advocating adoption of AMA model legislation, "An Act to Prohibit the Criminalization of Healthcare Decision-Making" (AMA Resolution 227; Prager 1998).

A further important issue remains, however. Is the shift toward criminalizing physician violence to be applauded? Are criminal sanctions preferable to civil sanctions in the kinds of medical cases that we have scrutinized? These, of course, are considerations of justice. A major argument for criminal sanctions is likely to be that of equivalence: if the harm inflicted with malice or through negligence is of the same order as that inflicted on innocent parties by street crimes, then the consequences to the perpetrators ought to be the same. The principle of just deserts thus mandates that the "criminal" violence perpetrated by physicians deserves the same kind of penalty and moral condemnation as other forms of criminal violence.

An alternative argument is that it is unfair to prosecute doctors under statutes, such as criminally negligent homicide laws, "that were never intended to criminalize mistakes in medical judgment or care" (Van Grunsven 1997:50; for similar reasoning on corporate prosecutions, see Cullen et al. 1987). In a related view, opponents of criminalization suggest that doctors lack the necessary "intent" to characterize their "mistakes" or "poor decisions" as criminal behavior (see, for example, Neumayer and Van Grunsven 1999). Such arguments, we should note, were used unsuccessfully in defenses against violent crime prosecutions brought against corporations and their executives (see, for example, Cullen et al. 1987). In the end, claims of a lack of intent do not shield prospective defendants from prosecution but are a legal matter to be settled in court. This is perhaps one reason why prosecutors have tended to indict physicians whose conduct perhaps has been egregious and enormously damaging: that is, resulting in patients' deaths.

Issues of utility, however, will also play a role: Will the public be safer if the egregious medical mistakes are socially and legally constructed as "criminal violence" and are prosecuted? A complicated policy debate is likely to ensue. In this regard, we raise two considerations: how criminal prosecutions might potentially affect (1) individual doctors and (2) the wider system of social control.

First, those who oppose criminalizing doctors' medical "mistakes" argue that prosecutions will cause doctors to focus not solely, as they should, on the patients' well-being but also on avoiding criminal liability (Van Grunsven 1997). They might be reluctant, for example, to treat the sickest or highest-risk cases. They also might become overcautious, spending excessive time and conducting unnecessary tests; in turn, this trend could cause medical expenses to escalate and resources to be allocated inefficiently.

Conversely, a limited number of salient prosecutions might create "perceptual deterrence" (Nagin 1998; Paternoster 1987) where none currently exists. In the past, in the total absence of prosecutions, doctors had no criminal punishment to fear, no matter how irresponsible their clinical practices. District attorneys, by selecting to prosecute the most serious cases, will not cause concern -among doctors who make "mistakes," but they may create incentives for especially wayward physicians to curtail their most reckless practices.

We admit that the extent to which white-collar offenders are deterrable by legal sanctions remains uncertain (see, for example, Paternoster and Simpson 1996; Weisburd, Waring, and Chayet 1995). This issue is likely to be complicated still further in the case of doctors, where the behavior targeted for deterrence is perhaps not intended nor due to rational calculation, but rather is the result of neglect or recklessness. Even so, there is evidence that at least among those lacking a strong moral code, intentions to offend may be diminished by the threat of a criminal sanction (Paternoster and Simpson 1996).

Second, opponents of criminalizing medical practices argue that the proliferation of prosecutions actually may weaken existing systems of professional control. In criminal cases, for example, prosecutors have been allowed access to peer-review files that traditionally have been kept confidential (Van Grunsven 1997). In this situation, physicians reviewing potentially faulty medical procedures—if they agree to participate in the review at all—may be reluctant to condemn colleagues' practices for fear that they may be consigning an otherwise "good doctor" to unwarranted prosecution (Prager 1998). There is also the possibility that when prosecutions occur, they will trigger an "oppositional culture" among doctors, in which physicians band together to define such intervention as illegitimate and characterize the doctors to which they are applied as scapegoats of politically ambitious prosecutors. If this is so, such resistance to control might create "defiance" and produce effects that undermine deterrence (see Braithwaite 1989; Sherman 1993). Indeed, as stated above, the AMA's response to criminalizing medical malpractice has been hostile: the Association says that it "decries" the "recent . . . indiscriminate use of criminal prosecutions against physicians" (Resolution 245).

Alternatively, even if criminal sanctions are applied only infrequently they might signal to doctors—and to medical associations—that doctors' failure to vigorously police their peers will subject all physicians to the growing threat of criminal liability. If this is so, then prosecutions might create stronger incentives for doctors to work proactively to show that criminal prosecutions are not needed. Such a possibility is suggested by a 1998 AMA editorial, in which the authors contend that harm to patients will not be reduced by "the flashy prosecution of a few doctors" ("Clinical Not Criminal" 1998:16). Instead they trumpet the "work of the National Patient Safety Foundation at the AMA. Its goal is to help the medical community to understand and rectify the often hidden factors that cause human error and system failures in health care organizations" (p. 16). In short, the possibility of an "iron fist" might create more and stronger "velvet gloves" aimed at preventing physicians' violence against the patients in their care.

◂ Endnote ▸

[1] One reviewer noted that the number of cases might be even less than 15 if a narrower definition of physician prosecutions is used: that is, by excluding the cases involving a foreign unlicensed doctor and the HMO, even though doctors were considered for prosecution. We might provide counter-arguments for specific cases, but instead we offer a broad response. As we discuss later, the key issue is not so much the precise number of prosecutions—whether 13 or 15—but the convergence, in a rather narrow period, of prosecutions that previously were rare or nonexistent. This convergence suggests not random or idiosyncratic events but an emerging social pattern that deserves attention and explanation.

◂ References ▸

Abramovsky, A. 1995. "Depraved Indifference and the Incompetent Doctor." *New York Law Journal*, November 8, pp. 3–10.

Addison III, F. W. and E. E. Mack. 1991. "Creating an Environmental Ethic in Corporate America: The Big Stick of Jail lime." *Southwestern Law Journal* 44:1427–48.

American Medical Association. 1995. Policy H-160.946. "The Criminalization of Health Care Decision Making."

———. 1998. Resolution 224. "Criminalization of Medicine."

———. 1998. Resolution 227. "Opposition to Criminalizing Health Care Decisions."

———. 1998. Resolution 245. "Decriminalization of Medical Decisions."

"Anesthesiologist Accused of Dozing in Surgery Found Negligent." 1996. *The Daily Record* (Baltimore), October 24, p. 17.

Bensel, F. P. and B. D. Goldberg. 1996. "Prosecutions and Punitives for Malpractice Rise, Slowly." *National Law Journal*, January 23, p. B7.

Benson, M. L. and F. T. Cullen. 1998. *Combating Corporate Crime: Local Prosecutors at Work.* Boston, MA. Northeastern University Press.

Benson, M. L., F. T. Cullen, and W. J. Maakestad. 1990. "Local Prosecutors and Corporate Crime." *Crime and Delinquency* 36:356–72.

Benson, M. L. and E. Walker. 1988. "Sentencing the White-Collar Offender." *American Sociological Review* 53:294–302.

Bonner, J. P. and B. N. Foreman. 1993. "Bridging the Deterrence Gap: Imposing Criminal Penalties on Corporations and Their Executives for Producing Hazardous Products." *San Diego Justice Journal* 1:1–56.

Braithwaite, J. 1989. *Crime, Shame, and Reintegration.* Cambridge, UK: Cambridge University Press.

Brennan, T. A. 1991. "Practice Guidelines and Malpractice Litigation: Collision or Cohesion?" *Journal of Health, Politics, Policy, and Law* 16:67–85.

Bucy, P. H. 1989. "Fraud by Fright: White-Collar Crime by Health Care Providers." *North Carolina Law Review* 67:855–937.

Clay, N. 1991. "Doctor's Trial Nears in Liposuction Death." *The Daily Oklahoman*, April 22.

"Clinical Not Criminal." 1998. *American Medical News*, March 23–30, p. 16.

Cohen, J., and R. Shapiro. 1995. "Environmental Crimes and Punishment: Legal/Economic Theory and Empirical Evidence on Enforcement of Federal Environmental Statutes." *Journal of Criminal Law and Criminology* 82:1054–1108.

Crane, M. 1994. "Could Clinical Mistakes Land You in Jail? The Case of Gerald Einaugler." *Medical Economics* 71:46–52.

Cullen, F. T., W. J. Maakestad, and G. Cavender. 1987. *Corporate Crime Under Attack: The Ford Pinto Case and Beyond.* Cincinnati, OH: Anderson.

"D.A. to Stay on Death Case Against Doctor." 1995. *People*, December 18.

DeBlieu, J. 1996. "It's a Crime: Misread Pap Smears Lead to Death." *Health* 10:82.

Dirmann, T. 1997. "Doctor Faces Trial in Liposuction Death." *The* (Riverside, CA) *Press-Enterprise*, October 3, p. B1.

———. 1998. "Some Guilty Pleas Filed in Surgery Trial: The Defendant Admits to Unlawful Practice of Medicine During His Cosmetic Operations." *The* (Riverside, CA) *Press-Enterprise*, May 22, p. B1.

"Doctor in Negligence Case Has His Sentence Eased." 1997. *New York Times*, June 28, p. 20.

Dolan, M. 1998. "Judge Acquits Rural Doctor of Murder of Infant Patient." *Los Angeles Times*, February 21, p. A1.

Dutzman, J. 1990. "State Criminal Prosecutions: Putting Teeth in the Occupational Safety and Health Act." *George Mason University Law Review* 12:733–55.

Engelberg, S. 1986. "Military Jury Sentences Surgeon to Four Years in Prison for Deaths." *New York Times*, March 4, p. A17.

Ensslin, J. C. 1999. "Doctor Wants License Reinstated: Anesthesiologist Seeks to Practice Medicine in California After Colorado Overturned Conviction." *Rocky Mountain News*, September 14, p. 12A.

Evans, T. D., F. T. Cullen, and P. J. Dubeck. 1993. "Public Perceptions of White-Collar Crime." Pp. 85–114 in *Understanding Corporate Criminality*, edited by M. B. Blankenship. New York: Garland.

Frank, J., F. T. Cullen, L. F. Travis, III, and J. Borntrager. 1989. "Sanctioning Corporate Crime: How Do Business Executives and the Public Compare?" *American Journal of Criminal Justice* 13:139–69.

Frank, N., and M. J. Lynch. 1992. *Corporate Crime, Corporate Violence.* New York: Harrow and Heston.

Friedman, L. M. 1985. *Total Justice.* New York: Russell Sage.

Garcilazo, M. and L. C. Merrill. 1995. "Abort Doc Describes Mistakes." *New York Daily News,* August 5, p. 8.

Geis, G., R. F. Meier, and L. M. Salinger, eds. 1995. *White-Collar Crime: Classic and Contemporary Views.* New York: Free Press.

Green, G. S. 1997. *Occupational Crime.* 2nd ed. Chicago, IL: Nelson Hall.

Hall, L. 1995. "Doctor Arrested in Firebombing of Wife's Home." *New York Times,* July 4, p. B6.

Hans, V. P., and M. D. Ermann. 1989. "Response to Corporate Versus Individual Wrongdoing." *Law and Human Behavior* 13:151–66.

Hillman, A. L., M. V. Pauley, and J. J. Kerstein. 1989. "How Do Financial Incentives Affect Physicians' Clinical Decisions and the Financial Performance of Health Maintenance Organizations?" *New England Journal of Medicine* 321:86–92.

Hills, S. L., ed. 1987. *Corporate Violence: Injury and Profit for Death.* Totowa, NJ: Rowan and Littlefield.

Holloway, L. 1995. "Doctor on Trial in Abortion Death Describes Fatal Procedure." *New York Times,* August 4, p. B2.

Howell, N. L. 1969. *The Search for an Abortionist.* Chicago, IL: University of Chicago Press.

Jesilow, P., H. N. Pontell, and G. Geis. 1985. "Medical Criminals: Physicians and White-Collar Offenses." *Justice Quarterly* 2:149–65.

———. 1993. *Prescription for Profit: How Doctors Defraud Medicaid.* Berkeley, CA: University of California Press.

"Kaiser Settles Texas Malpractice Case For $5.35 Million." 1998. *Mealey's Litigation Reports,* January 7, p. 3.

Kermode, F. 1995. *Not Entitled: A Memoir.* New York: Farrar, Straus, and Giroux.

Kilborn, P. T. 1998. "Voters' Anger at HMO's Plays as Hot Political Issue." *New York Times,* May 17, p. 1.

Klunder, J. 1987. "Physician Faces More Charges in Newborn Deaths." *Los Angeles Times,* June 12, p. 6.

Kocieniewski, D. 1993. "Convicted: Abortion Doc Guilty of Maiming Baby." *Newsday,* February 23, p. B1.

Kramer, R. C. 1992. "The Space Shuttle Challenger Explosion: A Case Study of State Corporate Crime." Pp. 214–43 in *White-Collar Crime Reconsidered,* edited by K. Schlegel and D. Weisburd. Boston, MA: Northeastern University Press.

Lewis, S. 1996. "Doctor Dozed in Other Operation." *Denver Post,* April 25, p. B6.

Lindsay, S. 1996. "Witness Tells How Doctor Failed to Act." *Rocky Mountain News,* October 9, p. 19A.

———. 1997. "Retrial of Physician in Death of Boy Grips Courtroom." December 3, p. 15A.

Lynch, M. J., M. K. Nalla, and K. W. Miller. 1989. "Cross-Cultural Perceptions of Deviance: The Case of Bhopal." *Journal of Research in Crime and Delinquency* 26:735.

Mann, K. 1985. *Defending White-Collar Crime: A Portrait of Attorneys at Work.* New Haven, CT: Yale University Press.

McKinlay, J. B., and J. D. Stoeckle. 1988. "Corporatization and the Social Transformation of Medicine." *International Journal of Health Services* 18:191–200.

McKnight, K. 1996. "Haunting Questions: The Sam Sheppard Case." *Akron Beacon Journal*, June 30–July 7.

Mokhiber, R. 1989. *Corporate Crime and Violence: Big Business Power and the Abuse of Public Trust.* San Francisco, CA: Sierra Club Books.

Musto, D. S. 1973. *The American Disease: Origins of Narcotic Control.* New Haven, CT: Yale University Press.

Nagin, D. S. 1998. "Criminal Deterrence Research at the Outset of the Twenty-First Century." Pp. 1–42 in *Crime and Justice: A Review of Research*, vol. 23, edited by M. Tonry. Chicago, IL: University of Chicago Press.

National Opinion Research Center. 1941. "Jobs and Occupations: A Popular Evaluation." *Opinion News* 9:3113.

"Navy Surgeon Convicted." 1986. *New York Times*, March 2, pp. 4–9.

"Navy Surgeon Convicted, Faces Prison in Deaths of Three Patients." 1986. *San Diego Union-Tribune*, February 27, p. A4.

Neumayer, L. A., and P. R. Van Grunsven. 1999. "The Criminalization of Medical Negligence." *Bulletin of American College Surgeons* (April).

"No Hearing on March 3 for Dr. Bruce Steir." 1999. *Refuse and Resist*, February 26.

"Oklahoma." 1990. *USA Today*, May 14.

Omstad, T. 1986. "Four Infants Die: Doctor and Aide Charged with Murder." *Los Angeles Times*, November 4, p. 6.

"One Doctor Is Cleared in PA Case." 1999. *New York Times*, April 27, p. A18.

"Pap Smear Deaths Draw $20,000 Fine." 1996. *Charleston Gazette*, February 23, p. 3C.

Paternoster, R. 1987. "The Deterrent Effect of the Perceived Certainty of Punishment: A Review of Evidence and Issues." *Justice Quarterly* 4:173–217.

Paternoster, R., and S. Simpson. 1996. "Sanction Threats and Appeals to Morality: Testing a Rational Choice Model of Corporate Crime." *Law and Society Review* 30:549–83.

"Patients, Doctors, Lawyers: Medical Injury, Malpractice Litigation, and Patient Compensation." 1990. *Harvard Medical Practices Study.* Boston, MA: President and Fellows of Harvard University.

Pontell, H. N., G. Geis, and P. D. Jesilow. 1985. *Practitioner Fraud and Abuse in Government Medical Benefit Programs.* Washington, DC: National Institute of Justice.

Pontell, H. N., P. D. Jesilow, G. Geis, and M. J. O'Brien. 1985. "A Demographic Portrait of Physicians Sanctioned by the Federal Government for Fraud and Abuse Against Medicare and Medicaid." *Medical Care* 23:1028–31.

Prager, L. O. 1998. "Keeping Clinical Errors out of Criminal Courts." *American Medical News*, March 16.

"Probation in Baby's Death." 1988. *Los Angeles Times*, February 19, p. 10.

Report of the Task Force on Medical Liability and Malpractice. 1987. Washington, DC: U.S. Department of Health and Human Services.

Roddy, D. B., and P. Hernan. 1999. "State Charges Polk Doctors." *Pittsburgh Post Gazette*, February 27, p. A1.

Rosoff, S. M. 1987. "Physicians as Criminal Defendants: Specialty Status and Sanctions." PhD dissertation, Department of Criminology, Law and Society, University of California, Irvine.

———. 1989. "Physicians as Criminal Defendants: Specialty, Sanctions, and Status Liability." *Law and Human Behavior* 13:231–36.

Rosoff, S. M., H. N. Pontell, and R. Tillman. 1998. *Profit without Honor. White Collar Crime and the Looting of America.* Upper Saddle River, NJ: Prentice-Hall.

Ross, E. A. 1907. *Sin and Society: An Analysis of Latter-Day Iniquity.* New York: Harper and Row.

Schudson, C. B., A. P. Onellion, and E. Hochstedler. 1984. "Nailing an Omelet to the Wall: Prosecuting Nursing Home Homicide." Pp. 131–45 in *Corporations as Criminals,* edited by E. Hochstedler. Beverly Hills, CA: Sage.

Schwendinger, H., and J. Schwendinger. 1975. "Defenders of Order or Guardians of Human Rights?" Pp. 113–46 in *Critical Criminology,* edited by I. Taylor, P. Walton, and J. Young. London: Routledge and Kegan Paul.

Shapiro, S. P. 1985. "The Road Not Taken: The Elusive Path to Criminal Prosecution for White Collar Offenders." *Law and Society Review* 19:179–217.

Shaw, J. I., and P. Skolnick. 1996. "When Is Defendant Status a Shield or a Liability? Clarification and Extension." *Law and Human Behavior* 20:431–42.

Sherman, L. W. 1993. "Defiance, Deterrence, and Irrelevance: A Theory of the Criminal Sanction." *Journal of Research in Crime and Delinquency* 40:445–73.

"Six Doctors Charged in Abuse of the Mentally Retarded." 1999. *New York Times,* February 27, p. A12.

Smith, R. 1998. "Abortion Doctor to Be Tried for Second-Degree Murder." *The* (Riverside, CA) *Press-Enterprise,* February 19.

Snyder, S. 1998. "When Doctors Bury Mistakes, Criminal Charges May Follow." *Arizona Republic,* December 15, p. Al.

Spolar, C. 1988. "Billig Cleared in Deaths of Three Patients." *Washington Post,* April 15, p. A1.

Steckner, S., and J. Snyder. 1999. "Abortion Doc Arrested: Biskind Charged with Manslaughter." *Arizona Republic,* January 13, p. Al.

Stoeckle, J. D. 1989. "Reflections on Modern Doctoring." *Milbank Quarterly* 66:76–89.

Susman, C. 1995. "When Doctors Err." *Palm Beach Post,* May 27, p. 1D.

Sutherland, E. H. 1949. *White Collar Crime.* New York: Holt, Rinehart, and Winston.

Swiggert, V. L., and R. A. Farrell. 1980. "Corporate Homicide: Definitional Processes in the Creation of Deviance." *Law and Society Review* 15:161–82.

Van Grunsven, P. R. 1997. "Medical Malpractice or Criminal Mistake? An Analysis of Past and Current Criminal Prosecutions for Clinical Mistakes and Fatal Errors." *DePaul Journal of Health Care Law* 2(l):1–54.

Vaughan, D. 1997. *The Challenger Launch Decision: Risky Technology, Culture, and Deviance at NASA.* Chicago, IL: University of Chicago Press.

Wagner, E. H., and T. Bledsoe. 1990. "The RAND Health Experiment and FIMO's." *Medical Care* 28:191–200.

Ware, J. F., W. H. Rogers, A. R. Davis, G. A. Goldberg, R. H. Brooks, E. B. Keeler, C. D. Sherbourne, P. Camp, and J. P. Newhouse. 1986. "Comparisons of Health Outcomes at an HMO with Those of Fee-for-Service Care." *Lancet* 1:1017–22.

Weisburd, D., E. Waring, and E. Chayet. 1995. "Specific Deterrence in a Sample of Offenders Convicted of White-Collar Crimes." *Criminology* 33:587–607.

Weisburd, D., S. Wheeler, E. Waring, and N. Bode. 1991. *Crimes of the Middle Classes: White Collar Offenders in Federal Courts.* New Haven, CT: Yale University Press.

Weiss, R. 1999. "Medical Errors Blamed for Many Deaths: As Many as 98,000 a Year in U.S. Linked to Mistakes." *Washington Post*, November 30, p. 1A.

Welkos, R. 1984. "Doctor Involved in Blinding Is Given a 4-Year Term for Fraud." *Los Angeles Times*, April 27.

Wheeler, S., K. Mann, and A. Sarat. 1988. *Sitting in Judgement: The Sentencing of White-Collar Criminals.* New Haven, CT: Yale University Press.

Wheeler, S., D. Weisburd, and N. Bode. 1982. "Sentencing the White-Collar Offender: Rhetoric and Reality." *American Sociological Review* 47:641–59.

Wolfe, S., K. M. Franklin, P. McCarthy, A. Bame, and B. M. Adler. 1998. *16,638 Questionable Doctors Disciplined by State and Federal Governments.* Washington, DC: Public Citizen Health Research Group.

Wright, J. P., F. T. Cullen, and M. B. Blankenship. 1995. "The Social Construction of Corporate Violence: Media Coverage of the Imperial Food Products Fire." *Crime and Delinquency* 41:20–36.

Wrightson, C. W. 1990. *HMO Rate Setting and Financial Strategy.* Washington, DC: Health Administration Press.

‹ 11 ›

Fraud Control in the Health Care Industry

Assessing the State of the Art

Malcolm K. Sparrow

More than $1 trillion is spent on health care each year in the United States, roughly 15 percent of the gross national product. The proportion of annual health care expenditures lost to fraud and abuse remains unknown because such losses are not systematically measured. But conventional wisdom, supported by recent Medicare studies undertaken by the Office of Inspector General, U.S. Department of Health and Human Services,[1] estimates that losses to fraud and abuse may exceed 10 percent of annual health care spending, or $100 billion per year.

Since 1992, when health care reform emerged as a matter of national debate, the issue of fraud control has received much attention. For example, health care fraud remains a top priority of the U.S. Department of Justice, with criminal convictions in 1997 increasing threefold over the 1992 total;[2] and over the past several years, the Federal Bureau of Investigation (FBI) has markedly increased the number of agents assigned to its health care fraud unit.

Reprinted from *National Institute of Justice: Research in Brief*, December 1998, pp. 1–11.

Such unprecedented attention to the issue of health care fraud produced many apparent successes. Coordinated actions involving Federal and State authorities as well as private insurers have succeeded in identifying health care fraud and abuse committed by major corporations. Nonetheless, little progress—in terms of practical improvements—seems to result. Not one of the industry officials interviewed in connection with this research thought the situation was under control or even in the process of being fixed. The majority thought existing efforts to control the problem barely scratched the surface, and how much fraud one found in the system depended only on how hard one looked:

- In 1994, the administrator of the Health Care Financing Administration (HCFA) acknowledged "good reason to believe" that the $5.4 billion in recoveries involving Federal health programs during that year was "merely the tip of the iceberg."[3]
- In March 1995, the FBI's director stated that intelligence showed cocaine traffickers in Florida and California were switching from drug dealing to health care fraud (the latter being safer, more lucrative, and less likely to be detected).[4]
- In early 1998, a scheme surfaced whereby more than $1 billion in phony medical bills using the names of unsuspecting patients and doctors had been submitted to scores of private insurers nationwide.[5]
- In July 1998, a Medicare contractor agreed to pay $144 million in civil and criminal penalties for concealing evidence of its poor performance in reviewing and paying claims of Medicare beneficiaries,[6] and receiving $1.3 million in Government performance bonuses to which it was not entitled.

Many instances of health care fraud suggest that existing control systems do not work the way we imagine they should. Often the manner in which schemes are revealed suggests detection is more luck than system. General Accounting Office (GAO) testimony to Congress has cataloged instances of fraud in the Medicare and Medicaid programs that, according to GAO, ought clearly to have been detected and stopped.[7] But in each case the schemes came to light only through tip-offs or whistleblowers, rather than through the operation of routine monitoring or audit.

In one case, a pharmacist from California had been billing Medicaid for improbably high volumes of prescription drugs and was being reimbursed without question, despite several recipients receiving more than 20 prescriptions per day.[8] For another patient, Medicaid paid for more than 142 lab tests and 85 prescriptions in 18 days.[9] All these transactions turned out to be fraudulent, yet none was picked up by routine monitoring or detection efforts.

In short, despite the level of political, legislative, and administrative attention paid to the fraud issue in the last several years, disturbing and somewhat surprising lapses in control persist.

The study summarized by this Research in Brief examined the health care industry's fraud control apparatus and asked, "Does it work?" and, if not, "Why not?" It assessed the assumptions, policies, and machinery comprising the health care industry's approach to fraud control in an effort to understand strengths and weaknesses and to offer some clues about how to make controls more effective.

Focus on Criminal Fraud

This study focused quite deliberately on criminal fraud as opposed to abuse, despite the difficulty of drawing a clear line between them. The reason for focusing on fraud rather than abuse (or billing errors, or "code optimization," or a host of other gray areas) is that fraud controls play to a distinctively different audience. Control systems may work very well in pointing out billing errors to well-intentioned physicians and may even automatically correct errors, adjust claims, and limit manipulation of billing codes. But those same systems may offer no defense against determined, sophisticated thieves, who treat the need to bill "correctly" as the most minor of inconveniences.

Most competent fraud perpetrators study the rule book carefully—probably more carefully than most honest providers—because they want to avoid scrutiny at any cost. So they "test" claims carefully, making sure they neatly pass all the established system edits and audits. Then, having found combinations of diagnoses, procedures, and pricing that "work" (i.e., trip no alarms and preferably pass through "auto-adjudication" to payment, avoiding human scrutiny altogether), they ratchet up the volume, carefully spreading the claims activity across different patients and across different insurers to avoid detection.

Many control systems are designed with only one audience in mind—honest providers, perhaps error prone, perhaps not up to date on administrative requirements and regulations, on occasions sloppy and disorganized, often confused by complex or indecipherable rules. For this audience, control systems serve the purpose of correcting errors, testing eligibility, matching diagnoses to procedure codes, checking pricing, and, if necessary, sending claims back for correction.

But effective fraud control systems must deal with quite a different audience: sophisticated, well-educated criminals, some medically qualified, some technologically sophisticated, all determined to steal as much and as fast as possible. They read manuals, attend seminars, and really appreciate all the help and training they can get in how to bill correctly, how to avoid prepayment medical review, and how not to "stick out" under postpayment utilization review.

That second audience is the one that counts here. The study evaluated fraud control assumptions, policies, and systems in terms of their effectiveness in deterring, preventing, and detecting *criminal fraud.*

What Makes Fraud Control Difficult and Complex?

Fraud control—in *any* profession—is a miserable business. Failure to detect fraud is bad news, and finding fraud is bad news, too. Senior managers seldom want to hear news about fraud, because such news is never good. Institutional denial of the scope and seriousness of fraud losses is the norm. Fraud control policies tend to be shortsighted and scandal driven.

The following seven factors largely explain what makes fraud control, in any environment, such a difficult and complex challenge.

1. What you see (i.e., what your detection systems show you) is never the problem. Most white-collar frauds fall in the category of "non-self-revealing" offenses. Unless they are detected close to the time of commission, they will likely remain invisible forever. Thus you see only what you detect. The danger, of course, is that organizations vulnerable to fraud lull themselves into a false sense of security by imagining that their "caseload" (i.e., what they detect) reflects the scope and nature of fraud being perpetrated against them. Often it represents only a tiny fraction, and a biased sample, of the frauds being perpetrated.[10]

2. Available performance indicators are at best ambiguous; at worst, perverse and misleading. If the amount of detected fraud increases, that can mean either the detection apparatus improved or the underlying incidence of fraud increased. The resulting ambiguity pervades much fraud control reporting.[11] Many other quantitative measures of fraud control success are ambiguous too. Successes in detection and prosecution can equally be viewed as failures in prevention. Some organizations boast of "record recoveries"; others say they prefer to deter fraud up front and regard chasing monetary recovery after the fact as a poor second best. Some organizations emphasize prevention to avoid having to admit that their detection systems are ineffective.

3. Fraud control flies in the face of productivity and service and competes with them for resources. A layer of fraud controls tends to slow down or complicate routine claims processes and creates too many categories for exceptional treatment. Officials responsible for high-volume claims processes want to think about the best way to handle the whole load. Investigators or fraud analysts want to think about the best way to handle the exceptions.

The savings from processing efficiencies may be small, but they are concrete and tangible. By comparison, the potential savings from enhanced fraud controls may be massive, but they remain uncertain and invisible. Bureaucracies usually choose concrete and immediate monetary returns instead of longer term, uncertain ones. So processing efficiency usually wins the battle for resources. As a senior HCFA official pointed out to the author, "Of course, the cheapest way to process a claim is to pay it."

4. Fraud control is a dynamic game (like chess), not a static one. Fraud control is played against opponents who think creatively, adapt continuously, and relish devising complex strategies. So a set of fraud controls that is perfectly satisfactory today may be of no use tomorrow, once the game has progressed a little. Maintaining effective fraud controls demands continuous assessment of emerging fraud trends and constant, rapid revision of controls.

5. Too much reliance is placed on traditional enforcement approaches. The strength of the deterrent effect depends on the probability of getting caught, the probability of being convicted once caught, and the severity of the punishment once convicted. For white-collar crimes all three of these are notoriously low; hence effective investigations do not necessarily translate into effective control. Many organizations fail to make the distinction between investigation (a tool) and control (the goal). Investigation focuses on detected cases, whereas the control function seeks to uncover and grapple with the invisible mass.

6. The effectiveness of new fraud controls is routinely overestimated. A false optimism is based on the hope that elimination of the types of scams most recently seen will mean elimination of the fraud problem. This fails to take into account the adaptability of opponents, who take only a few days, or weeks at most, to change tactics once they find a particular method thwarted.

7. Fraud control arrangements reflect the production environment within which they operate and thus address only the least sophisticated fraud schemes. Fraud controls are typically superimposed upon or embedded within high-volume, repetitive, transaction-oriented processes. Consequently fraud controls, consisting of a set of filters or branch points embedded within the transaction-processing operation, examine claims or transactions one at a time and usually in the same order in which they arrive.

This approach faces two major problems. First, the fraud control game is dynamic, so a static set of filters has only short-term utility. Second, most sophisticated fraud schemes are devised by perpetrators who assume the existence of transaction-level filters and who therefore design their fraud schemes so that each transaction comfortably fits a legitimate profile and passes through unchallenged. Fraud controls of this obvious "transaction level" type generally detect only the casual, careless, and opportunistic fraud attempts, not those of the serious dedicated criminal groups who quickly progress to a higher level of sophistication.

Exacerbating Factors in Health Care Insurance Industry

The factors above suggest that fraud control is a more complex and difficult challenge than is usually appreciated. Within the health care industry, additional factors exacerbate the problem.

Insurers seen by significant segments of the population as socially acceptable targets for fraud. Insurers are seen as "large, rich, anonymous, and as fair game for fraud in much the same way as tax authorities."[12] Health care fraud causes financial losses primarily to insurance companies and government bureaucracies, targets that engender little public sympathy.

Majority of health care fraud schemes "non-self-revealing." Many interviewees shared the common public assumption that explanations of medical benefits (EOMBs) sent to patients provide protection against provider fraud. But EOMBs do not have the effect one would hope, for a number of reasons:

- EOMBs are not sent to patients in many circumstances. Use of EOMBs is no longer routine within the Medicaid program. Under Medicare, EOMBs traditionally are mailed only when services require a copayment or Medicare refuses to cover a service. So, when services are approved and reimbursed 100 percent by the program, EOMBs normally have not been sent—in which case Medicare beneficiaries have no way of knowing what was billed under their names. Since 1981, EOMBs have not been used in connection with home health care services, now one of the most fraud-prone areas.

- Recipients of EOMBs have little or no financial incentive to pay attention to them. They are not, as in the case of a credit card statement, being asked to pay a bill.
- Many recipients cannot decipher the strange, computer-generated forms and have no incentive to try.
- Fraudulent suppliers find innovative ways to stop patients from reading their EOMBs, such as offering to buy back unopened EOMB envelopes or changing patient addresses on claim forms, thus diverting EOMBs to mailboxes under the suppliers' control.
- Many fraud schemes deliberately target vulnerable populations, such as the elderly or Alzheimer's patients, who are less willing or able to complain or alert law enforcement.[13]
- Even when beneficiaries call insurers to complain about bogus or questionable charges, the handling of beneficiary complaints often lacks the rigor required to uncover fraud.[14] The non-self-revealing nature of nearly all health care fraud schemes decreases the likelihood that authorities will be aware of the true scope and nature of the fraud problem.

Separation between administrative budgets and "funds." Investment in adequate fraud controls suffers significantly because program administration costs are budgeted separately from program costs (i.e., claims paid). This budgetary separation makes it virtually impossible to consider the notion of "return on investment" in allocating resources for fraud control.

The separation is most stark under Medicare Part A. The Medicare trust fund for Medicare payments under Part A is maintained by the 3.3 percent Medicare payroll tax, paid equally by employers and employees.[15] Medicare's administrative expenses, by contrast, come out of a "discretionary budget" from general tax revenues. In 1995 GAO observed that payment safeguards under the Medicare program produced at least $11 for every $1 spent; yet, on a per-claim basis. Federal funding for safeguard activities declined by more than 32 percent since 1989; adjusted for inflation, it fell 43 percent.[16]

In other governmental and nongovernmental programs, the separation, whether statutory or merely administrative, is powerfully manifested in employee culture and attitudes. Most officials care a great deal either about the costs per claim (where their goals and incentives all relate to efficiency) or about payment accuracy. Which one they care about depends on their specific responsibilities. Few managers find themselves in a position to understand the essential balance between them.

Respectability of the health care profession. The degree of trust society places (quite appropriately) in its health care professionals makes effective fraud control yet more difficult. Revelations about fraud are received by medical practitioners as an attack on the integrity of the profession and on its ability to police itself. Thus, the profession and its associations tend to play down the extent and seriousness of health care fraud and to oppose additional resources for investigation and review.

The respectability of the medical profession also presents notable problems to investigators and prosecutors. Investigators, lacking medical training, feel sorely disadvantaged when questioning physicians, whom they frequently experience as arrogant and condescending. And most prosecutors still avoid taking cases that require expert medical testimony, knowing they will be difficult, expensive, and relatively unlikely to succeed in front of a jury. Some prosecutors still display a broader reluctance to bring physicians—pillars of the community—to trial.

Perhaps most damaging, health care insurers extend the same kind of professional immunity and trust to all kinds of other provider groups whose members are not bound by a formal code of professional ethics—durable medical equipment suppliers, home health care agencies, medical transportation companies, physiological laboratories, etc. Payers accord such groups surprising latitude, paying claims on trust without any routine external verification of services provided.

Absence of clear distinctions between criminal fraud and other forms of abuse. Criminal fraud is clearly enough defined, requiring a deliberate misrepresentation or deception leading to some kind of improper pecuniary advantage. But when the deception or misrepresentation relates to the question of medical necessity, the distinctions between fraud and abuse become quite muddy.

Definitional ambiguities between criminal fraud and other forms of abuse produce some troublesome consequences for fraud control. First, they contribute to the medical profession's reluctance to unequivocally condemn fraudulent practice. (Nobody could be sure where along the continuum that condemnation, once mobilized, would end. Physicians may find it hard to condemn fraudulent practice among their peers if they cannot draw satisfactory dividing lines between what they might condemn in others and what they do themselves.)

Second, definitional ambiguities make it much more difficult to measure the problem systematically, because any measurement methodology would have to establish clear outcome classifications.

Third, definitional ambiguities provide an excuse for anyone who would prefer, for whatever reason, not to refer suspected "fraud" cases to an investigative unit. Many payment agencies, protective of their provider network and their program's public image, prefer to handle even quite serious cases through administrative action rather than turn them over to an investigative unit.

These impediments to effective fraud control—social acceptability of government and insurers as targets of fraud, invisible nature of the crime, separation of administrative budgets from "funds," trust placed in providers, and difficulties of separating fraud from other forms of abuse—are substantial. Add to them the seven elements noted previously under "What makes fraud control difficult and complex?" and the task of controlling fraud seems particularly complex, amorphous, and overwhelming.

Perhaps this helps begin to explain why health care fraud has not gone away despite the attention paid to it and why strenuous political and administrative efforts to bolster defenses have failed to provide a convincing cure. Another reason, which this study has established, is that the policies, systems, and machinery currently in place to combat fraud cannot possibly provide effective control. They are no match for the task.

Absence of Measurement

The health care industry differs from some other fraud control environments in its ubiquitous failure to measure the problem. The failure to systematically and routinely measure the scope of fraud is characteristic of the whole insurance industry—not just health care—and is not limited to the United States.[17] Measurement of fraud losses is quite feasible; it would involve standard sampling techniques backed by rigorous claims audits involving external validation procedures sufficient to identify fraud if present.[18] Success with such techniques has been demonstrated by the Internal Revenue Service in its efforts to measure and control fraudulent claims for tax refunds based on the earned income tax credit.[19]

Many interviewees believed that their companies' quality control procedures served the measurement function. However, without exception, such programs measured procedural compliance, accepting the claim as presented, and made no attempt to check the veracity of the information in the claim itself.[20] As Clarke's 1990 study of insurance fraud pointed out, "the essence" of any fraudulent insurance claim "is to appear normal and to be processed and paid in a routine manner."[21] One of the surprising truths of the fraud control business is that fraud works best when claims processing works perfectly.

Resource Allocation in the Absence of Measurement

In the absence of scientific measurement of health care fraud, the debate focuses on the size of the problem rather than on the search for solutions. Consequently, massive underinvestment in fraud control resources seems to be the industry norm.

Spending on payment-safeguard activities within the Medicare program totaled $441 million in fiscal year 1996. With a total Medicare budget of approximately $160 billion,[22] this represents an investment in fraud control of less than 0.3 percent of overall program costs—to tackle a problem whose size is estimated at more than 10 percent of program costs. These investments, small as they are, pay off handsomely. The special investigative units at Medicare contractors all save more than they cost, several producing savings-to-costs ratios as high as 14:1.

In the Medicaid program, total spending on the Medicaid fraud control units runs at roughly 0.05 percent of total program budget. The Federal Government offers to pay $3 for every $1 the States invest in their fraud control units, with a cap for Federal reimbursement at 0.25 percent of the State's annual Medicaid budget. Despite the $3-for-$1 offer, most States have for many years chosen to operate at a funding level far below the reimbursement cap.

A clear pattern emerges, spanning both commercial and public health insurance programs. The extent of fraud is never measured, merely estimated. The estimates are too soft to act as a basis for serious resource allocation decisions, so resources devoted to fraud control have to be based on something other than the perceived size of the problem. In practice, control resources are budgeted incrementally, with significant increases likely only if a fraud unit is visibly drowning under its caseload.

In practice, most fraud units, however small, are not drowning. The most likely explanation—which the field work for this study revealed all too clearly—is that the referral mechanisms do not work very well, producing the merest trickle of cases compared to the underlying size of the problem.

Assessment of Existing Fraud Control Apparatus

A central focus of this study's field work was to examine the units, functions, and systems that constitute existing fraud control arrangements: claims processing "edits" and "audits," claims development, prepayment medical review, postpayment utilization review, and special investigative units. These controls appear to be extremely useful for correcting providers' honest errors but ineffective as detection apparatus for criminal fraud. Fraud perpetrators can easily circumvent such controls by billing "correctly" and staying within the confines of medical orthodoxy and policy coverage.[23]

Claims processing edits and audits. These edits and audits enable the system to pay the right amount to the right person for the service claimed. They serve to correct billing errors and inappropriate billing procedures. And they reject claims if one or more of the provider, recipient, or procedure is somehow ineligible. But such systems do nothing to verify that the service was provided as claimed, or that the diagnosis is genuine, or that the patient knows about the alleged treatment. Rather, they assume the information presented is true and consider whether that information justifies payment of the claim.

Of the industry's standard edit and audit software modules, none is targeted on fraud. Generally, no attempt is made to create rules or logic to pick out "suspicious" claims for closer scrutiny or to detect claims containing deception or misrepresentation. The industry does not use fraud-specific prepayment edits or audits of any kind.

Claims examination. Once humans have a chance to inspect claims, the prospects for fraud detection and referral improve tremendously. Humans, given the opportunity, often notice the unusual or incongruous. The usefulness of this detection opportunity is constrained, however, because claims are suspended for review only if they trip a condition specified by the system audits. The model is "Systems Select: Humans Inspect." And the basis upon which claims are selected for review seldom has to do with fraud.

Prepayment medical review. This function's purpose is to establish medical orthodoxy and necessity and to determine whether the treatment is reimbursable. Often medical reviewers do spot fraud, but that is a fortuitous by-product of the fact that they are human and are looking at the claim, not because it is their job. Medical review and fraud detection are quite separate sciences. To escape attention from medical review, fraud perpetrators have only to base their false claims on medically plausible diagnoses and procedures and to stay comfortably within the confines of policy coverage.

Postpayment utilization review. Utilization review is currently the major tool used by the industry to detect fraudulent patterns of claims, with "provider profiling" being the predominant form of analysis. The degree to which postutilization review turns out to be a useful device for fraud control depends upon the degree to which fraud perpetrators use anomalous billing patterns. Of course, the smart ones do not.

Once again, this is not a criticism of postutilization review procedures per se. The principal purpose of utilization review is to review medical utilization patterns, both on an aggregate basis (to help formulate policy changes or provide needed provider and recipient education) and on an individual-provider basis (to eliminate medically inappropriate or unreasonably expensive treatment). As a fraud detection methodology, however, postutilization review procedures, with their strong emphasis on provider profiling, have certain limitations:

- They detect fraud only where it produces anomalous billing patterns. This makes them much better suited to detecting waste and abuse that does not amount to criminal fraud.
- Utilization review generally leads to scrutiny of only a few extreme outliers within each provider category, leaving the bulk quite safe from detection, even if the bulk is rotten.
- Most utilization review units prefer to inform and educate providers when they detect anomalous billing patterns, rather than investigate. So, as with prepayment medical review, fraudulent providers remain safe from investigation provided they change their tactics once "educated" about a particular practice.
- Utilization review procedures come long after payment has been made and so are useful only if there is a continuing relationship between payer and provider. The claims data forming the basis for provider profiles are usually at least 3 months old and in some cases more than 1 year old. Postpayment utilization review, therefore, comes far too late to be useful in combating the increasing number of fraud schemes run by fly-by-night operators. Storefront businesses, which fraud investigators say are increasingly prevalent, bill fast and furiously (creating extremely anomalous billing patterns) then disappear with the money long before postutilization review catches up with them. Against the threat of quick, high-volume, hit-and-run schemes, the only sure defense would be prepayment provider profiling, which would monitor each provider's aggregate billing patterns and billing acceleration rates before claims are paid. None of the sites visited had any form of prepayment provider profiling nor any prepayment method of watching for sudden surges in billings from individual providers.

Special investigative units (SIUs). The investigative units sit at the end of the referral pipeline, their cases coming from EOMB-stimulated beneficiary complaints, data-entry clerks or claims examiners, prepayment medical review, postpayment utilization review, or auditors. A small number of tip-offs from other insurers, from law enforcement agencies, or from anonymous telephone calls augment the volume of referrals.

Most investigative units work predominantly in a reactive mode, just about keeping up with the work that comes to them. Whichever mechanism produced the referrals, the investigator's job is the same: to investigate and to make cases. Following a traditional enforcement model, most of these units count their workload in terms of the number of incoming complaints or referrals and count their successes in terms of the number of cases made, settlements reached, aggregate dollars recovered, and convictions obtained.

Clearly, if the SIUs remain in a reactive mode, fed by largely ineffective referral pipelines, they will see the truth only dimly, partially, and probably very late. Without a clear focus on the goal of control—which would produce a much greater commitment to proactive outreach and intelligence gathering—SIUs can be no more effective than the referral pipelines that feed them their work.[24]

Lack of Coordinated Control Strategy

Lack of functional coordination and the absence of any coordinating strategy further handicap fraud control efforts.[25] At each of the field sites, the simple question "Who is in charge of fraud control?" produced bafflement and responses of either "no one" or "everyone."

The development of modern claims processing systems—highly automated, high-volume, highly efficient—seems likely to exacerbate whatever functional separations already exist and to diminish even further the prospects for coherent, effective, multidisciplinary fraud control strategies.

Effects of Electronic Claims Processing

This research also examined the impact of electronic claims processing on fraud and fraud control. Such systems exacerbate the problem of timely fraud detection. In essence, electronic claims processing creates the situation where an electronic signal received by an insurer triggers an electronic payment, often with no human intervention. The promise of administrative cost savings relies on the assumption that the majority of claims will be handled without human involvement. For fraud detection, increased speed of payment, coupled with the removal of human judgment, presents novel dangers.

One new threat involves computer-generated schemes utilizing hundreds or thousands of claims, each one carefully designed to pass through auto-adjudication to payment. Another threat involves the "quick hit" or "bust out" schemes, perpetrated by fly-by-night operators who steal millions in a relatively short period, then vanish.

Can Technology Provide Appropriate Safeguards?

Many officials express the belief that electronic claims processing systems can be made "fraud-safe" by implementing comprehensive batteries of up-front edits and audits to keep fraudulent claims out of the system altogether. If up-front preventive controls are good enough—so the theory goes—there should be less and less need for review or investigation. Many insurers are in the process of shifting resources from investigative units (labeled "reactive") into automated up-front controls (labeled "preventive"). The core of the emerging vision, therefore, could be termed *automated prevention.*

This vision, unfortunately, is fatally flawed in light of a sophisticated understanding of the fraud control challenge. It neglects the dynamic nature of the fraud control business, seriously underestimates the expertise and adaptability of the opposition, and overlooks the critical role that humans must play in any effective fraud control operation.

The vision of automated prevention assumes fraud control to be a static game; in fact, it is highly dynamic. Whatever the set of up-front controls, fraud perpetrators will quickly adjust their billing to fit. Any static set of controls only provides very temporary protection.

The vision also imagines that fraudulent claims can be distinguished from legitimate ones through analysis of the information they contain. Often they cannot. In most cases, the information content must be either compared with *other claims* to detect unusual patterns or checked against *external* information to verify its truthfulness.

However artfully constructed, automated defenses can never substitute for human common sense and will never be able to spot suspicious patterns that have not been seen before and for which they were not looking.

Automated defenses, especially when they rely mainly on "auto-rejects," provide the fraud perpetrator with complete information about what the detection systems can and cannot see. At the same time, they provide little or no opportunity for anyone *inside* the organization to gather intelligence about fraud perpetrators' latest schemes. Without a human "fraud control operation" to do the analysis, only one side in this game is gathering any useful intelligence.

Automatic rejection of claims up front is a fine tool for dealing with nonconformist billing practices or for rejecting claims containing obvious mistakes. The audience for such rejections is mostly honest and happy to be corrected. But relying on automatic up-front rejection of claims as the principal tool to fight fraud is naive. Usually, "auto-rejection" is a lame and feeble response to a new fraud threat, one that leaves the criminal perpetrator unscathed and free to try something different tomorrow.

The pervasive vision for fraud control under electronic prevention provides a diminishing (or vanishing) role for a human fraud control team. If this trend continues uncorrected, the advent of electronic claims processing will cement in place one of the major failings of fraud control systems today: no one is in charge, and no one is responsible for fraud control.

Effects of Managed Care

The study also briefly considered the advent of managed care and its implications for fraud and fraud control, showing that managed care will not provide a structural solution to the fraud problem, as many had hoped. Fraud will certainly take different forms under the various types of managed care contractual arrangements.

This study identified substantial difficulties law enforcement will face in dealing with managed care fraud and suggests that the criminal justice system will become less and less relevant to fraud control. At the same time, the new forms of fraud—involving diversion of capitation fees and resulting in inadequate medical care—may be more dangerous to human health than the types of fraud familiar under traditional fee-for-service arrangements.

Conclusions

Most insurers, public and private, do not systematically measure the fraud problem. They fly blind, remaining largely oblivious to the magnitude of the problem. This study failed to locate a single insurer that made resource allocation decisions based on valid estimates of the size of the problem. Massive underinvestment in fraud controls appears to be an industry norm.

Most insurers fail to designate responsibility for fraud control, and many equate it with investigation. They have no one responsible for playing the fraud control game and little prospect of effective coordination between different functional tools.

In terms of explicit strategy, many fraud units are bogged down in a reactive, case-making mode, unable to see the forest for the trees. At the other extreme, some proponents of electronic claims processing are in danger of proposing an extreme version of prevention, which threatens to eliminate human beings from the fraud control operation almost entirely, and which may decimate investigative and enforcement capacities. Insurers need a rational, integrating, control-oriented framework.

Most insurers, even if they believe in the value of proactive outreach and intelligence gathering, cannot find or protect resources for it. So they operate with a distorted and fragmentary picture of fraud, as revealed by largely ineffective detection and referral systems. And most payment systems remain vulnerable to multimillion dollar quick-hit scams because they lack the necessary prepayment controls.

Two developments are necessary before significant progress can be made in the battle against health care fraud: (1) the complexity of the fraud control challenge must be grasped and understood, and (2) the health care industry and public must learn the true extent of fraud in the American health care system. Without that knowledge, no one can justify the cost or inconvenience associated with operating appropriate controls. This study may help a little with the first. Only a commitment to systematic measurement can produce the second. Until these two developments occur, effective fraud control will most likely remain elusive.

◂ NOTES ▸

[1] Health Care Financing Administration, *Financial Report for Fiscal Year 1996*, Washington, DC: U.S. Department of Health and Human Services, Health Care Financing Administration, 1997; Health Care Financing Administration, *Financial Report for Fiscal Year 1997*, Washington, DC: U.S. Department of Health and Human Services, Health Care Financing Administration, 1998.

[2] U.S. Department of Justice, *1997 Annual Report*, Washington, DC: U.S. Department of Justice, 1997: 27. The crimes included submitting false claims to Medicare, Medicaid, and other insurance plans; home health care fraud; fake billings by foreign doctors; and needless prescriptions for durable medical equipment by physicians in exchange for a kickback from manufacturers.

[3] Vladeck, B. A., "From the Health Care Financing Administration: Medicare, Medicaid Fraud and Abuse," *Journal of the American Medical Association*, 273(10)(March 8, 1995): 766.

[4] Freeh, Louis J., Director, Federal Bureau of Investigation, Statement before the Special Committee on Aging, U.S. Senate, Washington, D.C., March 21, 1995, 2.

[5] Eichenwald, K., "Unwitting Doctors and Patients Exploited in a Vast Billing Fraud," The *New York Times*, February 6, 1998, A1.

[6] Pear, R., "Medicare Contractor Admits Longtime Pattern of Fraud," The *New York Times*, July 17, 1998, A10.

[7] Jagger, Sarah F., Director, Health Financing and Policy Issues, Health, Education and Human Services Division, General Accounting Office, "Medicare and Medicaid: Opportunities to Save Program Dollars by Reducing Fraud and Abuse," testimony before the Subcommittee on Human Resources and Intergovernmental Relations, Committee on Government Reform and Oversight, House of Representatives, Washington, D.C., March 22, 1995.

[8] Ibid.

[9] Ibid.

[10] Reiss, A. J., Jr., and A. D. Biderman, "Data Sources on White-Collar Law-Breaking," Washington, DC: U.S. Department of Justice, National Institute of Justice, September 1980: 91.

[11] Morey, Larry, Deputy Inspector General for Investigations, Office of Inspector General, Department of Health and Human Services, statement to the Subcommittee on Health of the Committee on Ways and Means, House of Representatives. 103rd Congress, 1st Session, March 8, 1993. Serial 103-3, p. 35.

[12] Clarke, M., "The Control of Insurance Fraud: A Comparative View," *The British Journal of Criminology*, 30(1)(Winter 1990): 2.

[13] Freeh, Statement, 4.

[14] General Accounting Office, "Health Insurance: Vulnerable Payers Lose Billions to Fraud and Abuse," Report to the Chairman, Subcommittee on Human Resources and Intergovernmental Relations, Committee on Government Operations, House of Representatives, Washington, D.C., May 1992, 23.

[15] Medicare Part B is funded from general tax revenues (roughly 75 percent) and from premiums paid by the elderly. See DeLew, N., "Medicare at 30: Preparing for the Future," *Journal of the American Medical Association* (July 19, 1995): 259–267.

[16] Jagger, "Medicare and Medicaid: Opportunities to Save Program Dollars by Reducing Fraud and Abuse," 12.

[17] Clarke, "The Control of Fraud: A Comparative View," 2.

[18] Ibid., 9.

[19] "EITC Compliance Study: Tax Year 1993," 5. The study was released publicly as an appendix to the Statement of Margaret Milner Richardson, Commissioner of the Internal Revenue Service, before the Subcommittee on Oversight, House Ways and Means Committee, U.S. House of Representatives, Washington, D.C., June 15, 1995.

[20] Gardiner, J. A., and T. R. Lyman, *The Fraud Control Game: State Responses to Fraud and Abuse in AFDC Medicaid Programs*, Bloomington: Indiana University Press 1984: 7.

[21] Clarke, "The Control of Fraud: A Comparative View," 1.

[22] Office of Management and Budget, "Analytical Perspectives: The Budget of the United States Government. Fiscal Year 1996." Executive Office of the President of the United States, Office of Management and Budget, Washington, D.C., 1995, 229.

[23] Ford, J., "Health Care Fraud: The Silent Bandit," *FBI Law Enforcement Bulletin* (October 1992): 2–7.

[24] General Accounting Office, "Health Insurance: Vulnerable Payers Lose Billions to Fraud and Abuse."

[25] Halperin, Donald M., "A Partnership Approach: A Prescription for Enhanced Coordination of Medicaid Fraud Detection and Prevention in New York State." New York State Senate, Albany, New York, June 1993.

‹ 12 ›

Maiming and Killing
Occupational Health Crimes

Nancy Frank

Work hazards are not new. "Members of primitive societies cut themselves and contracted anthrax while skinning animals, Roman slaves were exposed to mercury fumes in mines, and sixteenth century grinders suffered silicosis, or 'grinders' disease,' from inhaling silica."[1] Lead poisoning was common in many early trades, including printing, glass manufacturing, and ceramics.[2] As early as the eighteenth century, Bernardino Ramazzini, considered the founder of occupational medicine, understood the frequent connection between work and disease.

> "'Tis a sordid profit that's accompanied by the destruction of health. . . . Many an artisan has looked at his craft as a means to support life and raise a family, but all he has got from it is some deadly disease, with the result that he has departed this life cursing the craft to which he has applied himself."[3]

Industrialization increased work hazards. New processes and materials were introduced with little attention to their effects on health. In the late 1970s, the U.S. Council on Environmental

Reprinted from *The Annals of the American Academy of Political and Social Science*, 525 (January 1993), pp. 107–118.

Quality estimated that 700 new chemicals came on the market every year, and the National Institute for Occupational Safety and Health calculated that 880,000 workers were being exposed to carcinogens and other toxic substances in the workplace.[4] Recently the National Safe Workplace Institute estimated that 1 of 6 workers dies from an occupationally related disease.[5]

Increases in occupational hazards over the last 100 years have galvanized the development of public policy to deal with competing claims of employers, who want voluntary standards without government intervention, and workers, who demand government intervention to make workplaces safer. The first safety laws, passed after the middle of the nineteenth century, required employers to take minimal safety precautions, such as installing guards on machinery. State-mandated workers' compensation systems were established in the first decades of this century to settle disputes between employers and employees concerning job injuries. In 1970, a federal occupational safety and health program was enacted to deal with workplace accidents and to reduce exposure to hazardous materials. The 1980s saw a small number of criminal prosecutions of employers charged with causing the injury or death of workers, but administrative regulation remains the primary control mechanism for dealing with workplace-induced health problems.

In this article, I argue that the current policy emphasis on administrative regulation ignores the unique problems created by occupational diseases as opposed to occupational injuries. Attempts to prevent occupational diseases by regulatory action are hampered by uncertainty about the magnitude of the risks being addressed. Issues of uncertainty revolve around the question of whether potential hazards should be strictly regulated until proven safe or whether new materials or processes should be available until proven dangerous.

The article argues that expanded workers' compensation coverage, tort action, and criminal prosecution of employers are important adjuncts to the current system of regulatory enforcement and the limited availability of workers' compensation for occupational disease. Expanded workers' compensation would alleviate some of the burdens of regulatory uncertainty, while tort action and criminal prosecution might reduce some of the burdens of ineffective enforcement that now are borne by workers in the form of occupational illness and disease. To reach these conclusions, I discuss important differences between occupational injury and disease, review the development of legal control over occupational hazards, and assess the current state of occupational safety and health protection.

Hazards in the Workplace

Occupational hazards can be divided into two major categories: (1) traumatic injury and (2) physical deterioration and disease caused by repeated exposure to a particular process or material. Traumatic injuries include such things as broken bones, severed limbs, head injuries, burns, and acute poisoning. These injuries occur suddenly as a result of a massive exposure to force, heat, or toxic materials. A person falls and breaks a bone. A worker catches a sleeve in a whirling piece of machinery and loses an arm. The ceiling of a mine collapses; chemicals within a factory ignite and create an explosion; or a toxic spill poisons the nearby workers. Much progress has been made to reduce the occurrence of major accidents such as these, which can result in traumatic injuries.[6]

In contrast to sudden, traumatic injuries, other injuries and illnesses are caused by the slow accumulation of physical damage or exposure to debilitating conditions. Meat plant workers and computer operators can suffer numbness and eventual loss of hand and arm functions due to repetitive movements.[7] Long-term exposure to small amounts of a chemical can cause nerve damage or increase the risks of cancer. Chronic job-related stress may lead to heart disease, high blood pressure, and gastrointestinal problems such as ulcers or colitis.[8] Long-term exposure to asbestos fibers in the air can cause asbestosis and cancer.

At one time, many illnesses were not recognized to be occupationally caused, since workers developed symptoms gradually and only after long-term exposure.[9] It was easier to identify and control conventional hazards associated with traumatic injury. Consequently, prior to the 1970s, most efforts to curb occupational threats focused on safety, requiring guards on machines, safety precautions in mines and at construction sites, and other procedures designed primarily to avert sudden, traumatic injury. By contrast, occupational diseases were an enigma. Steven Kelman noted the difficulty of linking illness to occupation: "One cannot readily distinguish occupationally caused cancer or bronchitis from nonoccupationally caused versions of the same diseases. Certain symptoms (such as headaches, dizziness, or stomach pains) are extremely diffuse and may have countless causes."[10] In addition, the decline of workers' health has been viewed as an expected part of the aging process. As long as occupational disease was considered normal, there were few efforts to address the causes.

Evolution of Legal Controls

Legal protection for workers exposed to hazards on the job was extremely limited prior to the nineteenth century. Tort law—a civil action for injury caused by wrongful conduct—was the primary mechanism to compensate workers injured on the job through their employers' negligence.

Employers raised a variety of legal defenses to escape liability for negligence. They argued that injuries were caused by fellow employees; that employees had engaged in behavior that contributed to the risk; and that workers knew the job was hazardous. Many judges accepted these arguments, but by the end of the nineteenth century, workers were scoring important victories in civil suits against negligent employers.[11]

Typically, these suits concerned traumatic injuries. Long-term hazards resulting in occupational disease were less amenable to the remedy of tort action. Besides, workers often were unaware that their illnesses were caused by factors in the workplace. Even if they suspected workplace exposures, limited medical information about the effects of health hazards handicapped their efforts to prove causation and negligence.

Suits for traumatic injuries led to mounting legal and compensation costs for industry, and around the turn of the century some economic experts began to agitate for a workers' compensation system.[12] Under tort law, a considerable proportion of the money awarded an injured employee goes to the lawyer rather than to the injured worker. In addition, while some workers obtain large damage awards, most are unable to mount successful tort actions. Employers, for their part, are concerned about the costs of defending civil suits and having to pay damages to successful plaintiffs. These factors combined in the first half of this century to make a workers' compensation system appealing to a broad spectrum, and by 1949 every state had passed legislation creating such a system.[13]

Workers' compensation provides that employees no longer have to prove that employers were negligent. Instead, employers are required to carry insurance, or to be self-insured, to compensate injured workers, and when an injury is work related, the employee is entitled to compensation. Unless an employee can prove an intentional tort on the part of the employer, the workers' compensation system is the exclusive remedy for an injured worker.[14] In addition, proponents of workers' compensation anticipated that this no-fault remedy would provide for immediate compensation without the delays of the civil tort system. It offers compensation for lost wages, medical expenses, and rehabilitation services.[15]

Workers' compensation has reduced the level of workplace injuries, since insurers have an incentive to contain their costs by implementing safety programs. Safety experts have demonstrated that reducing workplace accidents reduces compensation costs and frequently improves overall worker efficiency.[16] Consequently, industry and many safety experts conclude that prohibitive regulations and government enforcement are unnecessary because wise companies invest in safety.[17]

Workers' compensation systems are not without problems. In most states, benefit levels are low, since workers' compensation was not designed to reimburse employees for all losses but only to provide temporary support until the worker could get back on the job.[18] Typically, workers receive only from one-half to two-thirds of their normal weekly wages, plus payment of hospital and medical expenses.[19] Some observers have argued that this has been an "unfair *quid pro quo*" because workers must give up their opportunity to go to court while, in exchange, they receive less compensation than would be possible under the tort system.[20] Injured workers also complain of delays in obtaining payments because of administrative inefficiency and disputes with employers. Employers frequently contest applications for compensation, arguing that the injury was not work related or that it is not covered by the compensation law.[21]

Such disputes have been especially common in cases involving occupational diseases. Initially, occupational diseases were not covered under workers' compensation schemes, but courts and legislatures gradually have included at least some occupational illnesses within the compensation system. As of 1978, all states provide some coverage. Employees, however, must prove the occupational nature of the illness to obtain compensation.[22] Much controversy continues about which diseases are occupational in nature. Only six states, for example, recognize stress and its physical effects as an occupational disease.[23]

Employers complain that compensation costs are too high and that rising medical expenses continue to drive premiums higher. Moreover, the growing gap between compensation levels under the workers' compensation system compared to jury awards has resulted in an increase in litigation and its associated costs.[24]

Federal Regulation

Most states at first invested only limited resources in the investigation of occupational hazards and in the enforcement of occupational safety and health standards. State regulatory efforts typically emphasize occupational hazards relating to falls, machinery mishaps, and fire. Few states have conducted investigations for occupational diseases.

This lack of attention to the risks of occupational diseases and other ill effects of exposure to chemicals, radiation, and hazardous substances in the workplace spurred efforts to create a federal regulatory agency. Accumulating research evidence was showing that workers exposed to certain chemicals were at increased risk of getting cancer and other debilitating or fatal diseases and that the number of workers exposed to these chemicals had grown exponentially.

The first federal action to deal with severe occupational hazards was the Federal Coal Mine Safety and Health Act of 1969. Among other things, the law set standards for coal dust in mines and provided federal compensation to miners afflicted with black lung disease.[25]

Shortly after the passage of the coal miners' bill, Congress enacted the Occupational Safety and Health Act of 1970 (OSH Act), which covered a wide range of workplaces across the country. Much of the debate before the bill's passage focused on the newly discovered issue of occupational disease. The statute created the Occupational Safety and Health Administration (OSHA), providing it with rule-making and enforcement responsibilities, and the National Institute for Occupational Safety and Health, which was to be responsible for research related to workplace hazards.

As part of an initial package of OSHA regulations, which was adopted from voluntary industry standards that had existed prior to passage of the OSH Act, 400 chemicals in the workplace were placed on the controlled list. But progress was extremely slow after this initial rule-making effort. From 1972 to 1978, OSHA promulgated only 10 new health standards, for asbestos, vinyl chloride, coke oven emissions, arsenic, benzene, cotton dust, and lead, among others.[26] Industry leaders continue to argue that the costs of complying with the new standards are prohibitive and that the risks from the chemicals are minimal so that in many instances implementation of newly promulgated standards has been delayed while industry appeals the rule making through the federal courts.

The technical and political challenges involved in developing new health regulations are enormous. Technical challenges include estimating the risks associated with particular processes and industrial materials; estimating the costs of reducing the risks; and estimating the health and economic benefits arising from regulation. Political problems include controversies about the economic costs of compliance and about whether chemicals should first be proved safe before use.

OSHA's Enforcement Record

OSHA enforcement is shared with the states, since the OSH Act gave the states the option of developing their own enforcement plans. OSHA is authorized to approve a state plan if its enforcement will be at least as effective as federal enforcement. Currently, 23 states have federally approved state enforcement plans.[27] The remainder are under federal enforcement guidelines and control.

Through most of its history, OSHA has relied on voluntary compliance rather than on threats and penalties. Negotiation and persuasion are used to gain compliance. Regulated businesses favor voluntary compliance, arguing that most violations are inadvertent and that they will be quickly corrected once regulatory officials point them out. Critics suggest that "voluntary compliance" is a political code word for a policy that allows companies to ignore standards set by law.[28]

The Reagan administration cut back on OSHA enforcement personnel, decreased the agency's use of citations and fines, and allowed companies to have penalties reduced if they corrected their deficiencies.[29] In early 1981, the administrator of OSHA ordered that follow-up inspections be decreased to 5 percent or less of all inspections. "They don't pay off," he claimed.[30] At the same time, penalties imposed by OSHA dropped significantly, from $25.5 million in fiscal year 1980 to $5.5 million in fiscal 1982.[31] During Reagan's first term in office, the number of federal OSHA inspectors declined from 1328 to 981.[32] A study by Public Citizen found that the number of workplace inspections declined 17 percent. Follow-up inspections dropped by 86 percent. Moreover, inspectors cited fewer violations and imposed less severe penalties.

The Reagan administration also allowed inspections of workplaces only if employers' accident records indicated that there was a problem.[33] This practice was implicated in the workplace death of Stefan Golab, an employee of Film Recovery Systems. Golab's death was the first case in which corporate executives were charged with murder for causing the death of an employee. Only two and a half months before Golab collapsed from cyanide poisoning, an OSHA inspector had examined the company's records and concluded that no on-site inspection of the plant was necessary. A full inspection of the silver-recovery operation might have discovered the high levels of cyanide and the inadequate safety equipment issued to employees.[34] Evidence of traumatic injuries may be found in company records, but it is less likely that hazards will be uncovered for which the harm takes many years to develop. On-site health inspections are the only means of monitoring a company's compliance with OSHA regulatory standards for exposure to chemical and other long-term hazards.

◂ Regulatory Standard Setting ▸

When researchers assess the risks created by exposure to a chemical or an industrial process, the resulting assessment is always tentative and involves a very high degree of uncertainty. Bayer and his colleagues, for example, studied the standard-setting processes for asbestos, lead, and coal dust and found that hazards were repeatedly ignored until the results of scientific testing became incontrovertibly certain.[35] Such an approach results in significant worker costs. Usually, until sufficient evidence is accumulated through scientific study to prove that something is hazardous, workers continue to be exposed to the suspected hazard and to suffer its effects.

The regulation of benzene, a chemical widely encountered by workers in the rubber, petrochemical, and steel industries, illustrates this burden. The initial benzene regulation adopted after the creation of OSHA was based on voluntary industry standards, allowing average benzene exposure of 10 parts per million (ppm), with an acceptable ceiling of 25 ppm and periodic excursions up to 50 ppm.[36] This standard was based on the toxic effects of benzene; the risks of leukemia from benzene exposure had not been considered.

During the 1970s, evidence of the leukemia peril from benzene exposure mounted, and in 1978 OSHA issued an emergency rule setting a new standard for workplace exposure to benzene. The new rule would have reduced the average allowable exposure to 1 ppm. Industries dependent on benzene in their production process, specifically the rubber and tire industry, argued that compliance with the standard would be too expensive. A federal appeals court agreed that OSHA had not demonstrated adequately that there was a significant health risk or that reducing exposure to the chemical was technologically feasible.[37] Consequently, the new standard did not go into effect until 1988, when research evidence had grown to proportions that could no longer be ignored or dismissed. The 1988 standard was identical to the one originally issued in 1978.

Because of the delay in implementing the 1 ppm limit, an estimated 9600 workers were exposed to benzene at levels between 1 and 10 ppm. In theory, once a regulatory agency, such as OSHA, sets a standard, worker exposures are expected to be reduced to that level. In practice, of course, standards are frequently exceeded. Consequently, an additional 370 employees were exposed to benzene levels above 10 ppm during this 10-year period. Based on these estimates, Nicholson and Landrigan concluded that between 30 and 490 deaths will occur because of the delay in lowering the standard from 10 ppm to 1 ppm.[38] Industry estimates suggest that businesses saved about $200 million because of the delay.[39] If rubber workers now suffer from leukemia due to benzene exposure, they bear the burden of "feasible" standard setting and ineffective enforcement of existing OSHA regulations.

As noted, OSHA is required by law to prove that a risk is significant before it may set a standard to reduce the risk. In the Industrial Union Department case, the Supreme Court suggested that a risk of 1 in 1000 was an appropriate rule of thumb for identifying significant risks. This criterion has been adopted in OSHA decision making. While OSHA has not specified a level of risk that it considers insignificant, it generally has not sought to regulate occupational cancer risks below 1 in 1000.[40]

The law also requires that hazards posing a significant health risk be reduced to whatever level is feasible.[41] This leaves unanswered, of course, how onerous the economic burdens to industry must be before the regulation is deemed economically infeasible. The question becomes, "At what point, if any, is it worth sacrificing the health of a discrete percentage of workers to preserve the economy of an industry?[42]

In the case of occupational hazards, the economic burdens of precaution, originally borne by employers, are usually shifted to consumers and ultimately diffused throughout society. In contrast, the burdens on workers of not regulating are not so easily shared. Although it is possible to compensate someone for lost earnings and to give monetary payments for pain and suffering, disease and death remain a very individual burden.

Because of this essential difference in the burdens associated with occupational hazards, it seems reasonable that they should be reduced at least to the level where the costs equal the benefits. The rest of us gain—in the form of lower prices, higher levels of employment, greater choices in the marketplace through social decisions to not regulate as tightly as we might. But we benefit at someone else's expense—those who get sick.

What is acceptable is a social decision that relies heavily on the context of what is being lost, what is being gained, and who benefits and who suffers. Decisions involve important societal values. Risking health for some compelling purpose, such as producing an essential product for which there is no substitute, is different from a similar risk taken merely to produce something that is a luxury or recreational item or one for which there are acceptable substitutes. On the other hand, banning exposures until a material has been proven safe may not be in society's best interests; banning chemicals for which there are no reasonable substitutes may be irrational and unnecessary. The burdens of protecting society's interests need not fall entirely on individual workers, however.

Distributive justice suggests that society should compensate workers for bearing the burden of uncertainty and the burden of acceptable or necessary risk. When it becomes societally inefficient to regulate any further, society is not absolved of responsibility for the residual illness and death suffered by individuals exposed to acceptable risks. Similarly, we need to provide remedies for workers in instances of ineffective enforcement of existing regulations, both to compensate the individuals and to deter regulatory violations.

Workers' compensation is a no-fault system, and the fact that an injury occurred at work is sufficient to justify compensation. In theory, workers should be receiving compensation for diseases caused by occupational exposures, even if those exposures are below what are deemed to be acceptable levels. In practice, workers usually are not compensated because of the limited coverage of occupational diseases under workers' compensation. A major obstacle to covering these diseases is the difficulty of determining whether the cause of an employee's illness is occupational exposure. When an employee falls at work, we do not need to determine whether it was a slippery floor or the worker's clumsiness that caused the fall. Because its occurrence at the workplace was obvious, there is no question that it is an occupational incident. In contrast, cancer has all sorts of causes, only some of which are related to occupational exposure to carcinogens.

An objection to a system of compensating workers as outlined previously is that many employees get cancer or other diseases who would have gotten ill even if they had not been exposed to a particular material in their work. The current system of compensation deals with this problem by denying compensation for most occupational diseases, putting the entire burden of uncertainty on the worker. An alternative approach is to require the worker to establish *prima facie* evidence of (1) an occupational exposure and (2) physiological damage consistent with the material or process alleged to have caused the harm. Workers should not have to prove, as they do now, that the occupational exposure is the cause of the illness.

The existing workers' compensation system also limits the availability of tort remedies for injuries caused by inefficient enforcement of existing regulations. Compensation statutes in many states prevent employees from suing employers unless they are able to allege that the injury was intentional or at least that the employer's acts were intentional and done with knowledge that injury was substantially certain.[43] As a result, the entire burden of ineffective enforcement falls on employees. In times of weak enforcement, employers are relatively insulated from being held accountable for injuries and illnesses caused by negligent and even reckless conduct. Expanded tort liability, however, would tend to maintain the proper standard of care even in the absence of effective regulatory enforcement, and tort remedies should be available to workers whenever exposures have exceeded regulatory limits.

Finally, criminal prosecution should continue to be used to punish willful violations, particularly in those instances in which workers are seriously injured, become seriously ill, or die as a result of an employer's reckless disregard of regulatory requirements. Where the regulatory system has failed to provide an adequate deterrent, criminal prosecution is an appropriate response. Where workers suffer harm due to the reckless or negligent acts of employers, they have a right to retribution.

◂ Conclusion ▸

Occupational health is protected through overlapping systems of standard-setting and enforcement. The tort system, workers' compensation, regulation, and—if only slightly—the criminal justice system establish a loosely coupled, overlapping network of control. The standards of conduct mandated by one system can be quite different from those mandated by another; this gap creates a number of difficulties. First, there is the obvious potential for inconsistency. When each authority adopts its own standards, they all tend to lose legitimacy, because differences between one set of laws and another make all appear arbitrary. Second, loose coupling creates difficulties for firms trying to determine the path they must follow. OSHA regulations may be voluminous, but they are also relatively clear-cut, giving companies specific guidelines about what is allowed and what is likely to get them into trouble. If firms comply with OSHA regulations but are nonetheless sued, forced to pay compensation, or prosecuted criminally, executives may be justifiably outraged by the lack of notice concerning the requirements of the law.

Overlapping systems of control provide checks and balances. When regulatory agencies fail to fulfill their mandate, when they are unresponsive to public concern about greater control of workplace hazards, then the workers' compensation, tort, and criminal systems should serve as a backup to raise the standard of conduct required of employers. In many instances, tort and criminal cases arise precisely because the regulatory system failed to set standards and provide effective control. Assault and homicide cases against employers in the last decade came about because prosecutors perceived the regulatory system to have broken down. These prosecutions forcibly remind employers that there are limits to what society will tolerate. The tort system serves the same function.

Concerned persons will continue to disagree about the precise level of risk at which the costs of a regulatory standard outweigh the benefits. Whatever the level finally adopted, some residual risk will remain that is judged too expensive to eliminate. The workers' compensation system must be reinvigorated and expanded to compensate for the harms that ensue. The tort system must be readily available to workers who suffer illness due to exposures beyond the legal limits. Criminal prosecution should be used judiciously to punish for reckless conduct that results in injury.

◂ NOTES ▸

[1] U.S., Department of Health and Human Services, Public Health Service, Centers for Disease Control, National Institute for Occupational Safety and Health, *Report on Occupational Safety and Health for FY 1985 under Public Law 91-596*,1986, p. 1.

[2] William Graebner, "Private Power, Private Knowledge, and Public Health: Science, Engineering, and Lead Poisoning, 1900–1970," in *The Health and Safety of Workers*, ed. Ronald Bayer (New York: Oxford University Press, 1988), p. 18.

[3] Samuel S. Epstein, *The Politics of Cancer* (Garden City, NY. Doubleday, Anchor Press, 1979), p. 76.

[4] *Ibid.*, pp. 69, 76.

[5] *Detroit Free Press*, 3 Sept. 1989.

[6] Margaret I. Bullock, *Ergonomics: The Physiotherapist in the Workplace* (New York: Churchill Livingstone, 1990), p. 3.

[7] *Ibid.*

[8] Stewart G. Wolf and Albert Finestone, *Occupational Stress* (Littleton, MA. PSG, 1986).

[9] Ellen Peirce and Terry Morehead Dworkin, "Workers' Compensation and Occupational Disease: A Return to Original Intent," *Oregon Law Review*, 67:649 (Summer 1988).

[10] Steven Kelman, "Occupational Safety and Health Administration," in *The Politics of Regulation*, ed. James Q. Wilson (New York: Basic Books, 1980), pp. 237–38.

[11] Lawrence M. Friedman, *A History of American Law* (New York: Simon & Schuster, Touchstone, 1979), pp. 409–27.

[12] Jodi Parrish Power, "Employer Intentional Torts in Virginia: Proposal for an Exception to the Exclusive Workers' Compensation Remedy," *University of Richmond Law Review*, 25:339 (Winter 1991).

[13] Nancy Frank, *From Criminal Law to Regulation: A Historical Analysis of Health and Safety Law* (New York: Garland, 1986), pp. 28–29; Power, "Employer Intentional Torts," p. 341.

[14] Power, "Employer Intentional Torts," p. 339.

[15] Nancy Kubasek and Andrea Giampetro-Meyer, "California's Radical Proposal: A Model for the Fifty States?" *Labor Law Journal*, 42:173, 174 (Mar. 1991).

[16] Frank, "From Criminal Law to Regulation," p. 55.
[17] *Ibid.*, p. 29.
[18] Institute for Civil Justice, *Annual Report*, April 1, 1991–March 31, 1992 (Santa Monica, CA: RAND, 1992), p. 63.
[19] Letitia Mallin, "Disease, Not an Accident: Recognition of Occupational Stress under the Workmen's Compensation Laws," *Columbia Journal of Environmental Law*, 13:357, 360 (Spring 1988).
[20] *Ibid.*
[21] John E. Bohyer, "The Exclusivity Rule: Dual Capacity and the Reckless Employer," *Montana Law Review*, 47:157, 160 (Winter 1986).
[22] Peirce and Dworkin, "Workers' Compensation and Occupational Disease," p. 657.
[23] Mallin, "Disease, Not an Accident," p. 360.
[24] Kubasek and Giampetro-Meyer, "California's Radical Proposal," p. 174.
[25] Curtis Seltzer, "Moral Dimensions of Occupational Health: The Case of the 1969 Coal Mine Health and Safety Act," in *Health and Safety of Workers*, ed. Bayer, p. 263.
[26] Kelman, "Occupational Safety and Health Administration," p. 248.
[27] *NewsBank*, 20 Sept. 1991 (EMP65:F8).
[28] Nancy Frank and Michael Lombness, *Controlling Corporate Illegality: The Regulatory Justice System* (Cincinnati: Anderson, 1988), pp. 89–93.
[29] Joan Claybrook and the Staff of Public Citizen, *Retreat from Safety: Reagan's Attack on America's Health* (New York: Pantheon, 1984), pp. 101–4.
[30] *Ibid.*, p. 103.
[31] *Ibid.*, p. 104.
[32] *Ibid.*, p. 100.
[33] *Ibid.*, pp. 101–4.
[34] Nancy Frank, *Crimes against Health and Safety* (Albany, NY: Harrow & Heston, 1985), pp. 21–25.
[35] Bayer, *Health and Safety of Workers.*
[36] Epstein, *Politics of Cancer*, p. 138.
[37] Susan J. Tolchin and Martin Tolchin, *Dismantling America: The Rush to Deregulate* (Boston: Houghton Mifflin, 1983), p. 118.
[38] W. J. Nicholson and P. J. Landrigan, "Quantitative Assessment of Lives Lost Due to Delay in the Regulation of Occupational Exposure to Benzene," *Environmental Health in Perspective*, 82:185 (July 1989).
[39] *San Jose Mercury*, 16 Oct. 1988.
[40] Joseph V. Rodricks, Susan M. Brett, and Grover C. Wrenn, "Significant Risk Decisions in Federal Regulatory Agencies," *Regulatory Toxicology and Pharmacology*, 7:314–15 (1987).
[41] *Industrial Union Department v. American Petroleum Institute*, 448 U.S. 607 (1980); *American Textile Manufacturers Institute v. Donovan*, 101 U.S. 2478 (1981).
[42] Tolchin and Tolchin, *Dismantling America*, p. 123.
[43] Power, "Employer Intentional Torts," p.155.

‹13›

Crime in the Waste Oil Industry

Alan A. Block
Thomas J. Bernard

This article focuses on a specific type of white-collar crime involving both the petroleum and the toxic waste disposal industries. A discussion of the recent origin of these crimes is followed by a presentation of one particular case. A causal explanation links the criminal behaviors to changes in the conditions determining economic self-interest in the petroleum and toxic waste disposal industries, and to changes in criminal law that defined those economically self-interested actions as criminal. Finally, an analysis of the actions of social control agents demonstrates the power of white-collar groups to influence the enactment and enforcement of criminal laws affecting their economic activities.

The Appearance of a New Type of Crime

In the early 1980s, an oil salvage dealer spread waste oil containing dioxin, a highly toxic chemical, over dirt roads in many parts of Missouri, especially in the town of Times Beach (*Time Magazine*, 1985). The dealer was later convicted of tax evasion in connection with the case (*New York Times*, 1983a), and the town of Times Beach was purchased by the government and abandoned.

While the problems of Times Beach are well known, less publicized cases involving mixtures of liquid toxic wastes and waste oil began appearing at around the same time. The Subcommittee on Oversight and Investigations of the U.S. House of Representatives (1982) conducted several hearings on the spreading of such mixtures both on country roads and in residential subdivisions. In 1982, Maryland state environmental investigators found the highly toxic chemical PCB in fuel tanks at a large truck stop. The Wilmington *Evening Journal* (1982) reported that over a million gallons of PCE contaminated oil had been distributed, and quoted an FBI official as saying that it may be part of a "mob operated distribution system for toxic waste that is hidden in fuel oil that may involve the entire northeast." A similar case turned up in Delaware, where the operator of a waste oil tank farm was indicted on state charges including theft and "violations of environmental regulations." According to the Wilmington *News Journal* (1984), the operator stored and probably mixed dangerous chemicals with the waste oil, which was then distributed as pure oil. In 1984, the State of New Jersey indicted several individuals and five corporations on charges that they mixed "toxic, ignitable and corrosive hazardous wastes" with an oil blend and sold the product as fuel oil throughout New England and the Middle Atlantic states (Kimmelman, 1984). In another New Jersey case, the B and L Oil Company and its president were convicted of selling as fuel a waste oil that contained various toxic substances (Brinkman, 1985).

All of these crimes involved the illegal disposal of toxic wastes by apparently legitimate waste oil dealers. No similar cases appeared before 1978, indicating that there may be broader societal conditions that explain the sudden appearance of this new type of crime. Prior to analyzing those conditions, a detailed case study of this new type of crime is presented.

A Case Study
The Mahler Operations

Russell W. Mahler had been in the petroleum industry for over thirty years, specializing in re-refining waste oil for almost the entire period. He owned and operated four waste oil refineries that produced about 6 percent of the total national output of re-refined lubricants. His general prominence and importance are reflected in the fact that for a number of years he defueled the Strategic Air Command bomber fleet and U.S. Navy ships and submarines in the northeast, as well as Air Force 1 (*U.S.A. vs. Russell Mahler* 1984). There is no evidence that he engaged in illegal activities in the petroleum industry until the late 1970s. After that time, however, he participated in a number of criminal activities related to the disposal of toxic wastes. The following account of his activities is taken from his testimony before the New York State Senate Select Committee on Crime, as well as other investigations by that committee (Marino, 1982; New York State Senate Select Committee on Crime, 1984).

In the summer of 1978, the U.S. Coast Guard discovered a small oil spill on Newtown Creek in Queens, New York. This creek forms part of the boundary between Brooklyn and Queens and runs into the East River across from the United Nations. The Coast Guard was able to trace the oil back to an overflowing catch basin on the property of Newtown Oil Refining Corporation, owned by Russell Mahler. This was one of the region's largest waste oil recovery facilities, with a reported storage capacity of over seven million gallons. A $1,000 fine was levied for the illegal discharge and the federal government spent $5,000 to clean it up.

The following winter, Newtown was bought by Hudson Oil, located on the Hudson River on the other side of Manhattan at Edgewater, New Jersey. Mahler was also the owner and president of Hudson Oil. After Hudson purchased Newtown, Mahler applied for a waste oil collector permit from the New York State Department of Environmental Conservation (DEC).

Mahler also owned and operated Northeast Oil Service in Syracuse, New York, which had a tank farm. This facility was licensed as a transfer station to collect and store waste oils for shipment to re-refineries elsewhere. On two occasions in 1976 and 1977, the firm had been fined for illegal discharges into the sewers. Beginning in March, 1979, large amounts of unusual discharge began appearing in a pump station below the plant. The sanitation department installed an automatic sampler to continuously test the water, but it was twice tampered with. They then installed a tamper-proof device and monitored it for three weeks without result. The device was then removed, and the following weekend they discovered that 40,000 gallons of waste had been dumped into the sewers.

City and state officials then inspected the facility. They found that all of the tanks had downspouts that emptied into the sewer system, which ultimately emptied into Lake Onandaga. Records from the plant indicated that a large variety of toxic wastes, including benzene, xylene, and toluene, were being brought into the plant. There were no records indicating how those wastes were removed from the plant. DEC later stated that these wastes were being dumped in various locations, including into the Syracuse sewer and into Newtown Creek. In addition, the Canadian Broadcast Corporation reported that Hudson had transported cyanide wastes from a plant in Montreal and flushed most of it down the Syracuse sewer. Later estimates were that this plant had been illegally dumping about 65,000 gallons of toxic wastes per month over an extended period of time.

As a result of these investigations, DEC turned down Mahler's application to renew the permits for several of his firms to collect waste oil. DEC's regional attorney also "advised" Mahler to stop his activities at the Newtown and Syracuse sites. Mahler's businesses, however, continued to operate without permits. In September, 1979, DEC warned its regional offices that these businesses (which by then numbered eleven different firms) were operating illegally and that they were "believed to be a flagrant violator of a number of sections of the Environmental Conservation Law." DEC, however, did not investigate further or take any action to close the firms down.

Following these events in Syracuse, truckloads of toxic wastes coming into Hudson Oil's Edgewater facility in New Jersey were directed by the dispatcher, with Mahler's knowledge, to take their cargos to an auto service garage in Pittston, Pennsylvania. Behind this garage was a bore hole connected to an abandoned mine shaft that ended at the Susquehanna River. Later estimates were that over three million gallons of toxic wastes were dumped down this bore hole over a two-year period (Rebovich, 1986:28). The operation was discovered in the summer of 1979, when vast quantities of the wastes spilled into the river. These wastes coalesced and spread over 30 miles down the river, nearly reaching Chesapeake Bay. The state of Pennsylvania then immediately shut down the Pittston operation.

Several years later, Mahler, the dispatcher at the Edgewater terminal, and the owner of the gas station were convicted for violating the state's Clean Streams Act. The three and their company were fined $750,000, and Mahler served a one-year prison sentence. Thus, Mahler had the distinction of becoming one of a handful of people in the nation who has actually served time in prison for such offenses (Smith, 1984). EPA supervised the cleanup of the site at an estimated cost of $10 million (Marino,

1982:12), and in 1982 took it off their priority list. However, heavy rains from Hurricane Gloria sent another 100,000 gallons of chemical wastes into the Susquehanna River at this supposedly cleaned-up site (*Time Magazine*, 1985:78).

After the closing of the Pittston site, Mahler and the New York DEC worked out a "consent order" at the end of 1979. Mahler acknowledged violations on "at least sixteen different occasions," paid a fine of $50,000, and posted bond of $250,000 against future violations. Mahler also reorganized his operations, bringing almost all of them together in a new company called Quanta Resources that was incorporated in Delaware. DEC allowed Quanta to operate in New York without a permit, and also agreed that it would "not seek penalties against Quanta for any violation occurring prior to the acquisition of Hudson's assets by Quanta." Thus, despite the fact that Mahler still owned the companies, he was no longer liable for any previous illegal actions. Mahler later expressed considerable amazement at DEC's willingness to allow him to continue operating, given their awareness of his prior activities (Marino, 1982).

The New York DEC then allowed Quanta to transport about 150,000 gallons of waste oil contaminated with high levels of PCBs and bromoform (a metabolic poison that can cause liver damage and death) from an illegal dump at Chelsea Terminal on Staten Island. This took place from January through March, 1981. During the summer of that year, investigators from the New York State Senate Select Committee on Crime and investigative reporters from the ABC News television show *20/20* learned that Quanta was delivering suspect fuel oil to apartment buildings in New York City. ABC obtained samples of the oil and had it tested in a private laboratory. The tests showed it contained extremely high levels of PCBs, as well as the bromoforms that had been discovered at the Chelsea dump. The New York Senate Select Committee later stated: "While conjectural, the Select Committee believes it is entirely possible that the exotic bromoform was obtained by Quanta at Chelsea and recycled as a means of disposing of it in callous disregard for human health" (Marino, 1982:14).

As a result of these disclosures, the New Jersey Department of Environmental Protection performed its own tests on the oil with the same results. Quanta soon filed for bankruptcy, and ABC broadcast the story on December 17, 1981. Mahler later pled guilty to conspiracy to defraud waste generators by illegally dumping their toxic wastes at the Edgewater plant and in New York City. He cooperated extensively with local, state, and federal investigators in return for an agreement in which the prosecution made no recommendation on sentencing, while the agencies with which he was cooperating requested that he be placed on probation, which was granted (*U.S.A.*

v. Russell Mahler, 1984). The city of New York was required to clean up the Newtown facility at a cost of $2.5 million after bankruptcy court agreed that the company could simply abandon the site (New York State Senate Select Committee on Crime, 1984:96).

Later testimony before the Select Committee indicated that when deliveries to Pittston were halted, the toxic wastes were diverted to several of New York City's landfills. The committee alleged that access to these landfills was achieved through "a wide conspiracy involving fraud (and) bribery . . ." (Marino, 1982). Quanta drivers allegedly made numerous trips to these landfills, where they attached slotted T-bars to the rear of the trucks and spread liquid toxic wastes over the roads inside the landfill or simply dumped it into holes dug by landfill employees with bulldozers. As a result of this investigation, one landfill supervisor was fired and later indicted for bribery.

Causal Analysis

◂ Economic Conditions and Criminal Laws ▸

A case history has been presented as an example of a type of crime that apparently is recent in origin but widespread in practice. Examination of events in the lubrication re-refining industry and in the toxic waste disposal industry reveals economic and legal conditions that explain the sudden appearance of this new type of crime.

The lubrication re-refining industry was a major part of the American petroleum industry in 1960, with over 150 companies producing about 18 percent of the nation's total lubricant consumption. By 1982, however, 90 percent of these companies were out of business, and the remaining companies produced less than 5 percent of the nation's lubricant consumption (McBain, 1982). There were many reasons for this dramatic decline in the re-refining industry. Lubricant oils were increasingly complex, with sophisticated additives to meet the needs of high performance engines. These additives account for as much as 25 percent of the total volume of the oil, and increase the cost and difficulty of re-refining (McBain, 1982). The quality of re-refined oils declined in response to this increasing complexity. This resulted in a decline in their use, including a ban on their use by the military and a drop in the price they would bring (Brinkman, 1985:48). Additional costs were also imposed on the industry by new toxic waste disposal regulations that increased the cost of disposing of the acid sludge that remained after re-refining (Hess, 1979). As a result, re-refined lube oil prices declined while costs were increasing and most re-refineries went bankrupt.

While the price of re-refined lube oils declined, the price of heating oil increased more than ten times (Brassart, 1982). The costs involved in preparing waste oil for burning are much lower than those involved in preparing it for re-use as lubricants. Straining and particulate settling are often sufficient (Jarvis, 1982), and at times trucks picking up waste oil may simply deliver it to residences and businesses for use as fuel with no treatment at all (Brinkman: 1985:70). Such waste oils are "recycled," but not re-refined. When treated lube oils are sold for heating fuel, the after-tax rate of return on investment is at least 110 percent (Brinkman, 1982). When untreated oil is sold the profit can be much higher since a dealer can acquire waste oil for between 0 and 20 cents per gallon and can sell it for between 80 and 95 cents per gallon (New York State Senate Select Committee, 1984:33). Thus, it was no surprise that the decline in the re-refining industry was accompanied by an expansion in the recycling of waste oil for use as heating fuel.

At the same time these events were occurring in the petroleum industry, a separate series of events was occurring in the toxic waste disposal industry. In 1976, Congress passed the Resource Conservation and Recovery Act (RCRA), which established a minimum set of standards and regulations for the control of hazardous wastes throughout the nation (Wilheim, 1981). The impact of this act was first felt in a drastic rise in the price of disposal. This was followed by the appearance of "midnight dumpers"—disposers who charged under-market prices because they simply dumped the toxic wastes anywhere and everywhere (Brown, 1984; Smith, 1984; Miller and Miller, 1985).

Many waste oils are contaminated with toxic wastes that must be removed and disposed of before the oil can be re-used for any purpose. This is a particular problem with polychlorinated biphenyl compounds (PCBs), a widely used but deadly substance that does not biodegrade (Kuratsune and Shapiro, 1984; Piasecki and Gravander, 1984). PCBs are difficult to dispose of properly, and also are difficult to detect and measure in waste oils (Xavier, 1982). Thus, it is possible to ignore their presence in the oil, particularly when PCB contaminated oils are to be used as fuel. In that case, the PCBs are simply dispersed in the atmosphere. Industries also use PCBs in other forms, and are faced with expensive disposal problems there. Xavier (1982) notes that "industry has found a convenient, simple, and cheap method of disposal" for these PCBs—they simply "dump it into their used-oils." Thus, PCBs may be deliberately introduced into waste oils that did not previously contain them.

A great many other types of hazardous wastes may also be dumped into waste oils as a means of cheap disposal. Brinkman (1985:49), for example, comments that:

> . . . unethical producers of hazardous wastes "hide" them in used oil to avoid the costs of proper disposal. When generators

> of used oil must pay a minimum of $1 per gallon to dispose of liquid hazardous wastes while recyclers are paying up to $.50 a gallon for used oil the temptation is hard to resist.

This practice was enhanced by the fact that Congress exempted waste oils from RCRA regulation in 1980 in an attempt to encourage the recycling of used oils (Arbuckle et al., 1985:73). Brinkman (1985) argues that the widespread bankruptcies in the re-refining industry are specifically attributable to the dumping of toxic wastes into waste oils, making them uneconomical to re-refine. Even if Brinkman's argument is not correct, it gives a sense of the extent to which illegal dumping of toxic wastes into waste oil was taking place.

While these contaminants pose insurmountable problems for legitimate re-refiners, they pose no problem at all for unscrupulous dealers who sell the oil as fuel. Whether or not these contaminants are flammable they increase the total volume of the oil to be sold. When burned, flammable contaminants may be transformed into other toxic substances that are dispersed in the atmosphere. Contaminants that are not flammable are simply dispersed into the atmosphere and lower the total amount of heat derived from the fuel. For example, analysis of a truckload of fuel oil delivered to a building in Brooklyn found that it contained (among other things) 102 pounds of metals, including lead, copper, aluminum, and zinc. In testimony before the New York State Senate Select Committee on Crime (1984:20), Russell Mahler gave a practical illustration of what that meant: "If you went to the roof of that building and had a 102-pound sack of fine powered metals over your shoulder and, over a period of four days, you threw it all out into the neighborhood, then the next load came in on the fifth day and you went up with another 102-pound sack of metal and threw that all over the neighborhood, that's what you would be getting."

Dealers may sell the fuel at regular prices to unsuspecting customers or may make mutually profitable arrangements with high volume purchasers who do not mind buying contaminated oil in return for lower prices. This is a particular problem in New York City, which has the highest fuel oil prices in the nation. Fuel oil dealers there have the greatest economic incentives to "cocktail" toxic wastes with waste oils and to sell the resulting mixture as fuel oil (New York State Senate Select Committee on Crime, 1984:128). At the same time, the owners of large apartment buildings have economic incentives to buy contaminated oil if they can get a cheaper price from the dealer, with little concern for public health because they do not live at the site at which it will be burned (Smith, 1984). A spokesperson for a regional trade association of fuel oil dealers estimated that at least 10 percent of marketed oil in New York is contaminated with toxic wastes (New York State Senate Select Committee on Crime, 1984). In the New York metropolitan area alone, this would amount to 300 million gallons per year.

In sum, the legitimate re-refining of waste oil for reuse as lubricants suddenly became uneconomical, threatening the entire industry with bankruptcy. At exactly that point in time, changes in the criminal law made the legal disposal of toxic wastes very expensive, which created economic pressure to dispose of toxic wastes by cheap but illegal means. Waste oil dealers already had facilities for the storage and disposal of waste products and could illegally sell a mixture of toxic wastes and waste oil as fuel with minimal chances of being caught. Thus, a new illegal means for making money was presented to waste oil dealers at the same time that their traditional, legal means for making money suddenly disappeared. The involvement of waste oil dealers in the illegal disposal of toxic wastes is explained by the convergence of these broader economic and legal conditions.

Within the context of generally accepted criteria for inferring causality (Labovitz and Hagedorn, 1976), it is appropriate to state that the broader economic and legal conditions *caused* the new pattern of crime. The economic changes in the petroleum industry and the legal changes in the toxic waste disposal industry are associated with the appearance of the new pattern of criminality and immediately precede it in time. A clear theoretical rationale establishes a causal relation between the legal and economic conditions and the criminality, and there is no apparent third factor that can simultaneously[1] explain the pattern of crime and the economic and legal conditions. Thus, in the present case, broader societal conditions directly caused individual criminal behaviors.

IMPLICATIONS

◀ THEORIES OF CRIMINAL AND DEVIANT BEHAVIOR ▶

Various criminology theories have been utilized to explain the motivations of white-collar criminals, such as differential association (Sutherland, 1949), anomie theory (Sherwin, 1963), and labeling theory (Waegel et al., 1981). In the present case, the white-collar crime appears to have been motivated by a relatively straightforward pursuit of economic self-interest, which itself was shaped by the particular economic and legal conditions associated with the waste oil industry. The theories that best describe this situation are "strain" (Merton, 1968) and "differential opportunity" theories (Cloward and Ohlin, 1960).

Both theories describe criminal behavior in terms of individual responses to structural limitations on economic opportunities related to lower-class positions. In the present case, however, the limitations on legitimate opportunities were generated by changing economic conditions in the petroleum industry and were experienced by those occupying higher class positions. Therefore, neither theory accurately accounts for the origins of the illegal opportunities in the present case: such origins lay in changes in the criminal laws on toxic waste disposal. The new illegal opportunities either consisted of the continued participation in the same (but now illegal and much more profitable) practices, or in the innovation of new methods of economical but illegal disposal of toxic wastes (see Rebovich, 1986:30).

This explanation is similar to that offered by Vaughan (1983) in her explanation of the Revco Medicaid fraud. In that case, the limitations on legitimate opportunities originated in the rejection of numerous legitimate Medicaid claims by the state welfare department and the illegitimate opportunity arose because a Revco employee had extensive knowledge of the welfare department's computer system. It is also consistent with more general arguments that the blockage of legitimate means to achieve any number of goals may generate pressure for white-collar deviance (Gross, 1978). Finally, it is consistent with a structural interpretation of strain theory in which individuals directly respond to structurally distributed opportunities to achieve goals, and are not necessarily psychologically stressed and frustrated (Bernard, 1987).

IMPLICATIONS

THEORIES OF SOCIAL REACTION

Recent sociological theory and research has also considered the official social control process which defines and responds to deviance (cf. Pfohl, 1985: 283–328). One concern has been the ability of powerful groups to prevent their own actions from being labeled as deviant (Lauderdale, 1980; Schur, 1980). In particular, Sutherland (1949) argued that white-collar groups are able to influence the enactment and enforcement of criminal laws so that their own economically self-interested actions are not defined and processed as criminal. A great deal of recent theory and research has examined criminal justice and regulatory responses to white-collar crime with this basic argument in mind (Braithwaite, 1985).

Recent research has focused more on the enforcement of laws about white-collar activities rather than on their enactment. Legislative bodies are often responsive to the activity of "moral entrepreneurs" (Edelman, 1964; Gusfield, 1967), and this responsiveness has been found with consumer protection legislation in general and toxic waste legislation in particular (Pertschuk, 1982; Williams and Matheny, 1984). The enforcement of those laws then is turned over to regulators who operate in a climate of interdependence with the regulated industry (Vaughan, 1982). An issue exists about whether compliance with the law is enhanced by this "conciliatory" atmosphere, or whether the absence of criminal sanctions renders the laws "symbolic" (cf. McGraw, 1975; Stone, 1982; Braithwaite, 1985).

In the present case, Congress repeatedly passed laws related to handling waste oils, but EPA refused to issue or implement regulations in response to those laws. In addition, EPA failed to carry out the enforcement procedures set up by Congress for the handling of toxic wastes, and finally dismantled its enforcement mechanism. The failure to enforce the laws did not appear to be associated with any overall efforts to elicit industry compliance with the legal standard, but rather appeared to be generated solely by industry pressure in support of its own economic interests.

When Congress passed the RCRA in 1976, it listed used oil as a hazardous waste and directed EPA to write regulations on the handling of these materials. Regulations were written but were not issued due to industry opposition (Brinkman, 1985). In 1980, Congress attempted to legislate a compromise to this stalemate by exempting fuel containing hazardous wastes from regulation under the RCRA statute while at the same time directing EPA to issue separate regulations to ensure the safe use of these oils. In January 1981, EPA proposed these regulations, which included designating waste oil a hazardous waste. The Reagan administration took office shortly thereafter and rescinded the proposal.

In 1984, Congress responded again to the inaction at EPA by enacting provisions regarding used oil and various other hazardous wastes (Hall et al., 1985:73–74). These provisions directed EPA to implement new requirements by November, 1986, or a congressionally formulated regulation would automatically go into effect. They also directed EPA to determine within two years whether waste oil would be identified as a hazardous waste.

In response to these provisions, EPA issued for comment in January, 1985, a set of regulations that again proposed listing waste oil as a hazardous waste (Graham, 1986). These regulations were to go into effect in November, 1986, in accordance with the congressional timetable and would have seriously compromised the economic viability of the re-refining industry. In the regulations issued on that date, however, EPA responded to widespread industry comments and decided not to list waste oil as a hazardous waste (*U.S.A. vs. Waste Management*, 1985). Generators of used oils (such as service stations) have no obligations under those regulations so long as the oil is sent to a qualified recycling center. Those who blend the used oil into a fuel and those who actually burn the oil must meet certain reporting and record-keeping requirements if the fuel exceeds specified levels of toxic substances.

In addition to failing to issue regulations, EPA failed to carry out the enforcement mechanism created by Congress for controlling toxic waste disposal. The mechanism centered on the creation of a "paper trail" composed of hazardous waste manifests that would accompany hazardous waste from generation to disposal. That "paper trail" meant that, at any point, regulators might check the manifests and determine whether the wastes were being properly handled. Once firms realized that their management of toxic wastes was subject to review and inspection, so the argument went, then they would avoid illegal disposal because it would be too risky.

That mechanism turned out to be useless because EPA regulators routinely failed to collect the manifests in the first place. Manifests that were collected formed a mountain of paper that proved impossible for the regulators to monitor. Regulators also failed to inspect hazardous waste sites even when there were known violations. That failure was demonstrated by a special GAO investigation which found 51 out of 65 licensed sites to be in violation of the law (*New York Times*, 1983b).

After President Reagan took office he instituted a policy of reviewing all regulations with the intention of relaxing the requirements and "decommissioning regulatory controls" (Jorling, 1981). Consistent with this policy, one of Anne Gorsuch Burford's first acts as the new head of EPA was to abolish the Office of Enforcement. She then implemented a series of contradictory and confusing enforcement policies that were later described by a House Subcommittee as motivated by "mismanagement, disregard, or indifference by top agency officials regarding their enforcement responsibilities" (Subcommittee on Oversight and Investigations of the Committee on Energy and Commerce, 1982:34).[2]

The general enforcement failures of EPA turned out to be highly profitable for toxic waste disposers. They were able to delay large capital expenditures necessary to improve disposal facilities, and at the same time to increase their fees substantially for disposing of the wastes. The accumulating capital gathered by the larger disposal firms was used to buy many of smaller firms across the country. The disposal industry in the United States therefore entered a period of intense centralization, perhaps the most significant RCRA accomplishment. At times, this centralization was highlighted by charges of price fixing and antitrust activities (*U.S.A. vs. Waste Management, Inc. et al.*, 1985:6278), but it moved inexorably forward.

At the state level, efforts to enforce toxic waste regulations were compromised by the lack of resources and facilities to enforce the law. New York State, for example, was the center of illegal activities in the waste oil industry because it had the highest fuel oil prices in the nation (New York Senate Select Committee on Crime, 1984). However, enforcement of these laws at the time of the Mahler case was the responsibility of three part-time officials. The maximum fine available under New York law was $1,000 per violation, and the average fine ran between $250 and $400 (New York State Senate Select Committee on Crime, 1984:88). State officials did not have the resources or facilities to impound trucks carrying hazardous wastes oils, and requests for additional resources were turned down by budget officials (New York State Senate Select Committee on Crime, 1984:115, 130–33).

In 1983, the New York State legislature passed a law defining the selling of toxic wastes as fuel a felony, and the New York DEC issued the first regulations in the nation to enforce this new law. In response to the new law, waste oil dealers organized themselves into the United Petroleum Association, filed a law suit against DEC opposing the regulations, and threatened a boycott. The regulations were then suspended (*U.S.A. v. Russell Mahler*, 1984:23).

So intractable were the enforcement problems that Nicolas Robinson, General Counsel and Deputy Commissioner of the New York DEC, made the astonishing argument that the government must begin subsidizing the re-refining industry or the problem would never be solved (New York State Senate Select Committee on Crime, 1984:129). This recommendation illustrates the measured view of an enforcement official at that time that enforcement itself was a lost cause and that violators could only be stopped by changing the economic incentives to which they were responding.

The enforcement mechanisms of most northeastern states have been solidified in the six years since the Mahler case (Rebovich, 1986:13–17). Nevertheless, Rebovich (1986:40) describes various ways in which white-collar groups retain significant power to influence the enforcement of criminal laws and regulations that affect their actions. Attorneys who previously worked for the regulatory agencies are hired by the firms to exploit their knowledge of loopholes. Law enforcement personnel may obtain part-time employment as security guards at offending companies. Inspectors are offered jobs by the industries they regulate, where overtures for these jobs are made well in advance of actual offers.

Finally, the absence of a federal standard leaves in place a fairly widespread pattern of interstate criminal activity involving waste oils that has developed since the Mahler case (Rebovich, 1986:43–46). Some states such as New Jersey regulate waste oils as a hazardous waste, while other states such as Pennsylvania do not. Waste oils in New Jersey may be blended with various toxic wastes and then legally classified as a toxic waste within the state regulations. They are then shipped across the river to Pennsylvania where they drop off the New Jersey books and are legally reclassified as waste oils under Pennsylvania laws. They then are shipped back to New Jersey under the Pennsylvania manifests and sold as fuel.

Conclusion

This article demonstrates a direct causal relation between broader societal conditions and individual criminal behaviors, consistent with a structural interpretation of strain theories. The relationship was demonstrated because the broader societal conditions abruptly changed at a particular point in time and that change was quickly followed by the appearance of a new pattern of criminal behavior. As such, the explanation meets the standard scientific criteria for inferring causality.

The article also describes a particular instance in which white-collar groups used their power to prevent their own economically self-interested actions from being defined and processed as criminal. This is consistent with the general arguments of conflict criminology (Vold and Bernard, 1986) and with Sutherland's (1940) more specific arguments about white-collar crime. It is interesting that, to the extent that industry groups are unable to prevent enforcement of the laws, the costs of enforcement were "socialized" by passing them on to consumer groups or back to the government. This pattern is evident in the Mahler case, where the costs of cleaning up the various sites were borne by governmental units despite the fact that Mahler continued to operate a profitable business at the time. In each case, those governmentally borne costs vastly exceeded the fines that Mahler paid.

Finally, in the present case, there is no evidence that the conciliatory relation between EPA and the waste disposal industry was associated with any enforcement effectiveness. EPA appeared to act like a "captured" agency (Sabatier, 1975) whose ultimate aim was to ensure industry profitability rather than to elicit compliance with the law.

Notes

[1] A possible alternate explanation would be that the appearance of this new type of crime reflects only changes in reporting practices, and not changes in the actual behavior of waste oil dealers or in the criminality of that behavior. We do not regard this as a serious alternate explanation. Cheap

and legal methods of toxic waste disposal were widely available prior to the enactment of RCRA, at least some of which were later defined as illegal under RCRA. Thus, there was no incentive to engage in illegal activities prior to the passage of RCRA. Nevertheless, see Reiss and Biderman (1980) for a discussion of the problems of engaging in causal analysis of white-collar crime in situations in which the law itself, and therefore reporting practices about violations of the law, undergo change.

[2] This enforcement policy was particularly apparent in the handling of the "Superfund" created by Congress in 1980 to pay for cleaning up hazardous waste sites. According to a Judiciary Committee (1985) report, all Superfund decisions had a political component. Some decisions were allegedly made to help Reagan congressional supporters, others to damage Democratic opponents, and others to reward "suspected polluters" who were major campaign contributors. The report accused the Department of Justice officials of conspiring with EPA officials and other members of the Reagan administration to withhold from Congress "documents such as enforcement strategy memoranda and statements of negotiation or settlement positions being utilized in ongoing litigation" under the false claim of executive privilege (Judiciary Committee, 1985:75).

◂ References ▸

Anderson, Jack with James Boyd. 1983. *Fiasco.* New York: Times Books.

Bernard, Thomas J. 1987. "Testing Structural Strain Theories." *Journal of Research in Crime and Delinquency*, 24(4).

Block, Alan A. and Frank R. Scarpitti. 1985. *Poisoning for Profit.* New York: William Morrow.

———. 1986. "America's Toxic Waste Racket." Pp. 115–26 in *Organized Crime: An Anthology*, ed. Tim Bynum. Willow Tree Press.

Braithwaite, John. 1985. "White Collar Crime," *Annual Review of Sociology*, 1:1–25.

Brassart, Patrick. 1982. "Industry Experience Around the World." Pp. 22–24 in *Used Oil: The Hidden Asset.* Washington: Association of Petroleum Re-refiners.

Brinkman, Dennis W. 1982. "Re-refining vs. Burning: How Do You Decide." Pp. 226–32 in *Used Oil: The Hidden Asset.* Washington: Association of Petroleum Re-refiners.

———. 1985. "Used Oil: Resource or Pollutant." *Technology Review*, 88:46–51.

Brown, Michael. 1980. *Laying Waste.* New York: Pantheon.

———. 1984. "Toxic Waste: Organized Crime Moves In." *Readers Digest* 125:73–78.

Cloward, Richard and Lloyd E. Ohlin. 1960. *Delinquency and Opportunity.* New York: Free Press.

Conklin, J. E. 1986. *Criminology.* New York: Macmillan.

Edelman, J. M. 1964. *The Symbolic Uses of Politics.* Urbana: University of Illinois Press.

Epstein, Samuel S., Lester O. Brown, and Carl Pope. 1982. *Hazardous Waste in America.* San Francisco: Sierra Club Books.

Graham, Janet. 1986. "An Overview of the New Policy on Waste Oil." *The Regulatory Information Service of Hazardous Material Management and Resource Recovery Program at the University of Alabama* 1(2) (Fall): 9–26.

Gross, Edward. 1978. "Organizational Crime: A Theoretical Perspective." Pp. 55–85 in *Studies in Symbolic Interaction*, ed. Norman Denzin. Greenwich, CT: JAI.

Gusfield, Joseph. 1967. *Symbolic Crusade*. Urbana: University of Illinois Press.

Hall, Ridgway M., Jr. and Nancy S. Bryson. 1985. "Resource Conservation and Recovery Act" in *Environmental Law Handbook*, 5th ed., ed. J. Gordon Arbuckle, G. William Frick, Ridgway M. Hall, Jr., Marshall Lee Miller, Thomas F. P. Sullivan, and Timothy A. Vanderver, Jr. Rockville: Government Institutes.

Hess, L. Y. 1979. *Reprocessing and Disposal of Waste Petroleum Oils*. Park Ridge, NY: Noyes Data Corporation.

Jarvis, Robert C. 1982. "Burning Used Oil." Pp. 224–25 in *Used Oil: The Hidden Asset*. Washington: Association of Petroleum Re-refiners.

Jorling, Thomas C. 1981. "Foreword: Hazardous Waste Regulation under the New Administration—Braking Past Progress." *Ecology Law Quarterly*, 9:522–23.

Judiciary Committee, U.S. House of Representatives. 1985. *Report on Investigation of the Role of the Department of Justice in the Withholding of Environmental Protection Agency Documents from Congress in 1982–83*. House Report 99–435. Washington: U.S. Government Printing Office.

Kimmelman, Irwin I. 1984. Press release, Office of New Jersey Attorney General.

Kuratsune, Masanori and Raymond E. Shapiro, eds. 1984. *PCB Poisoning in Japan and Taiwan*. New York: Alan R. Liss.

Labovitz, Sanford and Robert Hagedorn. 1976. *Introduction to Social Research*. New York: McGraw-Hill.

Lauderdale, Pat, ed. 1980. *A Political Analysis of Deviance*. Minneapolis: University of Minnesota Press.

Marino, Ralph J. 1982. *Case History of a Toxic Waste Dumper*. New York: New York State Senate Select Committee on Crime.

McBain, James A. 1982. "Industry Experience in North America." Pp. 30–32 in *Used Oil: The Hidden Asset*. Washington: Association of Petroleum Re-refiners.

McCaghy, Charles H. 1985. *Deviant Behavior: Crime, Conflict and Interest Groups*. New York: Macmillan.

McCloy, John J., Nathan Pearson, and Beverly Matthews. 1976. *The Great Oil Spill: Gulf Oil's Bribery and Political Chicanery*. Chelsea Books.

McGraw, Thomas K. 1975. "Regulation in America: A Review Article." *Business History Review*, 66:159–83.

Merton, Robert K. 1968. *Social Theory and Social Structure*. New York: Free Press.

Miller, J. and M. Miller. 1985. "The Midnight Dumpers." *USA Today* 113:60–64.

Nader, Ralph, Ronald Brownstein, and John Richard. 1981. *Who's Poisoning America*. Sierra Books.

New York State Senate Select Committee on Crime, Its Causes, Control and Effect on Society. 1984. *In the Matter of a Public Hearing on the Subject of Toxic Wastes*. New York, April 30.

New York Times. 1983a. "Salvage Oil Dealer Convicted in Tax Trial." July 23.

———. 1983b. "Waste Sites Found Violating U.S. Laws." October 6.

Pfohl, Stephen J. 1985. *Images of Deviance and Social Control*. New York: McGraw-Hill.

Piasecki, Bruce and Jerry Gravander. 1985. "The Missing Links: Restructuring Hazardous-Waste Controls in America." *Technology Review* 88:42–49.

Pertschuk, Michael. 1982. *Revolt Against Regulation.* Berkeley: University of California Press.

Rebovich, David. 1986. *Understanding Hazardous Waste Crime.* Trenton: Northeast Hazardous Waste Project.

Reiss, Albert J. and A. Biderman. 1980. *Data Sources on White-Collar Law Breaking.* Washington, D.C.: U.S. Government Printing Office.

Sabatier, Paul. 1975. "Social Movements and Regulatory Agencies." *Policy Sciences*, 6:301–42.

Schur, Edwin M. 1980. *The Politics of Deviance.* Englewood Cliffs, NJ: Prentice-Hall.

Sherrill, Robert. 1983. *The Oil Follies of 1970–1980.* New York: Anchor.

Sherwin, R. 1963. "White Collar Crime, Conventional Crime and Merton's Deviant Behavior Theory." *Wisconsin Sociologist*, 2:7–10.

Smith, Eleanor. 1984. "Midnight Dumping." *Omni*, 6 (March): 18ff.

Stone, Alan. 1982. *Regulation and its Alternatives.* Washington: Congressional Quarterly Press.

Subcommittee on Oversight and Investigations of the Committee on Energy and Commerce, U.S. House of Representatives. 1982. *Hazardous Waste Enforcement: Report.* Washington: U.S. Government Printing Office.

Sutherland, Edwin. 1949. *White Collar Crime.* New York: Dryden.

Time Magazine. 1985. "Toxic Waste." October 14: 76–87.

U.S.A. v. Russell Mahler. 1984. Sentencing Hearing before the Honorable Herbert J. Stern, May 10, Newark, NJ.

U.S.A. vs. Waste Management, Inc., et al. 1985. "Proposed Consent Judgement." *Federal Register*, 50(31) (Feb. 14): 6273–86.

Vaughan, Dianne. 1982. "Toward Understanding Unlawful Organizational Behavior." *Michigan Law Review*, 80:1377–1402.

———. 1983. *Controlling Unlawful Organizational Behavior.* Chicago: University of Chicago Press.

Vold, George B. and Thomas J. Bernard. 1986. *Theoretical Criminology.* New York: Oxford.

Waegel, W., M. D. Ermann, and A. M. Horowitz. 1981. "Organizational Responses to Imputations of Deviance." *Sociological Quarterly*, 22:43–55.

Wilhelm, Georgina K. 1981. "The Regulation of Hazardous Waste Disposal: Cleaning up the Augean Stables with a Flood of Regulations." *Rutgers Law Review*, 33:906–72.

Williams, Bruce A. and Albert R. Matheny. 1984. "Testing Theories of Social Regulation: Hazardous Waste Regulation in the American States." *Journal of Politics*, 46:428–58.

Wilmington *Evening Journal.* 1982. "Fuel Oil Scheme Spreads PCBs." June 24.

Wilmington *News Journal.* 1984. "Sealand Operator Indicted." December 15.

Xavier, Raymond A. 1982. "Detecting PCBs." Pp. 59–63 in *Used Oil: The Hidden Asset.* Washington: Association of Petroleum Re-refiners.

14

Government Breaks the Law
The Sabotaging of the Occupational Safety and Health Act

Harry Brill

Introduction

Corruption among public officials is generally associated in the public mind with such egregious behind-the-scene activities as taking bribes and kickbacks, colluding with private contractors who bilk the government or produce shoddy merchandise, and as revealed in the Iran/Contra scandal, complicity in narcotic trafficking. Yet in an insightful article on corruption pertaining to military spending, the important observation is made that "even if all the fat were trimmed and the crooks thrown in jail, the problem of corruption would not be solved" (*Dollars & Sense*, 1985:3). For corruption is rooted, the article maintains, in the military-industrial complex, which serves to benefit certain key institutions and those who control them at the expense of the public. More generally, when the driving force behind a program is not really intended to serve the public interest, but is mainly oriented toward pandering to special interests, it is inherently corrupt.[1]

Reprinted from *Social Justice*, 19(3): 63–81.

Because the institutional sources of corruption are intermediated through individuals, the inclination of the public and of many scholars has been to blame corrupt practices on the moral shortcomings of those who abuse their office.[2] This approach, however, is often misleading. Those who were opposed to the appointment, for example, of former CIA Deputy Director Robert Gates as CIA director complained about his devious and deceptive conduct.[3] Yet this is just what the CIA requires. Since among its important roles is to undermine democratic movements—an objective that is certainly not sanctioned by any statutes—the CIA would self-destruct if led by anyone who insisted upon integrity, freedom, and openness. Many other government agencies, including those with benign reputations, also require officials who are willing to neglect their moral and legal responsibilities to the public. Those who resist conforming are penalized and weeded out. Not by identifying personal proclivities, but by taking into account the underlying systemic and structural influences upon government agencies can we understand widespread corruption in government and its corrosive impact on democratic decision making.

If secret government tends to subvert democracy, the converse, open government, does not ensure uncorrupt and democratic conduct. Since corruption is the betrayal of the public trust by misusing public office to serve particular individuals or special interests, the widespread assumption among scholars and the public is that corrupt conduct is generally clandestine (Alatas, 1980:13).[4] However, corrupt practices in agencies within the executive branch and various independent enforcement agencies are routinely out in the open despite illegal conduct. Like behind-the-scenes corruption that feeds the nation's rapidly growing list of scandals, the misconduct of these agencies appreciably undermines the democratic elements of the U.S. political system.

Overt illegal conduct among enforcement agencies is endemic in liberal-democratic societies. Because the business sector is not omnipotent, it is unable to prevent many progressive laws from being enacted. If social-reform advocates completely lacked clout, all left-of-center bills would fail and, accordingly, there would be an absence of such legislation for public officials to flout. However, although the business community lacks absolute power, it exerts disproportionate influence, which it frequently employs successfully to prevent these statutes from being effectively enforced. The result is that enforcement agencies continually violate their legal duty to protect the public.

The influence of business is often also reflected in the various provisions of progressive statutes that dilute their effectiveness. Penalties for violations are often too lenient, remedial recourse is usually legally cumbersome, and agencies are given too much discretion. For these reasons, the failure of agencies to effectively enforce the law is often attributed to weaknesses in the statute. Yet even without amending the laws, the statutes are not empty boxes that agencies can fill any way they choose. Agencies cannot continually engage in a pattern of nonenforcement without violating the law. To do so is to abuse their discretion, which is illegal. Yet feeble enforcement of the laws is the rule. The Savings and Loan (S&L) scandals, the polluted environment, the myriad unsafe drugs, and widespread false advertising are among the grim testimonies to the lackadaisical enforcement practices of government agencies.

Even the most carefully constructed statutes do not compel agencies to enforce the law. The executive branch is adept at finding ways to break the law, and members of the judiciary, who are carefully selected by the executive branch and are usually confirmed by the Senate, generally validate the illegal actions of public officials. The continual pursuit of the perfect law, one that would impel agencies to adequately enforce statutes that regulate business conduct, is an illusory objective.

The unending abuse of the laws by public officials is camouflaged with legal rationalizations, which in part explains why the unlawful nature of their misconduct is often not apparent to the public. Also, because we associate corruption and illegal conduct with the actual commission of some objectionable act, when agencies do little or nothing about a problem, we do not regard it as illegal and certainly not criminal. Typical of the literature on corporate crime and violence is the lack of discussion on how the failure of public officials to perform their duties may make them accomplices to corporate crime.[5] Yet the failure to act when there is a legal duty to do so is illegal. When such an omission results in injury or death, it is a criminal offense (Henry, 1991:253–270).

The Occupational Safety and Health Administration (OSHA) is among the agencies that habitually violate their legal obligations. Although its exclusive responsibility is to protect the health and safety of working people on their jobs, the agency instead is far more responsive to business interests. As I will detail in the discussion of OSHA's conduct, OSHA commits with impunity both civil and criminal violations, which in turn encourages the business community to flout the law.

In particular, this essay will consider how OSHA ignores its legal obligations both to enforce health and safety regulations and to adopt new standards. Like many other government agencies that are unwilling to abide by their statutory duties, however, OSHA attempts to convey the misleading impression that it is behaving responsibly. Since OSHA's feeble enforcement record is accessible to the public, its contempt for the health and safety law—which it is required to enforce—cannot be hidden from interested parties, particularly from various watchdog organizations.[6] The judiciary, nevertheless, has protected OSHA against the legitimate demands of working people to obtain adequate enforcement of the health and safety act.

OSHA and the judiciary occasionally live up to their obligations. Many OSHA inspectors are serious about their responsibilities, but on the whole they are kept in line. Despite their weakness, working people and their organizations are not powerless. They occasionally have been able to compel OSHA to take strong action, though generally only after publication of flagrant business violations or the occurrence of a major industrial accident. Since OSHA's achievements are more highly publicized than its derelictions, the agency's record, and the judiciary's as well, seems far more in balance than they are in actuality. The truth is that OSHA and the judiciary have continually violated their statutory responsibilities, resulting in a great deal of harm to working people. OSHA's routine performance of its duties cannot be justified as a lawful exercise of its discretionary powers. Its conduct has been illegal, criminal, and therefore corrupt. To use Marcus Raskin's phrase, it is "violence clothed in the law" (1991:513).

The Problem

Tragically, the federal government's lackadaisical enforcement of the Occupational Safety and Health Act (the OSH Act) has been costing many working people their lives and physical well-being. As fines for violations are generally much lower than the costs of adequately correcting them, the business community realizes that they can get away with homicide and mayhem.

According to the National Safe Workplace Institute (NSWI, an independent research organization committed to advancing safety and health in the workplace), each year over 10,000 men and women are killed on their jobs and up to 70,000 workers become permanently disabled because of on-the-job injuries. Another 70,000 workers die of occupationally caused diseases. In the long run, about 25 percent of all workers will be either killed or seriously injured on their jobs or will die of job-related illnesses (NSWI, 1989a:2). Going to work, as more workers are learning, is not recommended for good health and longevity.

The OSH Act confers the legal authority for enforcing the law on the Secretary of the Department of Labor. The Occupational Safety and Health Administration (OSHA), a unit within the department, has been established to administer the act, and responsibility for the operation of OSHA has been delegated to an assistant secretary of labor. Thus, although articles and reports on workplace safety often refer to OSHA without mentioning the Department of Labor, OSHA is not an autonomous unit. In fact, other department officials, including the solicitor, play an important role in shaping OSHA's decisions. The agency is an integral part of the Department of Labor, and its practices reflect the policies of the Labor Department's secretary. OSHA's misconduct, then, is also the misconduct of the Department of Labor.

Critics of OSHA's lackluster performance have sought mainly to persuade Congress to amend the statute and to compel OSHA to adopt more health and safety standards. The OSH Act could certainly be improved and more regulations would be useful. A serious problem is that developing and finally approving regulations take at least four years, often much longer, not including a few additional years absorbed by court challenges (Shapiro, 1989:13–14). Moreover, most proposed regulations are never approved.

OSHA's Enforcement Record

Yet when we consider how little OSHA has accomplished by using the legal tools it already possesses, the faith that changing the legal text will significantly improve enforcement practices is unconvincing. Revising the OSH statute would prompt OSHA to find new strategies to circumvent it. Importantly, the judiciary can also be counted on to undermine the law.

Unions and other advocates of a safe workplace realize that OSHA could do much better without changing the laws. Yet they also believe that OSHA is generally law abiding and, therefore, reforming the OSH Act would influence the agency's conduct. Reform advocates have been urging Congress to adopt severe criminal penalties to discourage violations.[7] They maintain that the inadequate penalties of up to $10,000 in fines (recently increased to a maximum of $70,000) along with six months in prison for a first willful violation that causes death have discouraged the Department of Justice from prosecuting cases recommended by OSHA. Since the Department of Justice has not been prosecuting, OSHA has been reluctant, advocates claim, to refer cases.

True, OSHA has rarely recommended cases for criminal prosecution. Only one employer was ever sentenced to jail, for only 45 days (ESHG: Developments, 1990:13,050). Yet the claim that statutory limits on penalties discourage the Department of Justice from prosecuting employers conflicts with the department's own assertion that by criminally prosecuting violators under the Comprehensive Crime Control Act of 1984, it can ask for penalties of up to $250,000 for each individual and $500,000 for corporations (USCS, 1990d:60–61). Also, employers guilty of workplace homicide, who have knowingly jeopardized the safety of their employees, could serve long prison sentences under federal law if successfully prosecuted for second-degree murder or manslaughter.

Although the California OSH Act has certain advantages, the criminal penalties in California for homicide due to workplace accidents are not more stringent than the federal law. Yet while CAL/OSHA, which operates, after all, in only one state, has recommended 292 cases from 1981 to 1988 for criminal prosecution, the comparable figure for the federal government during this period is just 19. Almost 40 percent of CAL/OSHA's referrals had successful outcomes (NSWI, 1988a:15).

The enormous differences in enforcement practices cannot be understood by comparing the legal scriptures. Rather, those who are responsible for enforcing the federal statute are resistant to implementing the OSH Act. CAL/OSHA's enforcement record, incidentally, has been recently deteriorating as it, too, has been losing interest in properly enforcing the law. If the federal OSH Act is amended, those entrusted with enforcing a revised statute will attempt to ensure that progressive changes in the law will be undermined.

Although Congress has substantially increased maximum fines, OSHA has almost always imposed fines well below the statutory maximum for serious violations, including those resulting in death. Also, as OSHA's highly publicized megafines show, OSHA can count violations in ways that yield substantial fines. The agency on occasion tabulates the total number of violations by multiplying each violation by the number of employees. OSHA, then, has not lacked the tools to compel employers to obey the law.

The problem has been that OSHA has generally preferred to pamper employers rather than penalize them. The average fine for manufacturing companies in a recent year was only $34 (Weil, 1991:33). Proposed fines—if they are challenged, they are at least deferred, and almost always reduced—for construction accidents involving at least one fatality was under $1,000 in most cities (NSWI, 1989a:12). Worse yet, two out of five fatalities in the construction industry did not result in any penalty at all (*Ibid.*: 11).

Moreover, according to the General Accounting Office (the investigative arm of Congress), OSHA has been closing cases without requiring adequate evidence that violations were corrected. The agency only requests evidence. Also, OSHA discourages follow-up inspections. In 1989, only 6 percent of inspections were follow-up. OSHA's policy is to limit these inspections to 10 percent of all inspections (ESHG, 1991:2–3). Very few employers who are cited for violations, then, are under pressure to make any improvements at all.

OSHA has been not only irresponsible, it has also been breaking the law. As the statute gives OSHA considerable discretion—fines, for example, are not mandatory—the impression is that OSHA is abiding by the mandates of the OSH Act. Since OSHA must take into account many factors to guide its conduct, it needs considerable discretion. The use of discretion, however, is limited by law. Not only is a public agency prohibited from doing whatever it wishes, neither can an agency take actions that are allowed by the law, but are undertaken for the wrong reasons. According to the Administrative Procedure Act, if an agency's conduct is arbitrary and motivated by reasons not allowed by the law, it is abusing its discretion, which is illegal (USCS, 1989:432).

OSHA's enforcement practices are primarily motivated by its greater commitment to employers than to employees. Unlike the National Labor Relations Act, however, which is supposed to consider the interests of both employers and employees, the sole intent of the OSH Act is to protect workers. OSHA is required by law to respect the intent of the statute, which is to make the workplace healthier and safer for working people.

The agency's unlawful allegiance to employers is reflected, of course, in its lax enforcement practices. After more than 20 years of the OSH Act, the workplace remains dangerous. According to the Bureau of Labor Statistics, occupational injuries in construction, which is among the most hazardous industries, have increased over the past 10 years by 100,000 (Green, 1991:9). The industry continues to violate, with virtual impunity, safety standards that were known to be dangerous long before the OSH Act was passed.

The Illusion of Megafines

Yet frequently mentioned in the mass media is OSHA's imposition of megafines, which were first imposed during the Carter administration. These fines, exceeding $100,000, convey the impression that OSHA is serious about enforcement. Although OSHA publicizes these fines, the agency does not inform the public that they are later substantially reduced by as much as 96 percent (NSWI, 1989b:4). Moreover, the Department of Labor's Inspector General, who is responsible for auditing the activities of the department, found that because OSHA makes little effort to obtain what is owed to the government, the agency collects only a small amount of the fines due (NSWI, 1988b:22–23). OSHA's disinterest in fines violates both the Debt Collection Act of 1982 and its own regulation on collecting delinquent fines.

A record of final settlements imposed on various companies was requested by NSWI under the Freedom of Information Act. Despite the law, OSHA resisted complying. The Institute finally obtained the information it requested only after threatening to expose its recalcitrance, which was illegal, to the media and to Congress. The *Washington Post* columnist, Jack Anderson, correctly referred to OSHA's penalty approach as "a public relations binge" (Anderson, 1989:E19).

Tragic Events, Frivolous Response

OSHA's negligence has serious consequences; workers die or become incapacitated. In October 1989, a fire and explosion at a Phillips Petroleum Plant killed 23 workers and injured over 130 others. The incident was caused by the sudden release of several highly flammable gases. The Secretary of Labor acknowledged that the accident could have been avoided if recognized safety procedures had been followed. Among the violations were inadequate hazard communication, insufficient emergency exits, and insufficient respiratory protection. OSHA also found that Phillips Petroleum had ignored both its own procedures and standard industry practice (ESHG, 1990:2).

This accident could have been prevented by OSHA had it diligently enforced the law. OSHA knew that the company's facilities had serious safety problems. Before this event, OSHA's inspection of facilities in the region showed 18 killed and many others hospitalized (*Ibid.*). These accidents should have triggered a vigorous enforcement effort; but they did not. In fact, despite the irresponsibility of management, OSHA did not even recommend criminal prosecution. OSHA's conduct was predictable. According to an audit by the Inspector General of the Department of Labor, OSHA has generally failed to take appropriate action "against employers with significant histories of fatalities" (NSWI, 1988b:10).

In Chicago, an OSHA officer did not inspect a plant next door to the office because the company's records indicated a low injury rate. Yet conditions at the company's plant were described by a reporter as an industrial gas chamber. Several months after the OSHA inspection, an employee died of cyanide poisoning. The evidence showed a pattern of deception by management, which persuaded the State of Illinois to prosecute company executives for committing criminal homicide. A worker was instructed, for example, to remove the skull-and-crossbones symbol that warned of the lethal nature of one of the chemicals (Metz, 1988:16). Yet OSHA had been quite willing to settle for only a modest fine of under $2,400 (Committee on Government Operations, 1988:2). Each of three company defendants, however, were tried and sentenced by a state court in Illinois to 25 years in prison.[8] The sentence, though, was subsequently overturned on flimsy grounds.

◂ Rationalizing Inaction ▸

Advocates for a safe workplace complain that the paucity of standards is worrisome. They are convinced that the latitude of the agency to enforce the OSH Act is very limited. Yet the yearning for more and better regulations, although certainly appropriate, has been manipulated by the agency to detract from its poor enforcement practices. More often than many advocates realize, the problem is inadequate enforcement rather than OSHA's lack of a legal basis to act. Consider, for example, the approach taken by the agency, the media, and even advocates on the issue of protecting employees working in confined spaces. Accidents in confined spaces are responsible for about 3 percent of workplace fatalities. The main cause of death is asphyxiation. In addition, workers are killed because of mechanical failures they could not escape from in time.

OSHA expressed interest in a confined-space regulation as early as 1975, but to date one has not been adopted. The agency has claimed that the lack of a confined-space regulation has left many workers inadequately protected. It maintained "that the existing standards do not adequately protect workers in confined spaces from atmospheric, mechanical, and other hazards" (Federal Register, 1989:204080).

The media and advocates have echoed OSHA's claims. A caption in a front-page *Los Angeles Times* article read "Lack of OSHA Regulations—Confined-Space Deaths Blamed on Federal Delays" (Weinstein, 1989:1). Just before a public hearing on a detailed proposed confined-space regulation, a *New York Times* article discussed how family members of victims who were asphyxiated in confined spaces were to testify that their sons and thousands of others were killed because safety standards for confined spaces had not been adopted (Robbins, 1990:A17). The testimony of family members was arranged by NSWI, which was lobbying for the regulation.

The proposed regulation contains some very useful recommendations, especially a requirement that trained attendants regularly monitor confined work spaces. Yet OSHA already has an arsenal of regulations to protect workers confronted with hazardous conditions in confined spaces. In fact, the agency itself acknowledged that the "hazards encountered in permit spaces, such as exposure to electrical shock and contact with chemicals and machinery, are also encountered elsewhere in the workplace and are addressed, in general, by existing OSHA standards" (Federal Register, 1989:204080).[9]

Also, to prevent atmospheric contamination, employers must adopt "engineering control measures" such as proper general and local ventilation systems and must substitute less toxic materials (CFR, 1990a:401). When changing the workplace environment is not feasible, workers must be provided with appropriate personal protective equipment, including respirators (CFR, 1990b:400, 401). In addition, information on the hazards of chemicals used at work must be communicated to employees (CFR, 1990c:3867–3884).

Where recognized workplace hazards exist, OSHA's obligation to intervene is not limited to specific regulations. The OSH Act mandates a general duty clause to protect workers when no existing regulations apply. The clause declares that each employer "shall furnish to each of his employees employment and a place of employment which are free from recognized hazards that are causing or are likely to cause death or serious physical harm to his employees" (USCS, 1990b:37).

The courts rejected the contention of employers that the general duty clause is unconstitutionally vague. The Supreme Court, reflecting on the legislative history of the clause, maintained that it was intended "to deter the occurrence of occupational deaths and serious injuries by placing on employers a mandatory obligation independent of the specific health and safety standards to be promulgated by the Secretary" (U.S. Reports, 1979a:13). General duty citations could protect workers against exposure to toxics not covered by specific regulations. Although OSHA serves citations under the general duty clause for violations, including some for confined-space violations, very few are issued and the percentage given out began to decline in the 1980s (Morgan, 1983:298–302).

Still, imposing additional legal regulations on business, such as requiring attendants to monitor confined spaces, could provide OSHA with more and better tools to enforce the OSH Act. Certainly, no proposed standard deserves as long as 16 years of consideration. In fact, the Administrative Procedure Act specifies that agency action cannot be unlawfully withheld or unreasonably delayed (USCS, 1989:430). Since OSHA itself has officially recognized the importance of a confined-space regulation to saving lives, the failure of the judiciary to order OSHA to adopt the proposed regulation is a violation of the Administrative Procedure Act.

◂ Lopsided Due Process ▸

As already mentioned, OSHA's regulations are weakly enforced. When an OSHA compliance officer finds a violation, a citation is issued that identifies the nature of the violation and the period of time allowed to correct it. If an employer contests a citation, its enforcement is at least temporarily suspended.

Commonly, employers work out a satisfactory settlement with OSHA. Although employers can appeal OSHA orders, they generally don't have to.

Since the welfare of workers is directly affected by the outcome of these settlements, employees and unions need the opportunity to contest agreements that fail to adequately address their health and safety grievances. However, although employers can contest and appeal any aspect of a citation, employees and their representatives can only object to the time allotted to deal with the violations. They cannot challenge the adequacy of OSHA's abatement order itself.

Adverse decisions can be appealed to the Occupational Safety and Health Review Commission, an autonomous, quasi-judicial body whose three commissioners are appointed by the president with the consent of the Senate. Within the commission, administrative law judges initially hear cases, which can then be reviewed by the commissioners. These cases can afterward be appealed to a federal court. The commission was created as a concession to business. It provides business with an additional opportunity to contest adverse orders, or at least to delay their enforcement for a long while. Among the commission's contribution to business is its practice of throwing out OSHA fines (NSWI, 1990:5).

Except for allowing employees to contest the period of time that employers are allowed to abate violations, none of these legal routes are available to employees and their representatives. This dual system of justice, which is so generous to employers, but stints on employee rights, should have been declared unconstitutional. Employees are clearly being denied both due process and the equal protection of the laws. The denial of equal protection is especially ludicrous because the purpose of the OSH Act is to serve working people, not employers.

Since the federal appeals courts and the commission have deprived workers of their legal rights to protect their health in the workplace, the Supreme Court could have reminded these bodies of their constitutional obligations. Yet the high court was so thoroughly convinced that OSHA's right to withdraw a citation is unreviewable that it issued its opinion over the protest of two justices without giving those who objected an opportunity to present their side (U.S. Reports, 1985:3–8). Called a summary proceeding, courts use this judicial procedure to settle cases promptly when there is supposedly no basis for a legitimate legal dispute.

The assault by the judiciary on the due-process rights of workers, many of whom confront life-threatening working conditions, is extraordinary. It assures that very few cases will reach the courts because workers are made completely dependent on OSHA to file suits against uncooperative employers.

As employees and their representatives cannot challenge OSHA settlement agreements with employers, disputes initiated by working people cannot reach the commission or the courts. The experience of workers and their unions is vital to determining how safety and health violations should be abated. Like parties to any dispute, their testimony may or may not be persuasive. Yet allowing only employers to appeal adverse decisions unfairly tilts the scales of justice heavily toward business.

Even had the OSH Act mandated the dual system of justice, this policy would still be illegal because it is unconstitutional. Nowhere in the OSH Act are employees explicitly barred from challenging settlements. On the contrary, in the section of the OSH Act on contesting citations, it reads: "The rules of procedure prescribed by the Commission shall provide affected employees or representatives of affected employees an opportunity to participate as parties to hearings" (USCS, 1990c:201). Legally speaking, a party is anyone who is directly interested in the issue being considered and who has the fight, therefore, to be completely involved in any proceeding.

If the contrast between the statutory language and how it is interpreted seems startling, the commission and the judiciary have a prosaic explanation. The section of the statute on enforcement cites two grounds for appealing citations to the commission: first, when employers contest a citation, and second, when an employee or representative contests the period of time fixed in the citation for abating a violation. The courts have interpreted this to mean that employees are limited to challenging the time allowed for correcting a violation.

In 1982, the commission rejected this interpretation. The majority opinion explained that since the statute specifies that a citation should indicate the nature of the violation, the regulation that has been violated, and the time allowed to fix the violation, the time is not yet ripe for an employee to challenge a citation on a basis other than the reasonableness of the time period (OSHD, 1982:33,033).

The actual changes, if any, that employers are required to make in the workplace are determined later, when OSHA and the employer work out a settlement agreement. Only then does it become appropriate for employees to challenge the abatement method. After a Reagan appointment to the commission, the OSH Act was reinterpreted to exclude workers as parties to its proceedings other than to challenge the time allotted for abating violations (OSHD, 1984:34, 486–434, 489).

Employees can still challenge OSHA's delays and inaction on proposed regulations or amendments. Although a few battles on these issues have been won in court, these victories are illusory unless they are enforced. Since OSHA has been relieved of employee legal challenges to its enforcement practices and settlements, it can continue to abuse its discretion with impunity.

New Regulations? More Inaction

If standards are not followed, why do OSHA and the business community fiercely resist their adoption? First, regulations are not altogether ignored. Some employers take regulations seriously, while various unionized companies are under pressure from unions to conform to OSHA's standards. Many employers are repeatedly cited for infractions, however, and still do nothing to correct them. As fines are typically less expensive than the costs of remedying violations, they are not a deterrent. These fines, in effect, are fees charged for doing business as usual.

As health and safety regulations serve as the legal basis for citing employers, OSHA is continually urged to adopt new standards. In a detailed critical evaluation of the rule-making process, researchers funded by a grant from OSHA reported that the agency even lacked regulations on most chemicals that have been identified as carcinogenic by the federal National Cancer Institute (Shapiro, 1989:2).

OSHA has also ignored the law by failing to adopt stringent standards to adequately reduce the risks of exposure to hazardous substances. The agency even refused to strengthen its standard for airborne asbestos exposure until ordered to do so by a federal court. The serious health risks of being continually exposed to high levels of airborne asbestos is recognized by OSHA, which admitted that its own standard posed significant risks to workers. Yet in a court challenge by the AFL-CIO Building and Construction Trades Department, the agency's defense rested on its view that industry could not attain lower levels. As the court noted, OSHA's own records revealed that lower levels of exposure both could have and have been achieved. Appropriately, OSHA was ordered to reconsider promulgating a stronger regulation (Federal Reporter, 2d ed, 1988:1269, 1272–1273).

The Supreme Court, drawing on the legislative history of the health and safety statute, had ruled that OSHA is forbidden to engage in a cost-benefit analysis in deciding to issue regulations dealing with toxic materials (U.S. Reports, 1980:506–522). There was absolutely no legal justification for OSHA's refusal to issue a more stringent asbestos standard.

One would expect that an agency genuinely committed to minimizing exposure to toxics would be interested in warning those who come in regular contact with hazardous materials of the risks they encounter. Yet OSHA refused the request of unions to order companies that employ mostly non-English-speaking workers to use bilingual warnings and universal symbols on cartons containing asbestos. OSHA's hazard-communication regulations require warnings only in English. Yet the statute itself mandates "the use of labels or other appropriate forms of warning" so that employees are apprised of hazards in order to protect their health (USCS, 1990a:133). Clearly, OSHA is violating the intent of the statute, which requires that employees be informed rather than kept in the dark about the toxic materials they are working with.

The court ordered OSHA to develop a regulation that would warn non-English-speaking workers, but the agency did not comply. After a complaint was filed in court, OSHA was given a deadline. A regulation was finally issued that left it to employers to determine how to inform employees of the hazardous material they were exposed to. The new regulation did not require bilingual identification or even universal symbols on containers. Since the regulation lacks specifics and gives employers almost complete discretion, compliance can easily be evaded and violations can be difficult to prove. Nevertheless, the court found the new proposed regulation acceptable.

Misinterpreting the Law
The Supreme Court's Turn

Different governmental institutions take turns undercutting the rights of workers by ignoring the OSH Act. OSHA argued before the Supreme Court that since no safe level for exposure to benzene, a carcinogen, can be determined, then it should limit exposure to the lowest technologically feasible level. This approach was consistent with the section of the law just cited, which directs the Secretary of Labor to develop standards assuring that no employee's health would be adversely affected.

The Supreme Court, however, interpreted the OSH Act to require a standard based upon a finding of significant risk rather than mandating the lowest feasible risk (U.S. Reports, 1979:655). The high court still allowed OSHA considerable leeway. It ruled that OSHA should rely on the best available evidence without being required to support its findings with anything approaching scientific certainty (U.S. Reports, 1979:656). At least, OSHA is not expected to delay issuing standards until definitive studies are completed. In this instance, the high court was only acknowledging the segment of the law that actually states "on the basis of the best available evidence." Also, the Court stressed that the agency should feel free "risking error on the side of overprotection rather than underprotection" (U.S. Reports, 1980:656).

However, regulations based upon significant risk implies mandating higher levels of exposure to hazardous materials than regulations requiring the lowest technologically achievable levels. Also, since determining the adverse health effects of chemicals is expensive and takes many years, the Supreme Court's decision curtailed OSHA's ability to rapidly develop regulations. Yet nothing in the statute, as the dissenting Supreme Court opinion pointed out, refers to "significant risk." The statute's section on toxics is worded to minimize impairing the health of all workers exposed to hazardous materials. The high court did what only Congress is allowed to do—rewrite the law.

OSHA's advocacy of a strict regulation on carcinogens seems inconsistent with its anti-regulatory stance. In actuality, however, OSHA failed to present a strong case. Despite the considerable evidence of the adverse impact of even very low dosages of benzene, OSHA made no finding, as the Supreme Court noted, that evidence of exposure to benzene at levels set by the current standard or below had ever caused leukemia (U.S. Reports, 1979:634). The Court also noted that OSHA acknowledged that a study it had relied on to establish an emergency standard to reduce exposure levels did not support its view that benzene caused cancer at even much higher levels than the current standard permits (U.S. Reports, 1979:633). As OSHA's defense of the standard was weak, it would have required an unusually progressive court to have validated OSHA's proposal.

Misinterpreting the Law
The Commission's Turn

The commission and the judiciary have shown the same indifference to working people. In one case, for example, the commission cited a Supreme Court decision to justify rejecting an OSHA general duty citation given to an employer for inadequately protecting employees from exposure to a carcinogenic chemical (OSHD, Kastalon, Inc., 1986:35, 970–935, 982). As already mentioned, although the Supreme Court opposed a blanket policy of mandating the lowest possible level of exposure to toxics, it nevertheless indicated that OSHA was not obliged to show that a significant risk exists with anything approaching scientific certainty.

Yet the commission rejected the extrapolations from animal data as too speculative, including a DuPont study in which 100 percent of the dogs exposed to the chemical, called MOCA, contracted cancers, but none did in the control group. Moreover, industry experts agreed that MOCA is carcinogenic and one leading manufacturer urged the adoption of a standard for MOCA. OSHA had certainly established a significant risk. Although the Supreme Court tremendously diluted the statute's provision on exposure to toxics, the Court didn't annihilate it.

Misinterpreting the Law
OSHA's Turn

In 1972, the agency rejected a petition by a Hispanic-American organization to require employers to provide farm workers with toilets, drinking water, and hand-washing facilities. These basic amenities are indispensable to human health. OSHA's refusal to seriously consider the proposal clashed with the intent of the OSH Act. The judiciary eventually ordered a reluctant OSHA to adopt a regulation, but not until 14 and one-half years later (Shapiro, 1989:54). As the AFL-CIO's Safety and Health Director observed, "OSHA's list of achievements has been sorely outstripped by its shortcomings and reluctance to act" (Green, 1991:8). Significantly, OSHA has not taken any serious steps to enforce the new standard (Noble, 1988:A1).

Conclusion

In the corporate world, criminal homicide and the willful injury of working people are daily events. That little or nothing is done to punish these crimes exposes the fiction that in our so-called liberal-democratic society, the "rule of law" prevails. According to the rule of law, laws oblige everyone equally (Lowi, 1988:ix). Therefore, any employer guilty of criminal homicide in the workplace should be subject to as severe a punishment as anyone outside the workplace who was convicted of manslaughter or murder. The reality, of course, is that the opposite is true; corporate managers are, so to speak, getting away with murder.

The rule of law applies also to public servants. Among those guilty of criminal conduct are OSHA officials. Yet they, too, escape criminal prosecution for their illegal conduct, which is mainly reflected in their failure to take appropriate action. Legally speaking, omission is an offense when there is a legal duty to act. By repeatedly ignoring their legal obligations, OSHA officials continually violate the Occupational Safety and Health Act and the Administrative Procedure Act. The Administrative Procedure Act, in fact, specifically includes inaction as a legal violation. Also, those entrusted with enforcing the law have been continually violating the constitutional rights of working people to due process and equal protection.

These, by themselves, are only civil violations. However, when the willful failure to act contributes to injuries and deaths, it is a criminal offense. In particular, these public officials are guilty of complicity because their inaction has encouraged workplace injuries and deaths. A lifeguard who fails to make a proper effort to prevent an individual from drowning a bather is guilty of complicity. Among the legal grounds for complicity, which is liability for the conduct of another, is: "having a legal duty to prevent the commission of the offense, fails to make proper effort so to do."[10] Moreover, according to the federal statute, accomplices are as criminally liable as those who directly commit a crime (USCA, 1969:57).

OSHA officials have been legally entrusted with being the lifeguards of the workplace. By law, a crime of complicity does not require the accomplice to be on the scene when a crime has been committed. It is sufficient to demonstrate that OSHA officials have resisted making serious efforts to compel employers to correct health and safety violations despite the overwhelming evidence that these violations are appreciably threatening the lives of workers.

To dramatically improve the workplace would require empowering working people. In particular, workers and their chosen representatives would have to obtain the legal weapons needed to allow them to play a decisive role in changing working conditions.[11] Since the labor movement is weak, however, nothing significant can be won by first lobbying legislators for better laws. When workers are better organized and are making significant progress toward forcing employers to take their concerns seriously, only then can they successfully press for laws that reflect and consolidate the gains they have been achieving on the job.[12]

Yet the right to a healthy and safe workplace is a "subversive demand" (Navarro, 1991:54). It ultimately entails control over the process of production, which interferes with the logic of capital

(*Ibid.*). This incompatibility between the goals of workers and employers is irreconcilable. What begins, then, as a struggle by workers for social reform must eventually be transformed into a struggle to build a society in which protecting life and assuring justice are authentic and primary objectives of government.

◂ NOTES ▸

[1] For some excellent essays on the criminal conduct of the state, see Barak (1991). The essays attempt to recast issues of political economy into a criminological framework.

[2] See, for example, social scientist Syed H. Alatas (1980) and Fleishmann, et al. (1981).

[3] For a concise summary of Robert Gates' misconduct, see "Mr. Gates' Past, the C.I.A Future." *New York Times* (November 4, 1991):A18.

[4] For a clear, detailed discussion of the traditional concept of corruption, see Alatas' book (1980).

[5] For a comprehensive discussion of corporate crime, see Mokhiber (1988). Yet among the author's 50 recommendations to curb corporate crime, including stiffer penalties, none suggests prosecuting government officials for looking the other way.

[6] The National Safework Institute carefully, thoroughly, and aggressively monitors OSHA. Those who are interested in obtaining their research reports, which are for sale, should write to NSWI, 122 South Michigan Avenue, Suite 1450, Chicago, Ill., 60603.

[7] A major obstacle to legislating severe penalties is the belief that corporate illegal conduct generally violates civil law, but rarely criminal law. For a detailed discussion and persuasive refutation of this perspective, see Conklin (1977).

[8] For details, see Frank (1987).

[9] The belief that weak enforcement can be overcome by statutory amendments is widely shared by advocates of social reform. In late October 1991 under the auspices of the AFL-CIO, a worker testified before a congressional committee that he would not have lost his job for complaining to an OSHA inspector about unsafe work conditions if proposed legislation were in place. See O'Neill, Colleen M., "Workers Seek Voice in Workplace Safety," *AFL-CIO News* (November 11, 1991):4. However, the OSH statute already prohibits retaliatory dismissals, but OSHA rarely enforces this provision.

[10] This criterion for complicity is from the American Law Institute's (ALI) Model Penal Code, Section 2.06 (iii). In 1962, ALI completed an official draft of the Model Penal Code, major parts of which have been adopted by Congress and the legislatures of most states. ALI is an independent, influential organization of lawyers, judges, and legal scholars.

[11] For a thorough and persuasive case study of the serious weaknesses of liberal-inspired regulatory programs, which generally fail because they discourage the participation of those that these programs seek to benefit, see Noble (1986).

[12] For several excellent articles on the failures and successes of organizing around health and safety issues, see "Organizing for Health and Safety," *Labor Research Review*, 9 (Fall 1990):20. See also Judgins (1986).

References

Alatas, Syed H. 1980. *The Sociology of Corruption.* Singapore: Times Books.

Anderson, Jack. 1989. *Washington Post* (April 12).

Barak, Gregg (ed.). 1991. *Crimes by the Capitalist State.* Albany: State University of New York Press.

Code of Federal Regulations (CFR). 1990a. Part 1910.134.

_____. 1990b. Part 1910: 132, 134.

_____. 1990c. Part 1910: 1200.

Committee on Government Operations (CGO). 1988. "Getting Away with Murder in the Workplace: OSHA's Nonuse of Criminal Penalties for Safety Violations." 100th Congress, 2nd Session.

Conklin. John E. 1977. "Illegal, but Not Criminal." Englewood Cliffs: Prentice-Hall.

Dollars & Sense. 1985. "Corruption—Or Capitalism" (October).

ESHG (Employment Safety & Health Guide: Commerce Clearing House). 1991. *GAO Reports Weaknesses in OSHA Abatement Confirmation Process*, No. 1049.

_____. 1990. *Phillips Petroleum*, No. 989.

ESHG: Developments (Employment Safety & Health Guide: Developments) Commerce Clearing House. 1990. Senate Panel Hearings on Legislation to Increase Criminal and Civil Penalties for OSHA Violations.

Federal Register 54. 1989. "Permit Required Confined Spaces."

Federal Reporter, 2nd 838. 1988. Building Construction Trade Department, AFL-CIO v. Brock, Secretary of Labor.

Fleishmann, Joel L., Lance Liebman, Mark H. Moore (eds.). 1981. *Public Duties: The Moral Obligations of Governmental Officials.* Cambridge: Harvard University Press.

Frank, Nancy. 1987. "Murder in the Workplace." Stuart L. Hills (ed.), *Corporate Violence: Injury and Death for Profit.* Totowa: Rowman & Littlefield, 103–107.

Green, Arlee. 1991. "Worker Involvement Crucial to Job Safety, Labor Says." *AFL-CIO News* (March 18).

Henry, Stuart. 1991. "The Informal Economy: A Crime of Omission by the State." Gregg Barak (ed.), *Crimes by the Capitalist State.* Albany: State University of New York Press.

Judgins, Bennett M. 1986. *We Offer Ourselves as Evidence: Toward Workers' Control of Occupational Health.* Westport: Greenwood Press.

Lowi. Theodore J. 1988. Forward. Andrei S. Markovits and Mark Silverstein (eds.), *The Politics of Scandal.* New York: Holmes and Meyer.

Metz, Holly. 1988. "Death by Oversight." *Student Lawyer* (September).

Mokhiber, Russell. 1988. *Corporate Crime and Violence.* San Francisco: Sierra Club Books.

Morgan, Donald C. and Mark N. Duvall. 1983. "OSHA's General Duty Clause: An Analysis of Its Use and Abuse." *Industrial Relations Law Journal* 5:2.

Noble, Robert. 1986. *Liberalism at Work: The Rise and Fall of OSHA.* Philadelphia: Temple University Press.

NSWI (National Safe Workplace Institute). 1990. "Workplace Safety and Health" 3,11.

_____. 1989a. "Unmet Needs: Making American Work Safe for the 1990s."

_____. 1989b. "Unintended Consequences: The Failure of OSHA's Megafine Strategy."

______. 1988a. "Ending Legalized Workplace Homicide."

______. 1988b. "Failed Opportunities: The Decline of U.S. Job Safety in the 1980s."

Navarro, Vicente. 1991. "The Limitation of Legitimation and Fordism and the Possibility for Socialist Reform." *Rethinking Marxism* (Summer): 27–60.

Noble, Kenneth B. 1988. "Farm Workers Fault Lack of Enforcement of Sanitation Rules." *New York Times* (October 4).

OSHD (Occupational Safety and Health Decisions: Commerce Clearing House). 1987. Kastalon. Inc.

______. 1984. Pan American World Airways, Inc.

______. 1982. Mobil Oil Corporation.

Raskin, Marcus G. 1991. "The Road to Reconstruction." *The Nation* (April 22).

Robbins, William. 1990. "Grieving Relatives Gird for Federal Hearing on a New Rule for Job Safety." *New York Times* (January 30).

Shapiro, Sidney and Thomas McGarity. 1989. "Reorienting OSHA: Regulatory Alternatives and Legislative Reforms." *Yale Journal on Regulation* Vol.6.CA (United States Code Annotated)

______. 1969. Tide 18, Section 2.

USCS (United States Code Service). 1990a. OSH Act, Title 29, Section 655.

______. 1990b. OSH Act, Title 29, Section 654.

______. 1990c. OSH Act, Title 29, Section 659.

______. 1990d. Crimes and Criminal Procedure, Title 18, Section 3581.

______. 1989. (APA) Administrative Procedure Act, Title 5. Section 706.

U.S. Reports. 1985. *Cuyahoga Valley Railway Co. v. United Transportation Union*, Vol. 474.

______. 1980. *American Textile Mfg. v. Donovan*, Secretary of Labor, Vol. 452.

______. 1979a. *Industrial Union Department, AFL-CIO v. American Petroleum Institute*, Vol. 448.

______. 1979b. *Whirlpool v. Marshall*, Secretary of Labor, Vol. 445.

Weil, David. 1991. "Enforcing OSHA: The Role of Labor Unions." *Industrial Relations* 30.

Weinstein, Henry. 1989. "Lack of OSHA Regulations—Confined-Space Deaths Blamed on Federal Delay." *Los Angeles Times* (February 5).

‹ 15 ›

Organizational Crime in NASA and among Its Contractors

Using a Newspaper as a Data Source

Jurg Gerber
Eric J. Fritsch

‹ INTRODUCTION ›

Despite being less of a problem today that it was in the past, information on the extent of corporate and organizational crime is still difficult to find. The most commonly used and cited measure of the extent of crime in the United States, the Crime Index, includes only street crimes, and thus by definition excludes both white-collar and corporate crimes. Therefore, only a segment of all crimes is compiled in the Crime Index. Without such ready access, researchers are forced to collect their own data sets from a variety of sources. Commonly used sources include the records of federal agencies such as the World Trade Commission (e.g., Simpson,

Reprinted from *Social Justice*, 22(1): 75–88.

1986). In some instances, researchers may obtain access to court-related documents such as pre-sentence investigation reports (e.g., Weisburd et al., 1991).

Previously, we contributed to this process by suggesting the use of newspapers a data source (Gerber and Fritsch, 1993). Using the *Wall Street Journal* as our information base, we traced the corporate activities of General Electric (GE) throughout the 1980s. We were particularly interested in determining the value of GE's defense-related contracts, which violations it had allegedly been engaged in, the sanctions received for these violations (e.g., fines), and the consequences of such sanctions in terms of obtaining future contracts. Relying on what must be one of the most conservative records of white-collar crime, we were able to show that GE obtained defense contracts worth at least $43 billion during the 1980s, was accused of numerous unethical and illegal practices, admitted to having engaged in many of these practices, but suffered virtually no negative consequences. The fines it was required to pay were minimal (they represented .17 percent of the value of GE's contracts during the 1980s), and the company continued to receive contracts, even while nominally "banned" from new contracts.

Furthermore, we showed that GE was able to mitigate the negative publicity it received partially by nominating to its board of directors individuals who had extensive ties to the Pentagon and various branches of the federal government. Then we documented the participation of GE's directors in what had been termed the "power elite" by Mills (1956) and studied subsequently in detail by Domhoff (1983) and Useem (1984). In particular, we were able to show the existence of a "revolving door" that lets individuals move freely within the executive branch of government, the military, and corporate leadership.

The present project represents an extension of our earlier study by focusing on another agency, the National Aeronautics and Space Administration (NASA), which has the ability to award large sums of money to contractors who provide defense-related goods and services. However, although the GE study focused on a single corporation that had obtained contracts from one agency of the federal government, the Department of Defense, the current study is more ambitious in three important ways. First, we study all corporations that deal with a federal agency, NASA. Second, though our earlier study focused on the wrongdoing of the corporation alone, this study will also examine the illegal practices of the agency itself. Third, although the Pentagon is a national governmental agency whose interactions with corporations can easily be monitored through a national newspaper such as *The Wall Street Journal*, NASA has several regional centers. Hence, we decided that the regional press is of importance for this study. The current project will therefore demonstrate the feasibility of using the regional press as a data source for corporate and organizational crime.

◂ Methods ▸

One goal of our earlier study had been the development of a research technique that relies on an unusual source of white-collar crime data: *The Wall Street Journal.* This newspaper is the leading source of business news and maintains one of the most complete indexes of all major newspapers, yet it has been underutilized as a research tool for social scientists interested in white-collar crime. We further develop this research technique here by using a regional paper instead of a national newspaper. Our selection of *The Houston Post* was influenced by two factors. First, the publication had to be of regional significance. Since Houston is the location of the Johnson Space Center, which houses mission control for NASA, a newspaper from this city was a natural choice. Second, the newspaper must also have a detailed indexing system. The other major paper in Houston, *The Houston Chronicle*, does not and was thus eliminated from consideration.

For this study, we selected all articles published in the *Post* during the 1980s that dealt with NASA's budgets, its contractors, problems, allegations, and claims made against both the agency and the corporations involved with the agency. Excluded from the analysis were articles that did not deal with any of the above topics, but instead reported developments during individual space missions.

As we indicated previously, our research technique results in a conservative estimate of contracts awarded to corporations. It unlikely that all the contracts NASA awarded during the 1980s were recorded by *The Houston Post.* Smaller contracts are likely to have been omitted, but major projects awarded to corporations are likely to have been reported. Similarly, allegations of unethical or criminal behavior by either the agency or the contractors are likely to be under-reported by the regional news media. In an analysis of newspaper coverage of an oil spill in Santa Barbara, Molotch and Lester (1974) found that the activities most covered by the press were those that best suited the interests of oil companies and the executive branch of the federal government; environmentalists had much less access to the media. Given the importance of NASA and its contractors to the Houston economy, we would expect that local newspapers would be conservative in their reporting of organizational misconduct. Findings from this study are therefore likely to be biased in favor of the organizations involved.

To supplement our information, we consulted other sources of data. Such sources included governmental documents (e.g., Subcommittee on Space, 1991) that focus on NASA expenditures and its relationship with contractors, and secondary analyses of the agency (e.g., Vaughan, 1990).

White-Collar Crime, NASA, and Its Contractors

Whenever the focus of a study is on what is loosely called "white-collar crime," controversy arises over the nature and definitions of the acts to be analyzed. Unfortunately, definitions of what constitutes white-collar crime differ widely. While Sutherland (1940), the intellectual father of the concept, used a definition that was relatively broad and involved acts in violation of many different forms of law, his critics argued that only acts that violated the criminal law should be studied (Tappan, 1947). The problem with the second approach is that individuals who engage in white-collar criminal activities often have the power to affect legal definitions. Restricting the field of study to criminal violations eliminates behaviors of politically powerful perpetrators. It is thus necessary to study behaviors that are not legally crimes. Although such a procedure leads to some conceptual ambiguity, ignoring these behaviors would be more problematic. Instead of white-collar crime, concepts such as white-collar *illegality* (Shapiro, 1980) or white-collar *law breaking* (Weiss and Biderman, 1980) might have to be used by researchers.

We will use a definition of white-collar crime that is broad enough to allow for the violation of several forms of law, not only criminal law. Following Coleman (1994:5) we will focus on behaviors that represent a "violation of the law committed by a person or group of persons in the course of an otherwise respected and legitimate occupation or financial activity." More specifically, since our primary focus is on the wrongdoing of organizational entities, we will study "crimes committed with the support and encouragement of an organization whose goals it is intended to advance" (*Ibid.*:12).

Claims against NASA

NASA is accused of many things that can be construed as indications of white-collar crime: lack of fiscal responsibility, unethical practices, and general incompetence that borders on criminal negligence, to name a few. A claim that is raised repeatedly against NASA deals with cost overruns and fiscal irresponsibility. As can be seen from Table 1, NASA budget outlays for the 1980s totaled about $72 billion. Perhaps not surprisingly, numerous

Table 1:
NASA Budgets for Fiscal Years 1980–1989
(in Millions of Dollars)

FY 1980	4,852
FY 1981	5,426
FY 1982	6,035
FY 1983	6,664
FY 1984	7,048
FY 1985	7,318
FY 1986	7,403
FY 1987	7,592
FY 1988	9,092
FY 1989	11,051
Total	72,481

Source: Subcommittee on Space (1991:24).

Table 2:
Estimated Total Project Cost of Several NASA Projects
(in Millions of Dollars)

	Original Development Estimate		**1992**
	Date	*Range*	**Estimate**
Hubble Space Telescope	1/78	435–470	1,545
Gamma Ray Observatory	1/80	180–225	555–565
Ulysses	1/83	120–140	169
Tethered Satellite	1/83	40–50	145–150
Magellan	1/84	320–350	463
Advanced Communications Technology Satellite	1/84	325–425	499
Mars Observer	1/84	300–375	450–500

Source: Table is adapted from Subcommittee on Space (1991:20).

claims have been made that NASA has administered its funds in questionable ways. For instance, NASA's estimates for the total development costs of several projects have been much lower than later estimates. Table 2 shows some of the more spectacular underestimates of several projects. By 1992, the estimate for developing the Hubble Space Telescope was nearly four times the original amount, while that for the Mars Observer was about 50 percent higher than the original estimate.

Why were these estimates so far off the mark? It is conceivable that they were low due to unforeseen or unforeseeable circumstances. Conversely, the estimates may have been intentionally too low from the outset. It is possible that NASA officials perceived a need to underestimate the costs of various projects for them to be approved; true estimates might have led to a failure in obtaining funding for the project. Finally, estimates might have been initially correct, but turned out to be too low due to mismanagement and graft.

We have no data that would let us examine the possibility that estimates were intentionally low at the outset. However, claims are made repeatedly that NASA has financial problems due to incompetence, mismanagement, and graft, rather than to unforeseen circumstances. A relatively minor example is illustrated by the following claim in *The Houston Post* (1983a:13A):

> NASA also used a 5-passenger aircraft to ferry officials between Washington and Wallops Island, VA, where the space agency operates a research station, although the average passenger load was only 2.7 per flight, and it subsequently replaced this aircraft with a 9-passenger model.

As some critics point out, such waste may be the rule at NASA rather than the exception. According to a *Miami Herald* investigative report, one-third of NASA's budget is wasted. Examples of such waste include the following:

> the space agency routinely paid $30 for pins that should cost 3 cents, paid $159,000 for a $5,000 cooling fan and paid $256 to fly a contractor's dogs coast to coast (*The Houston Post*, 1986a:11A).

Along similar lines, the agency has also been criticized for its lavish hosting of VIPs during shuttle launches. For instance, it has been reported that NASA spent $1.5 million on VIPs for the first nine launches (*The Houston Post*, 1986b:5A).

Undoubtedly the most spectacular example, and also the most tragic, of NASA malfeasance of the 1980s involved the explosion of the *Challenger* space shuttle in 1986. It is unquestioned today that the immediate technical problem that led to the tragedy was the faulty design of the O-rings in the solid rocket booster (Presidential Commission, 1986). From a social science perspective, and specifically from the perspective of white-collar crime, it is noteworthy that the explosion was not an "accident," but rather an event that could have been anticipated and to some extent predicted. In fact, problems with the O-rings were known as early as 1977 (Vaughan, 1990), and the press reported within days after the explosion on memos that circulated around NASA at least a year prior to the explosion that the shuttle and its crew were in jeopardy in the future (*The Houston Post*, 1986c:3A). In addition, the press also reported that astronauts were not adequately informed of these dangers (Talley and Asker, 19836:20A).

What made this tragedy possible when NASA apparently knew for years that accidents were bound to happen? Part of the explanation may lie in Perrow's (1984) concept of *normal accidents*—accidents that involve advanced technologies and the way we handle them. Some technologies are so complex that their mere existence poses risks. Accidents are bound to happen, regardless of how careful we may be; given these technologies, and their potential organizational and systemic problems, the question is not *if* an accident will happen, but *when*.

An alternate explanation of the *Challenger* disaster, advocated by Vaughan (1990), may lie in NASA's organizational structure and decision-making processes. Although NASA was aware of technological problems with the O-rings, it did not extensively sanction its supplier, Morton Thiokol, since doing so would have been detrimental to the agency as it was dependent on the company. Furthermore, monitoring panels internal and external to NASA were not autonomous from the agency and thus could not meaningfully carry out their supervisory capacities.

NASA has largely been able to avoid monetary punishments stemming from its questionable practices. The federal government, as the party ultimately responsible, agreed to settle the claims of families of four of the members who died in the *Challenger* explosion. It contributed 40 percent of the approximately $750,000 paid to family members of the four victims (Simmon, 1986). Several more claims were filed against the government as a result of the *Challenger*, but they had not been settled by the end of the decade. According to our review of the press, at least $33.2 million were sought from NASA and the federal government in these suits. Considering that NASA's budget for the 1980s totaled more than $72 billion, even if the government were to pay the full $33.2 million sought by the plaintiffs, and even if this money were to come out of NASA's budget, the monetary settlement would be inconsequential (representing .04 percent of the budget for the decade).

It is possible that the negative publicity following the *Challenger* explosion might have had an adverse effect on subsequent funding decisions by Congress. However, even if that were true, the direct monetary consequences of NASA's organizational misconduct were negligible. The agency appears to have evaded negative sanctions to a large extent.

Claims against Contractors

Like any governmental agency, NASA not only receives money from tax revenues, but it also passes some of it on to contractors.

Table 3:
Contracts Awarded by NASA to Private Corporations
(in Millions of Dollars)

Year	Number of Contracts	Value of Contracts
1980	0	0
1981	0	0
1982	0	0
1983	1	2,000.0
1984	0	0
1985	3	1,011.5
1986	7	725.0
1987	8	8,846.0
1988	3	89.1
1989	2	134.0
Totals	24	12,805.6

Source: *The Houston Post*, 1980–1989.

Other agencies, such as the Pentagon, award many more contracts, for larger dollar amounts, than does NASA. However, as one of the agencies that is tied to national defense, the money NASA can award is substantial. As can be seen from Table 3, the agency awarded at least 24 contracts during the 1980s to private corporations, with a total value of over $12 billion. Most of this money was awarded in a relatively small number of contracts. The first award announced in *The Houston Post* during the 1980s was on September 8, 1983, when Lockheed received a two billion dollar contract to handle all space shuttle launch and landing activities for a six-year period. Lockheed, working with several subcontractors, replaced Rockwell, which had held the previous contract. However, only two years later, Rockwell received a $685 million award to handle "most day-to-day activities in the space shuttle program in Houston" (Asker, 1985:1).

Throughout the rest of the decade, the same few companies continued to receive the lion's share of contract money made available to private industry. Pratt and Whitney received a $182 million contract in 1986 for the development of "safer turbopumps for the space shuttle main engines" (Asker, 1986a:9). Lockheed landed a $655 million contract in 1987 to provide engineering support at the Johnson Space Center in Houston (Asker, 1987a:15), while later that year Morton Thiokol had its contract for space shuttle solid rocket boosters renewed in a contract worth $1.8 billion, despite its problems in the *Challenger* explosion (*The Houston*

Post, 1987a:1). Finally, through the remainder of 1987, five companies combined in a joint venture to land a contract that was worth a combined total of $6.25 billion. The corporations involved were Gruman Aerospace (Laws, 1987a), McDonnell Douglas, Boeing Aerospace, General Electric, and Rockwell (Laws, 1987b).

There is little doubt that private industry receives huge contracts from NASA. The question remains as to whether NASA, and thus taxpayers, receive fair value for their money. Even a cursory glance over press reports indicates that this is not the case. Repeatedly, claims are made that money has been misappropriated, that technology supplied to NASA has not lived up to promises made, and that contractors cheated in billing procedures. At the same time, it is alleged that contractors have not received any meaningful sanctions.

A specific example of corporate malfeasance includes missing target dates for the completion of contracts. Rockwell committed itself in 1972 to launching the first space shuttle in 1978, but missed that date by about two years. Eventually, it disputed having ever "scheduled" the first launch in 1978 (Maloney, 1980). When such delays occur, a common parallel development is cost overruns. A $18.9 million contract to design space suits for the shuttle was awarded to Hamilton Standard in 1977. At a later date, the contract was estimated to cost at least $236.4 million by 1985, a 12-fold increase (Maloney, 1982b).

Poor design of various parts is another frequent criticism aimed at NASA contractors. At times, the lack of quality may be the result of honest mistakes, while at other times, there is evidence (or at least there are allegations) of corporate wrongdoing. An example of the former includes problems with thermometers that forced an engine shutdown during a launch in 1985 (*The Houston Post,* 1985a). However, problems with the backpacks of space suits that forced the cancellation of a space walk in 1982 (Maloney, 1982a) and the failure of a space suit during the Sallie mission (Petty, 1982) were later traced to "poor workmanship and inadequate test and assembly procedures" (Petty, 1983:6). Similarly, NASA was forced in 1988 to ground 25 airplanes "after discovering suppliers may have used falsified strength and reliability data for fasteners used throughout the space program" (Kiely and Laws, 1988:1). It is at times exceedingly difficult to establish whether it is bad luck, poor design, or outright fraud that leads to problems. For instance, it was announced in 1984 that although it had originally predicted that space shuttle engines would be able to fly 55 missions without overhaul, the engines were "wearing out so fast that they needed repair after almost every flight" (*The Houston Post,* 1984:9).

Sometimes there are few doubts as to the culpability of corporate contractors. A Houston federal grand jury indicted ILC Space Systems for "claiming false labor costs on vouchers it submitted for its NASA work" (Manson, 1989:27). Similarly, Morton Thiokol was accused in 1987 of defrauding NASA when the agency paid for the hiring of 18 quality control and safety personnel for the company, but the money was used "as a slush fund for Thiokol" instead of being used for the hiring of the people (Palomo, 1987b:1).

NASA, the federal government, and in the case of the *Challenger* disaster, family members of the crew have sued the corporations for damages and sometimes have sought punitive fines against them. As is usually the case, claims filed against the corporations are initially much larger than what the eventual settlements provide. By far the largest claims made against the corporations were made in conjunction with the *Challenger*. Family members of the crew sought $2.5 billion from Morton Thiokol in compensatory damages in 1986 and 1987, while the company was sued for $2 billion in a suit filed on behalf of taxpayers for defrauding the government (Palomo, 1987a:14).

Settlements reached between the plaintiffs and the various corporations are modest by comparison. Although figures were not always precise, and the settlements were at times sealed, Morton Thiokol appears to have agreed to: (1) pay 60 percent of the approximately $750,000 awarded to each of four crew members' families due to the *Challenger* disaster (Simmon, 1986), with NASA paying the remaining 40 percent, (2) pay an undisclosed amount of money to family members of a fifth astronaut (Asker, 1987b), and (3) agreed to a reduction of $10 million in fees from NASA along with performing "$409 million worth of work at no profit" (Asker, 1987c:1). Similarly, Rockwell International agreed to pay the government $1.5 million for overbilling in 1982 (*The Houston Post*, 1982:14), and $1.2 million in 1985 for defrauding the Defense Department, which may have included NASA contracts (Walters, 1985:3).

All monetary settlements involving NASA contractors combined are almost certainly less than $20 million. Although this figure sounds impressive, it should be kept in mind that NASA awarded contracts worth at least $12.8 billion to private corporations during the 1980s. Fines and settlements therefore represent 15 percent of the value of these contracts; this represents hardly more than a licensing fee.[2] It is also noteworthy that the fines levied against the corporations and the settlements reached between NASA and the various plaintiffs are similarly minuscule.

Claims against Both Contractors and NASA

At times it is virtually impossible to ascertain if problems encountered in space travel are due to contractors' actions, to NASA's activities, a combination thereof, or simply to bad luck. One example of this includes problems with satellite launches in the mid-1980s. In a period of about 29 months, NASA lost five satellites. One satellite was lost in early 1984 when the rocket motors malfunctioned, motors that were described by their manufacturer as "almost fail-safe" (*The Houston Post*, 1983b:8). Three more were lost in a five-month period in 1984, again due to problems with the motors and the control systems (Harwood, 1984). Finally, another satellite was lost in April 1985 (Olafson, 1985).

Costs of such losses to taxpayers are difficult to estimate. First, satellites are normally insured through companies such as Lloyd's of London. During one 19-month stretch, insurers lost $600 million (*The Houston Post*, 1985b). Second, the satellites are often owned by private corporations and thus taxpayers are not directly involved. However, it seems likely that some of the costs will be passed on to taxpayers, either in the form of higher expenditures for NASA, or perhaps in the form of lower corporate income taxes due to higher insurance premiums faced by corporations.

◂ Discussion ▸

Our overview of NASA's activities and its relationship with its contractors has shown a considerable extent of illegal, unethical, and questionable practices. NASA controls billions of dollars and awards large sums to contractors, but there are constantly allegations of questionable activities. Apparently, at least as measured by newspaper coverage, there are few adverse consequences for either the agency, the corporations, or the individuals involved. For instance, corporations caught engaging in fraud appear to continue to receive contracts. Likewise, few if any individuals receive any meaningful sanctions. Indeed, sanctions were most likely to involve fines paid by the corporations—costs that might be passed on to the government in lower tax obligations. Indictments of individuals were rare and, as was the case with James Beggs, the former head of NASA who was included in an indictment of General Dynamics and four individuals associated with that company for fraud, most are eventually thrown out (*The Houston Post*, 1987b).

The question now is why this happens. Part of the answer may lie in the relationship between individuals in NASA and the corporations that receive contracts. In a discussion of problems encountered by regulatory agencies that attempt to control corporations, Coleman (1994:177) discussed not only the relative shortage of personnel, but also

> the fact that government employees receive much lower pay than they would in the corporate sector . . . The lure of a higher paying job in private industry has led many governmental staffers to cultivate the favor of private interests at the expense of their legal duty.

Professionals at NASA presumably represent their agency, and thus taxpayers, when they monitor contractors. However, newspaper coverage of the careers of NASA officials indicates that many end up in private industry, particularly space-related industry. Several individuals who were involved personally in the fateful decision to launch the *Challenger* in early 1986 eventually resigned from the agency and ended up working as consultants to NASA contractors or worked for them directly. At least one individual, Judson Lovingood, joined Morton Thiokol following his resignation from NASA (Haederle, 1988).

Closely related to the above is a general mutual dependence between the agency and the contractors. Whenever the agency is adversely affected by an organizational development, the contractors will suffer too. Martin Marietta announced in late 1986 the layoffs of about 700 employees as a result of the moratorium on space shuttle flights (*The Houston Post*, 1986d). However, the agency becomes likewise dependent on individual contractors. Following the *Challenger* explosion, Morton Thiokol, which had designed the faulty O-rings, was still eligible for a $75 million bonus for "superior performance" (Asker, 1986c). Maintaining good relationships with specific contractors is a necessity since they may be the only ones to provide specific services. The mutual dependence between the two can become so great that a contractor may even approach the courts to try to keep arrangements between the agency and itself secret. Such secrecy was required if Morton Thiokol was not to be "embarrassed" by documents detailing the relationship (Asker, 1987d).

◂ Conclusion ▸

This article is a continuation of a research project that seeks to develop the use of a not frequently used source of data for white-collar crime. In the first project, we used a national newspaper, *The Wall Street Journal*, to gather information on one corporation involved in national defense. This current study elaborates on the technique by studying all corporations that obtained grants from NASA, the organizational misconduct of the agency itself, and the use of a regional newspaper as the data source.

We are generally satisfied with this regional data source. Relying on *The Houston Post* for information, we were able to show patterns of mismanagement, incompetence, and graft that were responsible for NASA's financial problems during the 1980s. At the same time, NASA was largely able to avoid paying direct monetary penalties for its organizational misconduct. Similarly, the newspaper documented large contracts that were awarded to various corporations, extensive corporate lawbreaking, but again few meaningful sanctions against the corporations.

It should be reiterated that our research technique is probably biased in favor of NASA and the corporations due to the general tendency of newspapers not to be overly critical of locally dominant economic interests (Molotch and Lester, 1974). Nevertheless, the current study has shown the utility of our research technique; it is possible to study organizational crime using a local newspaper. Future research should be conducted that allows for the evaluation of the extent of the above bias.

◂ Notes ▸

[1] Delaying a launch is costly for NASA, but it is difficult to estimate what the exact costs are. In a launch that was delayed in 1981 by only a few days, NASA estimated that additional overtime expenditures, "reimbursement to the Department of Defense for launch and landing support," and similar expenses resulted in a total cost of at least $1.5 million (*The Houston Post*, 1981).

[2] In a remarkable coincidence, we found in our earlier study of General Electric's defense contracts that GE's fines represented 17 percent of the value of their contracts during the 1980s (Gerber and Fritsch, 1993). We therefore have further evidence that relatively little has changed since Geis' (1967) classic study of GE's involvement in the heavy electrical equipment antitrust case of 1961. He concluded that the fine levied against GE was the equivalent of a three dollar fine for an individual with an annual income of $175,000.

◂ References ▸

Asker, Jim. 1987a. "Lockheed Wins NASA Contract." *The Houston Post* (March 27): 15A.

———. 1997b. "McNairs Settle Shuttle Lawsuit with Thiokol." *The Houston Post* (May 8): 4A.

———. 1987c. "Thiokol, NASA Reach Accord." *The Houston Post* (February 25): 1A.

———. 1987d. "Thiokol Says NASA Pacts Are Private." *The Houston Post* (February 6): 12A

———. 1986a. "NASA Selects Firm to Develop New Turbopumps for Shuttle." *The Houston Post* (August 14): 9A.

———. 1986b. "Shuttle Settlements Anger Attorney in Suit." *The Houston Post* (December 30): 1A.

———. 1986c. "Morton Thiokol to Get $75 Million Bonus." *The Houston Post* (November 18): 3A.

———. 1985. "Rockwell Wins Pact for Shuttle." *The Houston Post* (September 13): 1A.

Coleman, James W. 1994. *The Criminal Elite: The Sociology of White-Collar Crime.* New York: St. Martin's Press.

Domhoff, G. William. 1983. *Who Rules America Now? A View for the '80s.* New York: Touchstone.

Gerber, Jurg and Eric J. Fritsch. 1993. "On the Relationship Between White-Collar Crime and Political Sociology: A Suggestion and Resource for Teaching." *Teaching Sociology* 21: 130–139.

Haederle, Michael. 1988. "Major Shuttle Figures Have Left Since Disaster." *The Houston Post* (September 25): 16A.

Harwood, William. 1984. "Satellite's Loss Deals Another Blow to NASA." *The Houston Post* (June 11): 7E.

Kiely, Kathy and Jerry Laws. 1988. Firms Turning Bad Bolts Loose on U.S.: Report." *The Houston Post* (July 31): 1A.

Laws, Jerry. 1988. "Age Bias Denied at NASA." *The Houston Post* (March 28): 8A

———. 1987a. "Gruman Awarded Space Station Funds." *The Houston Post* (July 3): 22A.

———. 1987b. "Space Station Jobs a 'Win-Win' for City." *The Houston Post* (December 1): 1A.

Maloney, Jim. 1982a. "Backpack Woes Persist in Tests." *The Houston Post* (November 19): 19A.

———. 1982b. "Cost of Failed Spacesuits to Rise 12 Times Above Initial Contract." *The Houston Post* (November 23): 18A.

———. 1980. "Rockwell Denies 1978 Shuttle Target Date." *The Houston Post* (December 25): 19A.

Manson, Patricia. 1989. "Houston Firm Faces 11 Counts on Overbilling." *The Houston Post* (July 7): 27A.

Mills, C. Wright. 1956. *The Power Elite.* New York: Oxford University Press.

Molotch, Harvey and Marilyn Lester. 1974. "Accidental News: The Great Oil Spill as Local Occurrence and National Event." *American Journal of Sociology* 81: 235–259.

Olafson, Steve. 1985. "$80 Million Shuttle Satellite Fails." *The Houston Post* (April 14): 1A.

Palomo, Juan R. 1987a. "Government Stays Out of Lawsuit over Shuttle." *The Houston Post* (June 5): 14A.

———. 1987b. "Morton Thiokol Employees Accuse Own Company of Fraud." *The Houston Post* (April 17): 1A.

Perrow, Charles. 1984. *Normal Accidents: Living with High-Risk Technologies.* New York: Basic Books.

Petty, John Ira. 1983. "Report Lays Blame for Space Suit Problems." *The Houston Post* (February 2): 6A.

———. 1982. "Sensor, Missing Locking Devices Stopped Space Walk, Officials Say." *The Houston Post* (December 3): 12A.

Presidential Commission on the Space Shuttle *Challenger* Accident. 1986. *Report of the Presidential Commission on the Space Shuttle Accident*, 5 Vols. Washington, D.C.: Government Printing Office.

Reiss, Albert J. and Albert D. Biderman. 1980. *Data Sources on White-Collar Law Breaking*. Washington, D.C.: National Institute of Justice.

Shapim, Susan P. 1980. *Thinking About White-Collar Crime: Matters of Conceptualization and Research*. Washington, D.C.: Government Printing Office.

Simmon, Jim. 1986. "Details of Shuttle Accord Withheld." *The Houston Post* (December 31): 3A.

Simpson, Sally S. 1986. "The Decomposition of Antitrust: Testing a Multi-level, Longitudinal Model of Profit-Squeeze." *American Sociological Review* 51: 859–875.

Subcommittee on Space, House of Representatives, U.S. Congress. 1991. 1992 NASA Authorization—National Aeronautics and Space Administration Budget Request for Fiscal 1992. Washington, D.C.: Government Printing Office.

Sutherland, Edwin. 1940. "White-Collar Criminality." *American Sociological Review* 5: 1–12.

Talley, Olive and Jim Asker. 1986. "NASA Withheld Concerns over Booster Seals." *The Houston Chronicle* (March 17): 20A.

Tappan, Paul. 1947. "Who Is the Criminal?" *American Sociological Review* 12: 96–107.

The Houston Post. 1987a. "Playing SRB Monopoly." April 21: 1B.

———. 1987b. "Unjust Indictment." June 29: 1B.

———. 1986a. "One-Third of NASA Budget Reportedly Wasted." March 17: 11A.

———. 1986b. "Agency Spent Almost $1.5 Million on VIPs Attending Shuttle Launches." June 12: 5A.

———. 1986c. "NASA Was Told Failure of Seals Was Possibility." 1987. February 9: 3A.

———. 1986d. "Space Supplier Jobs Cut by the Hundreds." September 4: 19A.

———. 1985a. "Bad Thermometers Caused Shuttle Engine Shutdown." August 13: 6A.

———. 1985b. "Destruction of Satellites Puts Insurance Losses Sky-High." September 15: 15A.

———. 1984. "Life of Space Shuttle Engines Proves Much Shorter Than Had Been Hoped." March 26: 9A.

———. 1983a. "Agencies Wasting Million in Aircraft Deals, Report Says." July 25: 1A, 13A.

———. 1983b. "Boeing Touted Troublesome Rocket as 'Almost Fail-Safe' Before Launch." April 16: 8A.

———. 1982. "Firm to Pay $1.5 Million in Shuttle Overbilling Suit." November 30: 14A.

———. 1981. "Delay Cost at Least $1.5 million, NASA Says." November 11: 1A.

Useem, Michael. 1984. *The Inner Circle: Large Corporations and the Rise of Business Political Activity in the U.S, and the U.K.* New York: Oxford University Press.

Vaughan, Diane. 1990. "Autonomy, Interdependence, and Social Control: NASA and the Space Shuttle *Challenger*." *Administrative Science Quarterly* 35: 225–257.

Walters, Robert. 1985. "Rockwell Caught Again." *The Houston Post* (November 16): 3B.

Weisburd, David, Stanton Wheeler, Elin Waring, and Nancy Bode. 1991. *Crimes of the Middle Classes: White-Collar Offenders in the Federal Courts.* New Haven, CT: Yale University Press.

‹ PART III ›

The Criminal Justice System and White-Collar Crime

Powerful groups often can prevent their actions from being defined as deviant—or at least prevent them from being treated as criminal. They can hide behind their respectability, or they can "buy off" the victim. Physicians, for example, have been insulated because their professional status provided a sort of "protective cloak." Unlike street criminals, physicians have high incomes and malpractice insurance. Victims of white-collar crimes committed by affluent offenders may prefer civil proceedings where they expect to be paid for their injuries. White-collar criminals generally have resources with which to pay for their crimes in money rather than jail time. Even if they are detected, they have many ways to avoid being labeled and treated as criminals.

Still, there is reason to believe that the struggle of law enforcement against white-collar crime may have somewhat greater success in the future. One reason to anticipate increased prosecution of white-collar crime has to do with the fact that public trust in "respectable" people (particularly high-status people such as CEO's, government officials, and professionals) has declined precipitously in recent years. Scandals have exposed a little of what goes on "behind the scenes," and the public, which was once more willing to put up with environmental pollution, dangerous workplaces, bungled surgery, or control of their finances by prestigious professionals or financiers, has been more inclined to demand its rights.

Of course, white-collar offenders are still in a position to influence legislation, insuring that their offenses are not defined as crimes, even after the public catches on to them. Even if laws are passed, if the enforcement agencies are underfunded, the laws won't be enforced.

Studies of regulatory enforcement have identified two types of enforcement strategies. The first depends on persuasion, while the second leans to prosecution. In the first of the articles dealing with the criminal justice response to white-collar crime, Nancy Frank presents a simple typology of four different approaches to regulation, based on whether an agency leans toward persuasion or prosecution and whether it has a centralized, formal administrative system with tight control over employees or a decentralized, informal administrative system in which employees have considerable autonomy.

Regulatory agencies that fall into what Frank calls the "service style" adopt a voluntary compliance approach. They provide services to the firms they are charged with regulating through technical advice by well-trained professionals. Those with a "watchman style" also rely upon persuasion, but they may be less inclined to "rock the boat" because they are staffed with poorly trained, unprofessional regulators intimidated by the agencies they are supposed to be regulating. Both styles seem to develop when the activity being regulated has low public visibility with no group challenging the dominance of the firms being regulated. The "watchman style" is probably more common, primarily because it is cheaper.

Those regulatory agencies with a "legalistic style" tend to be staffed with very competent inspectors and lean toward a prosecution strategy. These agencies seem to develop where there is an active and vocal conflict between different interest groups. Frank notes that the Office of Surface Mining was originally founded and first developed as a strong, "legalistic" agency but had to retreat to a conciliatory approach and become a "service style" agency because of a political backlash. This is a good example of the way in which powerful white-collar crime interests can force an agency to "back off." This happened to the Occupational Safety and Health Administration (OSHA). It began with a mandate to enforce the laws protecting workers and at first operated as if the laws were going to be enforced in a legalistic way by professional inspectors. It later retreated to either the "service style" or "watchman style."

Finally, Frank describes the "free agent" style, which allows inspectors to have greater independence than does the legalistic style of enforcement. She suggests that such a style tends to be the most effective but can only develop when there is general agreement that enforcement of the laws is beneficial and should be accomplished. One example of an enforcement agency that appears to approximate this style is the Securities and Exchange Commission (SEC). After the collapse of the stock market triggered the Great Depression, many people saw the dangers of too much criminal activity in the market. It is worth noting that the SEC was created with the support of those who controlled the stock market as well as those who wished to protect the investor.

Most of the articles in this collection discuss crimes of smaller corporations. We have not been able to examine in detail the crimes committed by major corporations of the United States. This is unfortunate. Sutherland's original work on white-collar crime focused on large corporations that dominated the U.S. economy; he found them to be "habitual criminals." For many years, prosecutions of white-collar crime involving corporations of any size were generally undertaken at the federal level. Local prosecutors tended to be intimidated by the major employers in town, and they had neither the training nor the resources to take on a corporation.

In their survey of local prosecutors, Michael Benson, Francis Cullen and William Maakestad found that prosecution of corporate crime at the local level is becoming more common. Consumer fraud led the list of "economic crimes" prosecuted at the local level, with false claims and insurance fraud close behind. Only environmental offenses, classified as "noneconomic crimes," were prosecuted as often.

White-collar crime is largely invisible, so how did the prosecutors learn about the criminal activity? Most of the offenses were reported through complaints by business and citizen victims. Sometimes reports came from local police or state regulatory agencies, and less often they came from the state police or state attorney's general offices. Prosecution of white-collar crime demands a greater commitment of resources than that required to handle street crimes, and prosecutors drop many cases because they are of low priority in a particular community. Local prosecutors, like other agents of law enforcement, are sensitive to the expectations of the particular community in which they live.

There are two ways that local prosecutors are working to develop resources to prosecute corporate crime. One is to put together teams of trained people from various agencies that can cooperate to analyze, investigate, and prosecute complex white-collar crimes. Another strategy is to create special units for economic crime so that prosecutors can learn to handle such complex cases by concentrating on them. Of course, this is only going to be possible if there are enough local prosecutors in a community to allow for some specialization.

Local prosecutors are more likely to drop the case if they feel that their personnel are not sufficient in numbers or training to handle the job. As with criminal cases, they are more likely to drop the corporate crime case if victims are not cooperative or if criminal intent appears to be difficult to establish. As we will see later, establishing criminal intent in a prosecution of a corporation is much more difficult than establishing it in the trial of an individual. In the presence of factors such as physical harm to victims, evidence of multiple offenses, large numbers of victims, or substantial economic harm, however, prosecutors seem more likely to try.

Many students of white-collar crime have suggested that prosecution is a stronger deterrent to white-collar crime than it is to street crime. White-collar crime is thought to be more calculated, and the offenders have more to lose than do street criminals, so it follows that seeing others prosecuted for something they contemplate doing would be more likely to deter them than it might deter street criminals. Local prosecutors seem to agree, prosecuting corporations on the theory that a conviction will set an example.

Interestingly enough Benson et al. discovered that some local prosecutors are arguing for a broader concept of their role, trying to control criminal activity through "problem solving" in the form of negotiated agreements that avoid criminal prosecution. This may suggest that they too would like to try the conciliatory approach so popular with federal agencies. Perhaps they are searching for a middle ground between prosecuting and doing nothing.

Of course, local prosecutors trying to prosecute corporate crime often find themselves up against excellent law firms with staffs that are well financed and better trained in corporate law than are the prosecutors themselves. What do prosecutors need in order to do a more effective job of prosecuting white-collar crime? They themselves suggest a need for a centralized clearinghouse that would allow them to draw on the experience of other prosecutors who have handled such cases. Computers offer the possibility of coordinating the work of different prosecutors working on similar cases, making it possible to analyze large amounts of information and to prepare a case for court. Benson et al. suggest the need for regional laboratories capable of assisting local prosecutors in analyzing chemical and environmental samples as evidence for prosecution. They also argue for increased publicity of white-collar prosecutions, taking the reasonable position that the public needs to be made more aware of how seriously prosecutors are coming to view these offenses. The authors are surely correct in asserting that greater public awareness is the key to developing the political will to deal with white-collar crime.

One of the major problems in trying to prosecute corporations is that the criminal law was developed to deal with the offenses of individuals. Even with increased public support for prosecution, there are many problems in applying the criminal law to huge, powerful corporations. Can a corporation have "intent" to commit a crime in the same way as an individual? How can its offenses meet the mens rea ("guilty mind") requirement of the criminal law if it has no mind apart from the minds of the separate individuals who work for it? While a legal entity, a corporation is not a living, breathing thing. Although it may own property, a corporation itself is not even a physical thing. It is a legal agreement. As Leo Barrile points out in his article, Lord Thurlow once complained that a corporation has "no soul to damn and no body to kick."

Barrile maintains that, when one considers the enormous magnitude of the problem, little progress has really been made in prosecuting corporations. Indeed, it sometimes seems like "ten steps forward and nine back." As far back as the New York Central case in 1909, the law has attempted to hold corporations responsible through concepts such as "vicarious intent." More recently, the legal concept of "knowing endangerment" has been used.

If the battle against white-collar crime is a struggle of workers, consumers, environmentalists and others against powerful corporations, respectable professionals, manipulative "insiders," and cunning fraudsters, what are the chances of winning at least part of the struggle against white-collar crime? White-collar criminals are much more powerful than street criminals, and they are much more sophisticated. While public awareness is necessary, the struggle against white-collar crime also depends upon legal redefinition and the willingness of enforcement agencies to do their jobs. As these articles show, law enforcement agencies follow different styles of enforcement. Prosecutors, even at the local level, are prosecuting more white-collar crime in criminal court, but the white-collar criminal, particularly the corporation, has some major legal and political advantages in the struggle.

‹16›

Policing Corporate Crime
A Typology of Enforcement Styles

Nancy Frank

In 1968, James Q. Wilson published *Varieties of Police Behavior*, an organizational study of police departments and the use of discretion by patrol officers. Wilson attempted to identify types of police organizations and some of the factors influencing a department to adopt one type of style over the other alternatives. His study was an important contribution to the study of policing because it identified variation in police organizations and performance. Today, the study of the enforcement of corporate crime[1] is at approximately the same level of development as was the study of community policing in the mid-1960s. Several excellent case studies of regulatory enforcement agencies have been carried out, but until recently, too few studies had been done to permit an examination of patterns of variation between such agencies. The typology developed here is offered as a step toward understanding variation between agencies in the ways they enforce the law.

Derived from Wilson's typology of styles of policing, it serves to illustrate the similarities between two forms of social control that

Reprinted from *Justice Quarterly*, 1(2): 235–251. Reprinted with permission of the Academy of Criminal Justice Sciences.

are typically viewed as being quite different from one another. Moreover, the typology is useful in sensitizing scholars of regulatory enforcement to a dimension of variation that has not received sufficient attention up to now: the organization of the enforcement agency. Enforcement agencies are dynamic, continually adapting to changes in their environments. This typology offers some predictions about the interactions between the enforcement organization and its environment.

These predictions are based upon a comprehensive review the literature on regulatory enforcement and my own preliminary research. While preparing to do systematic research on state and local food regulation enforcement, I have had a number of opportunities to talk with inspectors who have had a wide range of experience in regulatory enforcement. From these informal contacts, I made a number of observations that seemed to be echoed by the results of case-study research reported in the literature on policing and regulatory enforcement.[2]

The typology presented here is intended to provide a framework for the systematic development of hypotheses about variations in regulatory enforcement. In particular, this typology looks at how a given enforcement strategy is implemented through the formal and informal organization of the enforcement agency.

This article first describes the literature, which identifies two contrasting enforcement strategies, and suggests a wide array of potential explanations for the variation. Next, it identifies the two dimensions underlying the typology and explains why two variables were chosen. The last half of the paper provides thumbnail sketches of each type of enforcement style, with examples drawn from case-study research of regulatory enforcement.

◂ Persuasion versus Prosecution ▸

Contemporary studies of regulatory enforcement have identified two types of enforcement strategy—one which depends on persuasion and another that uses prosecution to obtain regulatory compliance. The persuasion strategy relies upon education, negotiation, and cooperation to gain compliance. The prosecution strategy, on the other hand, relies upon the imposition of sanctions to deter violations of the law. Researchers have noted differences between enforcement personnel and between enforcement agencies to the extent that they rely on persuasion or, conversely, prosecution to obtain compliance (see, e.g., Bardach and Kagan 1982; Blau 1963; Cranston 1979; Dickens 1970; Kagan 1978; Kelman 1981; Richardson, *et al.* 1982; Shover, Clelland and Lynxwiler 1982). With few exceptions (see, e.g., Bardach and Kagan 1982; Kelman 1981; Shover, Clelland and Lynxwiler 1982), studies of regulatory enforcement reveal a preponderance of persuasion-oriented agencies.

Frequently, researchers imply that this reliance on persuasion distinguishes regulatory enforcement from policing. Recently, however, commentators on regulatory enforcement have correctly noted that policing also entails a large amount of negotiation and discretion, an observation well-documented by research (Brown 1981; Gardiner 1969; Manning 1980; Wilson 1968, 1978). As Kagan (1983:10) notes, "Some police departments and some regulatory agencies lean toward legalistic strictness, at least for some kinds of violations and violators, while others are more prone to 'make exceptions,' more oriented toward informal conflict-resolution, conciliation, pressure and persuasion than toward law enforcement."

A large number of factors have been cited to explain this variation between agencies, both in the policing literature and in the regulatory enforcement literature. They fall into three general categories, (1) task and client characteristics (Bartrip and Fenn 1980; Cranston 1979; Carson 1979; Hawkins 1983; Kagan and Scholz 1983; Katzman 1980; Mileski 1971; Nivola 1978; Weaver 1977), (2) organizational characteristics (Blau 1963; Brown 1981; Manning 1980; Shover, Clelland, and Lynxwiler 1982; Truman 1940; Wilson 1968, 1978), and (3) the environmental context, particularly the political environment (Bernstein1955; Cranston 1979; Freedman 1978; Kagan 1978, 1983; Richardson, et al. 1982; Sabatier 1975; Shover, Clelland, and Lynxwiler 1982; Thomas 1980; Wilson 1968).

All these factors necessarily interact to influence the character of enforcement. For example, the research of Shover, Clelland, and Lynxwiler (1982) suggests that some organizational styles may be more sensitive to environmental constraints and pressures; and Kelman's (1981) research on occupational safety enforcement in the U.S. and Sweden suggests that the political environment may play an important role in shaping the organization of the enforcement agency. Similarly, Kagan (1983) notes that certain organizational factors, like recruitment and training, may make an agency more or less immune to external attempts to influence enforcement practices.

Indeed, these references to the interaction between the political environment and organizational factors in producing enforcement patterns suggest that one might look at organizational factors as the medium through which the political environment influences enforcement action. Wilson (1968) makes a similar observation with respect to the police. In his discussion of three styles of policing, Wilson emphasizes the organizational influences on police behavior and how these interact with the political culture to influence the degree to which police rely on formal or informal action (persuasion or prosecution). The typology developed in this paper explores these interactions and the role of the organization as either a conduit or a barrier between the political environment and agency practice.

CONSTRUCTING A TYPOLOGY

As noted above, studies of policing and of regulatory enforcement have discovered variability in the tendency of enforcement officers to rely on persuasion or prosecution. Both bodies of literature have also identified organizational influences on the enforcement behavior of individual officers and inspectors. These two dimensions of variation underlie Wilson's empirical typology of varieties of police behavior, although Wilson never elaborates his observations into a fully theoretical typology (see figure 1).

Figure 1
Wilson's Typology: Styles of Policing

	High Discretion	**Low Discretion**
Administrative Control	Service	Legalistic
Informal Norms	Watchman	X

One dimension is the degree to which enforcement officers exercise discretion. Some enforcement agencies tend to rely on a prosecution strategy, involving a stringent, penal, sanctioning orientation toward enforcement. Others adopt an accommodating, conciliatory orientation in which officers avoid taking formal action, relying instead on negotiation and informal action. The second dimension is the degree of formal administrative control exerted over officers in order to implement a particular enforcement strategy. In some enforcement organizations, the formal bureaucracy is highly developed, authority is centralized, and superiors closely monitor officer actions to insure the perpetuation of goals defined by superiors. In other enforcement organizations, the formal organization is a weak influence compared to the informal culture of the organization, the bureaucracy is not highly differentiated, and control of officer action is influenced by informal norms enforced through informal sanctions.

For the purpose of developing four ideal-types, these two dimensions have been dichotomized (see figure 2). Obviously, however, neither dimension is really a dichotomous variable. Thus, administrative control is actually considered in terms of greater or lesser degrees of centralization, hierarchical organization, rigid authority structure, etc.; and enforcement strategy refers to greater or lesser tendencies toward a stringent, deterrent orientation regarding enforcement, as opposed to an accommodative orientation.

Figure 2
Typology of Enforcement Styles

	Enforcement Strategy	
Administrative Control	**"Persuasion"**	**"Prosecution"**
	SERVICE	**LEGALISTIC**
Centralized Mechanistic Formal	Technical competence High political influence Emphasis on educational aspects of enforcement	High technical competence Insulated from political influence Unstable political environment
	WATCHMAN	**FREE AGENT**
Decentralized Organic Informal	Low technical competence Lack of initiative Industry-dominated political environment	High technical competence Insulated from political influence Consensus for enforcement

Although the following discussion of the four enforcement types as applied to regulatory enforcement is necessarily speculative and exploratory, it presents illustrations of each type drawn from the research literature on regulatory enforcement. The discussion begins with an examination of the two types that are probably the most frequently occurring empirical types, the Service and Watchman styles, both of which manifest a persuasion strategy for obtaining compliance.

Service Style

According to Wilson's typology, the Service style is characterized by a professional orientation. Administrative control is maintained through elaborate and detailed records by which officers' activities are monitored. The Service style is also characterized by the exercise of a good deal of discretion. According to Wilson, this style emerges out of administrators' sensitivity to "community" values, particularly the values of politically influential members of the community—the "Somebodies" in town (Wilson 1968:202–222). Wilson's name for this style indicates the primary orientation: service to the community, particularly those services desired by community notables.

Like the Service style police department, the Service style regulatory agency is characterized by a professional orientation. Inspectors are apt to be highly educated and knowledgeable in their fields. Administrators attempt to channel these skills toward service to the regulated industry. The centralized authority of the service agency is actively used by administrators to discourage or prevent inspectors from invoking formal action to induce compliance. As in the Service style police department, formal action is used—if at all—only as a last resort, when negotiations and repeated entreaties to correct the violation fail.

In lieu of formal action, enforcement officers following the Service style are instructed to provide technical consultation to the regulated firms. On the assumption, hope, or pretense that firms would comply if they only knew they were breaking the law and were told how to remedy the situation, education is stressed. In addition, firms that are under frequent surveillance or inspection may come to rely upon the Service style enforcement agency to notify them when their own quality standards have not been met. The firm is thereby saved the expense of maintaining its own in-house quality control team.

Administrators of Service style agencies are apt to be responsive to the political environment, which will probably be dominated by firms and industries regulated by the agency. The public will not be a significant referent for administrators (Sabatier 1975). The "Somebodies" whom administrators typically need to pacify are business people regulated by the agency.[3]

Administrators, responding to the prerogatives defined by the regulated industry, adopt a "voluntary compliance" philosophy and perpetuate it via the reward system of a mechanistic bureaucracy. The organization possesses the administrative control to reward "appropriate" behavior and philosophy. Therefore, those inspectors who adopt the persuasion strategy will be more favored for promotion and preferred assignments than those mavericks who insist on pursuing a prosecution strategy. In addition, a centralized administration may place numerous checks on inspectors' authority, and an inspector who invokes formal authority may be the subject of administrative discipline.

Within the research literature, Shover, Clelland, and Lynxwiler's description of later developments in the Office of Surface Mining exemplifies the Service style. According to Shover, Clelland, and Lynxwiler (1982:61), following Ronald Reagan's election to the presidency in 1980, the Heritage Foundation urged the new administration "to reduce the [Office of Surface Mining's] enforcement staff, to cut the agency budget, and to replace current OSM senior staff and regional directors with professionals 'more attuned to a rational program' of reclamation." The agency was reorganized to implement a persuasion strategy. The new leadership centralized the enforcement process. For instance, the new administrators required litigation to be approved by the central office in Washington. Through such centralization, field staff were stripped of enforcement authority, allowing administrators to exercise discretion and to promote regulatory leniency, "voluntary compliance," and non-enforcement.

Another example of a Service style agency is reported by Cranston (1979). In summarizing his work on consumer agencies in Great Britain, Cranston notes (1979:4):

> The local government character of consumer agencies is another factor which can be shown to have an important effect, for example, on how they exercise their discretion. In the past, prosecutions of consumer offenses had to be approved by a local committee. Since these often comprised a majority of businessmen, they were generally unfavourable to prosecution and so legal proceedings were approved in only the very serious cases.

Moreover, he adds (1979:14), "The careers of some enforcement officers suffered when they refused to bow to this type of pressure." Primarily, consumer agencies saw themselves as "advisors to industry," and this role was reinforced by administrative policies.

Watchman Style

Wilson's Watchman style of policing is also characterized by the ubiquitous use of discretion by patrol officers. But such departments lack a professional orientation and have only a few levels in the personnel hierarchy. There is little incentive or opportunity for advancement and consequently few administrative rewards. There is little administrative direction and a paucity of record-keeping. Few incidents are formally recorded, and the records that are kept are likely to be "skimpy and incomplete." Finally, the Watchman style police department is sensitive to the political climate. The shibboleth of these departments is "Don't rock the boat." Officers are expected to maintain a low profile and avoid controversy and confrontation. These norms are maintained primarily through the organizational culture rather than through rules and administrative directives, as are found in the Service style department.

Similar observations can be made in many regulatory agencies. Like the Service style, the Watchman style utilizes a persuasion strategy. In this case, however, the strategy emerges not from organizational policy directives but from a vacuum of administrative control. In the Watchman style agency, a widely held norm against prosecution serves to maintain a persuasion strategy, though little real persuasion may be undertaken.

The enforcement officers in a Watchman style agency typically possess only marginal competence. In addition, the organization provides little, if any, additional training to inspectors. As in the Watchman style police department, these characteristics are perpetuated through recruitment practices. As a consequence of their minimal technical competence, inspectors may tend to be more timid than highly skilled inspectors, particularly when they must interact with competent staff employed by regulated firms to supervise compliance. In such cases, inspectors may be easily cowed by the technical superiority of the industry representative.

Another consequence of marginal competence is that enforcement officers themselves may not fully comprehend the seriousness of violations or even how to detect violations. Finally, enforcement officers are given little training in the methods for initiating formal action.[4] The invocation of formal authority requires unfamiliar methods and may not appear to enforcement officers as a viable option. Thus, administrators do not need to control officers directly in order to continue the persuasion strategy. Instead, it is perpetuated indirectly through recruitment, socialization, and (non)training processes.

Because of the low technical competence of inspectors, many Watchman style agencies may be simply "going through the motions" of inspections. Investigations are routine, cursory, and brief. In some examples, inspection appears to be shifted to goals totally unrelated to the discovery and investigation of violations. For example, inspectors may be primarily interested in collecting license fees on their rounds of inspection. Also, like the Watchman style police department, the Watchman agency may experience more corruption than other styles, as has been charged of building inspectors in some cities. While the Service style agency at least keeps up an illusion of enforcement by keeping detailed records, in the Watchman style agency inspection reports are likely to be superficial and incomplete. Many violations will not be recorded even if they are observed, an unlikely event in any case.

An example of a Watchman style agency can be found in Richardson's et al., (1982) description of some trade effluent enforcement agencies in Great Britain. Noting the influence of the organizational environment upon the exercise of discretion, the authors also draw attention to similarities between policing and regulatory enforcement. They draw an analogy between the "peacekeeping" style of policing and the style used by trade effluent officers. The agency was highly decentralized and prosecution was extremely rare. "In Southern Authority it was hard to obtain any clear picture of the procedure which would have been followed in the event of a prosecution, because none had been brought for breach of trade effluent consent conditions since 1974" (Richardson, et al., 1982:134).

Within these agencies, officers adhered to a set of informal norms—"A 'good' trade effluent officer was one who could achieve compliance through cooperation and who did not need to resort to formal law" (Richardson, *et al.* 1982:185). Moreover, this norm was maintained primarily through the informal culture of the organization rather than through administrative directives. According to Richardson, *et al.* (1982:185), officers:

> complained that they had no clear picture of what was expected of them . . . Nevertheless, the vast majority shared the view that a co-operative approach to traders was condoned, while "throwing the book" at them or "waving the big stick" was not. Prosecution indicated failure.

This cooperative approach was sustained as much to win the approval of colleagues as of administrators.

Another example of a Watchman style is found in Swanson and Schultz's book, *Prime Rip* (1982), describing inspection and grading in the meat packing industry. According to testimony from court cases and legislative hearings, the supervision of these programs by the U.S. Department of Agriculture was extremely lax. Payoffs to inspectors were common, and there were few administrative controls of employees. At the same time, those few employees who attempted to maintain a prosecution strategy were harassed by their superiors and ostracized by their colleagues.

Legalistic Style

While Wilson's Watchman and Service styles correspond to a persuasion strategy, the Legalistic style corresponds to a prosecution strategy. Police officers in Legalistic style departments are likely to intervene formally, by making an arrest or urging signing of a complaint, rather than informally through conciliation or by delaying arrest in hopes that the situation will take care of itself. Wilson's Legalistic style emphasizes professionalism. Administrative direction and control are more pronounced than in the Watchman style. Like the Service style, the Legalistic style stresses detailed documentation of all incidents in which officers are involved. The Legalistic style emphasizes the rule of law and avoids political entanglements by deferring to the law.

Like the Legalistic police department, the Legalistic regulatory agency will recruit inspectors who have the competence and the professional orientation needed for enforcement. But rather than using that competence primarily to provide technical consultation, it is used to detect and document violations of the law. Similarly, the Legalistic style agency attempts to take policing out of politics. Strict guidelines and limits on discretion are one means of de-politicizing the agency, which attempts to step "above" political conflict by invoking the notion that it "just enforces the laws." The Legalistic agency is likely to have formal guidelines instructing enforcement officers when to bring formal action. These guidelines are likely to be weighted more heavily toward invoking authority than toward avoiding formal action. Checks on officer authority simply test the sufficiency of evidence against formal standards.

The Office of Surface Mining was founded and developed as a Legalistic agency. As Shover, Clelland, and Lynxwiler observed, to encourage maximum enforcement of the law, both statutory and organizational limits were placed on inspectors' discretion. The program was designed to emphasize obeisance to the rule of law (Shover, Clelland, and Lynxwiler 1982:42). Echoing a statement by a police administrator interviewed by Wilson, one of the architects of the Office of Surface Mining's enforcement program observed (Shover, Clelland, and Lynxwiler 1982:43), "One ought to do what the law says." Consistency was viewed as a necessary ingredient toward building a credible program that would deter violations.

Numerous examples of Legalistic style agencies may be found in Bardach and Kagan's (1982) indictment of the prosecution strategy. The U.S. Occupational Safety and Health Administration (OSHA) is a favorite example of this approach. Like the Office of Surface Mining, OSHA was designed to limit discretion and insulate enforcement decisions from political pressures, resulting in a relatively high rate of formal action against violators (Kelman 1981).

Free Agent Style

The Free Agent style was not identified by Wilson, but can be logically deduced from the two dimensions underlying Wilson's typology of policing styles. While there are few empirical referents for this style, it may provide a model for reforming excessively legalistic regulatory enforcement agencies.[5]

The Free Agent style requires technically competent staff who are also oriented toward law enforcement. Thus, the recruitment process is crucial to the development and continuation of the Free Agent style. Technical competence ensures the skills necessary for discovering violations; professional norms of strict enforcement result in a high rate of formal actions being taken by inspectors. As in the Legalistic style, the Free Agent style defers to the "rule of law."

The principal difference between the Free Agent style and the Legalistic style lies in the role and power of administrators. In the Free Agent style, administrators provide coordination and support services but do not exercise discretion in particular cases. The vigorous enforcement philosophy is supported by informal norms rather than by strict administrative control over inspectors' discretion. Investigators are accountable to the legislature and the courts rather than to agency administrators.

The Free Agent style characterized some of the early regulatory agencies. Prior to the turn of the century, inspectors were highly autonomous, often working independently of any administrative oversight. They were accountable only to the courts. In several of these agencies, Free Agent inspectors attempted to enforce the law stringently and frequently brought charges against violators. Their major frustration was the court system, which refused to convict or impose meaningful penalties (Bartrip and Fenn 1980; Carson 1979; Frank 1982).

A contemporary example may be found in the Securities and Exchange Commission. According to Freedman (1978), the prosecution strategy of that agency stems from a broad consensus among both regulated groups and the public that securities laws should be enforced. This consensus is translated into policy through the organizational culture of the SEC.

Discussion

This typology is directed primarily toward answering "how" rather than "why." Specifically, how is a particular enforcement strategy—prosecution or persuasion—implemented by an agency? A related set of questions might address the relationships between each of these four types and other kinds of variables. In this paper, two categories of such variables are addressed: (1) recruitment, training, and socialization of officers and (2) the political environment.

In the Watchman and Free Agent styles, a strong organizational culture is perpetuated by the recruitment and training practices of the agency (Cranston 1979:3). In Service and Legalistic style agencies, the formal organization will be more highly developed and influential.

The Service and Watchman style agencies are more likely to emerge when the activity being regulated has low public visibility (Sabatier 1975) and when no "public interest" groups challenge the industry's dominance of the political environment. The Watchman style, in particular, persists not so much through pressure from business, as from the lack of any countervailing pressure from the public. When the political environment is characterized by conflict between active and vocal interest groups, a Legalistic style is most likely to develop (Bardach and Kagan 1982; Shover, Clelland, and Lynxwiler 1982). Where the political environment is characterized by agreement that enforcement is beneficial and necessary, a Free Agent style may emerge.

But these relationships should not be viewed as prescriptive. Another set of relationships concerning the consequences of each style under differing circumstances must also be explored. For instance, although it is hypothesized that a Legalistic style is likely to emerge in a conflict-ridden political context, Shover, Clelland, and Lynxwiler (1982) suggest that its inflexible and strict enforcement may fuel business opposition, resulting in a backlash that would dismantle the agency.[6] Thus, although a Legalistic style may "naturally" emerge in an unstable political environment, it may not be the "best" policy choice under those conditions. Research on the consequences of varying enforcement styles may inform policy decisions concerning which style to implement in a given political environment.

By understanding the different organizational structures, one can identify targets for change. The typology suggests that the Watchman and Free Agent styles may be more resistant to change because their enforcement practices are embedded in the informal culture of the agency. A change in the leadership of a Watchman or Free Agent style agency may have little impact on how inspectors do their jobs, since the informal culture of the agency is stronger than available administrative controls. Therefore, transforming a Watchman style agency to a more rigorous enforcement posture would require supervision and formal checks on inspectors' discretion, or substantial retraining and resocialization of inspectors, or both. While retraining inspectors is a slower process for reforming the agency, it is likely to be more effective since it would engender less resistance than the creation of administrative controls and, when completed, would provide greater stability due to the commitment of inspectors to rigorous enforcement.

In contrast, the Service and Legalistic styles are more volatile and responsive to changes in personnel at the upper levels of the organization (see, eg., Shover, Clelland, and Lynxwiler 1982). The centralized administrative control can be harnessed for either a vigorous or a more conciliatory enforcement strategy. While sudden shifts in policy may cause morale problems among inspectors, the intensive administrative supervision that is normal in Service and Legalistic style agencies ensures that administrative directives are carried out nonetheless.

Finally, one might ask which of these four styles is most desirable. The answer, of course, depends on one's goals. From the standpoint of the regulated industries, the Service style appears to be the most advantageous—regulated firms receive advice about meeting regulatory requirements but are essentially free to accept or reject that advice. Regulatory requirements are rarely enforced, but firms that want to comply receive free expert assistance in overcoming problems. The single drawback of this approach, from the standpoint of industry, is that those firms that refuse to comply enjoy a competitive advantage, since they are not forced to pay the costs of regulatory compliance.

In spite of the advantages of the Service style to industry, however, many agencies, particularly at the state and local levels, adhere to a Watchman style. Businesses do not enjoy the free technical advice provided by Service style agencies, but are nonetheless insulated from vigorous enforcement. The Watchman style offers no direct benefits to industry, but poses no threat either. The Watchman style is prevalent because it is cheaper than the Service style—less qualified staff do not demand high salaries; a lower number of supervisory and administrative personnel likewise reduces staff costs; and training expenditures are minimal.

Advocates of strict enforcement criticize both the Service and Watchman styles as compromising the public health, safety, and welfare. During the 1970s workers, environmentalists, and consumer advocates organized opposition to the persuasion strategy in state regulatory enforcement agencies. These groups sought legislation that would limit the discretion of regulatory officials to ignore violations of the law. The result was the creation of several legalistic style federal agencies—for example, the Office of Surface Mining and the Occupational Safety and Health Administration. The strategy was less than successful, at least in the long run. The resentment by businesses of legalistic enforcement created an almost immediate mobilization of industry groups who sought to eliminate "over-regulation." Budget cuts and the appointment of administrators sympathetic to industry's complaints successfully rendered legalistic reforms ineffective.

An alternate option for advocates of strict regulatory compliance is the Free Agent style. The key advantage of the Free Agent style is that it disperses authority so that administrators are less vulnerable to pressure. Legislative prescription of training requirements and the explicit grant of enforcement authority to inspectors, rather than to the department or administrators, can provide the foundation for maintaining a Free Agent style. In a volatile political environment, or one dominated by business interests, the Free Agent style agency may suffer budget reductions and attempts by persuasion-oriented administrators to discourage enforcement. In addition, it is more likely to focus industry resentment on the inspector, straining relationships to the point of hostility. Nonetheless, a Free Agent style is more resistant to change than the Legalistic style. Moreover, the greater discretion afforded Free Agent style inspectors lessens the egregious problems of over-enforcement associated with the Legalistic style; thus, industry opposition will be both less intense and less credible.

◂ Conclusion ▸

This typology is offered to provide a framework for analyzing enforcement organizations. It identifies two important dimensions of variation between enforcement agencies. Thus, it may have heuristic value. If this typology can stimulate research on enforcement organizations and promote greater understanding of regulatory enforcement, it will have served its purpose.

◂ Notes ▸

[1] In this essay, I will use the term corporate crime to refer to illegal acts, whether criminal or civil, committed by corporations or individuals in the course of business.

[2] Ordinarily, it is preferable to present the results of original research, and to derive the typology from that research or to use that research to empirically verify a theoretically derived typology. This procedure is not practical in this instance. In order to verify the typology, research would have to be carried out on a large number of regulatory enforcement organizations. This would involve interviews with hundreds, and perhaps thousands, of inspectors, supervisors, administrators, and business people, in addition to an intensive background study of each organization. This is an undertaking of immense scope. I simply could not wait that long to present some theoretical ideas that seemed worthy of discussion and research. The patterns, between studies on policing organizations, published research on regulatory agencies, and my own unsystematic observations were too significant to ignore while I pursued several case-studies of my own. Therefore, although the empirical underpinnings of this typology are anecdotal and derivative, I believe it is important to represent this typology so that other researchers may also direct their research toward the questions the typology raises.

[3] The agency may not only be more sensitive to the concerns and wishes of industry as a whole, certain "somebody" firms in the regulated industry may wield more influence than "nobody" firms.

[4] It may be necessary to differentiate between three different kinds of knowledge and skill needed for competent enforcement. First, there is abstract scientific competence. Second, the enforcement officer must know how to apply that scientific knowledge to the discovery and investigation of violations. Third, there must be legal competence, knowing what constitutes a violation and how to proceed legally against violators.

[5] Bardach and Kagan's (1982) description of the "good inspector" corresponds closely to the characteristics of the Free Agent inspector.

[6] The typology might also be used to analyze the life-cycle of agencies. For example, opposition to the prosecution strategy of a Legalistic agency may result in new administrators being appointed who impose a Service style. Ultimately, however, they may alter recruitment practices and erode training so that the agency is transformed into a Watchman style, in which a persuasion strategy is perpetuated at lower administrative cost.

REFERENCES

Bardach, Eugene and Kagan, Robert. (1982). *Going By the Book: The Problem of Regulatory Unreasonableness.* Philadelphia: Temple University Press.

Bartrip, Peter, J. W. and Fenn, P. T. (1980). "The Administration of Safety: The Enforcement Policy of the Early Factory Inspectorate, 1844–1864." *Public Administration* 58:87–102.

Bernstein, Marver H. (1955). *Regulating Business by Independent Commission.* Princeton, NJ: Princeton University Press.

Blau, Peter. (1963). *The Dynamics of Bureaucracy: A Study of Interpersonal Relations in Two Government Agencies.* Chicago: University of Chicago Press, rev. ed.

Brown, Michael K. (1981). *Working the Street. Police Discretion and the Dilemmas of Reform.* New York: Russell Sage.

Cranston, Ross. (1979). *Regulating Business. Law and Consumer Agencies.* London: MacMillan.

Dickens, Bernard M. (1970). "Discretion in Local Authority Prosecutions." *Criminal Law Review*: 618–633.

Frank, Nancy. (1982). *From Criminal Law to Regulation: A Historical Analysis of Health and Safety Law.* Ph.D. dissertation, State University of New York at Albany.

Freedman, James O. (1978). *Crisis and Legitimacy.* New York. Cambridge University Press.

Friendly, Henry J. (1962). *The Federal Administrative Agencies: The Need for a Better Definition of Standards.* Cambridge, MA: Harvard University Press.

Gardiner, J. A. (1969). *Traffic and the Police.* Cambridge, MA: Harvard University Press.

Goldstein, Herman. (1977). *Policing a Free Society.* Cambridge, MA: Ballinger Publishing Co.

Hagan, J., J. D. Hewewtt and D. F. Alwin. (1979). "Ceremonial Justice: Crime and Punishment in a Loosely Coupled System." *Social Forces* 58 (December):506–27.

Hawkins, Keith. (1983). "Bargain and Bluff: Compliance Strategy and Deterrence in the Enforcement of Regulation." *Law and Policy Quarterly* 5 (January):35–73.

Kagan, Robert A. (1978). *Regulatory Justice: Implementing a Wage-Price Freeze.* New York: Russell Sage.

Kagan, Robert A. and John T. Scholz. (1983). "The 'Criminology of the Corporation' and Regulatory Enforcement Strategies," in *Enforcing Regulation: Policy and Practice*, ed. Keith Hawkins and John M. Thomas. Boston: Klower-Nijhoff

Katzman, Robert A. (1980). *Regulatory Bureaucracy. The Federal Trade Commission and Antitrust Policy.* Cambridge, MA: MIT Press.

Keiser, K. Robert. (1980). "The New Regulation of Health and Safety." *Political Science Quarterly* (Fall): 479–91.

Kelman, Steven. (1981). *Regulating American, Regulating Sweden: A Comparative Study of Occupational Safety and Health Policy.* Cambridge, MA: MIT Press.

Manning, Peter K. (1980). *The Narc's Game: Organizational Limits on Drug Law Enforcement.* Cambridge, MA: MIT Press.

Mileski, Maureen. (1971). *Policing Slum Landlords. An Observation of Administrative Control.* Ph.D. dissertation, Yale University.

Richardson, Genevra with A. I. Ogus and Paul Burrows. (1982). *Policing Pollution: A Study of Regulation and Enforcement.* Oxford: Clarendon Press.

Sabatier, Paul. (1975). "Social Movements and Regulatory Agencies: Toward a More Adequate—and Less Pessimistic—Theory of 'Clientele Capture.'" *Policy Sciences* 6:301–342.

Shover, Neal, Donald A. Clelland, and John Lynxwiler. (1982). *Developing a Regulatory Bureaucracy: The Office of Surface Mining Reclamation and Enforcement.* Washington, DC: U.S. Government Printing Office.

Swanson, Wayne and George Schultz. (1982). *Prime Rip.* Englewood Cliffs, NJ: Prentice-Hall.

Weaver, Suzanne. (1977). *Decision to Prosecute: Organization and Public Policy in the Antitrust Division.* Cambridge, MA. MIT press.

Wilson, James Q. (1968). *Varieties of Police Behavior.* Cambridge, MA: Harvard University Press.

Wilson, James Q. (1978). *The Investigators.* New York. Basic Books.

‹ 17 ›

Local Prosecutors and Corporate Crime

Michael L. Benson
Francis T. Cullen
William J. Maakestad

Crimes committed by and for business pose a serious threat to the health, safety, and financial welfare of consumers and workers as well as to the orderly functioning of the economy and the government. Commonly known as corporate or organizational crimes, these offenses raise special problems for detection, prosecution, and sanction.[1] Isolated efforts by individual enforcement agencies have proven inadequate against this type of crime, underscoring the need for a coordinated, multistrategy response from federal, state, and local levels of government.

Historically, the federal government has assumed primary responsibility for controlling corporate crime, but in the past two decades, local prosecutors have become increasingly concerned about this problem. In 1973 the National District Attorneys Association established an Economic Crime Committee to encourage local prosecutors to enforce white-collar crime laws and to enhance their

Reprinted from *National Institute of Justice: Research in Brief*, January 1993.

enforcement ability. By 1975, 43 district attorneys' offices were participating in the committee's Economic Crime Project.

Since the Economic Crime Project was begun . . . , local response to corporate white-collar crime has changed significantly. In the past, district attorneys concentrated almost exclusively on economic crimes such as consumer fraud. They are now prosecuting a wider variety of cases, including occupational safety violations and the illegal dumping of toxic waste. In nearly every state, prosecutors have sought criminal indictments against corporations, partnerships, and other business entities for noneconomic offenses.

This *Research in Brief* summarizes a National Institute of Justice study of local prosecutors' work against corporate crime. For the study, corporate crime was defined as "a violation of a criminal statute either by a corporate entity or by its executives, employees, or agents acting on behalf of and for the benefit of the corporation, partnership, or other form of business entity."

The first component of the study was a mail survey of 632 district attorneys with jurisdictions located in or near urban areas.[2] Completed questionnaires were received from 419 districts, a response rate of 66 percent. The survey data were merged with economic, social, and official crime data for each jurisdiction.[3] The second component of the study involved case studies in four jurisdictions: Cook County, Illinois; Los Angeles County, California; Dade County, Florida; and Nassau County, New York. In each jurisdiction prosecutors, regulatory officials, and representatives of various law enforcement agencies were interviewed regarding their views of corporate crime and their interactions with other law enforcement agencies.

Trends in Corporate Crime Prosecutions

One conclusion is that local prosecution of corporate crime is becoming more widespread. More than one-quarter of the survey respondents said that corporate prosecutions have increased during their tenure in office. One-quarter reported that they expected to prosecute more corporate cases in the future. Less than 1 percent had seen or anticipated a decrease in prosecutions.

Prosecutors in large jurisdictions (those with populations over 250,000) most frequently reported increased rates of corporate prosecutions. Roughly 6 out of 10 respondents in large jurisdictions said prosecutions had increased during their tenures in office, and a majority expected this trend to continue.

Prevalence of Corporate Crime Prosecutions

In 1988 two-thirds of the survey respondents said their offices prosecuted at least one of nine types of corporate crime (table 1). Although local prosecutors handled a wider variety of corporate crimes in 1988 than in previous years, economic crimes still made Consumer fraud was the most frequently prosecuted corporate offense, with 41 percent of the offices prosecuting at least one case of consumer fraud.

- False claims and insurance fraud followed as the most frequently prosecuted economic crimes, with 31 percent of the offices prosecuting at least one offense in these categories.
- Only one type of noneconomic crime—environmental offenses—was prosecuted as often as economic crime. In 1988, 31 percent of the offices handled at least one environmental offense.

  Most districts did not have data on the specific number of corporate offenses handled in 1988. For this reason, the prevalence of local corporate crime prosecutions can only be approximated (table 2).
- Typically, 15 percent of the districts handled more than three consumer fraud cases a year, while 20 percent of the districts handled one to three annually.

Table 1: Percentage of Offices Prosecuting Selected Corporate Crimes in 1988*

Corporate crime	Yes	No
Consumer fraud	41%	59%
Securities fraud	22	78
Insurance fraud	31	69
Tax fraud	16	84
False claims	31	69
Workplace offenses	11	89
Environmental offenses	31	69
Illegal payments	16	84
Unfair trade practices	8	92
Any corporate offense	66	34

*In 1988, did your office actually prosecute any of the following offenses?

Table 2:
Frequency of Prosecutions in a Typical Year*

	Frequency			
Corporate crime	**Never**	**Fewer than 1 case per year**	**About 1–3 cases per year**	**More than 3 cases per year**
Consumer fraud	32%	33%	20%	15%
Securities fraud	57	28	12	3
Insurance fraud	38	39	15	9
Tax fraud	61	25	8	6
False claims	40	34	15	11
Workplace offenses	68	25	5	1
Environmental offenses	45	34	13	8
Illegal payments	51	37	10	2
Unfair trade practices	75	18	3	5

*Typically, how often does your office prosecute the corporate criminal offenses listed below?

- About 10 percent of local prosecutors typically handled more than three false claims, insurance fraud cases, or environmental offenses per year.

  Prosecutors in the case study sites reported that most of their resources were allocated to combat economic offenses, but noted that environmental offenses were becoming more prevalent. As one prosecutor said, "The danger from this environmental stuff is much greater than what we have to worry about from drugs." Another noted, "A day does not go by without my hearing about some type of environmental issue on television or in the newspapers. The problems are immense."

Variation in Local Corporate Crime Prosecution

Because of their complex, technical nature, crimes committed in an organizational setting can be difficult to prosecute. Statistical analysis revealed three significant causes for local variations in corporate crime prosecution: availability of resources, community context, and regional differences. These all affected how aggressive local prosecutors were in responding to corporate crime.

Availability of resources. Because successful prosecutions often require substantial time and labor, the availability of resources has a significant influence on local activity against corporate crime. Large offices (as measured by the number of full-time attorneys) conducted more corporate prosecutions than small offices. Those offices that had joined an interagency task force to combat white-collar or economic crime or had established a special unit tended to be more active than offices lacking such arrangements.

Community context. The economic, demographic, and social makeup of the community also plays a significant role in determining the aggressiveness of local corporate crime prosecution. In the study, community context affected local prosecutors' attention and reaction to certain types of offenses. For example, prosecutors in Nassau County, New York, cited illegal disposal of medical waste as a significant environmental problem, while prosecutors in Cook County, Illinois, cited illegal disposal or abandonment of toxic chemicals by defunct metal-plating businesses as a typical problem. Local prosecutors tended to be sensitive to the specific problems, needs, and expectations of the communities in which they worked, much as are local police forces.

Regional differences. Regional differences also affect the amount of local activity taken against corporate crime. In general, prosecutors in western states tended to be more active against most forms of corporate crime than their counterparts in northeastern, midwestern, and southern states (table 3). Compared to offices in other regions, a larger percentage of western offices typically

Table 3:
Percentage of Offices Prosecuting More Than Three Cases per Year, by Region*

	Region			
Crime	**South**	**West**	**Northeast**	**Midwest**
Consumer fraud	11%	42%	16%	9%
Securities fraud	3	9	2	3
Insurance fraud	8	15	13	6
Tax fraud	7	9	2	5
False claims	9	30	12	7
Workplace offenses	3	2	0	0
Environmental offenses	3	33	9	6
Illegal payments	2	2	5	2
Unfair trade practices	1	28	0	2

*Typically, how often does your office prosecute the corporate criminal offenses listed below?

handled more than three cases per year of most corporate crimes.

The higher level of activity among prosecutors in the West may be due to the types of offices and communities they serve. First, the western offices sampled were located in districts with comparatively large populations. Along with their greater population size, these districts may have more business activity, and therefore, more potential offenses than districts in other regions. Second, the western offices tended to have more attorneys and investigators than offices in other regions. Third, legal or cultural factors unique to western states may cause local prosecutors to take a comparatively more vigorous approach to corporate crime. However, the true cause of regional variation remains unclear and deserves further investigation.[4]

Discovery of Corporate Offenses

District attorneys learned about corporate misconduct through a variety of official and unofficial sources. Most often, cases came to the attention of prosecutors after complaints by business and citizen victims. The second most common sources were the local police and state regulatory agencies, followed by the state police and state attorney general's offices. Federal law enforcement and regulatory agencies did not refer many cases to local prosecutors (table 4).

Table 4:
Frequency of Referrals from Selected Sources*

	Frequency			
Referral source	**Never**	**Fewer than 1 case per year**	**About 1–3 cases per year**	**More than 3 cases per year**
Local police	25%	40%	20%	15%
State police	41	37	16	6
State attorney general	40	37	16	6
State regulatory agency	28	39	20	14
Federal regulatory agency	71	22	6	1
U.S. Attorney's Office	72	23	5	0.3
FBI	63	29	7	1
Business victims	22	37	19	21
Citizen victims	18	37	23	22
Public interest groups	59	28	9	4

*In general, how often do the sources below refer potential corporate criminal cases to your office for investigation or prosecution?

Networking and Special Units

The Economic Crime Project discovered two ways for local prosecutors to augment resources and increase efficiency against corporate crime:

- Using interagency teams to analyze, investigate, and prosecute complex white-collar crimes. These networks typically include prosecutors; regulatory officials; and representatives from federal, state, and local law enforcement agencies.
- Creating special units for economic crimes, which allows prosecutors to develop the technical and legal expertise necessary to handle complex cases by concentrating on these types of crimes.

  This survey found that 24 percent of local prosecutors were using one or the other (or both) of these special control strategies.
- Twenty-three percent of the respondents had a special in-house unit in their office for investigating and prosecuting economic or white-collar crimes.
- Eight percent were involved in an interagency task force or strike group focusing on economic or white-collar crime.
- Of those involved in an interagency task force, 75 percent also had a special unit.

  The use of special control strategies varied by size of district and region of the country and was more prevalent in large jurisdictions than in small ones.
- Fourteen of the 30 largest offices were involved in an interagency task force, compared to only one of the 30 smallest offices.
- More than 70 percent of the respondents in large jurisdictions used one or more of the special strategies, compared to less than 10 percent of their counterparts in small districts.
- Special units and interagency networks were more common in western and, to a lesser extent, northeastern districts than in midwestern or southern districts.

Cooperation with Other Agencies

Jointly coordinated investigations are an integral part of networking. Local prosecutors reported collaborating most often with local police and state regulatory agencies on joint investigations of corporate crimes (table 5).

Table 5:
Frequency of Joint Investigations with Selected Agencies*

Agency	Frequency			
	Never	Fewer than 1 case per year	About 1–3 cases per year	More than 3 cases per year
Local police	29%	33%	22%	16%
State police	45	33	16	7
State attorney general	39	39	16	5
State regulatory agency	35	36	16	12
Federal regulatory agency	70	23	6	1
U.S. Attorney's Office	67	26	6	2
FBI	61	29	7	3
Another prosecutor	44	35	18	3

*How often does your office cooperate on joint investigations of corporate crimes with the agencies listed below?

- The highest number, 38 percent, reported working with local police on one or more corporate cases annually.
- Twenty-eight percent said they worked with state regulatory agencies on one or more corporate cases each year.
- At least once a year, more than 20 percent of prosecutors worked with the state attorney general's office and state police.
- Almost 20 percent of prosecutors cooperated with another jurisdiction at least once a year.

Joint investigations with federal agencies were rare. Less than 10 percent of the respondents said they worked with the Federal Bureau of Investigation (FBI), the U.S. Attorney's Office, or a federal regulatory agency as often as once a year. In three out of five offices, prosecutors never worked with these federal agencies.

Some prosecutors interviewed during the case study visits faulted federal investigative agencies for not referring cases to local officials. Although local prosecutors recognized the need for federal agencies to focus on large cases, they believed that some small, unpursued cases may have had significant local impact. While acknowledging different priorities, the prosecutors believed that too many cases have escaped enforcement. Better communication between federal and local officials could provide prosecutors with leads to pursue local cases not pursued by federal agencies.

However, despite growing recognition of the seriousness of corporate crime and widespread knowledge that traditional methods of law enforcement are inadequate, the development of coordinated, multistrategy responses from federal, state, and local governments remains more an ideal than a reality.

Constraints on Prosecutorial Discretion

Before deciding to proceed with a corporate case, prosecutors reported they considered many factors, including the type of offense, resources available, actions of other agencies, preferences of victims, and potential impact of the prosecution on the local community. Some of these factors limited the prosecutor's willingness to proceed with a corporate prosecution, while others increased it.

Factors that limited prosecution. The most important factors limiting local prosecution of corporate crimes were inadequate resources, legal constraints, and availability of alternative remedies.

- Seventy percent of the survey respondents were less willing to prosecute if state or federal regulatory agencies had already acted in a case.
- About 60 percent stated they probably would limit their willingness to prosecute if personnel were insufficient.
- More than 50 percent said they would be less willing to prosecute if victims were not cooperative or if criminal intent was difficult to establish in a corporate context.

The inadequacies of resources at the local level became apparent during visits to the case study sites. Even in relatively large well-to-do offices, prosecutors often did not have basic equipment. For example, prosecutors in one of the largest districts lamented that they did not have dictaphones and that memorandums, briefs, and other documents had to be written in longhand before office secretaries could type them.

An investigator in the same district pointed out that a car phone and an answering machine would greatly improve her efficiency and productivity, enabling her to receive and return calls as she traveled around the city working her cases. Without a phone, her time in the car was, as she put it, "mostly wasted." She and other interviewees noted that these items are standard equipment in all but the smallest private law firms.

On a more substantive level, prosecutors in one district commented that their ability to develop and dispose of environmental cases was seriously diminished by the lack of access to adequate laboratory facilities. For example, delays in identifying potentially toxic substances limited the prosecutors' options in responding to cases of illegal disposal or handling of toxic wastes. As one prosecutor explained, to "find out what's in a substance 6 months later is too late in an environmental case. How can you walk in [to a court] and [ask] for injunctive relief and say there's an immediate need to close this [business] down when you've waited 6 months? How can you do anything criminally—and talk about how bad this is—if our office lets it go 6 months at a time?"

Factors that increased prosecution. The factors most likely to increase a prosecutor's willingness to proceed against a corporate wrongdoer involved the nature of the offense and the characteristics of the offender. More than 90 percent of the respondents indicated they would be more willing to prosecute cases that involved the following:

- Physical harm to victims
- Evidence of multiple offenses
- Large numbers of victims
- Substantial economic harm

Only slightly less important were the education and deterrence functions of prosecution. More than 85 percent said the "need to deter other potential corporate offenders" would increase their willingness to prosecute. About 75 percent felt similarly about the "need to demonstrate publicly that the law applies equally to all offenders."

Goals of Prosecution

In general, district attorneys pursued different goals when prosecuting corporate as opposed to ordinary street crimes. In the case of a traditional street crime committed by an individual, the most important objective for local prosecuting tended to be either deterrence or incapacitation.

- About 33 percent of the respondents rated incapacitation or deterrence of the offender as the most important objective in prosecuting ordinary street crimes.
- Only 16 percent rated deterrence of other street criminals as the most important objective in this type of case.

In contrast, 40 percent of the respondents ranked deterrence of other offenders as the most important objective in pursuing corporate crimes. In the view of one experienced prosecutor:

> There's only one advantage to corporate prosecutions—in terms of its deterrence value, one prosecution is worth 500. I've prosecuted maybe 50 murderers, and I've never deterred a street murderer. I've probably prosecuted one industrial murderer, and I think we've deterred a whole lot of people—at least

> woke them up—so some people are tying to do the right thing. So even with a lack of resources, one corporate prosecution is much more valuable than one street crime prosecution.

Addressing the same issue, another prosecutor commented on environmental crime:

> Everybody agrees that criminal prosecution is the big hammer on environmental people. The proof is how loud they squeal when you file the case, and boy, do they squeal.

Despite the supposed moral neutrality of many corporate offenses, a notable proportion of prosecutors felt that corporate offenders deserve to be punished. Indeed, 35 percent ranked retribution as either the first or second most important objective in a corporate crime conviction. In contrast, less than 10 percent ranked retribution as the most important objective in prosecuting street criminals.

Most of the prosecutors interviewed at the case study sites echoed these opinions, arguing that corporate offenders were more easily deterred than ordinary street offenders. Furthermore, prosecutors expressed a strong sense of moral outrage over the "arrogance" and "callousness" of many business offenders, particularly those involved in repeated and intentional violations. For these offenders, the imposition of criminal sanctions for the sake of deterrence and retribution was regarded as appropriate, necessary, and deserved.

The Prosecutor as Problem Solver

While acknowledging the importance of convicting and punishing the guilty, some prosecutors interviewed at the case study sites articulated a broader concept of their role in the criminal process. In their view, the prosecutor's central function is reduction of criminal activity; deterrence is not merely a hoped-for byproduct of the punishment process. So, rather than devote themselves exclusively to the development of prosecutable cases, these prosecutors attempt to control criminal activity through alternative means, an approach that has been called "the prosecutor as problem solver."[5] Although it was more the exception than the rule, the case studies uncovered evidence that such an approach is not uncommon among local prosecutors.

For example, this strategy was used in a case involving a well-respected corporation that had violated a state law governing the transportation and disposal of toxic materials. Although there was enough evidence to pursue a criminal indictment, the prosecutor elected not to file charges. instead, he negotiated an agreement in which the corporation paid a substantial civil fine, donated money to a local hazardous waste project, and reimbursed the entire cost of the investigation. The money from the civil fine was used to fund a conference on environmental problems for law enforcement and regulatory officials.

In this case, the prosecutor believed that this approach both educated and deterred other potential offenders, while the conference fostered environmental awareness among local officials. Preventing other corporate environmental violations took precedence here over enforcing the law against a particular offender.

Policy Implications

In dealing with corporate offenders, local prosecutors often find themselves competing with well-financed and well-staffed law firms with vast financial and personnel resources, which can put up stiff legal obstacles for prosecutors to overcome. The effort is often expensive and time-consuming, especially for prosecutors who have limited staff and are facing these challenges for the first time. The following ideas on consolidating resources may be worthy of exploration.

Sharing information. Local prosecutors cited a need for a centralized information clearinghouse and brief bank to allow prosecutors to benefit from the collective knowledge and experience of their colleagues nationwide. For example, prosecutors in small communities could draw on the experience and wisdom of prosecutors in large urban centers. Such a clearinghouse could also contain information on alternative sanctions, innovative sentencing, and other enforcement techniques. it would be especially useful in relatively new areas of prosecution such as environmental and workplace-related crimes.

Automation. The potential of computers to coordinate work among investigators in different agencies could be more fully explored. Agencies often have cases stored in a computer data base, but have no way of knowing what cases other agencies are working on. A centralized computer data bank might be particularly useful to local prosecutors in situations involving certain types of financial fraud or in cases in which victims are located in widely scattered areas and offenders are mobile.

Many law enforcement agencies now use computers for record keeping and case management. These computer files could tell investigators when someone in their own agency is working on a particular case, thus reducing duplication of effort and facilitating information sharing.

Computer networks. Some prosecutors and investigators suggested that a local computer network linking agencies could provide access to a common data base of ongoing investigations and cases. The data base entries could contain information on the investigator (for example, name, telephone number, and agency) and information on the case (for example, victims, suspects, and modus operandi). Investigators could use this data base to obtain both information on the case and the name of the investigator to coordinate activities. Such a network would be particularly useful in large urban areas where multiple agencies in different jurisdictions often work in geographical proximity.

Many technical details would require careful consideration. For example, when a computer network is installed, files would need to be protected so that only the investigator entering a case into the data base could alter information pertaining to it; other investigators would need appropriate security clearances to read a file without altering it.

Regional laboratories. Regional laboratories to serve multiple local jurisdictions would make economic sense for hard-pressed prosecutors, and the feasibility of setting up such laboratories to analyze chemical and environmental evidence should be explored. These laboratories could analyze and identify chemical samples quickly, thus enabling local prosecutors to respond to cases that federal agencies may deem too small or too local in impact to pursue.

Publicizing of prosecutions. Finally, local prosecutors and other law enforcement agencies could take advantage of heightened public concern over corporate crime by publicizing their prosecutions of such offenses. The public needs to hear that local prosecutors regard these crimes as serious and to learn how to identify and report them. Ultimately, effective law enforcement depends on the support of concerned citizens who are willing to become involved.

Notes

[1] Corporate crime is a form of white-collar crime. The distinctive feature of corporate crime is that the offense is committed primarily for the benefit of an ongoing legitimate business enterprise, rather than for the individual who carries out the offense.

[2] The sample was drawn from a mailing list provided by the National District Attorneys Association. Districts were classified as urban if they were located in a Metropolitan Statistical Area (MSA), as defined by the U.S. Census Bureau.

[3] Data were abstracted from the *County and City Data Book (1988), Files on Diskette.* U.S. Bureau of the Census.

[4] A multiple regression analysis not discussed in this *Brief* confirmed the importance of resources, community context, and regional location in determining levels of activity against corporate crime. The dependent variable in the regression analysis was a scale measuring the overall level of activity against corporate crime. To construct the scale, the prosecutors' responses to the question on how often the office typically prosecutes the selected corporate crimes (see table 2) were assigned ordinal ranks and summed. The independent variables were number of attorneys, presence of a special unit, level of retail employment, and region. All of the independent variables exerted statistically significant effects and collectively explained 40 percent of the variance in the activity scale.

[5] Goldstock, R., 1991. "The Prosecutor as Problem Solver." Occasional Paper from the Center for Research in Crime and Justice, X. New York University School of Law.

18

A Soul to Damn and a Body to Kick
Imprisoning Corporate Criminals

Leo G. Barrile

Reflexive Statement

My grandparents came from rural villages in Italy to the United States at the beginning of the century. They settled in Lawrence, Massachusetts and took jobs in the textile and paper mills. They experienced the bloody attacks against workers and their families during the IWW led strike. Most of their children worked in the mills and luckily most of their grandchildren and great grandchildren did not. Two of my uncles, Nick and Armando, died in middle age from cancers contracted from the work conditions they were exposed to. I remember their long and painful deaths. I remember that Nick was already practically deaf from years of unprotected work near constantly clanking machinery, but the chemical fumes he was unprotected from were what eventually did him in. At the time, everyone saw my uncles' deaths and the families they left fatherless as facts of life, as the risks that sometimes accompany

Reprinted from *Humanity & Society*, 17(2): 176–199.

having a job. Even today, for some workers in blue collars not much has changed.

I was drawn to research on corporate crime, particularly corporate victimization of workers, largely because I see my uncles in those injured today. I see their families and the devastation that is largely preventable. Perhaps this has motivated my intolerance for those who advocate anything less than criminal penalties for those who knowingly disregard the lives of their workers. For Nick and Armando, this chapter is for you.

Introduction

It was Edwin Sutherland (1940) who first contended that socially harmful acts that were committed by corporations ought to be treated as crime or criminal behavior by sociologists whether these acts were considered criminally punishable by strict legal definition or not. Corporate crime is organizational white-collar crime. It consists of acts by the agents of legitimate businesses which violate criminal, civil, or regulatory laws or otherwise cause harm to workers, consumers or the environment. A case in point is the Johns-Manville company which for decades concealed its knowledge of the carcinogenic effects of asbestos on workers and failed to protect those who made, worked with, or used the product. Unlike occupational white-collar crime such as embezzlement, which is usually committed by individuals for their own benefit and often runs counter to the interests of the company, organizational white-collar crime enhances the company's capital accumulation and competitiveness (Michalowski 1985, p. 324), it is usually tolerated or even tacitly encouraged by upper management (Geis 1967), it is frequently done with management's knowledge of the harm and increased risks that will occur (Cullen, Maakestad and Cavender 1987, p. 41), and it is too often an endemic element of corporations and business practices (Needleman and Needleman 1979; Reasons, Ross and Patterson 1982; Ermann and Lundman 1992; Pearce and Tombs 1992). Individuals may benefit from corporate crime with promotions and increased salaries as Gilbert Geis (1967) found in his early research on the bid-rigging schemes of Westinghouse and General Electric, but the main outcome of the acts is the advancement of the company's interests. Richard Quinney called these acts crimes of economic domination because they help to preserve the superordinate position of the capitalist class by further appropriation of labor, resources and capital (Quinney 1980).

Until recently corporate crime, despite its devastating effects, remained closeted and invisible. Nearly all the cases of business-induced theft and harm were handled in civil and administrative courts and resolved with fines. In the rare criminal prosecutions, fines were also the most common penalty. In the even more rare cases of imprisonment, owners and operators of small companies or middle level managers, at best, from big companies served relatively short sentences. However, the Savings and Loan scandal and the growing grass roots environmental movement eroded some of the "halo effect" that those with high status, power, and legitimacy had in court and the legislature. The corporate veil which insulated most companies from criminalization was becoming transparent if not pierced.

Some social researchers argue that the public became more cynical about the corporate class as the cases of corporate disregard for health and safety became more apparent and more numerous (Simon and Eitzen 1986; Cullen, Maakestad and Cavender 1987). The rising sentiment of cynicism undergirded an incipient support for criminal prosecution of corporations. Cullen, Maakestad, and Cavender (1987) go so far as to contend that a Habermasian "crisis of legitimation" occurred during the 1970s because the state did little or nothing to prevent or punish corporate violence and fraud. Indeed the state had Watergate, Vietnam, and racial tensions shouting at its legitimacy.

However, the would-be legitimation crisis fizzled during the 1980s with the Reagan era. Ronald Reagan supported and implemented his version of laissez faire capitalism through massive deregulation of businesses. Reagan's evisceration of the budgets of federal regulatory agencies and his chaining of the justice department's reach in corporate matters allowed widescale corporate criminality to flourish. The HUD and S&L scandals were symptoms of this policy. Despite the environmental and health and safety movements, Reagan's popularity and legitimacy remained intact. However, his actions jolted the state's avowed role as intermediary between large businesses and the rights of individuals and communities. Reagan baldly and transparently promoted the interests of the dominant class disturbing what Poulantzas calls the "equilibrium" created by the state as arbiter between the public and the dominant class. In Poulantzas' words, "the modern capitalist state presents itself as embodying the general interest of the whole of society . . . " (Poulantzas 1975, p. 123).

Decimating the regulatory agencies was not the way to promote a democratic image of the state. Indeed, regulatory agencies, particularly the way they operate, perform a great function for the corporation. They act as a buffer between the corporation and zealous social reformers, consumer advocates, environmentalists, labor unionists, activist state and federal prosecutors, and socially aware state and federal legislatures, not to mention an angry public. In the present historical social formation, workers' and the general public's interests are more represented and more organized bureaucratically. Active regulatory agencies would at least appear to be containing corporate crime, and appeasing organized discontent.

Reagan's actions had the unanticipated consequence of forcing state and local judiciaries and legislatures to fill the political void. And they did. They brought corporations to criminal court, and as we will see, juries typically rendered guilty verdicts.

What of the hypothesized crisis of legitimation? Apparently, legitimation is not located in the state as a whole, but rather, as Poulantzas (1975) suggests, in relatively autonomous political forms, such as the executive, legislative, or judicial institutions. Indeed the popular push to use state courts for trying corporations may have come as a result of a declining faith in the arcane apparatus of the federal regulatory system and the comparatively greater influence that popular interest groups have on state and county court personnel through, for instance, the popular elections of judges, district attorneys, and state legislators. Typically, these middle levels of power, as C. Wright Mills referred to them, are more open to the dominated classes than are the closed political elites of the power bloc, the executive level of the political system, and the adjunct technoclass of policy advisors, researchers, and legal professionals.

And here is the hope for social change as realist theorists see it (Young and Matthews 1992): that groups, for example, of workers, consumers, and environmentalists can influence law and law enforcement to punish corporate agents and bring about greater social justice. This is what Karl Klare (1979) called constitutive law, and what Pearce and Tombs (1992) call "non-reformist reform," the empowering of capital-poor classes, substantially changing how corporate criminals are handled.

The environmental rhetoric of the Clinton administration is ever so encouraging. Yet it was a recessionary economy that drove the Clinton election much as it did Reagan's. The ultimate nightmare of the capitalist state be it run by a democrat or republican is that economic tailspins will lead to economic and political anarchy. It remains to be seen if the health and safety rhetoric of the Clinton administration, and the recently passed massive regulatory legislation and new federal sentencing guidelines for corporate crime will be subsumed to the goal of stimulating business growth by relying on the corporate class.

The potential disorder created by the demise of the economy may be at the basis of many sociologists' reluctance to advocate full criminalization for corporate misdeeds. Many advocate non-criminal approaches such as "compliance strategies," namely, encouraging corporations to obey regulations voluntarily or using reduction in fines to encourage compliance (Kagan and Scholtz, 1984; Sigler 1988; Stone 1975; 1985). Others such as Fisse (1971; 1991) Braithwaite (1982); Fisse and Braithwaite (1983) support such techniques as enforced self-regulation, negative publicity, and limited criminal and civil liability for corporations and managers. The main arguments against criminalization are that it will antagonize companies and perhaps drive them to more elaborate evasion schemes; that it is impractical to criminally investigate corporations; and that the vast majority of companies are either "good corporate citizens" or can be cajoled, shamed, or persuaded to comply. If all else fails or the acts are very serious, then some sociologists advocate corporate probation, the externally or internally supervised restructuring of goals and decision making within the organization (Gruner 1988; Geraghty 1979; Frank and Lombness 1988; Schwartz and Ellison 1982). Some see corporate probation as a strategy for making capitalist organizations more socially responsible, while others see it as a potentially radical attempt to change the relations of production (Schwartz and Ellison 1982). Punishing the corporation is akin to modifying a murderer's gun with rubber bullets instead of imprisoning the murderer. Apparently, many sociologists still cannot bring themselves to see corporate criminals as deserving of incarceration as street criminals. Present corporations are merely organizational conduits for those who are firmly entrenched with a capitalist business ideology. Corporate crime comes from the inherent drives to appropriate capital and exploit labor.

There is an enormous asymmetry in the relationship between the corporate criminal and the victim (Coleman 1992) which is not balanced by the present enforcement strategies, nor by sociologists' suggestions on compliance, shaming, or corporate probation.

The cases that I will discuss show the blameworthiness of corporations and their top managers. These cases cry out for just punishment which, as we will see, rarely if ever happens. However, the mere appearance of corporate class members in criminal court is encouraging. It is a first step at confronting corporate dominance.

Corporations and Executives in Criminal Court

During the 1980s there were substantial increases in the number of corporations and managers indicted, sentenced, and fined for crimes (though any increase would seem substantial because corporate prosecutions were rare). For instance, from 1983 to 1990 environmental criminal indictments more than tripled from 40 to 134 (Gold 1990). From 1985–1988 fines levied against corporations rose from one-half million dollars to seven million dollars (Goldberg 1991). The EXXON Valdez oil spill produced criminal fines several times that amount, a $25 million federal fine and a $100 million restitution payment not to mention the civil penalties of $900 million over 11 years (*New York Times* 1991). Also, a greater commitment appears to exist in the Justice Department and regulatory agencies such as the EPA which have begun, in the 1990s, to increase their investigative and prosecutorial staffs, establishing, for example, special environmental crime units. From 1982 to 1990, the justice Department increased its environmental unit staff from 3 to 25 lawyers, and the EPA increased its investigative staff from 23 to 60, and is planning eventually to reach 500 investigators (Cold 1990).

Despite these encouraging trends, very little actual progress in punishing or deterring corporate violence has occurred. Take workplace safety. Despite the fact that nearly 11,000 workers die each year from work related injuries, the Labor Department, from 1981–1989, referred only 44 criminal cases to the Justice Department and it in turn produced merely two convictions (Bros 1989, p. 289 using statistics from National Safe Workplace Institute, 1988). In American history only 16 cases of corporate homicide have been charged, only 9 of those made it to trial, and, in only three cases were corporate agents sentenced to prison (Bros 1989, p. 305). *In the 20 years that OSHA has existed not one person has actually served a prison sentence for violating the act* (Cohen 1989, p. 157). Moreover, corporations have recently obtained reversals of some of the few criminal prosecutions of the 1980s.

A case in point is Film Recovery Systems, Inc. (*People v. Film Recovery Systems, Inc.* 1985). Initially, this case appeared to be a model of how the law can be used to sanction corporate crime. The company and three of its agents, the president, plant manager, and foreman, were prosecuted for the death of a worker from cyanide poisoning. Hosts of sociologists and crime researchers referred to it as a watershed case. Unfortunately, the verdicts were reversed on appeal.

Film Recovery chemically stripped silver from x-ray film by using a mixture of water and sodium cyanide. The workers, most of whom were from Poland and Mexico, were never told of the cyanide and its dangers, nor were they adequately protected from toxic fumes in the processing. Most of the workers did not speak or read English and thus could not decipher the warnings on the chemical containers. Their supervisors purposely concealed the dangers from them, even to the point of removing the skull-and-crossbones labels from some of the containers. Most of the workers experienced dizziness, nausea, headaches, and skin and eye irritations every day. In 1983, Stefan Golab, a Polish undocumented worker, died at the factory from cyanide fumes.

In a bench trial in 1985, Film Recovery and its parent company Metallic Marketing, Inc., were convicted of involuntary manslaughter and 14 counts of reckless conduct and fined $24,000 each. Three of the company's agents were convicted of murder and 14 counts of reckless conduct, and received 26-year sentences. Two of the three were also fined $24,000 each. The judge ruled that the Film Recovery president and the managers knew that their acts would cause a strong probability of death or great bodily harm—conditions of murder in the Illinois statute.

On appeal the verdicts were set aside and a new trial was ordered, solely because of a technicality. The state appeals court concluded that since the evidence and facts used in both convictions were the same then they should not have produced different criminal convictions—murder for the managers and involuntary manslaughter for the corporation. (*Illinois v. Steven ONeill, Film Recovery System, Inc., Metallic Marketing System, Inc., Charles Kirshbaum, and Daniel Rodriquez* 1990). The usual reluctance to charge a corporation with murder because of its ostensible inability to serve a sentence or to be executed came back to haunt the trial prosecutors in this case. Now nine years after Stefan Golab died at work we still have no closure on his case.

Reversals on appeal are common in corporate criminal cases. Even in regulatory cases corporations have won some crucial appeals. For instance, in October of 1992, asbestos manufacturers successfully appealed the two-year-old EPA ban on asbestos products. These reversals remind us that corporate criminal convictions are rare. They are slow to come to court. They are cautiously prosecuted. And they are dragged on *ad infinitum* through the appellate system.

Is the criminal law experiencing *culture lag*? Does it need a statutory infusion to catch up to the new attitudes toward corporate criminality?

To some extent the notion of culture lag or legal lag is true. While federal and state criminal statutes have provisions for treating corporations as "persons," many courts have been reluctant to convict corporations for crimes beyond negligence, that is, crimes that usually require intent or *mens rea,* crimes such as assault and nonnegligent murder. Even cases of naggingly evident negligence have been reversed. A corporate version of mens rea needs to be formalized much as it was for organized crime under the federal RICO provisions (Racketeer Influenced and Corrupt Organizations Act).

Legal lag is evident in a case involving the deaths and injuries of workers in a Warner-Lambert chewing gum factory explosion (*People v. Warner-Lambert Co.* 1980; cert. denied, 450 U.S. 1031 1981). In the process of rolling and cutting gum, magnesium stearate dust and liquid nitrogen were used to prevent sticking in different operations. The factory was often thick with magnesium stearate dust, and this was noticed by the company's insurance inspector who stipulated that an effective exhaust system and better insulated electrical connections be installed to prevent an explosion. Warner-Lambert made some superficial changes but did not stop production and did not implement important safety modifications. Soon after, a small explosion, presumably caused by the liquid nitrogen's liquefaction of oxygen, set off a huge second explosion of the magnesium stearate dust which killed six workers and injured 44 other workers. In 1980, the company and four managers were indicted for second-degree manslaughter and negligent homicide. The trial court threw out the indictment, the appellate division reinstated it, and finally the New York Court of Appeals dismissed the indictment. The court of appeals reasoned that since the cause of the explosion could not be directly shown, the corporation and its managers could not have foreseen this "uncertain" cause of the explosion. The court ignored the issue of whether the conditions tolerated by the company posed a general risk of danger so great and so foreseeable that it was clearly an act of negligence (Koprowicz 1986, pp. 215–216). The court also held that the issue of work-related deaths was not clear in the statutes and that the legislature would have to more clearly define corporate criminal liability for the deaths of workers (Von Ebers 1986, p. 982). The court claimed, in effect, that state law lagged behind the changing attitudes toward corporate criminal responsibility.

The notion of collective responsibility still sounds foreign to the modern legal ear which is tuned to the frequency of individual intentionality long established in Anglo-American criminal and common law. Modern statutes reflect this. Few state criminal codes delineate a set of specific sanctions for corporations for specific crimes as is established for individuals. And while the new federal sentencing guidelines attempt to address corporate punishment, even if a corporation were convicted of first-degree homicide and even if there were aggravating circumstances, the corporation would probably be fined or placed on probation because the usual punishments indicated, imprisonment or the death penalty, are impossible to execute literally against a corporate entity, short of closing it down or quarantining its activities. As Lord Thurlow put it: the corporation has no soul to damn, no body to kick.

Ironically, corporations have argued for more than a century that they ought to be treated as "persons" under constitutional law. They contend that they should have the same rights as any citizen. For example, Dow Chemical argued in 1986 that it should be protected under the Fourth Amendment search and seizure provisions from the EPA's plane surveillance of its facilities to detect pollution (Nader and Mayer 1988). But no corporation has volunteered to be treated like a typical citizen for criminal prosecution. The corporation claims that the legal notion of personhood under the law is abstract and ambiguous when the argument shifts from privileges to criminal responsibilities and liabilities.

Despite the arguments about the soulless, mindless, ethereal nature of the corporation in the law, the courts have for more than eighty years attributed liability to corporations and managers for crimes.

In 1904 the New York Circuit Court found the Van Schaick company and several of its officers guilty of manslaughter in the deaths of 900 people who drowned when a steamboat caught fire and its life preservers failed. For its failure to furnish adequate firefighting and lifepreserving equipment the owner and the company were declared liable for violating the federal law on ship safety. No intent was necessary for conviction. The officers were convicted of aiding and abetting the violation (*United States v. Van Schaick* 1904).

In perhaps the most influential and precedent-setting case on criminal intent and corporations the *New York Central* (1909) case established the controversial principle of vicarious liability (*New York Central and Hudson River Railroad Co. v. U.S.* 1909). An assistant traffic manager for the company allowed certain customers to ship freight on the railroad for less than the statutory rates, effectively granting them an illegal "rebate" or bribe to use the railroad. The United States Supreme Court held that the corporation could be held liable for the acts of its agents when in their occupational role they illegally act in behalf of or for the benefit of their corporation. The civil law principle of *respondeat superior* (the superior speaks for his employees) was transplanted into criminal prosecutions. Justice Day argued that the intent of an employee acting in his job could be imputed to the company. A provision under the Elkins Act held that a corporate officer's actions could be taken as an act of the corporation as well as an act of the individual (212 U.S. 1909, pp. 494–496). Hence the corporation had *vicarious intent* or liability. Quoting Bishops New Criminal Law of 1892, Justice Day wrote " . . . [a corporation] can act therein as well viciously as virtuously." (212 U.S. 1909, p. 493).

In *New York Central* the contention that corporations could not be tried for crimes requiring intent had been pierced. The Court did mention that some crimes could not be committed by corporations and some legal scholars assume that this referred to specific intent crimes such as homicide (Foerschler 1990, p. 1293). However, the Court was likely referring to occupational white-collar crimes that are antagonistic to the corporation's financial interests, such as theft or embezzlement and other crimes occurring among employees such as rape, assault, and theft.

After *New York Central,* states began to include corporations in their statutes as criminally liable. However, some legal scholars and social thinkers have criticized the application of vicarious liability. Mueller (1957) argued that the corporation should be held liable only for the acts and intention of the "inner circle" of corporate officers. Since stockholders are affected by corporate liability they should pay the price only when those people who are truly entrusted with decision-making powers act criminally (Mueller 1957, pp. 40–41).

Indeed other countries have attempted to adopt this limited approach. In Great Britain, presumably, the agents of the corporation must be its "directing mind," its "alter ego," or the "organ of the company," before vicarious liability can be applied. Canada and Australia are attempting to apply similar standards. However, the notion of an agent with a directing mind in a large intricate organization is, in practical terms, difficult to apply. Large companies can and do have a huge advantage in criminal court over small companies because of the way that responsibility and decision making are typically diffused in bureaucracies.

Some contend that corporate criminal intent ought to be derived from the established policies, ideology, and corrective programs of a company. Brent Fisse (1991) argues that corporate blameworthiness should be tied to intent which could be measured by a company policy that permits wrongdoing and/or a lack of precautions or lack of due diligence in preventing the behavior from occurring. In a similar vein Pamela Bucy (1991) argues that a "corporate ethos" that encourages crime in corporate agents ought to be used to infer intent and corporate blameworthiness.

The problem with using policy and ethos is that they are easy for a corporation to contrive. Is image policy? Is public relations ethos? Hardly. Actions speak louder than avowed principles. And we can more readily deduce intent from the actions of employees than from some abstract purported policy or ethos.

In addition to criminal law, regulatory law contains provisions for misdemeanor and felony prosecutions of corporations and officers. Since regulatory law protects the public welfare, strict liability is used in many provisions. This means, for one, that a corporate officer who has responsibility over a worker who violates a regulatory law can be punished even if the officer did not know the actions had occurred. This is precisely what happened in the *U.S. v. Dotterweich* case (1943) where violations of the Food, Drug and Cosmetic Act (FDCA) made Dotterweich strictly liable. Similarly, in *U.S. v. Park* (1975) the president of a grocery chain was held liable for violations of the FDCA even though he had ordered a subordinate to correct the problem. Because the problem was not corrected strict liability fell on him. Similarly, the Clean Air and Water Acts, RCRA, and CERCLA have provisions for imprisonment and heavy daily fines. For instance, under RCRA (Resource Conservation and Recovery Act) fines of $50,000 per day and sentences of 2 years in prison are possible. Further, violations under the *"knowing endangerment"* provision of RCRA include a sentence of 15 years in prison and a fine of $1 million for life threatening actions. In 1980 amendments to RCRA incorporating knowing endangerment were passed into law, but it took 7 years after the provision and 3 years after the burden of proof was lessened in the act to gain a conviction. Knowing endangerment requires proof that a company knew of imminent danger of death or bodily injury. (See section 6928(e) of RCRA for a definition of knowing endangerment.) Any violations of the provisions of RCRA are federal crimes.

Protex Industries was the first conviction won and upheld under the knowing endangerment provision. Protex exposed employees to solvents used in cleaning recycled drums of toxics (*U.S. v. Protex Industries, Inc.* 1987). The EPA, FBI, and the federal grand jury found that Protex had violated the knowing endangerment provision of RCRA by exposing workers to solvents that affected their central nervous systems and increased their risk of cancer. Knowing endangerment is, for all intents and purposes, an attempt to find a substitute for mens rea without the same level of individual mal intent or criminal mind that is usually required. Using knowing endangerment, only the corporation's "actual knowledge" that its conduct will lead to serious injury or a substantial certainty of death, "imminent danger," is required. Interestingly, for purposes of prosecution, this "knowledge" can be ascribed only to the corporation as an entity not to individuals.

Protex argued that the notions of knowing endangerment and imminent danger were constitutionally vague as applied for criminal purposes in court, and that the EPA had failed to furnish them with the results of their tests. In short they pleaded ignorance. The Court and appellate court had no trouble establishing that Protex could have "reasonably expected harm" to occur to workers with a "substantial likelihood" in its workplace and that Protex had a "presumed knowledge" of the threat of its toxics and displayed a "willful blindness" to the consequences to workers in transporting, treating, storing, and disposing the chemicals.

The *Protex* case indicates the problems that arise when corporate liability is pushed beyond negligence. The Court literally had to redefine the mens rea element in the law to "knowledge of a substantial certainty of imminent danger" to fit the reality of the workplace. RCRA bent itself into a pretzel attempting to find an analogous notion of intent for corporations.

Many regulatory laws, like RCRA, contain enormously punitive sanctions. The EPA alone has over 100 convictions to its credit (*Industry Week* 1990). Unfortunately, regulatory agencies have been excruciatingly slow to bring cases to court and are enormously understaffed. The AFL-CIO estimates that there are 2,000 federal and state OSHA inspectors for 6 million worksites. Most will never be inspected.

The Reagan and Bush doctrine made matters worse. However, one of the unanticipated consequences of the Reagan policy was to stimulate the prosecutions of corporations in state courts. This created a controversy over "preemption." Did federal regulatory law preempt the states from taking action against corporations? A case in point is the *Pymm Thermometer Corporation* case (*N.Y. v. Pymm Thermometer Corp., People v. William Pymm, Edward Pymm Jr., Pymm Thermometer Corporation, and Pak Glass Machinery Corporation* 151 A.D. 2d 133; 546 N.Y.S. 2d 871; 1989; 1990; 561 N.Y.S. 2d 687; 59 USLW 2254; 14 OSHC (BNA) 1833). Pymm manufactures thermometers. Mercury contamination at the plant was always a problem. State and OSHA inspectors found that the workplace was contaminated and that workers were not issued protective masks. Also, Pymm was running a clandestine mercury reclamation business in a basement even more dangerous than its regular factory. Vidal Rodriquez, who worked in this basement, was exposed to mercury vapor levels 5 times the allowable limit without any ventilation. He developed neurological symptoms of mercury poisoning.

Pymm was accused of conspiracy, falsifying business records, assault in the first and second degree, and reckless endangerment. The jury returned verdicts of guilty on all these charges. The trial judge reversed the jury on the grounds that OSHA regulations preempted state prosecution. The appellate division reversed the judge, and the court of appeals affirmed the appellate's reversal of the judge and reinstated the jury's verdicts. The *Pymm* decision may actually be the watershed case that criminologists and legal scholars have been hunting for. A conviction of corporate officers for criminal assault.

One important conclusion that the appellate judges drew from the case was that federal regulatory laws set and control standards, but that they do not preempt general state criminal laws. In a famous civil suit brought by Karen Silkwood's husband against the company that exposed her to deadly radiation, the Supreme Court also ruled that federal law does not preempt state regulatory law (*Silkwod v. Kerr-McGee* 1984). Hence, federal regulatory provisions do not stand as obstacles to state criminal punishments, civil suits, or regulatory sanctions.

State prosecutions like *Pymm* have had to battle the corporation because of the inactivity and ineffectiveness of federal regulatory agencies, particularly OSHA. For example, workers from Pymm pleaded with OSHA to do something about their conditions, to no avail. And while the New York State Attorney's office intervened in Pymm, smaller and poorer state jurisdictions might not even attempt to bring such cases to court against large corporations. Furthermore, many states have less stringent codes than the federal government.

◂ Conclusion ▸

Regulatory agencies and the federal judiciary have, at their best, been slow, cautious, and reluctant to bring criminal charges against corporations. During the Reagan administration they were virtually absent. Few cases of corporate crime were actually punished or punished significantly. Poulantzas' point that the modern state contains the "effect of isolation," that it alienates the person from his or her real socio-economic relations of class is well illustrated by the relative invulnerability of corporations to real prosecution. Because of this, state criminal courts became more active in charging companies and their managers with crimes especially when workers or the public were injured or killed. The *Pymm* and *Film Recovery* cases are sterling examples of this phenomenon.

More importantly, community groups began to fill the void left by the state. Grass-roots community organizations and advocacy groups have shepherded an era of public involvement in the monitoring of corporate practices, particularly regarding the environment. Advocacy groups have lobbied for passage of strict environmental laws with "right to know" clauses. Community tracking committees have assumed central roles in scrutinizing the audits, the environmental impact statements, the toxic use reduction plans, and the evacuation plans of companies which produce or dispose of toxic materials. The message of groups advocating greater protection of workers, the environment, and consumers is receiving more support. There is apparently a healthy mistrust and cynicism in the public toward corporations and federal agencies. In the legal cases discussed above, most of the juries had no inhibition about punishing corporations and their managers. John Coffee's (1981) argument that juries might be impressed or intimidated by high status, powerful defendants and thus reluctant to find guilt (*jury nullification*) is simply not true of many trials.

Advocacy groups have been engaging in the kind of community involved policing of corporations that realist theorists advocate for street crime (Young and Matthews, 1992). However, as Pearce and Tombs (1991) point out, community groups need the support of committed social control agencies to match the immense power and economic influence of corporations.

Imprisonment of company managers for corporate crimes is an integral element in cutting the absolute power of the corporate class. It peels away some of the layers of legitimacy and invulnerability. Notwithstanding Braithwaite's argument that only "vice presidents for going to jail" will be imprisoned, serious sentencing of managers will inevitably cut a swath across the corporate hierarchy. Compliance models of enforcement, as Laureen Snider (1990) argues, merely reinforce the ideological, political, and economic dominance of the corporate class and the powerless relationship of regulatory agencies toward them.

The support of many academic and law professionals for nonpunitive, compliance-oriented strategies also fails to recognize the inherent criminogenic elements of oligopolistic capitalism. The rehabilitation of a "deviant" manager or the reorganization of a "defective" organization ignores the root causes of corporate criminality in the economic system and class conflict.

Imprisoning the corporate manager may seem like little more than a crime control approach, but it can have symbolic and political significance. If the corporate class is not beyond the reach of the law and prison, then some of the asymmetry in the relations between the capital rich and the capital poor might be reduced. More importantly, if community groups, grass-roots organizations, unions, and consumer groups can influence more legislation, enforcement and prosecution of corporate criminals, then a growing empowerment might occur and real challenges might be mounted against capitalist domination. This grass-roots use of criminal punishment is what Karl Klare (1979) envisioned as "constitutive law" and what Frank Pearce and Steve Tombs (1991) see as "non-reformist reform." The criminal punishment of the corporate class might be a rallying point for social justice and significant social change.

Corporate crime reveals the weaknesses and contradictions of oligopolistic capitalism. Imprisoning its purveyors attacks the first line of defense of the economic status quo. A constitutive law that involves the capital-poor in environmental, work, and product safety would empower these groups to form more egalitarian economic and political systems.

When social control agencies begin to punish corporate criminals in the same manner as street criminals, and when community groups are involved in developing economic policy, then the political system will have altered the relations between the classes and greater social justice will be possible.

◂ References ▸

Addison, Frederick W. 3rd and Elizabeth E. Mack. Spring 1991. "Creating an Environmental Ethic in Corporate America: The Big Stick of Jail Time." *Southwestern Law Journal* 44: 1427–1448.

Androphy, Joel M. 1987. "What Corporate Counsel Needs to Know about Criminal Investigations and Prosecutions." *Texas Bar Journal* 50: 998–1002.

Ballam, Deborah A. 1988. "The Occupational Safety and Health Act's Preemptive Effect on Criminal Prosecutions of Employers for Workplace Deaths and Injuries." *American Business Law Journal* 26: 1–27.

Bergman, David. 1990. "Recklessness in the Boardroom." *The New Law Journal* October 26, 140: 1496+.

Berry, Janis M. Summer. "Defence of Business, Individual Officers and Employees in Corporate Criminal Investigations." *Public Contract Law Journal* 19: 648–688.

Bixby, Michael B. 1990. "Was It an Accident or Murder? New Thrusts in Corporate Criminal Liability for Workplace Deaths." *Labor Law Journal* 41: 417–422.

Boston College Law School. 1988. "Pursuit of The Corporate Criminal: Employer Criminal Liability for Work Related Deaths as a Method of Improving Workplace Safety and Health." *Boston College Law Review* 29: 451–480.

Braithwaite, John. 1982. "Enforced Self-Regulation: A New Strategy for Corporate Crime Control." *Michigan Law Review* 89: 1466–1507.

Braithwaite, John. 1985. "Taking Responsibility Seriously: Corporate Compliance Systems." Pp. 39-61 in *Corrigible Corporations and Unruly Law.*, edited by Brent Fisse and Peter A. French. San Antonio, TX: Trinity University.

Braithwaite, John. 1989. *Crime, Shame and Reintegration.* New York: Cambridge University Press.

Braithwaite, John and Philip Pettit. 1990. *Not Just Deserts: A Republican Theory of Criminal Justice.* New York: Oxford University Press.

Bros, Carol L. 1989. "A Fresh Assault on the Hazardous Workplace: Corporate Homicide Liability for Workplace Fatalities in Minnesota." *William Mitchell Law Review* 15: 287–326.

Bucy, Pamela H. April 1991. "Corporate Ethos: A Standard for Imposing Corporate Criminal Liability." *Minnesota Law Review* 75: 1095–1184.

Clinard, Marshall B. 1990. *Corporate Corruption: The Abuse of Power.* New York: Praeger.

Clinard, Marshall B. and Peter C. Yeager. 1980. *Corporate Crime*. New York: The Free Press.

Cleaves, Robert E. IV, Esquire. 1990. "White-Collar Environmental Crime: Emerging Trends in Corporate Criminal Liability." *Maine Bar Journal* 5: 28–35.

Coffee, John C. Jr. 1981. "'No Soul to Damn, No Body to Kick': An Unscandalized Inquiry into the Problem of Corporate Punishment." *Michigan Law Review* 79: 386–459.

Cohen, George H. Fall 1989. "Preemption: Union Lawyer's View." *Northern Kentucky Law Review* 17: 153–175.

Coleman, James S. 1982. (1992). "The Asymmetric Society." Pp. 95–109 in *Corporate and Governmental Deviance. Problems of Organizational Behavior in Contemporary Society*. 4th ed. edited by Ermann, M. D. and R. J. Lundman. New York: Oxford University Press.

Coleman, James W. 1987, "Toward an Integrated Theory of White-Collar Crime." *American Journal of Sociology*. 93: 406–439.

Coleman, James. W. 1989. *The Criminal Elite*. New York: St. Martin's Press.

Cullen, Francis T., William J. Maakestad and Gray Cavender. 1987. *Corporate Crime Under Attack: The Ford Pinto Case and Beyond*. Cincinnati, OH: Anderson.

Curran, James D. 1986. "Probation for Corporations under the Sentencing Reform Act." *Santa Clara Law Review* 26: 785–808.

Dunmire, Thea D. 1989. "The Problems with Using Common Law Criminal Statutes to Deter Exposure to Chemical Substances in the Workplace." *Northern Kentucky Law Review* 17: 53–81.

Dutzman, Joleane. 1990. "State Criminal Prosecutions: Putting Teeth in the Occupational Safety and Health Act." *George Mason University Law Review* 12: 737–755.

Ebers David Von. 1986. "The Application of Criminal Homicide Statutes to Work-Related Deaths: Mens Rea and Deterrence." *University of Illinois Law Review* 3: 969–999.

Edelhertz, Herbert and Thomas D. Overcast. 1982. *White-Collar Crime: An Agenda for Research*. Lexington MA: D.C. Heath.

Edelman, Peter T. Fall 1987. "Corporate Criminal Liability for Homicide: The Need to Punish Both the Corporate Entity and Its Officers." *Dickinson Law Review* 92: 193–222.

Ermann, M. David and Richard J. Lundman. 1992. "Overview." Pp. 3–43 in *Corporate and Governmental Deviance: Problems of Organizational Behavior in Contemporary Society*. 4th ed. edited by M. D. Ermann and R.J. Lundman. New York: Oxford University Press.

Farrier, David. Oct. 1990. "Criminal Law and Pollution Control: The Failure of the Environmental Offences and Penalties Act 1989 [N.S.W.]." *Criminal Law Journal* 14:317–341.

Fisse, Brent. 1971. "The Use of Publicity as a Criminal Sanction Against Business Corporations." *Law Review* 8: 1733–1777.

Fisse, Brent. 1991. "Corporate Criminal Responsibility" *Criminal Law Journal* 15: 166–174.

Fisse, Brent and John Braithwaite. 1983. *The Impact of Publicity on Corporate Offenders*. Albany: SUNY.

Foerschler, Ann. 1990. "Corporate Criminal Intent: Toward a Better Understanding of Corporate Misconduct." *California Law Review* 78: 1287–1311.

Friedlander, Steven L. 1990. "Using Prior Corporate Convictions to Impeach." *California Law Review* 78: 1313–1339.

Gattozzi, Lynn M. 1986/87. "Charitable Contributions as a Condition of Probation for Convicted Corporations: Using Philanthropy to Combat Corporate Crime." *Case Western Reserve Law Review* 37: 569–588.

Geraghty, James A. 1979. "Structural Crime and Institutional Rehabilitation: A New Approach to Corporate Sentencing." *Yale Law Journal* 89: 353–375.

Gruner, Richard. 1988. "To Let the Punishment Fit the Organizational Sanctioning Corporate Offenders through Corporate Probation." *American Journal of Criminal Law* 16: 1–106.

Gold, Allan R. 1991. "Increasingly, Prison Term Is the Price for Polluters." *New York Times* Friday, Feb. 15.

Goldberg Andrew M. 1991. "Corporate Officer Liability for Federal Environmental Statute Violations." *Boston College Environmental Affairs Law Review* 18: 357–379.

Griffin, Craig L. 1989. "Corporate Scienter Under the Securities Exchange Act of 1934." *Brigham Young University Law Review*, 1227–1259.

Hans, Valerie P. 1989. "The Jury's Response to Business and Corporate Wrongdoing." *Law and Contemporary Problems* 52: 177–203.

Harris, Christopher, Patrick O. Cavanaugh, and Robert L. Zisk. 1988. "Criminal Liability for Violations of Federal Hazardous Waste Law: The 'Knowledge' of Corporations and Their Executives." *Wake Forest Law Review* 23: 203–236.

Humphreys, Steven L. Winter 1990 "An Enemy of the People: Prosecuting the Corporate Polluter as a Common Law Criminal." *The American University Law Review* 39: 311–354.

Jones, S. Douglas. 1990/91. "State Prosecutions for Safety-Related Crimes in the Workplace: Can D.A.'s Succeed Where OSHA Failed?" *Kentucky Law Journal* 79: 139–158.

Kagan, R. and J. T. Scholtz. 1984. "The Criminology of the Corporation and Regulatory Enforcement Strategies." Pp. 67–96 in *Enforcing Regulation* edited by K. Hawkins and J. Thomas. Boston: Kluwer Nijhoff.

Klare, Karl. 1979. "Law Making as Praxis." *Telos* 40: 123–135.

Korpics, J. Joseph. 1991. "*United States v. Protex Industries, Inc.*: Corporate Criminal Liability Under RCRA's 'Knowing Endangerment Provision'" *Houston Law Review* 28: 449–486.

Koprowicz, Kenneth M. 1986. "Corporate Criminal Liability for Workplace Hazards: A Viable Option for Enforcing Workplace Safety?" *Brooklyn Law Review* 52: 183–227.

Kramer, Evan N. 1989. "This 'Old Corporation Dog' Can Hunt: The Realized Doctrine of Corporate and Association Criminal Liability in Texas." *Texas Tech Law Review* 20: 179–202.

Kynes, James H. and Stuart C. Markman. *1989.* "Corporate Internal Investigations for Federal Criminal Wrongdoing." *The Florida Bar Journal* 63: 57–59.

Kynes, James H. and Stuart C. Markman. 1990. "Corporate Internal Investigations for Federal Criminal Wrongdoing." *Federal Bar News & Journal* 37, 5: 282–284.

Maakestad, William F. 1990. "Corporate Homicide." *The New Law Journal* 140: 356–357.

Magnuson, Jay C. and Gareth C. Leviton. 1987. "Policy Considerations in Corporate Criminal Prosecutions After *People v. Film Recovery Systems, Inc.*" *Notre Dame Law Review* 62: 913–939.

Maher, Fred. Mon. June 22, 1987. "Statute of Limitations Begins Upon Death." *Pennsylvania Law Journal* 425: 1 & 10.

McDonnell, Xavier K. Fall 1989. "Criminal Liability for Workplace Accidents." *New England Law Review* 24: 293–331.

Metzger, Michael B. and Charles R. Schwenk. Fall 1990. "Decision Making Models, Devil's Advocacy, and The Control of Corporate Crime." *American Business Law Journal* 28: 323–377.

Michalowski, Raymond. 1985. *Order, Law, and Crime: An Introduction to Criminology.* New York: Random House.

Miester, Donald J. JR. 1990. "Criminal Liability For Corporations That Kill" *Tulane Law Review* 64: 919–948.

Milne, Robert A. 1988/89 "The Mens Rea Requirements of the Federal Environmental Statutes: Strict Criminal Liability in Substance but Not Form." *Buffalo Law Review* 37: 307–336.

Nader, Ralph and Carl J. Mayer. 1988. "Corporations Are Not Persons." *The New York Times*, Saturday, April 9.

Needleman, Martin L. and Carolyn Needleman. 1979. "Organizational Crime: Two Models of Criminogenesis." *The Sociological Quarterly* 20: 517–528.

New Law Journal. 1989 "Manslaughter and Corporate Crime." *The New Law Journal* 139: 931–932.

New Law Journal. 1990. "Manslaughter in the Tunnel." *The New Law Journal* August 3, 140: 1108–9.

Niekamp, Thomas J. 1987. "Individual Liability of Corporate Officers, Directors, and Shareholders for Violations of Environmental Laws." *Ohio Northern University Law Review* 14: 379–391.

Pearce, Frank and Steve Tombs. 1992. "Realism and Corporate Crime." In Roger Matthews and Jock Young, *Issues in Realist Criminology*. Newbury Park, CA: Sage.

Porter, Richard H. 1990. "Voluntary Disclosures to Federal Agencies: Their Impact on the Ability of Corporations to Protect from Discovery Materials Developed During the Course of Internal Investigations." *Catholic University Law Review* 39: 1007–1033.

Poulantzas, Nicos. 1975. *Political Power and Social Classes*. London: New Left Books.

Quinney, Richard. 1974. *Critique of the Legal Order*. Boston: Little, Brown.

Quinney, Richard. 1977. "The Study of White-Collar Crime: Toward a Reorientation in Theory and Research." Pp. 283–295 in Gilbert Geis and Robert F. Meir, *White-Collar Crime: Offenses in Business, Politics and the Professions*. New York: Free Press.

Quinney, Richard. 1980. *Class, State and Crime*. New York: Longmans.

Rapson, Roxanne R. Jan. 1991. "Mens Rea Requirements under CERCLA: Implications for Corporate Directors, Officers and Employees." *Santa Clara Computer and High-technology Law Journal* 6: 377–405.

Reasons, Charles, Lois Ross and Craig Patterson. 1982. "Your Money and Your Life: Workers' Health in Canada." *Crime and Social Justice* 17: 55–60.

Reilly, David J. "Murder, Inc.: The Criminal Liability of Corporations for Homicide." *Seton Hall Law Review* 18: 378–404.

Reiner, Ira and Jan Chatten-Brown. 1989. "When It Is Not an Accident, but a Crime: Prosecutors Get Tough with OSHA Violations." *Northern Kentucky Law Review* 17: 83–103.

Rush, Fred L. Jr. 1986. "Corporate Probation: Invasive Techniques for Restructuring Institutional Behavior." *Suffolk University Law Review* 21: 33–89.

Schwartz, Martin and Charles Ellison. 1982. "Criminal Sanctions for Corporate Misbehavior: A Call for Capitalist Punishment." *Humanity and Society* 6: 267–293.

Sigler, Jay A. and Joseph E. Murphy. 1988. *Interactive Corporate Compliance: An Alternative to Regulatory Compulsion.* New York: Quorum.

Silets, Harvey M. and Susane W. Brenner. 1986. "The Demise of Rehabilitation: Sentencing Reform and the Sanctioning of Organizational Criminality." *American Journal of Criminal Law.* 13:329–380.

Snider, Laureen. 1990. "Cooperative Models and Corporate Crime: Panacea or Cop-Out?" *Crime and Delinquency* 36: 373–390.

Stern, Yedida Z. 1987. "Corporate Criminal Personal Liability: Who Is the Corporation?" *The Journal of Corporation Law* 13: 125–143.

Sutherland, Erwin H. 1940. "White-Collar Criminality." *American Sociological Review* 5:1–12

Tigar, Michael E. 1990. "It Does the Crime But Not the Time: Corporate Criminal Liability in Federal Law." *American Journal of Criminal Law* 17: 211–234.

University of Michigan. 1987. "Reckless Endangerment of an Employee: A Proposal in the Wake of Film Recovery Systems to Make the Boss Responsible for His Crimes." *University of Michigan Journal of Law Reform* 20: 73–905.

University of Toledo, College of Law. 1986. "Imposing Penal Sanctions on the Unwary Corporate Executive: The Unveiled Corporate Criminal." *University of Toledo Law Review* 17: 383–396.

Vaughan, Diane. 1983. *Controlling Unlawful Organizational Behavior Social Structure and Corporate Misconduct.* Chicago: University of Chicago Press.

Volz, Elizabeth Beebe, and Bernard A. Penner. 1991. "Prosecuting Violation." *The Maryland Bar Journal* 24: 10–12.

Washington University. Fall 1986. "Can a Corporation Commit Murder?" *Washington University Law Quarterly* 64: 967–684.

Washington University. 1990. "Recent Developments in Corporate and White-Collar Crime." *Washington University Law Quarterly* 68: 779–818.

Wylie, Michael I. June 1991. "Corporations and the Non-Compellability Right in Criminal Proceedings." *The Criminal Law Quarterly* 33: 344–363.

Young, Jock and Roger Matthews. 1992. *Rethinking Criminology: The Realist Debate.* Newbury Park, CA: Sage.

Zald, Mayer N. 1978. "On the Social Control of Industries." *Social Forces* 57: 79–102.

◂ LEGAL CASES CITED ▸

Illinois v. Steven O'Neill, Film Recovery Systems, Inc., Metallic Marketing Systems, Inc., Charles Kirshbaum, and Daniel Rodriquez Ill. App. 3d, 550 N. E. 2d 1090 (1990).

New York v. Pymm Thermometer Corp. 135 Misc. 2d 565.

New York Central and Hudson River Railroad Co. v. United States. 212 U.S. 482 (1909).

People v. Film Recovery Systems, Inc. Nos. 84 C 5064 and 83 C 11091 Cir. Ct. of Cook County Ill. June 14, 1985.

People v. William Pymm, Edward Pymm Jr., Pymm Thermometer Corporation, and Pak Glass Machinery Corporation 515 N.Y.S. 2d 949; 151 A.D. 2d 133; 546 N.Y.S. 2d 871; 1989 N.Y. App. Div. Lexis 13537, 76 N.Y. 2d 511; 563 N.E. 2d 1; 1990 N.Y. Lexis 3345; 561 N.Y.S. 2d 687; 59 USLW 2254; 14 OSHC (BNA) 1833.

People v. Warner-Lambert Co. 51 NX 2d 295, 414 N.E. 2d 660, 434 NNS. 2d 159 (1980), cert. denied, 450 U.S. 1031 (1981).

Silkwood v. Kerr-McGee 464 U.S. 238 78 LE 2d 443–476, 104 S Ct 615, (1984).

United States v. Dotterweich 320 U.S. 277 (1943).

United States v. Park 421 U.S. 658 (1975).

United States v. Protex Industries, Inc. No 87-CR-115 DC Colo March 4, 1987.

United States v. Van Schaick 134 F. 592 C.C.S.D.N.Y 1904 159 (1980), cert denied, 450 U.S. 1031 (1981).

◀ Index ▶